A SCRAPBOOK *of* MEMORIES

ASHOK CHOPRA has occupied some of the hottest seats in the Indian book trade – executive editor of Vikas Publishing House, vice-president of Macmillan India, publishing director of UBS Publishers, executive director and publisher of India Today Book Club and Books Today, as well as chief executive and publisher of HarperCollins *Publishers* India. Currently, he is chief executive of Hay House Publishers India. He lives in Gurgaon, near Delhi.

Presently he is working on his next book: *The Ageing Loins.*

Praise for A *SCRAPBOOK OF MEMORIES*

'He's been a Sherpa to some of the brightest minds in the country. Ashok Chopra, the publisher, has toiled with the marathon men and women of the Indian literary world. He's lugged their baggage of dreams and ideas to the peaks of success. He's untangled their monstrous egos and scattered petals in the path of the "Queen of Indian Fiction", as he describes Shobhaa Dé. He's saved his writers from the frostbite of indifferent reviews and descent into sudden oblivion ... He documents the many twists and turns of his astonishing career ... He's been able to dazzle us with his fervour for the great and the glorious ... He creates a series of vignettes that are often quite irresistible ... If the earlier portions of the book brim with the froth of human interest, the last part is invaluable. There's sweetness about Ashok Chopra's interventions that makes one enjoy his journey.'

—***India Today***

'A gripping collage of memories spanning a forty-year career of Ashok Chopra wherein he had the opportunity of publishing the top-notch authors of India.'

—***BBC***

'A publisher's anecdotes about the people he has worked with in a career spanning four decades and their idiosyncrasies .... Maybe a hundred vintage sketches from Indian publishing recalling standout people of the last four decades and memorable events .... Episodic, anecdotal, even whimsical, the *Scrapbook* format highlights the situations Chopra has been in and the people he has worked with in four decades of publishing .... There are insights into the lives of the rich and famous who do books or become their subject. Chopra refreshes with his plain talking, a rather rare trait in the world of commissioning editors, who do like to keep up appearances in order to nurture deathless friendships. One wonders why the unnerving disclosures in this book do not mark a closure to Chopra's lively career in Ink Street. In less capable hands, this would have been an act of professional suicide.'

—***The Indian Express***

'An encyclopedia of the world of publishing, where Ashok Chopra has gone down memory lane to pick out many memorable stories, including a few disappointments, some astonishments, everlasting friendships and complex working relationships. It is a world he shares with his readers by narrating stories of acquiring manuscripts, of several gambles that failed to mature into concrete deals and of the satisfaction of not burning his fingers in a failing project. Without hiding facts, he has recollected countless moments that would stay in the mind for a while and might often come back when you see the book on the shelf. Stories like these make the read interesting as they give an idea of power struggle, ego tussles and network building that form the bedrock of the publishing business. Chopra has woven the narrative in delicate thread that perfectly paints the picture.'

—***The Times of India***

'Ashok Chopra's close association with the publishing industry is thoroughly reflected in his latest book ... He has a microscopic eye for detail. And an ability to know just where to cut things out. And it reflects in his written word.'

—***The Hindu***

'Unfurls like a contemporary Bayeux tapestry of India's literati. Everyone who wanted to be anyone is there. He reveals his authors' idiosyncrasies with discretion, their writing habits with patience, and their impatience with genteel derision. He analyses the Indian publishing industry with geometric precision ... A fascinating, riveting read, faultless in construction, tone and content, moving without being mawkish.'

—***Friday Times*, Pakistan**

'Ashok Chopra's book *A Scrapbook of Memories* raises some very pertinent questions and goes on to answer them in quite a plausible manner .... In chapters devoted to subjects relating to publishing, Chopra discusses at length such issues as sourcing manuscripts. He also writes about book launches and their usefulness (or lack thereof) in selling the publications. He rightly concludes that word-of-mouth recommendations contribute largely to the sales of books.'

—***Dawn*, Pakistan**

'Recaps a journey that began in Chandigarh. He writes about the life and times of authors, artists, actors, literary agents and painters — some of whom he published, others he interacted with. He gives us stories of their inner worlds — some known, others largely unknown.'

—***The Tribune***

'We recommend ... *A Scrapbook of Memories*. Written by a veteran of the publishing industry, this is a memoir about interactions with authors, celebrities and celebrated authors. Ashok Chopra's experiences while commissioning books by some of the most celebrated authors of our age are given in detail along with delicious vignettes. These profiles of authors not only serve to outline the dimensions of Chopra's career but the tensions that accompany the job of a publisher. In detailing the coaxing and pursuit of people to write on time, emerges an interesting memoir that offers an insight into how publishing works.'

—***The Asian Age***

'A roller-coaster ride through Indian publishing for nearly 40 years. [A] candid and colourful memoir.'

—***The Pioneer***

'The 416-page book is an encyclopedia of the world of publishing.'

—***The Sentinel***

ASHOK CHOPRA

A SCRAPBOOK *of* MEMORIES

MY LIFE WITH
the RICH,
the FAMOUS
and the SCANDALOUS

HarperCollins *Publishers* India

First published in hardback in India in 2015 by
HarperCollins *Publishers* India
First published in paperback in 2016 by
HarperCollins *Publishers* India

Building 10, Tower A, 4th Floor, DLF Cyber City, Phase II,
Gurugram Haryana – 122002, India
www.harpercollins.co.in

1 2 3 4 5 6 7 8 9 10

P-ISBN: 978-93-5264-112-3
E-ISBN: 978-93-5177-096-1

Printed and bound at
MicroPrints India, New Delhi

To
Taarini and Jesse,
the loves of my life.

For
Lakh Sikand
whom I miss, even today,
immensely.

A book must be the axe for the frozen sea within us.

– Franz Kafka

Contents

Part Two

Part Three

Part Four

Preface

A Journey with and through the Written Word

WHO IS A BOOK PUBLISHER?

Is he (the he could well be a she) a dilettante who acts as a middleman between an author and the market, a kind of a facilitator who paves the way for a potential writer to sell his ideas to a select audience? Is he a businessman because publishing is both an art and a business if it has to survive in the harsh business climate of today? Is he a man-about-town who needs a wide range of contacts with the intellectual community and the business world, bringing both together for his own private gain?

A publisher is a man of many parts who can't be slotted into a specific category. Perhaps, it may be easier to state what he is not if only to dispel some notions in the popular mind. A publisher is not a scholar or a pure intellectual who lives on ideas alone; he may have his head in the clouds but is firmly rooted to the ground. He is not a typical businessman who is looking to make a quick buck but he is in the business all the same on a long-term basis. Every successful publisher has been a businessman under the cloak of intellectual pursuits. Clearly, he is a combination of all the questions listed above, and more, with an unerring instinct for what the reader wants, combined with communication skills that would seduce authors to join him in a venture that needs collaborators such as editors, designers, printers and distributors.

A publisher is not born but made and his journey without maps brings him in contact with creative artists who have their own quirks and idiosyncrasies. It is true that the strangeness of human beings is no great news in our times, but a publisher, and his authors, are a breed apart. Their encounters, at times anecdotal, offer an insight into their thinking – call it their psyche, if you like – which helps us understand them better.

This is not an autobiography. Nor a memoir in the truest sense of the word. It is my journey with, and through, the written word; a journey with the life and times of authors, writers, poets, singers, composers, lyricists, actors, directors, literary agents, publishers and their publishing houses, artists, painters and designers – a few of whom I published, others whom I met and interacted with. It is a journey comprising stories of their inner worlds – some known, others mostly unknown.

– A.C.

Part One

Life is not what one lived, but what one remembers and how one remembers it in order to recount it.

– Gabriel García Márquez

1

Chandigarh

A City That Never Was

Chandigarh was my first love. It gave me my first girlfriend and my first kiss; my first university degree and my first job; my first salary cheque and my first rejection slip; and my best growing-up years and lifelong friends. It is the city that made me discover the romance of the written word. From here started a journey that took me into the hidden and secret, fascinating and enthralling, mysterious and enigmatic, eerie and nebulous world of many creative artistes – all of whom have been, and are, an essential part of our literary and cultural world today.

I always picture a city in terms of colour. Mumbai is sea green, Jaipur pink. Delhi is reddish white, Kolkata filthy grey. Chandigarh was born rosy with a tinge of light green. The light green was in the shimmer of its distant Shivalik range of mountains whose shadows covered the huts, the houses, the large bungalows (which the locals call kothis), roads and trees. For most part of the year its sunshine is cool. It filters through the clouds and the trees like the smile of an Arab woman from behind her veil. While in the winters its sunrays are soaked up like sponges, it's only in the summer months that it casts off its veil as the sunshine pours down shamelessly. As the city grew, the rosiness was lost. It soon became, on one side, a city of green and white – green hedges and white beards – while on the other, of more glitz, sound and thunder. Unlike their neighbours in Himachal Pradesh, who, because of the sky that hangs low, muffling the large green state under its heavy weight, move noiselessly, the robust Chandigarhites are noisy and boisterous, roaring with laughter till the blue sky overhead resounds with reverberations.

Chandigarh was built as an organic city – functional like the human body. The northern part is its head, comprising three giant buildings: the oval-shaped legislative assembly with its plush interiors and stained-glass windows; on its left is the sleek eight-storey civil secretariat on stilts – a honeycomb of ministers, clerks, secretaries, peons and that demigod, the bureaucrat; on its right, the concrete high courts of Punjab and Haryana. From here runs the two-way, long road to Sector 22 – the spine of the city. The overbusy Sector 17 is its stomach; the Rose Garden and the Leisure Valley its lungs. And the hairy legs and arms of Chandigarh are its downtown and mushrooming towns of Panchkula and Mohali, and the grumbling shopkeepers, the ever-growing slum and ragged dwellers, respectively.

Chandigarh has a head, lungs, stomach, arms and legs but no feet. A visitor to the city becomes totally immobile. No one knows when and where the local buses run. Their routes and timings are a secret. The bearded taxi driver is ferocious in his talk and outrageous in his fare demands. The autorickshawallah is mostly unwilling and grumbling for he goes on the routes he wants to and not where you have to.

An oval lake, spacious gardens, flowering trees and warm colours made somebody christen Chandigarh, 'The City Beautiful'. Whoever did so must have had a wicked sense of humour – for today, just about sixty years after its birth, Chandigarh has everything but beauty.

The French architect, Le Corbusier, had designed the city so that its architecture could mould the people's taste. He retained the solid texture of the concrete, its roughness, muscles and veins and tried to break its drabness by bright yellows, reds, blues and turquoises. Not once did he realize that the steel-gutted Punjabis and the fierce Haryanvis would mould the architecture to suit their own tastes.

Soon the sleek secretariat was transformed by ugly plywood platforms, partitions, torn posters, musty files, dingy corridors and foul-smelling urinals. Burly sword-wielding jathedars (Sikh preachers), dhoti-clad Punjabi farmers and large-turbaned Haryanvi Jats coupled with swarms of petitioners roamed the corridors whose unswept and unclean corners were painted with paan spit. The lifts cracked and creaked carrying loads of perspiring clerks and peasants, the uncountable sycophants and favour-seekers surrounding the ministers and the all-powerful bureaucrats. The sprawling Panjab University campus and the overcrowded Postgraduate Institute of Medical Education and Research (PGIMER), across the road, became political platforms full of intrigues and counter-intrigues.

Then came another blow. On Tuesday, 1 November 1966, Chandigarh was married to three feudal lords. The three warring husbands – Punjab, Haryana, and the Union territory – aspiring for the sole proprietorship of this delicate beauty, mauled and battered it badly, in true Punjabi and Haryanvi styles. Political dharnas, agitations and rallies became the order of the day. Checkpoints, barriers, barbed wires, metal drums and wooden obstacles were erected all along the beautiful, wide roads. The young city was fortified. Police and mounted Central Reserve Police Force (CRPF) personnel stood guard. Everyone who was anyone moved around with a battery of gun-wielding security guards in siren-blowing, beacon-flashing vehicles. The number of security personnel sanctioned to an individual became the barometer of status. The beauty queen had turned into an ogre. 'The City Beautiful' turned into 'A Shitty Beautiful'.

In this atmosphere of shame and discontent, the morale of the peace-loving Chandigarhites ebbed and a mounting sense of despair, disillusionment and frustration took over, which soon gave way to cynicism and everyone adopted the 'chalta hai' attitude. Instead of growing into a young, bewitching beauty, Chandigarh, being a young planned city of India, couldn't stop the problems its adolescence brought. As inevitable and unsightly as a teenager's acne, the city started sprouting slums and shanties – the vote banks of our politicians – all over like button mushrooms in wooden trays, no different from those in Delhi, Mumbai or Kolkata.

Cities do not grow overnight. It takes at least a hundred years for any city to develop. Chandigarh, once a barren landscape, developed with amazing speed. The intellectual cream of Punjab, the artistic and cultural figures, the socially conscious and sophisticated minds, the politically powerful and the rich made it their centre of activity. Yet, it never became a city! In fact, the entire Punjab (as well as Haryana) is a rural town, a mammoth village. Chandigarh was the Punjabi's only hope of a city with its own pulse, speed, tensions and cross-currents of cultural, political and social clashes. It should have been like Lahore (now in Pakistan), which even in the early 1940s had a population of just 700,000, but was a city with tremendous character. It had a wide variety of writers, publishing houses, well-equipped bookshops, art galleries, printing presses, newspapers and magazines in various languages, an age-old university, famous educational institutions, theatres, film studios and a great tradition of literary and artistic life.

Even today, Chandigarh lacks all these elements. The little art and culture that exist are shut in its theatres and museums. There is no tradition of clubs or associations of writers, painters, poets and actors. Those that exist are convenient platforms for a 'step up the ladder', or for settling personal scores or exchanging petty political and social gossip. And this was the city to which theatre-historian Balwant Gargi gave a superb tradition of theatre and set up a full-fledged Department of Indian Theatre at the Panjab University. If today, theatre artist Neelam Mansingh Chowdhry is still carrying on the tradition in a culturally barren environment and against all odds, it is through sheer willpower and determination. It is the city to which a one-time unknown and lowly paid government servant Nek Chand Saini gifted a masterpiece of a creation – The Rock Garden – a fantasy designed over decades of sheer hard work and dedication, at times against bureaucratic resistance.

The hard core elite of Chandigarh comprises a hundred-odd families – affluent and arrogant industrialists, westernized sardars in their SUVs, assorted culture vultures, conceited journalists, boisterous university professors who make a virtue of their knowledge, empty-headed and noisy politicians and pompous bureaucrats – all trying hard to run each other down. No function, be it a marriage, house-warming, birth, funeral or a reception, is ever complete without the presence of these hilarious, entertaining, comical, outrageous and downright trite tribe.

Yet, all is not lost for Le Corbusier's Chandigarh. Such was the imaginative layout of the French master that a city initially meant to house just about 100,000 people does not give a feeling of suffocation. It still manages to breathe, despite its population of over 1.1 million, because of its great lungs – the Rose Garden and the Leisure Valley. The master left enough margins for the roads (margs), central streets and the side lanes to have been widened three times over and yet look natural and proportionate in the general layout of the city. Given a chance, Chandigarh can still pursue its way in a sprightly manner.

Le Corbusier's design and architecture of Chandigarh have evoked sharp reactions but few have been as vocal as the eminent painter-architect Satish Gujral. I recall an evening at Balwant Gargi's house on Kasturba Gandhi Marg in New Delhi, in November 1976, where the conversation somehow got diverted to the making of Chandigarh. There was Satish Gujral with his graceful wife Kiran, Manmohan Singh, a secretary of the Department of Education and Culture in the Government of India, the famous Bharatanatyam dancer

Indrani Rahman, the celebrated writer Uma Vasudev, artist Jatin Das and some others. Manmohan, who wore colourful, oversized turbans, belonged to the Punjab cadre of the Indian Administrative Service (IAS) and had seen the birth and growth of Chandigarh and claimed, like every second bureaucrat of those days boasted, to have personally known Le Corbusier. (A few even went to the extent of telling anyone who cared to listen that their houses had been 'especially designed by Le Corbusier' – something which all knew was a total fabrication of their imaginations.) He also dabbled in birdwatching and wrote poetry, which few read but no one understood, though they all praised it to his face. Locked in a heated discussion with Satish, he said that Le Corbusier loved India and had a dream … a vision … a passion for it. Chandigarh was his gift to our country. Satish disagreed and asserted that India had been saddled with third-rate architecture – miserable, colourless and baseless. A sheer disgrace …

Everyone around was shocked into pin-drop silence. But, there was no stopping Satish:

> Listen! [Edwin] Lutyens created the most beautiful Indo-British architecture, a classic of our times – Rashtrapati Bhavan, the Secretariat, and Parliament House, with a mile-long vista of lawns and pools. He took care of the angles of mosques, mausoleums and ruins and integrated those in Delhi's body.... Lutyens hated India, but gave us a beautiful capital. [Le] Corbusier loved India, but gave us third-rate Chandigarh.
>
> 'Have you seen Nek Chand's Rock Garden?' Satish asked. 'See it! It's a miracle. You know I am quite an egoist, but Nek Chand has made me feel so small. Nobody in India has a more original vision and greater genius than Nek Chand. His garden is a fantasy. You cannot plan such a garden on paper. It has been designed stone by stone, shrub by shrub, pebble by pebble, stump by stump, over decades. Chandigarh is fortunate to have Nek Chand. [Le] Corbusier is shit.... Art is not democratic. Intellectuals like you have destroyed our architecture. For you architecture

> is social science, making buildings to house the maximum number of people at the lowest cost. You see everything through a calculator. You have neither the eyes to see the beauty of the form, nor the mind to understand the design and visual aspect which determine sculpture, painting, architecture and graphic arts. But the intellectuals speak for hours at seminars without understanding.... It's amazing how ignorant and pretentious our intellectuals are. They are the worst enemies of [the] visual arts. They should be shot in a public square to silence their stupid tongues.[1]

No one dare dispute Satish Gujral's well-argued opinion!

2

Satish Gujral

Painter of Images. And Words

Satish Gujral has known me since I was born. He and my father, six years older to him, had known each other since school (Mayo School of Arts, Lahore, now The National College of Arts) days where they shared a room in the hostel. Later, they also worked together in their respective first jobs with the Punjab Government in Simla (now spelt as Shimla) after the partition of the country. Eighty-nine-year-old 'Uncle Satish', who was impaired of hearing at the age of eight, is a painter, sculptor, muralist, graphic designer and architect of immense repute who has consistently experimented with art and expressed his ideas in numerous ways.

Uncle Satish has a great sense of humour and is a fabulous raconteur. Possessing an elephant's memory to this day, he tells me, and others, unforgettable stories of my childhood, including how my first birthday was celebrated at government expense, which even my parents never told me. He can churn out jokes and gossip, as also real-life incidents and political analysis, with equal ease. One always looks forward to an evening with him full of spellbinding anecdotes on politics and politicians, local gossip about the city's who's who, love and sex, art and culture, punctuated with bawdy jokes. For him 'painting is a mindless act, a ritual in which an artist's own participation is no different from the audience's.... The same tantric principle of creative energy.'[1]

Explaining this phenomenon he says: 'Look at the masters – look at [William] Shakespeare or [Muhammad] Iqbal or [Pablo] Picasso. It was not thoughts or ideas that these giants gave us, but something much greater, something much more – an electric shock. But to shock others they had to first shock themselves. By an uncanny power they arranged their words, their art in a manner that their lines, their colours burnt, sang, hissed and stung. By their very touch, ordinary thoughts and clichés turned into revelations ... moving, original, pregnant with rare beauty'.[2]

As apparent in the previous chapter, Uncle Satish has very definite views on a subject, which no one can change, nor can any amount of conviction alter. He is also a great listener. And of course, above all, a thinker. While explaining or giving his view, he hates interruption. He considers the famous author Ved Mehta 'a second-rate writer reading whom is like locked in conversation with a second-rate mind. He is boring. His writing has an artificial, false ring. He is blind but he insists on describing the features of a man, the colour of his jacket, the cut of his beard.... Just a big fraud!… I can name so many of them who hate India, but have nothing else to sell except India. Who would read Ved Mehta if he were to write about New York?'[3]

For years I had been trying to persuade Uncle Satish to write his autobiography. He was not receptive to the idea. Then, on the evening of 26 September 1991, on the small lawn of the second-floor apartment of film historian Aruna Vasudev in Defence Colony in New Delhi, where we had gathered for dinner, the conversation got diverted to Raj Thapar's book *All These Years: A Memoir*,[4] which had been released just a fortnight earlier. It was getting wide press coverage and was being discussed extensively in Delhi's social circles.

I spoke to Satish, once again, trying my best to convince him that he too should write. I don't really know what happened but within a month, when I happened to meet him next, he agreed to do not one but two books – a coffee-table volume comprising most of his works and, of course, his autobiography.

The World of Satish Gujral: In His Own Words[5] was planned to be the first release. Satish wrote a text of about 10,000 words to go with it as a prelude, which he wanted to be edited by Rohini Singh, who had already edited over a dozen volumes of Khushwant Singh and the works of writers like S. Nihal Singh, Inder Malhotra, Uma Vasudev and Vasant Sathe. The brilliant designer, Gopi Gajwani, was to design the book and also take some photographs. I warned Gopi and Rohini to tread cautiously as Satish had never allowed anyone to tamper with his work, and was quite clear in his mind as to how the book was to be laid out. Satish's only condition was that the book be printed in Singapore. It was.

The result was a 'very handsome book' and Chu Bong, the head of world-famous Toppan Printers in Singapore, took personal care during its production. For the editor, Satish wrote: 'I am deeply indebted to Rohini Singh for the tenderness and affection that she fused in her editing'.

The short text of the book was gripping and was quoted by many reviewers. As Satish had told me: 'If the first 500 words of my text can't hold a reader then it means it's shit'. The opening lines were:

> A child prodigy I never was.
>
> Certainly not the type who preferred to suck brushes instead of their mother's breasts.
>
> Nor can I count myself among those inspired souls who are seized by mysterious visions on touching a box of paints, or the stub of a pencil.
>
> A fascination for colours and graphic expression, it is too well established, is inherited by almost all children. And if some overindulgent parents see, in this common quirk, visions of

having sired another Picasso or Leonardo da Vinci, I would hate to shatter their illusions …

While the first book was under production, Satish started writing his autobiography. He was obsessed with it and worked on it, day and night, with a one-track mind. Once the first draft of two chapters was ready, he sent it to me. The result was amazing. He had not written, but painted words. The sentences flowed on paper like colourful strokes of his brush on canvas. The imagery was unique. The scenes exceptional. It was like nothing I had read before. The same evening I went over and told him so. I was excited that the baby had finally been conceived and started dreaming of the day when it would be born … when I would publish and release his book.

However, it was not to be so!

A couple of months later, Raseel, the immensely talented and charming younger daughter of Satish and Kiran, invited me for dinner. 'The parents are also coming', she informed. Dinner at Raseel's was always fun, especially if Uncle Satish was there – intimate, cosy, with good food served elegantly, and of course lots of laughter over gossip and tearing apart of reputations.

During the course of the evening Satish said to me: 'Last week we went to meet Khushwant Singh and I mentioned casually to him my autobiography. Khushwant has offered to edit it and I think my book will benefit a great deal with his inputs. It will mean a lot to me. However, he feels that since he is associated with Penguin Books it would be proper only if Penguin were to publish it. He is going to talk to you about it. But I thought it would be better if I talked to you first and explained my position.... Under the circumstances can you revert the rights to me and release me from the contract?'

I was dazed. Speechless. My drink suddenly tasted like ditch water. How was I to tell him that this was a child I had waited for, for years … that we had conceived it together … that a divorce during pregnancy was unthinkable … that there was a certain vision I had for it.... But I also knew that Uncle Satish had made up his mind and no amount of talking to convince him to the contrary would help.

The next morning, I signed the letter cancelling the agreement and reverted the rights to him. And had it hand-delivered to his residence.

On 1 March 1998, *A Brush with Life: An Autobiography* was released by Satish's elder brother I. K. Gujral, the then prime minister of the country, in the presence of the who's who of Delhi's glitterati. But Khushwant was not there. For, by then, the two had fallen out, with relations severely strained. The issue: whether Khushwant's name was 'to be or not to be' on the cover as co-author.

Khushwant insisted. Satish resisted. Finally, both relented and as per a compromise formula, Khushwant's name went only as 'Edited by Khushwant Singh' below that of Satish Gujral as the author, on the cover. An upset Khushwant did not attend the release function; nor did he want anything to do with the book on which he 'had worked for months together'. I was not even invited.

How the book fared in the market I don't know, but I do recall having put it aside after reading just about thirty-forty-odd pages. These were not the pages I had read in their infancy, wherein Uncle Satish had painted words with his favourite brush and vibrant colours. These were not the pages with flowing rhythms. The rustle and the silken texture had got lost somewhere. The painter's poem had dissolved into the writer's prose. The next morning, I gifted it to Balwant Gargi, for it was not a book I could even adopt as a surrogate child for my bookshelf.

3

Balwant Gargi

The Ornamental Cactus

I first met Balwant Gargi on 11 June 1971 through a common friend, guide and philosopher, Tara Chand Gupta. He was fifty-five; I twenty-two. It was a relationship that lasted through thirty-two years, till Gargi passed away on 22 April 2003. It was a love-hate relationship – though more love and a little hate, for Gargi had literally inducted me, like a couple of others, into his small family.

Tara Chand Gupta, an active member of an underground revolutionary party during the early 1940s, was a childhood friend of Gargi. Both hailed from the remote sandy village of Neeta Khandan in Bhatinda district of Punjab, famous for its over 1,800-year-old Gobind Qila (fort) where the first and last woman ruler of both the Sultanate and Mughal period (1236–40) of Indian history, Razia Sultan, was imprisoned. Both went to jail together. Both wanted to be writers. Tara Chand Gupta, who had an eye and ear for news and hidden facts, established himself as a journalist of some repute in north India. His motto was simple: 'Someone, somewhere is trying to hide something. That is news. Rest is all public relations.' Gargi, who had an eye for every pretty lass and an ear for their hidden stories of woe or praise, established himself as a 'theatre historian' and director of some repute. He did go on to create history in the world of English and Punjabi literature.

Gargi shunted between Delhi, where his heart was, and Chandigarh, where his work was. In 1972 he established the Department of Indian Theatre on the Panjab University campus, and thus kept the kitchen fires burning in his modest three-bedroom, W1 bungalow, allotted by the university on the sprawling campus, behind the stone-walled, open-air auditorium of the department, sandwiched between the boys' hostels No. 1 and 2 – named Mehr Chand Mahajan Hall and G. C. Chatterji Hall, respectively.

In Delhi he had a small, single-storey, one-room house on 27 Curzon Road (now known as Kasturba Gandhi Marg). This long, rectangular room was his study, sitting room and, at night, or even during the day, if the occasion demanded, a bedroom. It was furnished with straw mats and cotton cushions of varied colours, low furniture, a study table with an overused electric typewriter on it, a telephone that was constantly ringing and a low divan where Gargi, dressed in his colourful and striped lungi-kurta, would sit cross-legged every morning, constantly clearing his throat while dictating to his secretary, who hammered away furiously on the keys. Behind the secretary's table hung a large framed print of Pablo Picasso's *Blue Nude* of 1902. If 'small is beautiful', his home certainly was one – full of character, immense energy and great atmosphere. It was like a small beehive yielding a great amount of honey.

Outside, in the small verandah with Arab arches, hung a framed poster of Joan Miró's beautiful *España 82* in black, green and burning yellow. Vine and red bougainvillea clambered up the courtyard wall onto the road outside. There was a takhatposh (wooden bed), always covered with a colourful Phulkari, where many evenings were spent over drinks and dinner. Whether his wallet had anything in it or not – more often not – Gargi was a generous host who kept an open home both in Delhi and Chandigarh.

In Chandigarh, as Neelam Mansingh Chowdhry writes, 'evenings at Gargi's were memorable, with famous writers and directors who were passing through the city meeting at his home for either a quick meal, a chilled glass of beer or a visit to the washroom. It was a roster of the who's who that represented an interesting cross-section of the literary and artistic life of the country. For me it was more of a whetstone, where stray conversations and accidental encounters made me feel that I was coming into my own. Writing my own history, finding the argot that would transform my world'.[1]

Gargi, who had earned fame early both at home and abroad, was always wanting to shock people. His first Punjabi play *Loha Kutt* (The Blacksmith, 1944), about the double elopement of a daughter and mother in a blacksmith's family, was a real shocker for its time. *Saelpathar* (Petrified Stone, 1949), *Kanak Di Balli* (Stalk of Wheat, 1968), *Dhuni Di Agg* (Fire in the Furnace, 1977) were just a few that followed. Each of these highlighted filial hate, sex, violence, betrayal and death, which, in fact, were his obsessions. In the US he taught theatre at the University of Washington, published two books, *Theatre in India* and *Folk Theatre of India*, both of which got good notices and earned him the label of 'theatre-historian of India'. It helped him get the prestigious assignment of writing the entry on Indian theatre for the *Encyclopedia Britannica*.

As Neelam Mansingh Chowdhry observed: 'His life seemed to be a kind of template of how a Bohemian artist should behave. Unconventional dress, iconoclastic social behaviour, numerous affairs and his tempestuous marriage to the beautiful Jeannie was the stuff that fed our imagination.... He had a mincing step and a low blurred raspy voice that gave the impression that he had a spittle caught between his teeth. Short and square, his bald pate had a ruff of wispy hair growing across, making him look like a cross between a gnome and a sad clown. I still cannot figure out how he acquired the image of a Don Juan. Over the years, meeting him either in Delhi or Bombay, I invariably saw him squiring a sexy crumpet draped over one arm and knew that his reputation of being a ladies' man was confusingly true. Many women fell in love with Gargi: some genuinely loved him, others did so for the privileges this association could bring. These women then became footnotes in the history of his momentous romantic life.... Gargi would tell us the stories about his life, his travels, the plays he had written, the ones he was going to write; all the while urging us to move ahead untrammelled by our history and tradition. He exhibited a disdain for convention, community or family. I did not understand what was being said, but each sentence sank somewhere within me and remains with me until today.'[2]

It changed my outlook towards life, my thinking, my vision completely.

His book, *The Naked Triangle: An Autobiographical Novel*, was published in 1979 by Narendra Kumar, the chief of Vikas Publishing House, New Delhi, who had a nose for manuscripts. It went into three reprints. In it he laid it all bare, 'sparing neither himself nor the women he loved. He exposed himself with the same ruthless candour as he denuded them of their pretentions and pettiness.'[3] Friends, former university colleagues, students, acquaintances, his estranged wife Jeannie, all had been denuded at one go. While many of his former girlfriends heaved a sigh of relief for not having been exposed, some felt cheated for not having got even a mention in the book. It created many a storm including a legal battle accompanied by a stay order from a Chandigarh court, which, needless to say, gave immense publicity to the book.

In this 'bare-all, dare-all, part reality and part fictive construct', Gargi used real names and characters, situations and events, and disguised them under the garb of 'an autobiographical novel', except for one. As soon as the extracts were published in the Sunday magazine section of *The Tribune* in Chandigarh on 20 May 1979, Chandigarhites were up in arms against the man who had given them the tradition of theatre over the years. 'How could he do that?' they all seemed to be asking. It was a betrayal of one and all.

Prominent Punjabi author and Gargi's old friend Sant Singh Sekhon, known for his historical plays including *Mittarpiara* (Beloved Friend) which won him the Sahitya Akademi Award in 1972, who had given an endorsement for the book, without even reading it, along with the likes of eminent and award-winning writer-director from Hollywood Elia Kazan, Khushwant Singh, Amrita Pritam and

Mulk Raj Anand, wrote to me (I was the editor of the book at Vikas) on 20 May 1979, saying:

> Seeing the comments of Khushwant Singh and Mulk Raj Anand, I was persuaded to write a few words.... Today, after reading extracts in *The Tribune*, I asked to be shown a typed manuscript. On going through it I strongly feel that the novel did not deserve my commendation. Therefore, I request you to kindly refrain from printing my comment.... This so-called novel is so unfairly defamatory about a lady who had the misfortune, perhaps, to love him. I want to disassociate myself from any line of opinion about the 'novel' – *The Naked Triangle.*

Amrita Pritam, the first prominent Punjabi woman poet, who went on to win many awards in her six-decade-long career, including the Padma Vibhushan and the Jnanpith Award and a nomination to the Upper House of the Indian parliament, the Rajya Sabha, was next to react. She came to know the contents of the book through her friend, the Punjabi writer and Gargi's friend of long, Ajeet Caur. Amrita was furious. She called me over to her place 'urgently'. That evening, her live-in companion, the soft-spoken and gentle artist Imroz, whom I met at the entrance itself, cautioned me about Amrita being in a foul mood. She was, in fact, livid and withdrew the endorsement saying: 'I could never imagine that Balwant would stoop to such a level.... I don't want my comments to be published under any circumstances. I don't know how *you* could publish such a book!' The fact that I was just an employee at Vikas who worked on the book as an editor was lost to her in the fit of anger. Mulk Raj Anand, one of the pioneers of Indo-Anglian fiction and author of such famous works like *Untouchable* and *Coolie*, was upset as well for having been 'misled' into giving his comments on the book, but did not make an issue of it. Apparently, Gargi had collected endorsements for the book just on the basis of a brief narration.

Strange as it may seem, endorsements, as a general practice in our country, are given away as a gift, or a favour, from one brother or sister author to another, generally without reading the manuscript. And some of the big names are equally guilty of it.

The book had already been printed and bound – 3,000 copies – waiting to be distributed. This was a crisis situation. Narendra Kumar gave instructions to reprint the jacket, deleting the endorsements of both Sant Singh Sekhon and Amrita Pritam, and 'pulp' the original one.

However, that was not the end of it. Later, much later, it came out that the endorsement given by Elia Kazan was never given for the *The Naked Triangle* but for a short story and an anthology of profiles that Gargi was planning and had shown to him. Khushwant Singh was the only one who insisted on reading the manuscript before giving his comments to be carried on the back cover of the book. Since he had read the manuscript, he was also the first one to review it in his syndicated column – 'With Malice Towards One and All' – thereby jumping the deadline given to other newspapers and magazines. He wrote:

> I don't recall when I first met Gargi, except that it was in the house of a good-looking lass whom he had succeeded in leading astray from the straight and narrow path of matrimony.... He was certainly an engaging talker and had the knack of surrounding himself with attractive women and persuading quite a few that a Dunlopillo mattress was not necessary to make bed an exciting place.... I did get to read an anthology of profiles that he published. They were the wittiest pieces of prose I had ever read. They were obviously designed to hurt and succeeded in doing so ...
>
> Balwant Gargi is like a cactus flower. He hurts anyone he touches. In *The Naked Triangle* he barely conceals the identity of the people he writes about. Some are mentioned by their real names.

In *The Naked Triangle* Balwant Gargi had spared no one. The well-connected Mrs K. Atma Ram was described as 'the horsy principal of the local Government College for Women … [who] by her sheer physical weight dominated Chandigarh art circles and pronounced judgements on theatre and literature with great arrogance. This cultural ogress with her squeaky voice had the power and charm to melt down the hardest bureaucrat.' His previous, immediate boss, the university vice chancellor, R. C. Paul, was described as '… a strong-jawed ex-wrestler … who looked like an officer of the Baluch Regiment'. Eminent scholar-poet Mohan Singh Diwana was referred to as 'a pale-bearded lobster'. The dean of university instruction and his team as 'dull-witted, mulish and arrogant buffoons'. An IAS officer, who was once Gargi's close friend, was mentioned as 'luxuriously fat … sipping whisky, smoking and pouting. She kept a small, loaded pistol in her cleavage…. She had sensitive lips … enormous breasts and buttocks … an IAS hippie she was the spoilt daughter of bureaucracy.' About Professor M. M. Puri he wrote:

> During the Emergency various forums were being set up: Artists' Forum, Doctors' Forum, Writers' Forum, Lawyers' Forum, Teachers' Forum…. Campus teachers vied with one another to champion Indira Gandhi's 20-point programme and fought for the secretaryship of the forums. Intrigues and counterintrigues. Finally, an ultra leftist-cum-rightist-cum-infra factionist grabbed the position … Professor M. M. Puri of the political science department…. Once, at a get-together at my house a heated discussion took place. M. M. Puri, a left-wing professor with a Lenin-beard said: 'We are gutless … the so-called intellectuals. After teaching for 20 years in a university, we lose not our hair but also our potency … now look at me. Do you think I believe in these new forums? But I am the first to be there. We are with Indira Gandhi. But I tell you that if the Chinese came, we will be with the Chinese, or the Americans.'

Puri moved the court for a perpetual and mandatory injunction seeking to 'restrain the printing, circulating, distributing and selling of the book....' As was bound to happen, the sales jumped. Everyone, from Chandigarh to Mumbai, seemed to be discussing the book. There were two particular party scenes – one at Satish Gujral's house in Delhi and the other in Mumbai where the then famous film story and script writer, and now lyricist, Javed Akhtar, was present – that became the talk of the social circles. Excerpts from the Delhi party scene:

> There were ten of us at [Satish Gujral's] party ... Jayshree was sipping a Martini and smoking a cigarillo. Her Dravidian lips and bosom jutted out. In her plushy voice she condemned bourgeois art and championed the cause of left-wing Naxalities.
>
> Blowing out a cloud of smoke she held Satish's hand. 'Why don't you give me that painting?'
>
> He snapped: 'Why should I? What have you given me? I have never gifted a painting. It's worse than whoring! ...'
>
> Jayshree retorted: 'Don't talk rot! You have become a bourgeois painter. What is the purpose of your paintings? They don't touch the masses ... just decorative designs. No ideas.'
>
> Satish laughed bitterly. 'What's an idea? If ideas made art, Plato would make a greater poet than Shakespeare. Van Gogh painted a pair of old shoes and made it look holier than the face of Madonna. But I know the painters who paint Madonnas and succeed in making her look worse than old shoes. Don't try to pump your newly learnt Marxism-Leninism into me. I have had enough of it in my time. It has taken me years to learn that greatness does not lie in painting beautiful things but painting things beautifully.... It's the power behind the brush which gives it the form of art. Not ideas, not feelings, not inspiration. Just power ... a magical creative power ... A lady asked Picasso, "You have great power in your lines. How do you paint?" Picasso replied, "Madam I don't paint with my brush; I paint with my penis".'

Satish's face became intense, his nostrils flaring. 'Picasso was not joking. He meant it. One paints from the pit of one's navel ...'

Jayshree held Satish's hand and pouted: 'You are mean. Why don't you give me that painting, louse!'

Satish looked at her and something flashed in his head. He said: 'All right, on one condition. You stand on that stool, strip and walk to that painting.'

Amidst cigarette fumes and cackles, Jayshree got up, walked defiantly to the stool and stood hipshot on it. She cast a theatrical look at the audience, her lips half-opened. She paused for a moment, gauging our reaction, a suspense for all of us ...

Jayshree looked at us with impish glee and gave a throaty laugh. She then jerked her head and started peeling off her clothes one by one – sari, petticoat, blouse – and stood in her bra and pink panties. The party enjoyed the game of striptease, cheering and giggling with excitement. Jayshree swung her head, undid her bra and flung it away, releasing her enormous silky breasts topped by dark aureoles and nipples. A sensation ran through us, of wonder, of admiration, of charged joy. Women shouted: 'That's all.'

Satish thundered: 'No!'

Jayshree laughed, jiggled, kicked off her panties, and rotated like a model. What we saw was a glimpse of the inky plumage of her crotch.

She walked with a swagger, making her breasts bobble, and stood on her toes to reach the painting. In the crazy light of the room were seen her long ivory hands with polished black nails and her golden-olive buttocks, like the two halves of a musk melon.

She removed the painting, picked up her clothes and disappeared into the other room.

After a few minutes she walked in beaming, wrapping her sari around her.

Satish had not bargained for this. He was perspiring with shame as if it was he who had been stripped.

Though Gargi had not used the real name, all knew who Jayshree was. What had been a small, private affair, seen by a few, was now public knowledge. Naturally, 'Jayshree' was hopping mad.

Gargi of course justified his book and 'hubris' by saying to one and all: 'The women that I have loved have been immortalized in my book, they have become every man's fantasy. I have lifted them from their middle-class anonymity and made them into archetypes. They will be remembered for generations to come … I have glorified them by exposing them … this exposure is not of corruption or blackmarket, it is not a political exposure. It is an exposure of my soul, their soul, of their body, or their art, of lovely breasts and naked conversations. I describe them like this because I love them. And love them dearly.'

I asked him: 'You have described your friends ruthlessly. You have called an artist friend "a dead monster". About a well-known socialite, you have said: "her breasts are so glamorous that they should be kept in a museum". Aren't these outrageous expressions?'

'This is how I see them. I cannot see them from their viewpoint. I describe things, I believe, without malice or without the intention of hurting anybody. All are my friends, some very dear,' he replied.

Years later, in 1992, Gargi decided to write 'a sequel' to *The Naked Triangle*, not for Vikas Publishing House as, by then, much had changed there. To summarize: By the early 1980s Vikas had grown into a household name. Its head, Narendra Kumar, led a small, dedicated and enthusiastic team from the front at the functional 5, Ansari Road offices in New Delhi. He was a great boss to work for – hard-working, ever-smiling and always accessible, hospitable and generous. However, success does a lot of things to lot of people and Narendra Kumar was no exception. From an expert in developing and maintaining author–publisher relationships, he turned into an arrogant and a pompous brat.

Sometime in the summer of 1980, Narendra Kumar and Sharda Chawla, the graceful and ever-young-looking wife of Vikas's parent company owner C. M. Chawla, decided to move out of the group's headquarters at Ansari Road – the hub of Indian publishing industry – to the inhospitable terrain of Sahibabad, across the border in Uttar Pradesh. A move that baffled one and all, it was reminiscent of the eccentric sultan of Delhi, Muhammad bin Tughlaq (1325–51), who shifted his capital from Delhi to Daulatabad at much expense and time only to return to Delhi. The Vikas shift was a monumental folly by all standards. Two giant-sized sheds were erected – one for warehousing of books, the other for the staff. Hot, dusty and inhuman conditions prevailed. Narendra Kumar and Sharda Chawla, who had since the inception of Vikas worked from two small-sized rooms in Ansari Road, made for themselves giant-sized halls – each larger than perhaps the entire former Vikas premises. Ironically, this full-of-life and energetic man of action, ever visible on the Indian publishing scene, got lost behind a giant oval desk. With it the sun had set on Vikas. And Narendra Kumar!

Gradually, one by one, the senior staff, including me, quit. And, one by one, authors too started bidding goodbye.

By the mid-1980s, the publishing scenario in the country too was changing. By December 1991, the grim-looking C. M. Chawla, who had long forgotten how to smile, too decided to enter the publishing business, in defiance of Vikas, and develop a parallel list – a move that surprised many. He hired me for the job. His company, UBS Publishers' Distributors, was a giant in the business of book distribution and exports. He was the one who had started Vikas, a company, which he had, for all practical purposes, lost or handed over to his wife Sharda and Narendra Kumar years back, depending on which way one looked at it. It was only on the morning of 5 May 1992 when, in a swift operation carried out with military precision, Chawla rose, phoenix-like, to overthrow Narendra Kumar and take back Vikas. It was a coup, carried out in complete secrecy, which even his so-called lieutenants did not know about. And Narendra Kumar, the man who had changed the face of Indian publishing not so long back, who had been responsible for building the imprint of Vikas into a brand across the length and breadth of the country and overseas, was left disgraced and humiliated, with his little-known private imprint Har Anand Publishers as his crutch.

Released on Friday, 1 October 1993, *Purple Moonlight* was finally neither a sequel to *The Naked Triangle* nor as hurtful to one and all. By then Gargi had mellowed considerably. However, it was autobiographical and, as I had written in the blurb, a collage of happenings interlaced with passion, greed, lust and danger, wherein Gargi described his emotional and artistic world: sexual adventures in Moscow in the 1950s, tender evenings with the Nobel Prize winner Doris Lessing in a foggy London, a night in a Russian prison, mehfils (gatherings) at Mulk Raj Anand's, unlimited parties in the company of writer-historian-novelist Khushwant Singh and artist Satish Gujral, and film actress Parveen Babi's intelligent ravings. Towards the end of the book, Gargi mused 'over life and death, loneliness, the mockery of time, the destructive nature of beauty'[4] and much else. Perhaps, he was predicting his own future.

To go back to Neelam Mansingh Chowdhry: 'In 1996, he decided to shift back to Chandigarh, the city he had romanced in his youth with the hope of recapturing its beguiling spirit. His calling card, when he had first arrived in 1969, was talent and originality, and the city had lavished its love on him. But things had changed; his friends from his earlier days had either passed on, or moved out or just ignored him. His students had climbed into their professions, and did not have the space to accommodate an aging Lothario. The rejection of the "insider" by the "outsiders" who had indulged his intellectual conceit in the past was a hard reality to digest. The truth of the matter was that no one was ready to forgive him his trespasses and *The Naked Triangle* had made him a social pariah. He moved to Bombay, to be with his son Manu. Languishing in a cruel and harsh city, he slowly decayed and then faded, an old, gaunt man barely recognizable, struck with memory loss. Memory is identity, and by losing this, he lost himself.'[5]

However, coming back to *Purple Moonlight*, it was 'unputdownable' and a commercial success, which gave him fairly good royalties at a time when he badly needed money. The book resonated with me, as I was a part of a few events described in it, one of which stands out in my mind even today – a meeting with the Hollywood writer-director Elia Kazan.

The sixth International Film Festival of India (IFFI) held in New Delhi during 3–16 January 1977 was a grand affair. Three of the most prominent and influential film-makers in the history of cinema were on the jury – the Italian Michelangelo Antonioni, the legendary Japanese Akira Kurosawa, who was to win the Academy Award for Lifetime Achievement in 1990, and the Greek-American Elia Kazan, who went on to direct twenty-one actors to Oscar nominations, winning nine of them.

Three-time Academy Award winner, Elia Kazan, one of the most honoured and influential directors in Broadway and Hollywood history who gave the world many legendary actors like Marlon Brando, landed in New Delhi on the afternoon of 1 January 1977 from Bombay (now Mumbai), where he was on a short holiday along with his then girlfriend, the actress Barbara Loden. Within a day he had reportedly got tired of watching bad films and decided, instead, to go around Delhi. Balwant Gargi, who had helped the film directorate get Kazan to India called me (I happened to be visiting Delhi from Simla where I was posted with the *Indian Express* as its state correspondent), to say that Elia was in town and asked if I could play host to him for a day as he himself was busy with the festival. Playing host to him? It was something I couldn't have ever dreamt of. Excitement written all over, I landed at Gargi's home next morning. Elia was already there, sitting on the wooden takhatposh covered with a colourful Phulkari, in the courtyard.

Pleasantries over, Kazan said: 'Call me Elia…. Barbara wants to go to the Cottage Emporium [then situated in the old colonial structure next to the Indian Oil Bhavan on Janpath] and then go to the state emporia [on Baba Kharak Singh Marg].'

'What would you like to do?' I asked.

'Can you take me to a Hindu cremation ground? I would love to go there,' he replied.

We drove to Nigambodh Ghat – the old and ever-busy crematorium on the banks of the Yamuna on the Outer Ring Road, behind the historic seventeenth-century Red Fort. There were over a dozen pyres burning.

'This place is real busy. I am glad you brought me here …'

He stayed there for four to five hours, observing the performance of various rituals associated with the last ceremonies of the 'departed souls', noting, once in a while, a point or two in his little notepad, 'inhaling the fumes', unmindful of the vast amount of smoke and ash flying around from the lit pyres.

Later in the afternoon, just when I was wondering when Elia would get up, I heard music. As the sound came closer, I saw a large group of mourners, carrying a decorated bier with a local seven-member band playing a joyous number from a recently released music track of the J. Om Prakash film *Apnapan*, which had hit the bestseller list: '*Aadmi musafir hai, aata hai jaata hai*' ... Elia was somewhat baffled and looked at me inquiringly. I explained that in the case of a very old person passing away, who had seen a 'full life' and spent the last days without suffering or illness, the family – children, grandchildren, and perhaps even great-grandchildren – and friends 'celebrate' the person's life, after death, instead of the traditional mourning.

A discreet inquiry revealed that the person happened to be an old lady whose age nobody seemed to know for sure. She had lived a 'good life', was much cared for, and loved, by all nineteen members of the family who lived under one roof and ran a common kitchen.

Both Elia and I were taken to be a part of the large gathering and given samigri (kindlings) and asked to offer it on the burning pyre.

Later, as we drove back, Elia was in a pensive mood. He said: 'I love it … it's so pure … so sacred … almost sacroscant…. You Hindus have a great, a noble ritual of burning the dead. You give back to the earth what you get from it…. It's so pure … so refined. Thank God, you don't leave the carcass beneath the earth but clear it so beautifully…. The fire destroys everything, the good and the evil, at the same time. Not like us…. We are like barbarians, who put the body in a coffin, bury it in the earth and let it rot. I hate to think that insects and worms will eat the eyes or ears of a loved one. Imagine, after me, some rodent crunching my skull and various species of insects having a merry feast with my brain as their pudding! ... Eeeks! Just thinking about it gives me the creeps….'

Gargi referred briefly to this incident in *Purple Moonlight*. So did Elia in his brilliant autobiography *A Life*.[6] According to Elia:

> I've known two ceremonies of the dead that I admired, and I admired them because they were celebrations, not objects of hysterics, breast-beating, and overpraising a dead person. One was in India, just outside old Delhi, and I watched from the time they sat the old lady, whose life they were celebrating, in her favourite chair on the makings of a great bonfire. I was invited to add a few pieces of kindling, then I watched the flames consume her, sat by patiently with the members of her family and her friends until the ashes were powder, then were gathered and emptied into the flood of a river close by, along with all the flowers that had been brought to the place. It was beautiful, it was final, and it cleared the earth of a carcass.

Actually, Elia had got it a little wrong. With so many pyres burning we had got involved in two different ceremonies of two different families. The second was of a family that had come to collect the remains of their departed one who had been cremated a day earlier. Elia saw how these were picked, cooled in a bucket of water mixed with milk, collected in a bag and then immersed in the Yamuna river, amidst the chanting of prayers by family members and the local priest, just behind Nigambodh Ghat.

My meeting Elia, and spending a day with him, is one memory I have treasured to this day.

In designing the cover of *Purple Moonlight* lay another story.

Gargi wanted a full nude. That was not possible as various complications could arise, including a legal one. I told him so. He was upset. Finally, it was decided to have a topless woman … of course, not a photograph but a painting. I suggested one by the artist Jatin Das. The seventy-three-year-old eminent painter, lecturer and muralist Jatin Das is an innovative artist who has explored 'new and dynamic ways of depicting human figures. His paintings mainly revolve around the various aspects of a man-woman relationship such as crisis, contacts, disclosure, emotional tensions etc. The treatment of human forms in his paintings is exceptionally great and the colours seem to be charged with emotional tinges. The linear arrangement and brisk brushwork further add a unique dimension to his work'.[7]

Jatin was reluctant. Apparently, Gargi had said something nasty about him to some common friends who had carried it back. One soporific morning, I landed at Jatin's Nizamuddin apartment in Delhi and talked to him. A large-hearted man, he agreed immediately. Everything that Gargi had said had been forgotten in a moment. There and then Jatin started drawing. He was charged. His hands moved fast on the paper as a voluptuous woman, on her knees, displaying enormous breasts with heavy dark nipples, thick black hair falling on her back and enormous buttocks, emerged. It was beautiful, but not what I had in mind for the cover. It was too heavy. Dark. My woman on the cover had to have the most kissable lips and much more grace with exquisite contours, slim arms, sensuous large firm breasts and beautiful thighs. She would have to look like the most desirable woman.

Jatin drew again. This time he got it. Or so I thought. But he himself was not satisfied. He then said: 'OK, *mere dost* [my friend]. I know what you want. Come tomorrow and take it ... it will be ready.'

The next morning, Gargi and I went to Jatin's, braving heavy rain. Both of them shook hands and, to Jatin's credit, not once did he bring up the subject of the nasty comments made by Gargi. Instead, he welcomed him with his usual warmth and a big hug. And there it was – beautiful – a dream sketch … in black and white. Gargi had it coloured on the sides in vibrant greens, reds, blues and yellows, with Jatin's permission, by his former colleague and talented artist, Mahendra, at the Department of Indian Theatre in Chandigarh.

With the final sketch in hand, I asked Jatin if I could have the other two also. Generous as ever, he just picked them up and gave them to me. Overwhelmed, I didn't know how to thank him and have not been able to do so to this day. Jatin, I hope you are reading this: Thank you, thank you very much. I had always wanted to own a Jatin Das and you would always say: '*Mere dost*, take whichever you want … for you 50 per cent off … and pay me whenever you can … even instalments would do.' Finally, you gave me three. That too gratis! And, even today, I don't know how to thank you.

Years later I gifted one to my friend Om Arora. The other two occupy a place of pride in my house next to the nudes by Akbar Padamsee and Suhas Roy, and a beauty by none other than M. F. Husain.

The masterly Rock Garden (above and below) in Chandigarh, designed by Nek Chand Saini (right), over decades of hard work and dedication, at times against bureaucratic resistance.

My prized possessions: two early oil paintings by Satish Gujral, made in 1949 and 1950, respectively, which I have inherited from my father.

The sketches that painter Jatin Das made (above) for the cover of Balwant Gargi's *Purple Moonlight,* and the final cover of the book.

The sketch that M.F. Husain made for me at the India Today Group's office in Okhla in 2002.

The full cover of General V.P. Malik's book, *Kargil: From Surprise to Victory*, which I published at HarperCollins India in 2006. It continues to be in print, with a new paperback edition out in 2010.

4

M. F. Husain

The Generous Gifter

I AM ONE OF THE LUCKY FEW TO OWN SOME GOOD WORKS OF ART and that too for free. These include two from Satish Gujral, one from M. F. Husain and three from that genius, R. K. Laxman.

The two from Satish Gujral were not gifted to me, but to my father, from whom I inherited them. One of them is a 'Mother and Son' watercolour, which was apparently drawn by Uncle Satish and coloured by my father B. R. Chopra. The other, a 1949 four-by-four, oil on canvas, has the backs of three women – the writer Uma Vasudev in the middle with writer Ved Mehta's two sisters Omi and Nirmal on the left and right, respectively. Apparently, Satish Gujral, in those days, was smitten by Uma, who never even looked at him during her daily evening walks with her two friends, on the Mall Road in Simla. Much later, in 1995, Uncle Satish had the art restorer and author, Rupika Chawla, restore this painting for me and had it beautifully reframed.

M. F. Husain's was a different story. Maqbool Fida Husain was undoubtedly the most famous, charismatic, controversial, nationally and internationally celebrated Indian painter of the twentieth century, who became a victim of the ever-increasing 'mob culture' so very prevalent in India today. It was all because 'he treated the Hindu gods and goddesses as visual stimuli rather than deities, depicting them unclothed and often in sexually suggestive poses'.[1] These hurt the Hindu nationalist groups who mounted a hate campaign against him. Ironically, these paintings, when first done in 1970, went unnoticed but hit the headlines twenty-six years later in 1996, when *Vichar Mimansa*, a little-known socio-political monthly magazine, published them.

It was on 22 August 2002 when Baba (as I called Husain), dressed in his usual white khadi kurta and a Nehru jacket, barefeet, with a long paintbrush in his hand and a cotton, long sling bag on his shoulder, accompanied by Amitabh Kant, the then head of Kerala Tourism, came to see me unannounced in my office in Okhla, a locality in south Delhi. By this time I was working with the India Today Group and had started its Book Club, to which, later, was added its publishing imprint Books Today. The visit was a pleasant surprise as I had not met Baba for nearly four or five years.

Husain had apparently been commissioned by Kerala Tourism to do a series of paintings to promote the state's tourism industry, which it now wanted published as a coffee-table book, with an introduction by the well-known writer Shashi Tharoor. 'I want it out in ten days as I have to take at least 400 copies with me to Belgium on Monday, 2 September, to be released at the Festival of India,' Husain ordered.

'Baba, *ten* days for a coffee-table book, to be designed, printed and bound?' I protested.

'I don't know all this … I know you can do it … so let's start …'

Amitabh Kant intervened: 'I have come to complete all written formalities that you may have … we will buy 2,000 copies … the rest you can sell in the market.' I was left with no choice.

My office was in the pre-press reprography department of Thomson Press. I asked its head for its schedule and costing. By then word had gone around that Husain was in the premises and there was much excitement all around. By the time the costing could be worked out I asked Husain: 'Baba, I am meeting you after so many years and that too you have come to my office, can you write something for me?'

'Write? Why? Let me draw something for you,' he replied. 'Give me paper and some colours.'

In a publishing house or the repro there is no dearth of paper but colours were not available. Husain took out a black marker pen from his waistcoat pocket and asked: 'What would you like me to draw?'

'Just a beautiful woman ... reading a book,' I answered.

Husain made one, signed it, and handed it to me. Even today the drawing occupies a place of pride in my home. And yes, the Thomson Press staff, once again as all too often, did a superb job and met Husain's deadline. On the morning of 2 September Husain came with Amitabh Kant to see the printed book. He told Amitabh: 'Didn't I tell you only he can do it?'

That was my last meeting with Baba. His compliment has been a prized possession with me – more valuable than any painting, a treasure for a lifetime.

However, a couple of months later, Husain sent one Rashda Siddiqui, to me. She had compiled a large collection of Husain's work – paintings, sketches, photographs, poems, conversations, interviews – over 3-4 decades and wanted them published in the form of a large coffee-table book. Later I realized that she had the largest collection of Husain's works in her possession, gifted by Husain over the years.

Rashda was Husain's 'closest friend' since long, and remained so till his last days – a friend who genuinely cared for him, travelled with him, and looked after him and all his interests. With age she had put on an enormous amount of weight, yet, one could visualize what a beauty she must have been in her youth. My friend Seema, daughter of the well-known Urdu writer Ismat Chugtai (Nannu to me), who had known Rashda since her Lucknow days, summed her up in two words: 'real stunner'. To me it seemed like an understatement!

This 284-page hardbound, *In Conversation with Husain Paintings,* sponsored by Rabo Bank and published under the Books Today imprint, had a black-and-white Husain sketch of Rashda, dated 8 February 1977, on its the cover. Rashda had 'peppered' her book with 'interviews, conversations, amusing anecdotes', which brought out the 'warm, mischievous aspect of Husain that few knew about'. The book gave an insight into the making of Husain's well-known series on Mother Teresa, Satyajit Ray, on umbrellas and horses, and so much more. A warm, loving tribute, by a Husain-obsessed friend and loyal companion.

On seeing the advance copy, Husain called to thank me and said he was sending me 'that sketch you liked'. It was a black-and-white drawing of a painting from his book on Kerala (published on p. 25) that I had indeed liked very much – a sketch of a Kerala woman – nude, with her rounded buttocks and the left breast with an erect nipple – sitting on the side of a boat, with the tusk and the right leg of a baby elephant across her left arm.

However, the sketch never reached me.

Soon Husain, who was termed as 'the Picasso of India' by *Forbes* magazine, whose highest-selling painting fetched $1.6 million in a 2008 Christie's auction, went into a self-imposed exile in Qatar. One of the original members of the Bombay Progressive Artists' Group, founded by F. N. Souza, he died in a London hospital on 9 June 2011, at the age of ninety-five, with his wish to breathe his last in India unfulfilled.

5

F. N. Souza

The Ungrateful One

UNGRATEFUL AUTHORS ARE A DIME A DOZEN BUT LUCKILY I have had to face just a few of them. They are all sweetness when picked up, launched and groomed by a publisher. Once they reach the shore, they kick the boat and the boatman that brought them there without any qualms. The first one that I can think of was the artist F. N. Souza (1924-2002).

As mentioned in the previous chapter, Francis Newton Souza was a founding member of the Bombay Progressive Artists' Group and the first post-Independence artist from India to achieve high recognition in the West. According to art historian Yashodhara Dalmia: 'Souza's expressionistic style sought to illustrate both low-life and high energy. Be it the sluts or the suits, the seamy side of life or the steamy, the gnomish, pox-scarred boy from Goa went on to become one of the first Indian artists to be feted in the salons of Europe.'[1]

According to the famous English painter and art critic John Berger, his style 'was deliberately eclectic: essentially Expressionist in character',[2] but 'also drawing on the post-war Art Brut[3] movement and elements of British Neo-romanticism'. According to Dalmia: 'At the heart of Souza's creativity was the belief that society's destructive aspects shouldn't be suppressed, they should be aired and confronted. Be it the hypocrisy of the church, the corruption of the upper classes or the repression of sexuality in a country that has a Khajuraho, he was uncovering the underbelly of existence.'[4]

Souza was a colourful personality who led an eventful life, arousing a great deal of social and media interest. His works had, by the mid-1970s, been exhibited in various world capitals. A number of books had been published on him in Europe and America and in various volumes on art he figured as one of the masters of modern art. After Souza's death on 28 March 2002 in Mumbai, his works sold for over a million dollars each. In fact, in 2008, his painting *Birth*, done in 1955, set a world auction record for the most expensive Indian painting sold till then at a price of $2.5 million (Rs 11.3 crore) at a Christie's auction. It was bought by Harmony Arts Foundation, run by former film actress Tina Ambani, wife of the business tycoon Anil Ambani of the Reliance Group.

In November 1977, Vikas approached him for his autobiography. Souza agreed. A contract was signed a couple of weeks later and the book, to be illustrated with Souza's works, was tentatively slated for a 1979 release.

On 28 January 1979, Souza (who was then in the USA) sent the manuscript, handwritten, by airmail, under a high insurance cover, along with sixty-two drawings. While we waited to receive the manuscript news came in on 3 February that the Delhi customs had seized the entire packet containing the manuscript and the drawings on charges of 'obscenity'. Our men at the customs certainly have a queer sense of morality. Their private views often obscure their official judgement of 'obscenity'.

It became a unique case, which was picked up by the international media and finally featured in Parliament too. On 23 March 1979, the Congress (I) member in the Rajya Sabha and a well-known author himself, Shrikant Verma, made a forceful address:

> ... a painter speaks not only through words but through sketches and drawings. The assistant collector of customs in New Delhi has confiscated the manuscript [and] drawings .... It is a disgrace for the entire government that the customs of this government

> are so backward that they have taken upon themselves the task of the censor, that they have become the custodians of public morality, that they can ban a book in this manner. They have confiscated 62 drawings as they consider these to be obscene … [will they confiscate] the presents the dignitaries bring with them if the customs consider them obscene? If the drawings of Souza can be detained by the customs why not the paintings of the great masters of the twentieth century in Europe and America?
>
> If we were to agree to the standards adopted by the Delhi customs for considering a certain work of art as obscene and erotic then what shall we do when we are confronted with our own temples at Khajuraho and Konark? Are we going to hang our heads in shame? Today, we have a backward mind as reflected in the Delhi customs.

On the other end, sitting in New York, Souza was getting more and more anxious, and quite naturally so. His life's work had been detained. He would keep on writing letters, send telegrams, telex messages and call regularly, unable to understand why it was taking so long to get the manuscript and drawings released. To quote one letter:

> … how do they [customs] function there? The official is acting outside his jurisdiction as a custodian of public morals. His duty is to collect revenue on dutiable goods and to prevent contrabands entering into the country. The manuscript he is arbitrarily detaining has not been legally declared contraband. The drawings are an integral part of the text. The writings and the illustrations dovetail into each other. The drawings are not photographs which may or may not be regarded as obscene. I don't know how the law there stands on that issue. But these drawings are works of art and the law is clear on that.

The law indeed was clear and this was very much evident from the *Akbar Padamsee And Ors* vs *Union of India And Ors* case, Bombay, 1950. The art world was shocked when the Bombay police had raided Akbar Padamsee's studio. Padamsee had taken the matter to the Bombay High Court, which gave 'a judgment phrased in terms of a tribute in the artist's favour'.

Souza was right when the wrote: 'If every petty official uses his own judgement it would make nonsense of the legal precedent. Would this ignorant official have detained my manuscript if the illustrations were line drawings of Khajuraho? In fact, my drawings do not consist of representing sexual intercourse as Khajuraho does. But in my next volume I intend to depict sexual intercourse in the illustrations if only to get rid of the Victorian laws which still persist in our land and create harassment by petty officials. I will depict even intercourse which abounds in our ancient Sanskrit culture.'

Souza was more upset about the fact that Atal Bihari Vajpayee, the then minister of external affairs, had inaugurated an exhibition in India's consulate in New York at which Souza's works were proudly exhibited for the public – the same works that the Indian customs officials had now detained. He thought of writing to Prime Minister Morarji Desai but dropped the idea on the advice of Narendra Kumar. He wrote to me: 'I don't think approaching the Prime Minister will do any good. He is an old fogey recycling his own urine, and seems to be bent upon imposing prohibition on beverages other than what he believes are potable ...'[5]

Finally, on 29 March 1979, the customs released the manuscript and the drawings after taking 'expert advice', which 'does not consider this work of art as obscene'. However, the question that remained unanswered was and is to this day: Can the customs department be given the authority to judge what is objectionable in art? It is all very simple to detain the works of an artist by declaring it 'obscene' and releasing it later by saying 'expert opinion has been taken which certifies that the said work is not obscene'. If a nude is interpreted as 'erotic' and declared 'obscene' and thus 'objectionable', the entire art heritage of Europe of the last two centuries will have to be done away with. And what will happen to our art – ranging from Pahari miniatures to the scenes from the Kamasutra to the temples of Khajuraho?

Obscenity in art is a controversial and a sensitive question. Only those with finer sensibilities and artistic vision can decide what is and is not 'obscene'. The issue cannot be left in the hands of a few policemen and customs officials!

However, Souza's book never saw the light of the day.

Knowing that Narendra Kumar had gone out of his way to get the manuscript released from the customs in New Delhi, Souza perhaps started thinking that Vikas could not do without his 'gold mine' any more. As he wrote to Kumar on 11 April 1979: '… there is no doubt that my autobiography will be the most sensational book (and full of wit and learning) to come out of India when it is published.' He raised his financial demands considerably and started dictating terms. He now wanted the autobiography in three volumes without a single word deleted. As he said, 'My work does not need any editing. Not a single line, or word can be deleted. I will not accept any changes.' That was indeed the last straw. A decision was taken to drop the entire project, even though by then the handwritten script had been typed and editorial work started.

A book on the life and times of one of our greatest artists, which would have been a valuable addition to any shelf, died before being born. For me it was a great personal loss for I was eagerly looking forward to working on it.

6

Dom Moraes

The Devil within Authors

FRIDAY, 8 AUGUST 1980, 8.30 A.M. AN OLD, BRUISED AND battered DLY taxi was heading towards 1, Safdarjang Road, New Delhi, residence of the prime minister of India, Indira Gandhi. Its lone passenger, impatient and tense, kept ordering the old Sardar driver in his half-English, half-Bombay-Hindi to drive faster, or he would be late for his appointment with the prime minister, as he constantly kept on looking at his watch. The passenger was the famous poet-writer Dom Moraes, then editor of *Sunday Standard*, the widely circulated Sunday issue of the *Indian Express* newspaper published from a dozen-odd cities across the country. He held in his hand an elegantly gift-wrapped copy of his latest book *Mrs Gandhi*, published the world over by Jonathan Cape. Dom, who was to present the book to the prime minister, was already visualizing the fanfare and publicity that would be splashed in the media the next day.

What happened was just the opposite.

There was no press. No photographers. To make matters worse, at the prime minister's residence, he was kept on tenterhooks about his meeting. It was well past his appointment time when, finally, he was quietly advised that the prime minister was about to leave for office, and to snatch a moment with her, it would be best to meet her where her car was parked.

Dom stood on the steps and as soon as he saw Mrs Gandhi, he walked towards her white official Ambassador car. Though already in a low mood at the reception meted out to him, he greeted her.

'Yes?' she enquired, rather curtly.

'Madam, I have brought my book to present to you,' he said.

'Book? What book? I don't need it. I don't read gutter stuff. Take it away,' she replied, while getting into her car and driving off. It was all over in just about ten seconds.

The snub came as a big shock to Dom. Dejected and crestfallen, he went straight to the *Indian Express* building on Bahadur Shah Zafar Marg and entered the office of executive editor Arun Shourie, with whom I happened to be sitting. Dom narrated his tale of woe to us. Arun suggested that since Indira Gandhi had refused to accept the book why not present it to him. Dom did so. The book, which went into Arun's large book collection, had the following inscription in it:

For the subject of these words
Dom

Dom Moraes, despite all his shortcomings, was a literary phenomenon of our times. He was precocious and immensely gifted. At the age of nineteen, his first book of verse, *A Beginning* (1957), appeared which won him the prestigious Hawthornden Prize in 1958 – the first non-English writer and also the youngest ever to win it. The book won him admiration from such distinguished poets as W. H. Auden and Stephen Spender. According to writer Deepak Tandon: 'Deeply influenced by the Welsh poet Dylan Thomas [also known as a roistering, drunken and doomed poet] and the Surrealistic school, Moraes' is a highly personal poetry, with a persistent confessional tone and the self-probing or a tortured soul. His verse often creates a haunted world in which classical, Christian, medieval and fairy tale myths are mixed and dragons and dwarfs, Cain and the unicorn, the tomb of Mycenae and Christ come together. He finds himself unloved and forlorn'.

Son of the legendary editor and author, Frank Moraes, Dom was born in a Goan Roman Catholic family and had an excruciating childhood and adolescence because of his mother's frequent bouts of insanity, which were a persistent nightmare for him. He was an accomplished essayist and a true stylist in the subcontinent who produced more than thirty volumes of poems and prose.

Dom's biography of Indira Gandhi was slated for an international release on 6 September 1980, in London. The embargo for publishing the extracts was 8 June 1980. Narendra Kumar of Vikas Publishing House, where I worked as its executive editor, bought the rights for publishing, distribution and marketing of Dom's biography of his 'proclaimed heroine' for the Indian subcontinent, directly from Jonathan Cape in the UK. It was a big book and timing was of great essence. We at Vikas were going all out with our promotional campaign, which included publication of excerpts in well-circulated journals – a normal practice for any publisher. Excerpts and serializations of books in newspapers and magazines are a big business in the West. In India, however, it is just the reverse. The media gets away with the argument: 'Look at the publicity we are giving you.'

Vikas gave the serialization rights to the then largest circulated weekly magazine *Sunday* edited by the young and energetic M. J. Akbar. The *Sunday* issue of 8 June 1980 carried the first extract as a cover story. It was well received and the issue got sold out. However, Dom was most unhappy. Early next morning he called me and expressed immense displeasure, stating that Vikas had no right to give out any extracts.

No amount of reasoning with him, as also later with his charming actress wife, Leela Naidu, whom I knew well, helped. Dom threatened legal action. Two days later, Dom again called to say that he would be in Delhi on Friday, 13 June, and asked if we could meet over lunch at York's restaurant in Connaught Circus. My boss Narendra Kumar felt that I should meet him and see what Dom had to say.

We met over Dom's favourite kadai-chicken, which I had introduced him to a couple of years earlier. We talked about his two forthcoming books from Vikas – *The Seventh Person* and *Collected Poems.* Apparently, on 18 December 1970 (much before I joined Vikas) Dom had signed an agreement with Narendra Kumar for five books. Of these three, *My Son's Father*, which was released as a hardbound in the UK in 1970, was released in India in paperback on 17 January 1971; *From East and West* was released in hardback on 21 January 1972; and *The Tempest Within: An Account of East Pakistan* on 17 November 1972 in hardback.

A brilliant conversationalist with a great knack for amusing stories, the soft-spoken Dom did not bring up the subject of the publication of extracts of *Mrs Gandhi*. Neither did I. Perhaps he had seen reason, I reported to Narendra Kumar.

I was wrong!

Six weeks later, on 30 July, Narendra Kumar received an official letter, under 'Registered A.D.'[1] saying that the permission for publication of excerpts to *Sunday* magazine and elsewhere (by then some other regional newspapers had started carrying extracts) 'had been given without the author's permission' and he was within his rights to take legal action. On 6 August 1980, Narendra Kumar replied, saying:

> … being the Indian publishers, Vikas Publishing House had full rights to get the book widely reviewed and publicised in order to generate adequate demand to justify the edition. I hardly need to say that you as the author and we as the publishers ought to work closely to ensure the success of the book.
>
> Incidentally, serialization in India does not involve big money and I am sure you as editor of *Sunday Standard* are aware of it. While the amounts received are negligible, the publicity thus generated is of greater significance.

The same day Narendra Kumar also wrote to M. J. Akbar:

> ... Although we have traditionally all rights relating to co-publishing arrangements, Dom Moraes is creating confusion about the serialization rights. May I request you that no further excerpts from this book *Mrs Gandhi* be published till you hear from us....

The next morning I too wrote to Dom saying that since he 'did not bring up the serialization subject at our last meeting over lunch on Friday, I presumed that the matter was resolved. Your letter dated 30 July to Mr Narendra Kumar has thus come as a shock and I wish you had discussed the matter with me. He has already replied to you, thus I don't need to add anything more. However, I would like to assure you as the author of the said extracts, that the amounts received from *Sunday* would be passed on to you.'

All correspondence was being copied to Jonathan Cape in London.

On 3 September 1980, we at Vikas received a friendly but business-like response, without any imputation of any impropriety, from Dom's literary agent in London, Ms Dinah Wiener of Curtis Brown Limited:

> ... As agents of Dom Moraes I have in my possession copies of your recent correspondence with Jonathan Cape Ltd. Although we, of course, congratulate you on selling an extract from *Mrs Gandhi* to *Sunday* magazine, I think you are not aware of the fact that Curtis Brown controls serial rights of this title. I would therefore be most grateful if you could send me the cheque for the amount you receive from *Sunday* for the extracts, so that I can arrange for payment to be made to Dom Moraes.
>
> Thanking you,
> Ms Dinah Wiener
>
> P.S. I would like to wish you every success with the sales of *Mrs Gandhi* in India.

Meanwhile, the book was not getting the kind of reception that one was hoping for. It was dismissed as a 'poor exercise in egotism'. Word had also travelled fast that Indira Gandhi had found the book distasteful and had refused to accept a copy from the author. Normally, even the most illiterate sycophant and party worker would have paid anything to possess, and be seen around with, a copy of the book in order to show his loyalty. Ironically, this time the loyalty was shown, by one and all, by disapproving the book and openly speaking against it, even by those who had not read it or did not know how to read. According to reviewers, the book was a damp squib. We were hugely disappointed. Dom was immensely dejected.

On Thursday, 18 September 1980, Dom came to the Vikas office to meet me. Samuel Israel, the editorial consultant, was also present. Dom was still seething with anger. I failed to convince him that the subject was closed now as agreed upon with his agents Curtis Brown. He left, threatening dire action against Vikas.

The action came on Sunday, 5 October 1980, when Dom used the columns of his newspaper the *Sunday Standard*, to settle his 'scores'. He wrote: '… very few Indian publishers have any kind of principles at all and the writer seems to have come to the conclusion that arguments with sharks does not clear the water … good publishers never treat authors as chattels: there is usually, after some years, a friendship between the author and his publisher … I am not sure whether this is the case in India. Here a book is taken as a product, and its author a kind of factory.'

A controversy was bound to erupt. Even the vernacular press had a field day. The Federation of Indian Publishers (FIP) was belligerent. Its then president, Vishwanath, wrote a strong letter to S. Mulgaonkar, then editor-in-chief of the *Indian Express*: 'I would like to raise the question of the propriety of publishing slanderous material against the publishing community wherein specific names have been mentioned….' The controversy led to other issues. A *Hindustan Times* report went to the extent of saying: 'Mr Moraes is still a British passport holder and a man who lived abroad longer than in India….' Another paper commented: 'Obviously, for Mr

Moraes, Vikas is only a pretext to attack Indian publishers. Perhaps his antagonism towards Indian publishers is a part of his general dislike for all things Indian. One cannot forget that Dom gave up his Indian citizenship in protest against India's action in liberating Goa. If Moraes has chosen not to give up British citizenship in protest against the neo-colonialist policies followed by Britain, it is certainly his business. But he should know that his readers are not gullible fools.... Dom has taken upon himself a role which would thrill those who still believe in the discredited doctrine of the white man's burden. Everything Indian evokes his ire and anger.'

Dom's article was a meaningless piece of unjustified condemnation. His thesis was shocking and his conclusions sweeping when he implied that 'very few publishers have any kind of principles'. The main question being debated was: 'Is it ethical for an editor to use the columns of his paper to settle personal scores?'

Soon, as normally happens, skeletons came rolling out of the cupboard. Vision Books revealed that on 6 July 1977, Dom had signed an agreement with them for the biography of Mrs Gandhi, and taken a 'sizeable advance against its royalties'. Vision announced the book in its September newsletter. Seeing the announcement, Jonathan Cape wrote to Vision that Dom had already licensed exclusive world rights (including India) to them, through the literary agents Curtis Brown. Vision Books was stunned. It wrote to Dom reminding him about the contractual obligation and the advance given for it. Dom, in exchange, sent a portfolio of his already published articles to be recycled and dressed into a book. Vision refused. It never got back the advance. Vikas too got neither the two books nor the balance of the advance back.

Few people learn from past mistakes. And I am one of them.

By April 1984 I had left Vikas to join Macmillan India, the reputed publisher of educational books, which was being run by S. G. Wasani, who had turned the group around from a loss-making publishing house to a highly profitable one. In fact, if Narendra Kumar at Vikas taught me what hard work is all about, it was Wasani from whom I learnt the business of running a publishing house. For him nothing mattered but 'the bottom line'.

Sometime in end-1985, Wasani informed me that he was negotiating with the Nirlon Group for publishing the official pictorial biography of cricketer Sunil Gavaskar. The book was to be published and released in early 1987, by which time Pakistan was supposed to be touring India for a Test series. The group was now looking for a good author and three names were being considered, including that of Dom Moraes. Without thinking I told Wasani to suggest Dom, if Sunny agreed. Later that evening, I spoke to both Dom and Leela. It was like old times – warm and friendly. The incident relating to *Mrs Gandhi* was left behind.

Dom was excited about the Gavaskar project. The money was good, and that too at a time when he needed it. I don't know the details and how it was all worked out, nor was I privy to them, but a few weeks later, Wasani informed me that Dom had been signed on.

Many issues crept up between Sunny Gavaskar and Dom, initially during the various interviews conducted by Dom and later, during the writing of the book. However, these got resolved gradually, except for one that was quite a controversial remark made by Russi Mody of Telco. Sunny objected as the remark was 'not only derogatory but also factually incorrect'. I don't recall what it actually was but Dom threatened legal action if it was deleted. Sunny too was adamant. Finally, the particular comment was deleted, as some others, by which time Sunny had somewhat lost interest in the book. And so had Dom.

To make matters worse, this 206-page, coffee-table book in colour was tackily designed, poorly printed and badly bound. Perhaps, wanting to make an extra profit, instead of commissioning a professional designer and having it printed and bound in Singapore or Hong Kong where such prestigious projects were sent those days, Wasani had it printed at the Macmillan India Press in Injambakkam, on the outskirts of Madras (now Chennai). The press, which was equipped with basic machines and used for printing low-priced school textbooks, had neither the capacity nor the capability, nor even the expertise to take up such a prestigious project on machines which printed only textbook covers in colour. It was a disaster – simply a case of penny wise and pound foolish.

On Friday, 20 February 1987, late in the evening, I met Sunny and his wife Marshneil in the Jai Mahal Palace hotel in Jaipur, that incomparable palace hotel, set amidst 18 acres of lush green, beautifully landscaped Mughal Gardens. The Indian cricket team was staying there for the third Test match with Pakistan (21-25 February 1987). Needless to say, both felt very disappointed and upset with the poor production quality of the book they were so eagerly looking forward to. Over dinner they were relatively quiet. It was clear that they felt immensely let down. Sunny gave me a VIP pass for the match and asked me to bring a few copies to the stadium the next morning – just in case he needed to present some.

As was fixed, I reached the Sawai Man Singh Stadium early next morning, with five copies, which I handed over to Marshneil along with two gift-wrapped copies, which Sunny wanted to be released by the then president of Pakistan, General Muhammad Zia-ul-Haq, who had especially flown into Jaipur for a few hours to inaugurate the match, on his way to Ajmer Sharif. To my surprise, Marshneil informed me that they had decided not to have the biography released but just present a copy to President Zia and that too by their eleven-year-old son Rohan. After the introduction of the two teams, Rohan presented the book to President Zia who handed it over to one of his aides – a formality which did not go unnoticed.

India won the toss and opted to bat. Opener Sunny Gavaskar got out to the very first ball of the match from Pakistan captain Imran Khan, caught by Javed Miandad. A hush fell over the stadium. The second copy of the gift-wrapped book fell out of Marshneil's lap as she put both her hands to her mouth and stood up. Quietly, I slipped out without even saying goodbye to her.

7
Dev Anand

The Romance of Losing

One thing publishing teaches you is never take any book project for sure, even if the agreement is signed, even if an advance has been paid, till you have the manuscript in your hands. I have, over the years, been assured of many book projects, even signed some, which finally were published by someone else.

However, there are two books in particular, which I was looking forward to publishing but never could. Those were the books by Khushwant Singh (see Chapter 11) and the matinee idol, Dev Anand.

There is a little pain, some hurt and regret, even today.

Every time I notice Dev Anand's *Romancing with Life: An Autobiography* on my bookshelf, I am reminded of what could have been and, yet, could not be, though with a slight feeling of guilt also. Over the years, every time I met Dev Saab, as he was popularly known, he would tell very interesting stories about his life and times, and every time I would urge him to write his autobiography. His usual answer would be: 'But where is the time ... perhaps one day.

Let's see....' Always oozing with energy, Dev Saab had the artfulness of a born raconteur. Even though most of the conversation was more or less one-sided, he always said something new for me to learn from. His one big lesson, which he imparted to all, and many benefited from, was the message: 'Always be positive. Forget your yesterday. Live now. And only *now... now, now, now*.... Have you seen my film *Hum Dono*? If not, see it. There is a song, "*Main zindagi ka saath nibhata chala gaya, har fikr ko dhuein mein udata chala gaya*". It's a beautiful song penned by Sahir Ludhianvi. I follow that. I leave every worry behind and move on.' But a message that has remained vividly in my mind is: '*Kabhi nahin bhoolna ki haar mein bhi ek nasha hai*' (Never ever forget that in defeat too there is a great high).

Every time I came out after meeting Dev Saab I would feel pepped up, full of energy, younger, with a resolve to leave the past behind and move on. But it was easier said than done.

Once I suggested to him that since he had no time, why not give the job to a biographer. 'No', he said immediately. 'How can someone else write about me ... that life ... the experiences ... the emotions ...the loves ... the highs and lows ... everything? Only I know what I have gone through and only I can feel it. And only I can describe it. My life is not a dinner party where the chef will cook and serve to everyone. No. No. I will have to write it my way ... full of feeling, passion, emotions, the way it all happened ... as I saw it ... as I experienced it. I will give it to you the way I faced life ... raw ... beautiful ... full of blood and tears and laughter. I will write about my films, my loves, my successes, my failures ... yes, my failures also ... beautiful failures they all were ... each one of them. Remember, *Haar mein bhi ek nasha hai*. Which other person can describe all this? Nobody can. Nobody should. It's Dev Anand's life. And only Dev Anand can, and will, write his journey ... for he has romanced with it.'

Then suddenly it happened! I don't recall exactly when, but it was perhaps in the summer of 2003 that Dev Saab informed that he had made up his mind to write. I knew this was the *now* moment he always talked about. Now he would do it and nothing could stop him. And he did it. His dedication to writing his autobiography was exemplary. Always a late riser who would reach office after noon, he would check on his normal office routine and then start writing. Undisturbed. Dressed in his ankle-high trousers, his landmark jacket and a colourful scarf, he would sit on the corner sofa of his spacious but somewhat chaotic office where every corner was loaded with files, papers, magazines, posters, books, awards, framed posters of his films on the walls, and what not. He wrote in longhand, page after page, day after day. He was like a man obsessed. Whenever I called he would say: 'You have to come and see what all I have written … Do let me know when you are in town next … we will go over it and you tell me how it reads.'

I did meet him twice. He read out some portions but not once would he trust me with the pages to read. He had become like a child who had got his favourite toy, which he wanted to show off but not let any one else touch it. His reading page after page was earnest passion for what he had set out to create. On 12 October 2006, my old colleague from UBS Publishers' Distributors ,Vivek Ahuja, called to say: 'Call Dev Saab. He has finished his autobiography.'

I did. Dev Saab, excited as always, said: 'Come down whenever you can and we can talk. On 14 October 2006, I flew down to Mumbai. The heavy rain that evening was a big dampner to my reaching the Navketan office in Pali Hill. Little did I know that another, bigger dampner awaited me!

We had hardly settled down, when Dev Saab showed me the manuscript and said: 'I have finished it. Look at this: 964 pages, all in longhand … look at the blisters I have got on the sides of these two fingers from holding the pen and pencils, day after day, month after month, for hours each day…. Wait till you read it. You will love it … I have put everything I had into it …'

For nearly two hours Dev Saab talked about his book … read out extracts from the manuscript … explained scenes and what photographs he had selected to go in to it … how he would like to release it in Mumbai, Delhi, London, New York, Toronto … how he was already thinking of making the book into an international film. Finally, he said: 'We must publish the book fast. I am already selecting the photograph to go on the cover. So you should urgently talk to my lawyer Mohan Dewan in Pune to settle the terms and conditions.'

'Lawyer? Why should I talk to a lawyer, Dev Saab? It's been between you and me. Always was!'

'Yes, but you work out the contract formalities with him. He is a very good person … a friend … I have briefed him about you. Just talk to him.'

I came back a bit disturbed not knowing what it was all about. Later, I learnt that it was Dewan who would have the final say, and that he was also talking to other publishers. I felt let down and decided to talk to Dev Saab again. Before I could do so Dewan called: 'How much will you pay?' he came straight to the point.

'I don't know. I can't say anything without reading the entire manuscript. I don't even know the extent of the book, how many pages will it come to, how many photographs will be there, how much will we price it at,' I replied.

'But you know about it.... How much will you pay without reading it?' he asked again.

'Nothing. Without reading I can't offer anything.' I answered.

I knew the project had slipped out of my hands.

I must admit that to this day I have not forgiven myself for losing a project I had dreamt of for years … which I had instigated Dev Saab to write. I should have bid for it, for it was a professional deal and, after all, Dev Saab was not wrong in signing with the highest bidder or with a bigger imprint. *Romancing with Life*, published by Penguin Books India in 2007, went on to become a success. It taught me a lesson: 'A little ego can be dangerous.' I have not forgotten Dev Saab's words 'forget the past', nor learnt anything from them. His other words, '*Haar mein bhi nasha hai*', were good for him, but not for me!

A year later, on 30 June 2008, I bumped into Dev Saab in the lobby of Astoria Waldorf in New York, where I was staying for the annual meet of Hay House – the publishing house I work for. We exchanged pleasantries as he checked in. Late that night Dev Saab called and asked me to come down to the lobby. Astoria Waldorf is a landmark luxury hotel on the famous Park Avenue in New York. As one enters the hotel, on the left are the reception desks while on the right is the famous Peacock Alley – a bar restaurant. In the middle of the lobby is a giant antique clock, dating back to the nineteenth century, around which Peacock Alley hosts the much anticipated, and well-attended, weekly Sunday brunch. He looked at the clock and reflected: 'Finally, it is all about time ... life is after all just a moment in time.'

We talked of this and that. He never mentioned anything about *Romancing with Life*. Nor did I. While I was still living in the past, with the old hurt, perhaps he had already moved on to his next project. Obviously, I had not learnt anything from his words: 'Forget your yesterday. Live now. And only *now... now, now, now....*'

That was the last time I met Dev Saab!

8

Shalimar

The Mega Fiasco

In 1977, the Hindi film industry was going through a great deal of excitement, and intrigues and counter-intrigues were rife. Everyone seemed to be trying to outsmart the others. All because of a film project called *Shalimar* and its young director, hitherto unheard of in India, Krishna Shah.

Born in 1938 in India, a graduate of Yale and the University of California (Los Angeles), Shah was the first Asian-American writer, producer and director who won critical acclaim on Broadway and in Hollywood. On Broadway, he had directed and co-authored, with the famous Alan Paton, a South African play *Sponono*. On Off-Broadway he adopted and directed, besides other hits, Nobel Prize winner Rabindranath Tagore's *The King of the Dark Chamber*, which ran for over a year and won two OBIE (Off-Broadway Theater) awards.[1] Shah's *River Niger* won many international awards at various film festivals. However, he could never make it to the 'A' grade of Hollywood directors.

When Shah landed in Bombay to announce that he would be making a big-budget film with top stars from Hollywood and Bollywood, he became a star himself, who was lapped up by the media – both national and international. The Hollywood star list included Rex Harrison, Italian actress Gina Lollobrigida, the sex symbol of the 1960s and 1970s, and John Saxon, with award-winning Harvey Genkins as the cinematographer. From India, Shah wanted Amitabh Bachchan and Zeenat Aman. He had already signed Shammi Kapoor, O. P. Ralhan, Aruna Irani and Premnath for the film to be made in Hindi and English simultaneously. Shooting was to take place in Mysore (now Mysuru) and Bangalore (now Bengaluru). Bollywood had never witnessed anything like this before and everyone, it seemed, wanted to hitch on to the *Shalimar* bandwagon, where money was overflowing. Everything was going great till Shah got the information that Amitabh Bachchan had said no to the project, who he felt had been brainwashed by a rival camp. Though disappointed, without losing any time, he signed the next best of the times, the ever-dependable Dharmendra.

The *Muhurat*, to be followed by a gala dinner party was organized on Thursday, 7th April 1977 on the lawns of the prestigious Race Course (Turf Club) in Bombay. Everyone who was anyone in the film, social and media world was invited. Buxom Gina Lollobrigida, who was put up in a special suite of the Taj Mahal Hotel, decided to make an imposing entry dressed in a red-and-gold, low-cut dress, showing off her ample bosom and legs right up to her thighs. Zeenat Aman, who had got wind of Gina's dress, not to be outdone, decided to time her entry after Gina, thus reversing the planned protocol of the event. And what an entry it was, in an even lower-cut, long, blue-and-silver-gown slit on the sides even higher! It was a grand battle of the boobs with the cleavages and thighs in severe competition. The victory margin, if any, was thin and sharp, depending on who saw whom from which angle. The media had a field day and Krishna Shah's happiness knew no bounds.

But it was shortlived!

The party may have been a great success, but it was clear to everyone that the highly experienced, fifty-five-year-old Gina had been outwitted by the relatively inexperienced, twenty-seven-year-old Zeenat, who had walked off with the evening. If Zeenat was amused that night, Gina certainly was not. The first thing she did on reaching back home, perhaps, even before she unpacked her bags, was to opt out of the film.

Krishna was devastated. He immediately flew to Los Angeles to talk to her but came back having signed in place of the voluptuous Gina, an old-looking, shrivelled, passionless and temperamental, Sylvia Miles, a little known actress in Hollywood whom no one had even heard of in India. Apparently, she had acted in the television serial, *The Dick Van Dyke Show* (in the 1960s), but she was known more for her two-minute role in *One Life to Live* (1968), a six-minute one in *Midnight Cowboy* (1969) and *Farewell, My Lovely* (eight minutes in 1975) – though she had got an Oscar nomination each for the last two. Years later, she was also seen in films like *Go Go Tales* (2007) and *Sex and the City* (2008).

Rex Harrison landed in India with his girlfriend and forty-two pieces of luggage, which the customs detained. Rex was furious and threatened to go back. How Shah managed to get them released I don't know. Not to be outdone, O. P. Ralhan came with forty-three pieces of luggage, which contained, besides his attire, other necessary and unnecessary items, forty-three pairs of footwear, including Kolhapuris, in different colours and designs and made of different materials ranging from leather, suede and jute. He made it a point to inform the media about it so that it would not go unnoticed by Rex Harrison. While popular film columnist Devyani Chaubal gave all the details in her column 'Frankly Speaking' in *Star & Style*, O. P. Ralhan saw to it that the magazine did reach Rex Harrison in his room.

Along the way the overambitious Shah decided that as was done in many a case in Hollywood, he would like to novelize the film script and have it published simultaneously with the film's release. This is how Vikas Publishing House came into the picture. Narendra Kumar flew down to Bangalore to sign the agreement for Vikas while Krishna Shah signed on behalf of Laxmi Productions. Dharmendra signed as the witness. According to this agreement dated 18 March

1978, while Vikas was to bear the editorial and production costs, the *Shalimar* production banner, Laxmi Productions, was to bear the entire cost of advertising and publicity for the book. In addition, all publicity materials of the film were to carry a slogan announcing the book also. The handsome fee for the writer would also be paid directly by Laxmi Productions. It was a great business deal for Vikas.

Or so one thought!

Big names, bigger plans were rolled out. Krishna Shah's first choice was the renowned novelist R. K. Narayan who immediately said no to it. Finally, Manohar Mulgaonkar, well known for his books like *Distant Drum* (1960), *Combat of Shadows* (1962), *A Bend in the Ganges* (1964), and *The Men Who Killed Gandhi* (1978), was signed to novelize *Shalimar* much to the surprise and embarassment of the Indian literary world. Mulgaonkar later mentioned to me that the money along with the perks were too good to let it pass. It certainly was an unheard of amount those days. I would say perhaps even today.

Ambitions grew. It was decided that along with the English edition, the novel would also be published in Hindi and Urdu simultaneously. Greed has no limit, and Vikas, which had never done any book in the vernacular nor was it equipped to do so, offered to take over and was handed the job without any thought or planning by Krishna Shah.

The film's shooting was going as per plans and so was the writing of the book. Mulgaonkar stationed himself in Bangalore where he was put up in the same hotel where the stars were staying to meet the deadline. After the day's shoot most of the senior stars and crew (excluding Rex Harisson who would eat in his suite) would meet in the private dinning room of the hotel for dinner, which Shah would proudly call the 'Shalimar family dinners'. One night, as I sat next to O. P. Ralhan exchanging pleasantries, I noticed Mulgaonkar, opposite me, sitting next to Sylvia Miles. Suddenly, one saw Sylvia fling her large plate of hot soup on Mulgaonkar and walk off in a huff. No one knew what the provocation was. Dressed in high heels and a long, flowing gown, Sylvia had just taken a few steps when she tripped on her dress and fell straight on her face. John Saxon and some others helped her up and led her out of the dining room. Ralhan and I gathered some table napkins to help Mulgaonkar wipe off the soup from his face and clothes, and helped him to his room. Later, Ralhan, who was in the habit of calling everyone kabutar (pigeon), asked: 'What did the kabutar say to the kabutari?' Shammi Kapoor and Ralhan had a good laugh over the incident.

At Vikas, all caution had been thrown to the winds. Sales and marketing plans for the book were big and the talk even bigger and more boastful. In a nation where the average print run of a book is just 2,000-3,000 copies, nearly 20,000 copies each in English, Hindi and Urdu, simultaneously in hardbound and paperback, were in the press. Along with the normal trade outlets, it was decided to explore unconventional ones. A tie-up was entered with Indian Oil, whose major petrol pumps across the country were to display and sell the book. It was on 'sale-or-return' basis, that is, whatever sold would be paid for, balance returned.

On the evening of Thursday, 28 December 1978, the multi-starrer *Shalimar* had a gala premiere in Bombay and was released across the country the next day. A day later, it had a grand but chaotic premiere at India's first 70-mm cinema – Sheila, in Paharganj, Delhi, owned by the Kaushiks. The same afternoon at 4 p.m. the novel *Shalimar* was released in its three language editions at a modest function at the Indian Oil filling station on Aurobindo Marg, now sandwiched between that beautiful 1754-built sandstone and marble mausoleum called the Safdarjang Tomb and the ugly glass-and-steel structure of Rajiv Gandhi Bhavan housing the headquarters of the Airports Authority of India. The chief guest was Zutshi (whose full name I forget now), the head of Indian Oil for north India.

The rest is history!

Shalimar, the film, sank within a week at the box office. *Shalimar*, the book, never even took off. The only consolation, if one can say that, was that *Shalimar* the film got nominated that year for three *Filmfare* awards – Best Music for Rahul Dev Burman, Best Playback Singer (Male) for Kishore Kumar and Best Playback Singer (Female) for Usha Uthup. The novel *Shalimar* had no consolation whatsoever. For weeks later, the atmosphere in Vikas was like that of a cremation ground. Egos, big plans and bigger and boastful claims had all fallen on the ground like deformed pigeons. Voices could hardly be heard. It seemed as though suddenly tongues had got fixed with rubber soles. For months after that the sales, accounts and warehouse staff was kept busy with tracking the returns, storing them, which is an expensive exercise, and issuing credit notes.

The funniest, or saddest, were the returns from Indian Oil. The new, 'unconventional' experiment was a complete disaster. The total sales, from across the country, never even touched the 100-mark. Most of the stocks came back with greasy marks, dog-eared pages, dirty and damaged – obviously, the only readers were the staff at the filling stations. Finally, the entire stock was disposed off as raddi (waste).

A few months later, while watching the Hollywood multi-starrer blockbuster *The Towering Inferno* at Delhi's Archana Theatre in Greater Kailash with Narendra Kumar and his wife Vinita, I ordered some peeled salted groundnuts during the intermission, which was quite common those days. Ironically, each of the paper packets in which the nuts were served was a page from the *Shalimar* book!

Quite a nutty end to a nutty project!

9
Raju Bharatan

The Film Music Encyclopedia

Over the years I have published quite a few books on cinema, mostly biographies, including those of Satyajit Ray, Dilip Kumar, Pran, Madhubala, Naushad, M. S. Subbulakshmi, to name a few. However, the most exciting project of them all was the biography of Lata Mangeshkar by Raju Bharatan, known as the film music historian of India, who wrote on film music and cricket with equal ease.

Raju has what they call an elephant's memory – 'phenomenal depth in terms of recall value; … masterly in recalling almost every song composed in the Hindi music industry between the 1940s and 1990s, complete with the details of the singers, lyricists, film directors and composers. An incredible record of film music's passage from uncertain infancy and creative adolescence to an adulthood that Bharatan would consider almost delinquent'.[1]

I recall an incident, which was narrated to me by Khushwant Singh. As editor of *The Illustrated Weekly of India*, an appointment was fixed for him by his deputy, Raju Bharatan, to meet the legendary Lata Mangeshkar in Bombay. During the course of the evening, Khushwant asked Lata which was her first film song recording. According to Khushwant: 'Lata had no idea. After trying to recall she gave up and said: "Why don't you ask Raju. I am sure he would know it'". Yes, Raju did. Not only that, he also knew which instruments had been used and which raga the song was based on.

Once Raju took on the Lata biography there was no looking back. We gave a deadline and he met it. And in that period he just breathed and lived Lata, 24x7, till the book was complete. And that is the pattern he adopted in all the subsequent books he did for me – *A Journey Down Melody Lane* (2011) and *Naushadnama: The Life and Music of Naushad* (2013) – both of which I published for Hay House. His only problem is that with so much of information and knowledge of his subject, he never knows what to put in and what to leave out.

Initially, *Lata Mangeshkar: A Biography* was slated for release in February 1995. As Raju was working on the book, came the news that another publisher – Rupa – too was bringing out a biography of Lata being written by Harish Bhimani, a well-known voice-over artist and a friend of the Mangeshkar family. The vital difference of course was that Raju's Lata was unauthorized while Bhimani's Lata was 'authorized'. Raju had already discovered his Lata while Bhimani was still 'in search' of his Lata. Raju's Lata was pure and authoritative, while Bhimani's totally raw, lacking depth and detail.

The race had started and who would win was the main question. Schedules were advanced and shifts increased. Raju was writing and sending the text to us chapter by chapter, and chapter by chapter it was being edited, typeset and proofread. Dushyant Prasher, an extraordinary talent, agreed to design the cover. And what a cover he made – a real gem. The words 'Lata Mangeshkar' were in solid 24-carat gold paint. Thanks to Shobhaa Dé, her cousin Gautam Rajadhyaksha, that ace photographer who had perhaps photographed every icon of Bollywood, sent me an exquisite photograph of Lata, and that too free of cost. Lata was in a cream silk sari with a broad colourful zari border in gold, green, yellow, red and black. Certainly, the most beautiful photograph of Lata ever taken. Prasher set the photograph into a piece of green Italian marble and put a thin gold border around it. To add to its quality, the book was gilt-edged – the gold for appropriately honouring Lata, the legend.

The 386-page biography was released on 12 October 1994, far ahead of Bhimani's book. To his credit, R. K. Mehra, the Rupa chief, was gracious to call personally to congratulate me on the release of the book and compliment on its production quality. The book was reviewed extensively by the national press. The first to review it was *India Today* in its issue of 15 December 1994. Madhu Jain in her review titled 'Missing Note' wrote:

> … Breathless, staccato, Raju Bharatan's prose hurtles forward like a cricket commentary with his protagonist knocking down all adversaries en route, until her ascension as 'the tuneful symbol of national integration', 'the goddess of song', the voice of India's plaintive soul…
>
> The book is a gold-mine of information on the film music industry – a veritable who's who and who did what to whom, the off-screen sonorous factories which gave Indian cinema its soul, lilt and rhythm…. Even the chapters are broken up as successive struggles for supremacy between Lata and those who helped her or came in her way to the top and her long battle to remain there.
>
> So, whether it's eclipsing Noorjehan or Suraiya at the start of her career; or the short-run races with almost all also-rans such as Vani Jairam and Suman Kalyanpur; or the more recent tussles with Anuradha Paudwal; or even the ego hassles with music composers such as Naushad or Pandit Ravi Shankar, Raju tells his story in the vocabulary of a battle.
>
> ... There are enough nuggets here though. For instance, the singer's noisy – but genuine – *kolhapuri chappals* which announced her arrival long before she appeared, her unflinching ambition as she did the rounds of composers, her metamorphosis from an echo of Noorjehan into a singer with a well-rounded voice of her own which could take in the flavour and inflections of the entire country.
>
> Needless to say, the book has been packaged and produced beautifully, its gilt edge appropriate for honouring Lata.

On 14 October 1994 I sent an advance copy of the biography with a large bouquet of flowers and a box of sweets to Lata, through our UBS Bombay office. Everything came back. 'Not accepted', I was informed. Later, Raj Singh Dungarpur, who shared a close relationship with her, told me that Lata was so upset with the book that she wanted to take legal action and stop its sale; he, however, was able to dissuade her from doing so.

Why Lata was upset is still a mystery for me!

About a month or so after the release of the book, I heard of a strong rumour that was doing the rounds – that Raju had taken a 'sizeable amount' from Gulshan Kumar, the then head of T-Series Super Cassettes, to promote his protégée and 'close friend' Anuradha Paudwal, who was getting well established as a playback singer. This was indeed shocking!

Gulshan Kumar had indeed grown powerful enough to say 'why wait on Her Majesty VIP Lata, when the "super" Anuradha was now there'. And Anuradha too had grown into 'a cheetah of a girl', as Raju described her in the last chapter of the book, who had already been adjudged 'Savvy woman of the year 1991' for 'her gumption in being the first to rebel against the Mangeshkars'. She had thundered, in print, under her own signature, that the Mangeshkars, Lata and Asha, frightened her once, but not any more – that she was taking both of them on in one stroke and let the devil take the hindmost!

Did this rumour against Raju have any base? In Chapter 17, page 363, titled 'Her Queendom for a Song', Raju had written:

> Frailty, thy name is a woman! Emergency, thy name is a woman! Monopoly, thy name is a woman! Hence, the Indira Gandhi Puraskar, I suppose to Lata Mangeshkar in 1994. But the emblem came two years too late. For 1992 had seen the Mangeshkar monopoly smashed to smithereens. Anuradha Paudwal,

claiming the pedigree to be as eminent a Maharashtrian as Lata Mangeshkar, had managed to accomplish what Vani Jairam, Sulakshana Pandit, Hemlata and Runa Laila failed to do. Anuradha cut like a rapier through the Mangeshkar tapestry. Even while Kavita Krishnamurthy, Alka Yagnik, Sadhna Sargam, Anupama Deshpande *et al* were content to perform as children of a lesser god, Anuradha threatened to dub the all ready songs of Lata Mangeshkar, no less, in *Radha Ka Sangam* (starring Juhi Chawla).

On page 375, Raju had written:

After this public attack, a theme picked up by every second paper to satiate a hungry weekend readership, the Mangeshkar image took a lot of burnishing. 'I will never stop singing', Lata hit back at that elaborate function, arranged in 1992, to celebrate her 50 years as a singer. But the issue no longer was whether Lata would stop singing, it was whether the public would stop hearing Anuradha.

This cheetah of a girl had first shown her 'spots' with Usha Khanna's *Madhuban khushboo deta hai* on Padmini Kolhapure in Saawan Kumar's *Saajan Bina Suhagan*, Jaidev's *Zindagi, zindagi, mera ghar aana, aana zindagi* on Sharmila Tagore in *Dooriyaan* and Raghunath Seth's *Yeh paudhe, yeh patte, yeh phool, yeh hawayen* on Deepti Naval in *Ek Baar Phir*. Now, in one panther leap, Anuradha had sprung to centre stage – a stage designed, as it turned out, for the most direct, most aggressive assault on the Mangeshkars in 40 years. It was an assault by the new Super Cassettes monopoly on the old HMV monopoly. One a screaming youthful monopoly. The other a seemingly ageless monopoly. One having nothing to lose. The other having everything to guard. It needed a Kishore Kumar to break the Mohammad Rafi spell. It needed merely Anuradha Paudwal to show Lata Mangeshkar to be as vulnerable from the outside. As Lata huffed and Asha puffed, the Mangeshkar monopoly was no more.

I did not buy the rumour line that was going around. The fact was that in the same book, in the same chapter, Raju had balanced it all by asking:

> Anuradha Paudwal might have got special treatment at Super Cassettes. But has it really helped her grow as a singer beyond a certain point? When Naushad employed Anuradha's vocals as a counter to Lata and O. P. Nayyar utilized them as a rejoinder to Asha, the Paudwal girl saw how much she learnt, how much she grew in just two films. Their vocal vocabulary, Anuradha found, was further enriched when she went to Shiv-Hari in the one film in which they were not under compulsion to use Lata. Anuradha needs to move out to such teacher-composers if she is to go beyond her Lata fixation.
>
> Sadly, Anuradha Paudwal is today caught in her own T-Series vortex. She finds she can neither advance nor withdraw. That is Anuradha's destiny …

If Raju had been 'paid' by Gulshan Kumar, would he have written all this against him? Certainly not. Rumours are rumours and should be ignored. I did the same. Later, I commissioned Raju for two other projects, *A Journey Down Melody Lane* and *Naushadnama: The Life and Music of Naushad*, which were released in 2011 and 2013, respectively. Presently, he is working on two more projects. Both for me – one slated for release in 2014 and the other in 2015. The fact is Raju is Raju – the one and only film music authority whom even top composers of the day like Naushad and C. Ramchandra, O. P. Nayyar and Shankar, Dada S. D. Burman and Ravi, invited to listen to their latest composition and give his views. He is the man whose writing has influenced and enriched, informed and educated, three generations of Hindi film music lovers.

10

Dominique Lapierre and Larry Collins

Joie de Vivre

If you go through the websites of authors Dominique Lapierre and/or Larry Collins or their listings on Wikipedia, there is one book that is not listed: *Mountbatten and the Partition of India.* Yet this book was published by Vikas Publishing House, New Delhi, in 1982.

Lapierre and Collins had tasted success early with their first book together – *Is Paris Burning?* in 1965. They never looked back, giving one international best-seller after another – *Or I'll Dress You in Mourning* (1968), *O Jerusalem!* (1972), *The Fifth Horseman* (1981) and twenty-four years later, during which period they both wrote solo, they once again joined hands to publish *Is New York Burning?* (2005). But it was *Freedom at Midnight* – 'the story of the Indian independence in 1947 and the subsequent assassination of Mahatma Gandhi in 1948' – that made their name and that of their Indian publisher Vikas, which had dared to buy the Indian reprint rights, and that too during the internal Emergency imposed in June 1975. This move made them household names amongst the literate and political classes of the country. As authors they captured the imagination of the country. They do precede the blockbusters of today and can still compete with them.

After the international success of *O Jerusalem!*, which sold over thirty million copies, Lapierre and Collins travelled to many countries, over three years, spending over $300,000 researching the story of the partition of India. It was another huge success for them. However, they had a lot of research material left, which they had not been able to use in the book. From a historical and political perspective, it was important material. The Vikas head, Narendra Kumar, came up with the idea of publishing the balance research material. Lapierre and Collins agreed and signed an exclusive contract for a series of four volumes, featuring four different aspects of the partition and the role of the last viceroy in India, Lord Louis Mountbatten, in it.

The first in the series – *Mountbatten and the Partition of India, Volume 1* (*22 March-15 August 1947*) – was published in hardcover, on 12 April 1982. As was their norm, this 192-page book carried Collins's name first and Lapierre's after him for the English editions and the other way around for the French volumes. Within a fortnight of its publication came a controversy in whose centre were the two authors; Vikas Publishing House; the Broadlands Archives Trust, founded by Lord Mountbatten to administer his extensive estate; Lord John Brabourne, an award-winning producer-director and son-in-law of Lord Mountbatten who was the principal trustee of the archives; and strangely enough, the Crown itself, represented by Her Majesty's Stationery Office (HMSO).

Soon after the book's release, the trust sought to block its import into the UK, claiming that the material used in the book was its property and 'its publication without permission is liable to legal action'.

Mountbatten and the Partition of India dealt with a vital period of modern Indian history, the independence of the country, and its partition into India and Pakistan. The account by Collins and Lapierre of the last momentous days of the Raj was 'given in a combination of personal interviews with Lord Mountbatten conducted over many hours, and a selection of personal and official documents culled from the Mountbatten Archives'. The entire drama of the partition and the transfer of power was captured in Mountbatten's own words and through his meticulously recorded detailed reports to the Secretary of State for India in London.

The question that arose was: Did Larry Collins and Dominique Lapierre commit a breach of trust in reproducing and publishing confidential material obtained from Lord Mountbatten in the course of researching *Freedom at Midnight* in another book on the same subject?

Collins and Lapierre said: 'No'. The trust said: 'Yes'. The Crown said: 'We hold the copyright.' Vikas claimed: 'The Government of India is the successor state, and thus legal heir, to all assets of the British Empire in India. HMSO and the Trust can claim no right to ownership'.

The ensuing exchange of 'confidential' letters and notices must surely be one of the most riveting in contemporary publishing history. On Wednesday, 5 May 1982, the solicitors of the Broadlands Archives Trust sent a letter to Messrs Garland Ford Ltd, the distributors of Vikas in the UK, stating:

> ... In 1972 the above authors [Larry Collins and Dominique Lapierre] approached the late Earl Mountbatten of Burma in connection with their proposal to write a book about the last days of British India and independent India and Pakistan. This book was published as *Freedom at Midnight*. Lord Mountbatten agreed to assist the above authors in their work and this essentially involved: (1) access to Viceregal Governor-General papers (including private reports and letters to His Majesty the King); and (2) access to his own confidential and private recollections. The basis of this agreement is set out in the correspondence passing between Lord Mountbatten, Sir Burke St. Trend[1] and the authors. In particular the authors expressly agreed:
>
> 1. to undertake like obligations as those imposed on Mr. H. V. Hodson[2] when writing *The Great Divide*;

2. Not to publish in full or in part any of the said documents in which access was given. Those papers were private and unpublished;
3. To submit that manuscript in draft to the Secretary of the Cabinet. In reliance upon, and in consideration of these promises, Lord Mountbatten and the Senior Trustee of the Trust agreed to give access to, and did give access to, the said papers from Broadlands and Lord Mountbatten agreed to disclose his recollections aforesaid.

   In the event it appears that your clients' new book (a) plainly reproduces these Viceregal papers (including Lord Mountbatten's private reports) and (b) extensively uses and quotes Lord Mountbatten's recollections given for *Freedom at Midnight*.

The solicitors of the trustees of the Broadlands Archives Trust wanted an undertaking 'pending resolution of the matters with the Trust not to publish or distribute howsoever any work which reproduces the said copyright documents and said confidential information'.

Meanwhile, Lord John Brabourne, as principal trustee of the archives, wrote directly to the authors, Collins and Lapierre, seeking confirmation that 'no material from the Archives are used in [your] book' and asking for 'reasons why you believe you have the right to publish a second book' on the subject.

A week later in a legal notice to Vikas Publishing House in New Delhi, Her Majesty's Stationery Office said that they 'for their part were pained to note from a recent advertisement in the *Bookseller* that the publication, which is to be in two volumes [at that stage only two volumes had been officially announced], contains material which appears to be subject of the Crown Copyright and there is no trace here of permission having been given for its publication … permission to reproduce from official materials should normally be obtained from this office'.

It was now clear that though the trust and the HMSO had acted independently, their effort appeared to be coordinated. Distribution of the book got held up pending a resolution of this issue.

On 6 July 1982 Vikas replied to the HMSO:

> We are clearly amazed at being asked to explain why we should be documenting the history of our own country! The book is a historical study, and the documents contained in it public documents that have either been published already [by the HMSO in its *Transfer of Power*[3] volumes] or been referred to extensively in public writings. And having been published by the HMSO they, as official documents, have entered the public domain. Vikas would thus be obliged if the HMSO could indicate, specifically, which of the documents reproduced in the book are copyright of the Crown. In any case, the said papers relating to Lord Mountbatten's term as Viceroy and Governor-General of India, were the property of the Government of India, India being the successor state.

In its reply dated 23 August 1982 the HMSO said: '… the book contains extracts of materials which are verbatim extracts of reports sent by the Viceroy of India to Her Majesty's government, and that, as such, they would appear to be covered by Section 18 of the Copyright Act, 1911….'

The Trust, it seemed, always closed in when it came to anything in print regarding Lord Mountbatten. According to the *Sunday Times* of 1 August 1982, which was following the story and the developments around it closely: '… [It] jealously guards the wealth of material that Mountbatten left behind him…. Meanwhile, another book has just been quashed by the Broadlands Archives Trust and the HMSO. Several thousand books will be locked in Vikas' warehouse while anxious scholars of the post-war period wait to see the outcome of this latest debacle.... The Broadlands Trust and the HMSO are remarkably guarded about the copyright problems. Lord Brabourne refuses to comment while HMSO simply confirmed that it has written to Vikas in India expressing their feelings.'

Two years earlier, in February 1980, the trust, together with Lord Brabourne, took British historian Richard Hough, author of the best-selling biography *Mountbatten: Hero of Our Time*,[4] to court on similar grounds, adding that advance publicity for his book implied that it was an 'authorized' version. An expensive and protracted battle ensued, eventually settled out of court by Brabourne and Hough.

The main question debated, and left unanswered, was: Was not Lord Mountbatten, in authorizing Larry Collins and Dominique Lapierre to keep, for a protracted length of time, large parts of those documents, violating the terms of the trust that governs the deposition of his papers in the Broadlands Archives? If so, the entire case would have been a matter of public knowledge in the course of legal proceedings and thus would also destroy the basis on which the archives had been built and could give Her Majesty's government reason to demand the papers back or to place other terms on them governing their use.

The real source of Lord Brabourne's indignation was revealed later. The media, quoting 'reliable sources', pointed out that if the book got distributed, popular British papers like the *Daily Express* and the *Daily Mail* would also seek permission to serialize extracts from the book. Under the then existing terms, these rights belonged to Collins and Lapierre with the provision that 'should the authors make use of the same, the publisher would be entitled to one-third of the monies received'.

Lord Brabourne was 'greatly concerned' about this particular clause as he had already made a substantial pre-publication serialization sale to the *Sunday Times* in June that year. Hence, under the circumstances, were the other papers to serialize extracts from the book, it would jeopardize his relationship with the *Sunday Times*.

The case dragged on with several notices served, replies given, questions raised, some answered, others left unanswered. The ultimate loser was the book – *Mountbatten and the Partition of India*. It just died a slow death in the London warehouse of the distributors Messrs Garland Ford. The second volume, on which editorial work had been completed, never came out. The main question remained unanswered: Can any individual or institution claim copyright on history?

I first met Larry Collins on 2 June 1972 in Simla (now Shimla) through that wonderful, polite and soft-spoken Mian Goverdhan Singh, the highly knowledgeable librarian at the Himachal Pradesh Secretariat library housed in Ellersilie in Chhota Simla. Collins was in Simla – the summer capital of the British Raj – during the course of his research for *Freedom at Midnight*, co-authored, once again, with Dominique Lapierre.

Mian Goverdhan Singh had placed before Collins an enormous amount of material, including some rare gazetteers of the late 1800s and early 1900s. While a couple of appointments of Collins had been fixed by the British Council in Delhi, he wanted to meet some old-timers who had lived through and witnessed the 'glory' of the Raj days. He was also keen to see some old, historical buildings. That is where I came in.

I took him to the Wildflower Hall, 13 km north of Simla, which had seen better days as the residence of the British commander-in-chief of Indian armed forces, Lord Horatio Herbert Kitchener, during 1902–09, and was being run as a 'premium' hotel by the state government. Lord Kitchener, 'the man who won fame for his imperial campaigns and played a central role in the early part of the First World War had lived here and spent lavishly landscaping the wilderness'.[5] Situated on the National Highway 22, which runs right up to Kaurik, on the Hindustan–Tibet Road, Wildflower Hall, at a height of 2,510 metres, was originally constructed as a bungalow in 1864. Its first owner was G. H. M. Batten, private secretary of the viceroy of India, Edward Robert Lytton, 1st Earl of Lytton. Later, it was claimed to be the favourite retreat of the viceroy, Lord George Frederick Samuel Robinson, the 1st Marquess of Ripon (Lord

Ripon). In 1909 Lord Kitchener sold it to one Robert Holtz whose wife demolished the building in 1925 and erected a fine three-storey hotel. After Independence, in 1947, the premises were taken over by the government and run as a hotel by the Himachal Pradesh Tourism Development Corporation. On 4 May 1993, the hotel was gutted in a fire, then rebuilt, and today it is run as a 'luxury hotel' by the Oberoi Group – certainly one of the finest hotels in north India.

Collins was fascinated by The Gaiety Theatre on the Mall, the Rothney Castle – the one-time residence of Allan Octavian Hume, father of the Indian National Congress – on the Jakhu Hill and the Barog railway station. Barog was set up during the building of the 2'6"-guage, 96-km-long Kalka-Simla railway line which became operational on 9 November 1903. The railway station was named after one Colonel Barog, an engineer involved in building the railway track and its tunnel number thirty-three, which is the longest of the 103 tunnels along the line. The story goes that Barog started work on this roughly 1-km-long tunnel by digging and blasting from both sides of the mountain. However, due to a calculation error, the two ends of the tunnel – supposed to be the straightest in the world – did not meet. Colonel Barog, who was fined one rupee, could not stand the humiliation, and committed suicide. Buried near the incomplete tunnel, the area was named after him.

Barog railway station developed into an important midway point for rest and breakfast or tea, depending what time of the day one was travelling. Over the decades, it retained its importance and hosted the viceroys and their families down to bandmasters who would shift to Simla for the summers. Today, of course, while the old building stands weeping for the days gone by, the restaurant is little more than a tacky joint – unclean, unswept, with unwashed and stinking toilets and a filthy kitchen that caters refreshments to passengers in an even dirtier dining room.

Collins and I travelled down in the once famous 'rail motor' – a rail bus, which was used to transport the upper-class travellers from 1927 onwards. Since gradually the number of travellers shifting to Simla for the summers increased, so did the number of rail motors to four, between 1927 and 1930. Needless to say, Collins was highly disappointed with both the rail motor and the Barog station.

Davicos, once an elite restaurant, housed on the first floor of an old elegant 1882 building on the Mall Road, in a giant-size hall without a single pillar supporting it, was what fascinated Collins. Here he met Choor Singh, the immaculately dressed head waiter, who had seen the 'grand days of the Raj' and served many a VVIP for nearly half a century, both pre- and post-Partition.

Amongst the old-timers, I shortlisted three other persons for Collins to meet – Pandit Hari Ram Sharma, Abdul Majid Khan and Lala Chandu Lal Sood. They were amongst the most prominent faces of Simla. Pandit Hari Ram was a veteran Congress worker, who, one heard, had never sought any benefits for himself and was happy running his small business of distribution of newspapers and magazines. His shop was more like a reading room, for he never objected to us young students picking up a newspaper, reading it and keeping it back neatly on the sale counter. In fact, he encouraged us. By the early 1970s, he was a disillusioned man, and felt, like many others of his age who had fought for the freedom of the country, betrayed by the new breed of Congressmen. He refused to comment on the state of the nation but loyally stuck to his homespun khadi kurta, churidar pajamas and a waistcoat. Similarly attired, but with a sherwani, Abdul Majid Khan, a former diplomat, was a staunch Gandhian, who, without fail, till his last days, could be seen paying his respects, with folded hands, to the life-size statue of Mahatma Gandhi on the Ridge next to the Simla Municipal Library building every afternoon when he came into town and evening when he went back home to Sanjauli, on the outskirts of Simla. (I must mention here that the library building is a real gem. Completed in 1860, it is in the Tudor style of construction with sections of the structural woodwork left decoratively exposed). The third, Lala Chandu Lal Sood, was the seniormost advocate from the Raj days, who was still practising, though only on important and prestigious cases. Always elegantly dressed in fine-cut, three-piece suits and 'Tootle' neckties, the cigar-smoking 'Lalaji', as he was popularly known, was a man of very few words. Till he thundered in the courtroom, of course. He was looked upon with great respect by the younger lawyers and immensely feared by his opponents.

While both Pandit Hari Ram and Abdul Majid Khan met Collins in the small shop-cum-office of Rama News Agency on the Mall Road, Lalaji met him late in the evening in his first-floor office, from where today, his impeccably attired son Rakeshwar Lal Sood, a senior advocate at the Himachal Pradesh High Court, and grandson Arjun run their respective practices.

Whether Collins got anything worthwhile out of these meetings I don't know, but none of them got any mention, or acknowledgement, in *Freedom at Midnight*, when published three years later in 1975. Except, of course, for Lady Hermoine May Montague, 'grand lady' of Simla. And, that too, 'incorrectly'.

Collins was keen to meet Lady Montague and had been referred to her by the British Council in Delhi also but had not been able to get an appointment with her. A Britisher by birth and 'with a good lineage', she had been born in Gujranwala, near Lahore (now in Pakistan) and brought up in Calcutta (now Kolkata). After studying in England for seventeen years she made up her mind to return to her first love – India. 'Even if I have to swim back, I will', she told her family members, who failed to persuade her to stay on in England and complete her higher studies. Once back, this 'stunning beauty', who lived a good life, loved theatre and ballroom dancing, used to shunt with the royalty and the government between Calcutta, Delhi and Simla and lived through the Raj days right into the post-Independence era. Her 'cottage mansion' Northwood, which was considered a 'masterpiece', had been designed by none other than the famous architect Roland Hotz.

Getting through to Lady Montague was never easy. She apparently had 'no telephone', and if she had, no one knew the number. A letter – properly written on a letterhead and sealed in a proper envelope, and only then would it be entertained – had to be left at the counter of the now 134-year-old, Gainda Mull Hemraj Agency, a well-known daily provisions store on the Mall Road. Her staff, who visited the shop every alternate day, would pick it up and get a reply two days later – again, left at the counter from where one could pick it up. That was her personal postal-cum-courier service!

Having known her a little, I wrote to her on Saturday, 3 June 1972, with a personal request that since Collins was on a very brief visit, 'a reply by telephone or through her Man Friday for a next day meeting, would be most appreciated'. No telephone came. The appointment was given, through the counter at Gainda Mull Hemraj, for 'high tea' at 5 p.m. on Tuesday, 6 June.

Lady Montague was waiting for us in the study of Northwood, where we were greeted by her favourite companion Jacko with the words: 'Hello.... Come in. My name is Jacko and I am an African Grey.... It's a long, long way to Tiffany'. Jacko, a parrot, was a great imitator, who could, among other things, recite the full 'Jack and Jill' poem, imitate anyone coughing or the creaking of a door, equally well.

On Saturday, 4 December 1975, by which time *Freedom at Midnight* had been released, become a best-seller, and had evoked good amount of controversy, I got a letter from Lady Montague inviting me for 'high tea' on Monday, 6 December.

She was furious!

'I have been quoted absolutely wrong by that friend of yours, Larry Collins. What I said has been distorted by him to suit his own writing,' she said with an obvious feeling of hurt.

> Firstly, I was eighty-two years old when Collins came with you to talk to me and not eighty-seven as he has written. How dare he increase my age.... A gentleman does not get a lady's age wrong. And that too a British gentleman. And he refers to my family as dogs, cats and servants, as if they are any odd dogs and cats picked up from the streets ... and how can he call them my

servants? They are my helpers and one is my khansama [cook] … and each one of them has a name. And I had specially mentioned this to him….

See here, on page 269 he writes: 'While the summer capital of the Raj celebrated, she sat at home weeping, unable to bear the sight of another nation's flag going up that pole where her beloved Union Jack had flown'. It is absolutely incorrect. I was not in Simla but in Jaipur at that time and was delighted to see the handover. Why would I have tears in my eyes? We were not a conquered race who had been defeated in a battle for me to have had tears running down my cheeks. We were glad to give India everything we had including the army messes and its shining plates…. A British woman never cries in public, so there was no question of my having tears on that eventful day….

But he wrote correctly that I am up most of the night for I enjoy the radio because one gets a clear reception. It's so much quieter … often the sunrise finds me reading or writing. But despite that I am up and about and agile. See, at this age I have no ailments whatsoever and am able to walk easily, even today at eighty-five, without a stick or any help from anyone. I have no false teeth and don't need reading glasses. I neither drink, nor smoke, nor eat rich food. My only indulgence is one pastry every afternoon and a good piece of chocolate every day!

That was the last time I met Lady Montague. Nor did I ever meet Larry Collins after his visit to India in 1972. Lady Montague died on 26 July 1985 leaving her estate and her favourite parrot Jacko to Pronoti Singh, the charming wife of Kanwar Ratanjit Singh of Kapurthala, who today runs Shimla's most exclusive holiday property 'Chapslee' – certainly worth a stay if one can afford it, for it will be love on the first night itself. Pronoti has used a part of the estate to build a senior section of her Chapslee School. The main cottage is being maintained in its original avatar.

Over the years I met Dominique Lapierre, regularly, during his trips to India, as he was a Vikas Publishing House author, where I worked (since 5 April 1978) as its executive editor.

Call it joie de vivre, panache or simply *le grand passion*, Lapierre is, first and foremost, a super salesman. I have yet to come across any other author who can promote himself so well. The nearest that comes to him is Shobhaa Dé who, in the words of a Bruce Springsteen song, too has 'action and the motion', and can always hold people spellbound. Like a typical intellectual, Lapierre's ideas are clinical and precise like some kind of a Cartesian logic and his gestures – eyes, face and hands – expansive, maybe to complement what words can't exactly describe.

During the course of our conversations, mostly informal, Lapierre would explain his ideas and books, clarify what he called historical works based on facts that couldn't be disputed. Of course, he never did elaborate what he meant by 'facts' or whether 'facts' could be chosen to fit a theory.

During a conversation at my house on 16 February 1991, he told me why he had left journalism to take up writing as a career. 'Challenge', he said in one word. '*Is Paris Burning?* was the challenge Parisians had to face when confronted with Adolf Hitler; *Freedom at Midnight* was the challenge that the Indian people faced with the British to bring down the biggest empire of all times. *Beyond Love*, the medical challenge that doctors have to face to combat the AIDS virus.' It was challenge that drove Lapierre on, something that the heart felt or an intense passion that kept him going despite the cancer he had been operated on for in 1990. It was again the challenge despite overwhelming odds, 'call it the *joy of life*', and it is this theme that provided him with the inspiration and the theme for all his writings – whether done jointly with Larry Collins or solo.

Once I referred to his books *Is Paris Burning?*, *O Jerusalem!* and *Freedom at Midnight* as historical fiction, to which he said: 'No, first of all I think one misunderstanding should be cleared – my history books are history books. They are not fiction ... there is *no* fiction in it. I have never really written any historical fiction. With Larry I wrote *Is Paris Burning?* which is pure history about how Paris was liberated after the war. *O Jerusalem!* is about the state of Israel in 1948. The same was the case with *Freedom at Midnight*. There is no fiction in it. It is pure history. Larry and I have written only one novel titled *The Fifth Horseman*. It is a novel, not historical fiction. *The City of Joy* is placed in a slum in Calcutta. It is by no means history. It's a story. *Beyond Love* depicts the fight against AIDS. It's a story. It's history. But in no way do I accept the term historical fiction. To write this book was my biggest challenge. I had to become a scientist myself because it was a difficult research. I had to read and read on the subject so as to be able to ask a lot of questions to the doctors, researchers and scientists.... There is no imagination in it at all. There is no fiction work in it at all. It was pure factual research of a great moment of history...

'I am more interested in histories and biographies than in strict fiction. I always like reading a well-written book by a reputed historian.... However, historians sometimes may be great researchers but they don't know how to write and that is too bad, because history is so fascinating; it has all the ingredients for a good story. No novel can ever compare to the richness, the tapestry that history can bring out. There are many writers that I admire – in the field of novels, for example, Ernest Hemingway. John Steinbeck for me is a real model; a writer like André Malraux, a great lover of India, was also a model for me. Jean Paul Sartre was another great model. He used this gimmick of simultaneously telling scenes happening in different parts of the world to different actors at the same time. I was always fascinated by it and now I follow it myself.'

Whether a writer has absolute freedom to use history anyway he or she likes, Lapierre stated that it all depends on how the author introduces his or her work. 'If it is introduced as a novel, as a work of fiction, then he can take his inspiration from any facts in history that he wants, provided he does not cheat his reader and tells him or her that these are pure, accurate facts, when in actuality, he is presenting a product of his imagination, with some historical background.'

Converting books into films has seen many a conflict between the author and the film-maker and there is rarely a case of any consensus between them. Many of Lapierre's books too have been made into films – *Is Paris Burning?* starring Kirk Douglas, Glen Ford and Alain Delon and directed by René Clément; *O Jerusalem!* directed by Elie Chouraqui and *The City of Joy* scripted by Mark Medoff, who wrote *Children of a Lesser God*. 'How much licence would you allow your director and scriptwriter to depart from the text?' I asked.

'Writing and filming are two different expressions. Take the example of *The City of Joy*. If one was to film most of the book, one may need fifteen or twenty hours. Filming has to compress the story into a very limited number of characters, perhaps not more than five or six, because that is what an audience can associate with. In a film that lasts about two hours a screenwriter is bound to make a choice when he is adapting a book. The problem is whether he protects the spirit of the book or not. For each of my books, particularly *The City of Joy*, the film scripts have beautifully expressed what I wanted to say. And if the script dropped some parts of the book, some scenes, which I really loved, I realized why so. That's the law. That's the rule'.

Speaking of films, few know that in 1990, after having approved the script for a television film on her, Mother Teresa refused to give the 'green signal'. Lapierre felt let down and immensely disappointed. He had 'no idea why and how the decision was taken by Mother to cancel it.' He tried to meet her to clear misunderstandings, if any. But she would not meet him. In fact, on 9 January 1991, he even brought the matter to the notice of Pope John Paul II, requesting him to intervene and settle the matter. But nothing happened till 1996 …

In December 1982 Mother Teresa had agreed, after nearly two years of persuasion, to sign a contract 'granting' Lapierre 'exclusive permission to undertake a motion picture which will portray my life'. By early 1984 she changed her mind when two other producers from Italy were prevented by Lapierre from making a similar film citing the exclusivity clause. In fact, Mother was quite upset about it. According to Sunita Kumar, who was a long-time associate of

Mother Teresa: 'Yes, Mother did sign the contract … it was done so in good faith, without reading it carefully. She didn't realize Lapierre wanted exclusive rights and she had no intention of giving him sole permission.'

Shortly afterwards, Mother's office, on legal advice, served Lapierre a notice terminating the contract of December 1982 saying: '… the contract was not valid since it had not involved any consideration (payments).'

Dominique persisted: 'I was still very keen to make the film on her … I had to … it was like a mission … my life's aim.' Finally, on 13 October 1988, Mother sanctioned the script of my film. But …

Once again Mother backed out, writing a three-page letter on 7 November 1990 withdrawing all permission. Lapierre did not know the reason and felt hurt. But according to Sunita Kumar: '… this time Mother agreed on the clear understanding that the script would be approved by her. A year or so later she was shown the script which she said 'no' to. I don't know what was objectionable as I did not go through it with her; but it was like a work of fiction.' This is when Lapierre wrote to the Vatican.

The Vatican replied through a letter written by Joaquín Navarro-Valls, head of the media office of Pope John Paul II: 'From … reading of this manuscript, we can see the tremendous formal beauty of this film … I would imagine that the delicacy of Mother Teresa's feelings might induce her to consider that some details of the film should be modified. But I find that it is precisely those "commercial" aspects which permit the Christian message to be transmitted.'

Yet, it was not till 1996 that Mother finally agreed and shooting started for the film, the rights to produce which had been bought, meanwhile, by the Los Angeles-based Hallmark Entertainment.

The film was premiered on American television on prime time Family Channel on Saturday, 5 October 1997, as also on several European channels. It was publicized as 'Mother Teresa's authorized cinematic biography'. The Missionaries of Charity was, however, quick to issue a statement: '… Mother Teresa denies authorizing the film.'

A lot of questions arose. Most of them remained unanswered. Did the Vatican have a final role in the making of the film? How come Hallmark publicized it as an 'authorized cinematic biography' when the Missionaries of Charity not only denied the same but also levelled a charge that 'the film is inaccurate and very Hollywoodish'? If Lapierre had indeed been given a go-ahead by Mother, why was the film shot in Sri Lanka and not in Calcutta? Lapierre never answered the questions.

Whatever the truth, which will not be known now, the film was lauded immensely by the press and the public. It won the 'Audience Award' at the 1998 Art Film Festival in Cannes. The British-American actress, the 'authoritative', Geraldine Chaplin, walked away with a lot of praise. Daughter of the famous Charlie Chaplin who had been seen in films like David Lean's *Dr Zhivago* and Robert Altman's *Nashville*, she perhaps drew on her experience as a convent-educated schoolgirl in Switzerland and her once-held desire to become a nun.

Finally, the heat and dust settled down. A film whose making had been surrounded in so much controversy and considerable delay had survived. Sister Nirmala Joshi, mother-general of the Missionaries of Charity, announced: 'We have no objection to the Dominique Lapierre film on Mother Teresa *In the Name of God's Poor.*' The Archbishop of Calcutta, Henry D'Souza, saw the film and wrote to Lapierre on 1 May 2000:

> The video film *Mother Teresa: In the Name of God's Poor* has been seen by me. We are fortunate to have this film that brings to life the years 1947 to 1979 and which portrays it as faithfully as it can … I am aware that Mother Teresa had deep reservations about allowing the film to be made. She had given permission for it initially hoping that it would serve the cause of the poor. Later, she picked up reservations about the script which appeared derogatory to the congregation she had left and seemed also to exploit the poor who she was serving …
>
> I am happy to see that the final project takes care of these reservations and allows deep appreciation both for the

> congregation she left as well as the poor for whose cause and service she gave her life.
>
> I believe that you [Dominique Lapierre] have done much to preserve the rich heritage of an extraordinary individual who lived in our midst, sanctified whatever she touched and brought hope to distressing situations.... The film *Mother Teresa: In the Name of God's Poor* will certainly touch the hearts of many and enrich all by the sublime sacrifice of our dearly beloved Mother Teresa.

Though it took fifteen years (1982 to 1997) 'of profound suffering', Dominique Lapierre had achieved what he had set his heart, soul and mind to. He was a happy man. He wrote: 'We [Dominique and his wife who shares the same name Dominique] are so happy that our Mother Teresa film is getting such recognition with the MC [Missionaries of Charity] sisters.... All our best wishes to you. Thank you for your prayers.'

What a journey it had been – long, arduous, bumpy, and full of intrigues and counter-intrigues!

'Why do your projects become so controversial?' I once asked Lapierre.

'I don't think they are controversial', he explained. 'It's just that some people like to make them controversial. That's a part of the game, I suppose. What can I say? Personally, I think my books and even the Mother Teresa film are very informative. They are told in a way that is accessible to a very large audience. In the world of today, when we are so busy, when we have so little time, I think it is the duty of an author to write a book in such a manner that people enjoy the writing. If some people think a book is controversial on some point, it is their business, but I can tell you that no one has ever written to me, or ever wrote to Collins, that such and such passage is wrong in a particular book ... that the facts are incorrect. Yet, there was controversy in India regarding *Freedom at Midnight*, whose release coincided with the Emergency of June 1975. At that time, the only way to have your name in the newspapers was to write that the authors were writing controversial stuff.'

Since the early 1970s, Lapierre has had a love affair with India. Half of his royalties are donated to support several of the projects he runs in India in the field of development or in medical action.

As he put it: 'I always wanted to do something which Mahatma Gandhi would have approved of ... I wanted to work for the lepers and I found a home in Kolkata which shelters 250 lepers, all children from some of the poorest slums. We have expanded the home to include spastic children and all those affected by polio. Perhaps, it's just a drop in the ocean but as Mother Teresa said: "If that drop of water was not in the ocean, the ocean would miss it". For me Kolkata is there like India is there, always with me. For me it is hope. I need to go there in order to survive.... My visits to India bring me the values of hope, the sharing, the compassion of courage that we in the West, where we have everything, have lost. I don't want to write about the dirt and filth of Kolkata. For me, even in that dirt and filth, there is something great – the hope of the common man.'

About the intimate coming into his books, Lapierre feels that he tries 'to depict events objectively, as impartially as I can. But there is no doubt that I am more attracted by certain characters than others and I depict them in a way that they themselves have impressed me. I want my reader to be as impressed as I was. I think there is a lot of me in every one of my books. In *The City of Joy*, spending so much time in the slums with rats, cockroaches, filth and junk, but with extraordinary people, was for me one of the greatest experiences of my life. The book is a resolve of a personal experience, a personal encounter with certain values in life. Even in *Beyond Love*, some of the doctors, the scientists, who are my heroes, are people with whom I had spent days and weeks and obviously there was a rapport, sympathy, affection between them and me to be able to bring forward the epic that they were trying to construct. You have enough to destroy humanity, and to get there are dedicated people doing all sorts of experiments with it. This is something extraordinary and if I was not myself warmed up, all excited by what they were doing, my book would really be cold and a flop, a document which would not interest people.'

Ingredient has always been very important to Lapierre. In his home in France, there is a piece of cardboard on his desk on which are written three words: Colours, Noises, Smells. He explained that every time he sits at the desk to write a scene he asks himself what did he see, what did he hear and what did he smell: 'because the world is multidimensional and you owe the reader the story in multidimensions'. That technique of taking it all to the reader, of making the tapestry richer in texture is very important to him as a writer. But 'the social purpose is not', for the message comes out of the story itself.

In 1988–89, Lapierre was detected with cancer. An operation was inevitable. He shared with me some moments of the operation morning: 'When I was laid on the operation table, before being put to sleep, I heard the voice of one of the boys that I had met in the City of Joy. He is called Ranjit, affected by polio, completely paralysed. But his will to live, the smile, his looks signified Life with a capital L. There on the operation table I heard his voice and he gave me the energy to go through the whole thing. Kolkata is such a part of my consciousness now that I think I must have been a rickshaw-puller in my last incarnation'.

11

Khushwant Singh

The Man for All Seasons

If there is one author whom I have met the most, read the most – almost every word that he has written – published the most, travelled with the most, wrote about the most, earned out of the most, through whom I met the maximum number of authors, writers, poets, scholars, artists, socialites, who recommended the maximum number of authors and their manuscripts to me, most of which sold well and some became best-sellers, it was that man for all seasons – Khushwant Singh.

I first met Khushwant Singh in the winter of 1962, when I was a student in Simla, through his book *I Shall Not Hear the Nightingale*. This 1959 novel had a black-and-white photograph of The Ridge area and the historic Christ Church of Simla on its cover, which actually drew me to it. As the years went by, various editions of the book got different covers. By 1972 it had the Golden Temple of Amritsar in sepia, which later was changed to colour through that beauty of a photograph by Raghu Rai. The publishers stuck to that cover till, five reprints later, in September 1979, a photograph of a nightingale replaced Raghu Rai's photograph. Then, as happens with most books, this too went out of print. However, on 2 December 1997, Ravi Dayal Publisher gave a rebirth to the book with a totally different cover – featuring an illustration by Suddhasattwa Basu showing a

Sardar standing in front of a British judge in his chamber. Today, a new title is being sought from the readers for its future editions as was announced at the Khushwant Singh Literary Festival in Kasauli on 10 October 2014.

'Readers who get nothing out of fiction probably haven't yet found the novelists who see and feel the world as they do. And they should keep on searching, for there is nothing so exhilarating, so mind-blowing, as to experiencing other lives through the same sensibilities, the same curiosities, the same inclinating preoccupations, moods and responses as one's own – to say nothing of finding one's half-formed thoughts expressed and confirmed', critic George Strickland wrote about Stendhal. 'Reading a novelist who is the same sort of person as oneself (plus genius) is like going on a world tour without leaving home.'[1] Above all, if we discover these writers ourselves, we have a special and a lasting place for them in our heart and imagination – to whom we go back time and again to discover things that we never thought existed in the text before.

The excitement of discovery also has a subversive element. Simla, where I was born and brought up, the Simla of the 1950s and the 1960s, was still heavily dominated by the Raj culture; the Englishman's critical presence was so powerful that it was not possible for us to conceive of the possibility of an Indian writing a contemporary novel about a situation that wasn't all that far back in time.

It was Khushwant Singh who revealed to us a world beyond the small talk of the Mall Road in Simla and beyond the lazy and gossipy loiterings on the Ridge, a world peopled by ordinary non-English-speaking Punjabis – people just like us in a world like ours. Khushwant's descriptions of the world were so realistic that for those who longed to explore something beyond their own confines, his novel *I Shall Not Hear the Nightingale* was greatly tempting.

Like most novels of the period, the freedom struggle, Partition and the Raj provide the central themes. This novel is set in 1942-43, at the height of the Quit India movement. The national movement has its impact on the family of a Sikh magistrate, loyal to the Raj. Unknown to the father, the son has turned terrorist; if proven guilty, he would be hanged. The deputy commissioner, an Englishman, understands the family's anguish and offers the boy a choice: betray his comrades or go to the gallows. While this drama is being played out, life carries on just the same for the rest of the people with its loves, passions and glorious uncertainties.

As far as the theme is concerned, it is commonplace. But what attracted me – and I suppose this has been the reason for the novel's immense popularity – were two factors: first, the question of choice and, second, the exhilarating irreverence, which pays no respect to the so-called good taste or false sentiments.

All great novels raise the question of choice of what a critic has described as 'the mechanism of minimal hope.' In other words: 'You can go on living if you do this or that to your satisfaction'. But the doing involves a choice so hideous and degrading, that it diminishes the humanity of the boy and the magistrate's family members, who would have to make the decision. The father has to choose to let his son die; the informer has to betray his comrades in order to live. To live was to choose to be less human. What would one do in such situations? Turn to God?

Or does one simply accept the inevitable? There are no easy answers. To each his or her own, because every one of us has to make peace with the Maker or ourselves. The open-ended conclusion of the novel draws many readers to it.

No story is ever told as if it is the only one: there are wheels within wheels and wheels outside wheels. For many readers it is the 'wheels' outside that interest most. Some reviewers have criticized Khushwant's characters as 'crude', a stricture of which I could never see the validity. He described the world as he saw it, put in the novelist's imagination and let us know what it was all about. But behind all this put-on 'hardness', there is a profound and compassionate insight into the lives of ordinary people, especially women in a society that denied them choice, autonomy and dignity.

All fiction has its autobiographical roots, spreading through, in this case, the provincial world, limited and, in some ways, claustrophobic. Memories of terrorist activity in the 1940s (it was Punjab first and Bengal later) must have provided grist to Khushwant's mill. But its juxtaposition with social attitudes and its play on the interlocking concepts of caste, community and political attitudes make the novel much more than a thriller.

Khushwant's keen awareness of our capacity for self-delusion and his frank avowal of the unworthiness of many of our motives could be shocking only to those who are themselves suffering from massive self-delusion.

Introduced to him in 1962, I first formally met Khushwant Singh ten years later in Bombay on 9 May 1972, in his office at the Times of India Building, where he was the star editor of *The Illustrated Weekly of India*. I had just finished my postgraduation in mass communication from Panjab University in Chandigarh and had written an article on 'Punjabi Theatre'. Without looking at it Khushwant said: 'You have written such a long article on a subject that does not exist ... why don't you write a short story and send it to me?'

I did. He accepted it. He rewrote it and published it – my first major byline.

That was the start of my association with him which lasted forty-two years, through his days after the *Weekly* with the *National Herald*, *New Delhi*, *Hindustan Times* and as a columnist, till he passed away at the age of ninety-nine on 20 March 2014. Over these years, as he became one of the highest-selling Indian authors, I took full advantage of this phenomenon and can today claim to have published the maximum number of his titles – thirty-seven –

under various imprints, and also co-authored a volume with him[2] in addition to two volumes on him: *A Man Called Khushwant Singh* (1996) and *The Legend Lives On …* (2014).

I have often been asked what made Khushwant Singh 'tick' with a cross-section of readers? Was it his posturing as the 'Sultan of Sleaze', which, in actuality, hid a scholar of history, whose fields also passionately included nature and literature? Was it his genuine unritualistic religiosity and deep spirituality? Or was it his persona as a champion of lost causes that endeared him to millions?

Who knows, for the answers are manifold. John Maynard Keynes, the noted British economist, once asked: 'Who can paint the chameleon?' There are aspects of Khushwant Singh that remain irretrievably hidden because it is impossible to pin down the chameleon-like character who refused to be boxed in.

Whatever the answer, he was, first of all, any publisher's pride. Why did publishers seek him out? What charisma did he possess that the bottom line of a publishing house looked a little more hopeful after his books were added to its list? The answer is simple: The ability to sell right down the line, coupled with the fact that at a time when memory spans are becoming shorter, time for reading books less, and the life of a book 'somewhere between butter and yogurt', Khushwant's books have a long shelf life. Readers may or may not agree with his views but they all read him – usually line to line, again and again. Why so? Because of his acerbic pen, his wit and humour, and his ability to laugh at himself. His writing provided entertainment, even if it was little bawdy, information that few have and education that all love to acquire.

Then there are the bread-and-butter intellectuals' issues for the ordinary reader caught in the trappings of life. More than any other writer in India, before and since, Khushwant realized the value of humour in the lives of most of us, and he understood, above all, that language had to be simple and close to the bone. To paraphrase an expression from Raymond Chandler's essay, 'The Simple Art of Murder', Khushwant Singh took writing out of upper-class snobbery and dropped it into an alley. He wrote for the people with a sharp, aggressive attitude to life, who have known the seamy side of things because they live there. If, in the process, Khushwant became 'a bit too much', it never bothered him because that was the way he saw the world around him and wished to represent it. And the reader too laughed along with him and faithfully read his books even if a majority of them were old wine in new bottles – recycled and compiled from his columns.

Leaving aside the 'recycled books' and most of his later novels, two books merit serious consideration – *Delhi: A Novel* (1990) and his autobiography *Truth, Love and a Little Malice* (2002).

Over the last six decades, much, too much, has been written on Khushwant Singh's novel *Train to Pakistan* (1956) whose jacket designs too have undergone various reincarnations. Few know that the novel was originally published under the title *Mano Majra*. The name did not click. Nor did the book. The publishers, Grove Press, US, then changed the title to *Train to Pakistan*. The rest is history!

The title for any book, or even a film, is very important. There are numerous cases in the world of publishing where a change in the title has led to a book, which was not moving at all, becoming a best-seller. One of the famous examples being Robert James Waller's novel *Love in Black and White* published in 1992. The novel was about to disappear without notice when its publishers, Warner Books, USA, decided to rechristen it as *The Bridges of Madison County*. It worked. And how! It became a publishing phenomenon with over fifty million copies sold worldwide. Clint Eastwood went on to buy the rights and made a film of the same title with Meryl Streep in the female lead in 1995. Khushwant's *Train to Pakistan* too was made into a film by Pamela Rooks in 1998.

For me much of the power that *Train to Pakistan* derives is from Khushwant's descriptions of nature in its various moods. From the following extracts a reader can feel the intensity, 'the sheer unfathomable beauty of nature and yearning to become one with it':

> Monsoon is yet another name for rain. As its original Arabic name [*mausam*] indicates, it is a season. There is a summer monsoon as well as a winter monsoon, but it is only the nimbus south-west winds of summer that makes a *mausam* the season of the rains. The winter monsoon is simply rain in the winter. It is like a cold shower on a frosty morning. It leaves one chilled and shivering. Although it is good for the crops, people pray for it to end. Fortunately, it does not last very long ...
>
> The sun goes on, day by day, from east to west, scorching relentlessly. The earth cracks up and deep fissures open their gaping mouths to ask for water; but there is no water – only the shimmering haze at noon making mirage lakes of quicksilver. Poor villagers take their cattle out to drink and are struck dead. The rich wear sunglasses and hide behind chicks of Khus on which their servants pour water.
>
> The sun makes an ally of the breeze. It heats the air till it becomes the loo and then sends it on its errand. Even in the intense heat the loo's warm caresses are sensuous and pleasant. It brings up the prickly heat. It produces a numbness which makes the head nod and the eyes heavy with sleep. It brings on a stroke which takes its victim as gently as breeze bears a fluff of thistledown.
>
> Then comes a period of false hopes. The loo drops. The air becomes still. From the southern horizon a black wall begins to advance. Hundreds of kites and crows fly ahead. Can it be...? No, it is a dust storm. A fine powder begins to fall. A solid mass of locusts covers the sun. They devour whatever is left on the trees and in the fields. Then comes the storm itself. In furious sweeps it smacks open doors and windows, banging them forward

and backward, smashing their glass panes. Thatched roofs and corrugated iron sheets are borne aloft into the sky like bits of paper. Trees are torn up by the roots and fall across the power lines. The tangled wires electrocute people and start fires in houses. The storm carries the flames to other houses till there is a conflagration. All this happens in a few seconds. Before you can say chakravartyrajagopalachari the gale is gone. The dust hanging in the air settles on your books, furniture and food; it gets in your eyes and ears and throat and nose.

This happens over and over again until the people have lost all hope. They are disillusioned, dejected, thirsty and sweating. The prickly heat on the back of their necks is like emery paper. There is another lull. A hot, petrified silence prevails. Then comes the shrill, strange, call of a bird. Why has it left its cool, bosky shade and come out in the sun? People look up wearily at the lifeless sky. Yes, there it is, with its mate! They are like large, black and white Bulbuls with perky crests and long tails. They are pied crested cuckoos who have flown all the way from Africa ahead of the monsoon. Isn't there a gentle breeze blowing? And hasn't it a damp smell? And wasn't the rumble that drowned the birds' anguished cry the sound of thunder. The people hurry to their roofs to see. The same ebony wall is coming up from the east. A flock of herons flies across. There is a flash of lightning which outshines the daylight. The wind fills the black sails of the clouds and they billow out across the sun. A profound shadow falls on the earth. There is another clap of thunder. Big drops of rain fall and dry up in the dust. A fragrant smell rises from the earth. Another flash of lightning and another crack of thunder, like the roar of a hungry tiger. It has come![3]

If *Train to Pakistan* and *I Shall Not Hear the Nightingale*, coupled with some of his short stories, are considered 'modern classics',

Khushwant's *Delhi: A Novel*, I feel, is his crowning achievement. It is a stupendous saga of the origin and development of the city of Delhi, 'a colossal attempt to record the evolution of a historical city through the ebb and flow of time recorded in verifiable history. On its gigantic canvas, the novel crystallizes a large continuum of time and a remarkable magnitude of historical action that went into the making of a great city' – today the capital of India.

Having had the advantage of reading the final draft of the novel during its various stages of writing and typing, I was the first one to have reviewed it for *Sunday*, the magazine section of the *Hindustan Times*, in its issue of 14 January 1990, a few months before the novel was released on 1 May 1990. This review did bother the publishers, Penguin Books India, as also other magazines and newspapers, for not observing the embargo.

When one sets out to write over 800 years of Delhi's history in close to 400 pages, as Khushwant did, the result is potted history interspersed with wild imaginings to fill in the gaps and merge historical facts with fiction. To an extent this is true of almost all historical fiction and the novelist has a licence to do what he wants with facts. The most recent example is of a series of historical novels (five volumes released so far on each of the first five Mughal emperors, while the sixth on Emperor Aurangzeb is slated for release in September 2015), *Empire of the Mughal*, by Alex Rutherford (the pen name of Diana Preston and her husband Michael). But in the case of *Delhi*, the line between history and fiction is particularly thin; it is, in many ways, a fevered imagination and the wildest sexual fantasies that bridge the gap between history and literature.

Khushwant's novel is recounted in the first person. Its central character is a very queer one called Bhagmati. She is said to be a hijra (hermaphrodite) having both male and female reproductive organs. And yet she is nowhere portrayed as any different from a typical prostitute from the red-light areas. Bhagmati symbolizes Delhi down the ages – a harlot who is first abandoned by her parents, then systematically raped and buggered by many invaders, till she subsequently rapes and buggers all those who remain behind.

Khushwant quotes the great nineteenth-century poet Mirza (Asadullah Baig Khan) Ghalib in a dedication at the start of the novel:

> I asked my soul: What is Delhi?
> She replied: The world is the body and Delhi its life.[4]

The selection of this particular couplet echoes the author's own near obsession with Delhi, a subject particularly close to his heart and about which he wrote a great deal. He strongly believed that for all its vicissitudes, the city still remains dear to all its denizens. As he says in the opening lines:

> I return to Delhi as I return to my mistress Bhagmati when I have had my fill of whoring in foreign lands. Delhi and Bhagmati have a lot in common. Having been misused by rough people they have learnt to conceal their seductive charms under a mask of repulsive ugliness. It is only to their lovers, amongst whom I count myself, that they reveal their true selves.[5]

It is the unfolding of Bhagmati's personality that holds the key to the central concerns of the novel.

Khushwant's novel, which was over twenty years in the writing, cannot and should not be taken just as a sexual or scatological piece of writing, as was implied by some critics. It is much more than that. Khushwant has simply used sex as a symbol to reveal what Delhi's personality is. Despite Bhagmati's waywardness, she comes across as a warm, empathetic and generous human being who needs to be understood. He takes the reader on a journey 'through time, space and history to "discover" his beloved city' and, in the process, to meet 'a myriad of people – poets and princes, saints and sultans, temptresses and traitors, emperors and eunuchs – who have participated in (and have been witness to) the major historical forces that have shaped and endowed Delhi with its very special mystique ...'[36]The novel has a great deal of information of historical importance on Delhi – details perhaps unknown to even old Delhiites. Khushwant's research for historical actuality has interwoven the passage of time with those personalities who are a part of Delhi's history, including the sixth Mughal emperor Aurangzeb, the invader Nadir Shah, poet Mir Taqi Mir, the last Mughal Bahadur Shah Zafar, down to the father of the nation Mahatma Gandhi, the iron man Sardar Patel and Indira Gandhi, to name a few. The only problem the reader finds is that the act of procreation, in psychedelic colours, is almost omnipresent and seems to be almost an obsession with the author. For example, even when portraying Zafar in the midst of the 1857 turmoil, the author could not help plugging in: 'We took a large spoon of aphrodisiac that Hakim Ahsanullah had prepared for us. A little later we took our Begum with the same passion with which we had consummated our first union.'

A narrative in the first person singular has its own pitfalls as it can easily turn into a series of monotonous monologues. When an author is dealing with recorded history, the problem is compounded. Khushwant's *Delhi*, however, does not suffer from these flaws. It is, as all of Khushwant's works, immensely readable. He skilfully introduces an interlude after every major sequence. Some have argued that this device has been intended to provide relief from the narration 'of the so-called dry-as-dust facts of history'. The fact is that even when providing the bare facts of history, Khushwant has given us, in his inimitable style, food for thought in a simplistic and easily comprehensible manner. For example, in the chapter, 'Aurangzeb Alamgir: Emperor of Hindustan', Aurangzeb seems to dispute the verdict of the historians who came after him, saying: 'Misguided historians have written many falsehoods about the way we came to acquire sovereignty over Hindustan while our father Shah Jahan was still alive. They have maligned our name as a scheming self-seeker and plotter. They forget that the holy book says, "God is the best of plotters. We serve but the instrument of his design".'[7]

Similarly, in the last but one chapter, titled 'The Dispossessed', the narrator, while talking about Mahatma Gandhi's fast because of the Hindu–Muslim riots, says: 'On the sixth day of his fast the old man complains that he can't piddle. I would like to ask him "what happened to all the orange and lime juice you drank?" He babbles as if only half-awake. The radio says he is dying. Thousands turn up as if their real fathers are dying. They tell him that they have been fasting with him – their fathers, mothers, wives and children too. They submit petitions saying they will not molest Muslims; they will get out of mosques and Muslim homes, even welcome Muslims returning from Pakistan.'[8]

Each episode and each incident is observantly detailed – a perfect blend of expression and thought. Take the skill with which Khushwant portrays the change of mind undergone by Nihal Singh in respect of a captured Muslim woman, jihadin Anwar Bai. Says Nihal Singh:

> The sun is about to set. It will soon be dark. I will have her first as I am the Sahib's orderly. Then I will have some sleep and let the others take their turn. Then I will have her the second time; then a third time. In the early hours, I will take her to the dump and shoot her. We have a saying: first quench your thirst then spit in the well.
>
> But the woman asks to be allowed to say her prayers. He has no objection.
>
> She goes down on her knees, presses her forehead on the ground a few times. Then she sits back on her heels and holds the palms of her hands in front of her as if she is reading a book. Her face glows. We stop making jokes about her. Her eyes filled with tears; they run down her cheeks and onto her muslin shirt. We stop talking. Her lips stop moving. She runs the palms of her hands across her tear-stained face. She turns her face first to the right and then to the left. I know Musalmaans do this to bless people on either side; we are on the right side. She takes out a rosary from her shirt pocket and tells the beads. By now it is almost dark. She puts the rosary around her neck and stands up. 'Sardar Sahib, I am ready.'
>
> Everyone is besmitten with shame. Nihal Singh leads her to

> the spot they had captured her from and asks: 'Can you find your way from here?'[9]

Another equally well-written scene is the one in which Khushwant brilliantly portrays the assassination of Mahatma Gandhi with whom he feels he had a deep emotional attachment:

> When the old man comes out for his afternoon meeting he seems very happy. And why not! He has one arm resting on one girl, the other on another. Both girls are young and pretty. He jokes with them. His jokes are very silly. One girl gives him a carrot. 'So you are giving me cattle-food!' says he. Everyone laughs …
>
> I edge up closer to him. I like being closer to him because I get into the pictures in the newspapers and show them to my mother. People stand up to greet him. Someone shouts: '*Bolo bolo*'; others respond: '*Mahatma Gandhi ki jai.*' The Old Man grins and says *namaskar*.
>
> And then everything happens so suddenly that I have to go over it again and again to make sure I really saw it happen. A stout, young fellow muscles his way through the crowd, pushes aside the girl who tries to stop him, bends down as if to touch Gandhi's feet, draws a revolver from the folds of his *dhoti* and before anyone can guess what he is up to pumps three bullets into the old man. Thah, thah, thah!
>
> Gandhi's hands remain joined as if he is bidding *namaskar* to the world. He says, Ram, Ram. Then he crumbles down in a pool of blood.
>
> A fit of madness comes over me. I jump on the man and bring him down. I tear his hair off his scalp; I bash his head on the ground and call him all kinds of names: mother-fucker, dog, bastard, son-of-a-pig. A policeman grips me by the neck, pushes me aside and grabs the fellow. There is a lot of confusion. I jostle my way out of the crowd and run away. I start crying – running and crying, crying and running. I sit down on the pavement and slap my forehead with my hands and yell *hai, hai, hai.* A crowd

> of people gathers around me. They ask me very kindly: 'Son, why are you crying?' I look up at them through tears and reply: 'My Bapu is dead.' They make chuckling sounds of sympathy. One says: 'You must be brave. You must stand by your mother. You must carry on whatever work your Bapu was doing!' Then he becomes very serious and asks, 'How did your Bapu die? Was he seriously ill.'
>
> 'No, he wasn't ill at all. I killed him with my own hands. I killed him. Then I slapped by forehead and yelled *hai, hai*, I murdered my Bapu!'[10]

A historical novel of this kind, which encompasses nearly six hundred years of a city's history, can be judged only in two ways. First, for its literary merit. Second, for its historical authenticity. The literary distinction he has certainly earned. As for historical authenticity, though no novel can ever be read too closely for accuracy, *Delhi* cannot be faulted in this regard, for, as Khushwant once told me, he had not taken any liberties with historical facts. 'I have tried to tell the story of Delhi from its earliest beginnings to the present times. Its staple is history.'

Records chronicled by eyewitnesses furnished him with the primary source; hence he chose the first-person narrative to tell the story. 'History provided me with the skeleton. I covered it with flesh and injected blood and a lot of seminal fluid into it. In fact, I put in it all I had in me as a writer: love, lust, sex, hate, vendetta and violence – and, above all, tears. I did not write this novel with any audience in mind. All I wanted to do was to tell my readers what I learnt about the city, roaming amongst its ruins, its congested bazaars, its diplomatic corps and its cocktail parties. Once I started working on it, I had to pick and choose episodes which tell the story from A.D. 1008 up to the assassination of Indira Gandhi [on 31 October 1984] and the riots that followed, which I decided would be the cut-off point,' he informed me.

A major point of criticism against the novel has been its overdose of sex, often lurid. Did he want to let himself loose or was he treating sex as a symbolism for violence against Delhi, I asked him? Khushwant said: 'Both. Sex is an integral part of life – the most important factor. I have never had any inhibitions in writing as explicitly as I can about it and I don't think I have done any more than any of the modern writers who have written on similar themes. I would only compare it to a liqueur chocolate – you have a sugar coating which is the fiction. Then there is the real stuff – the liqueur inside, the sex. I am a dirty old man. I will remain one and I will write like one. So, I have tried to make it as heady as it is sweet. Through it you get the information on Delhi in as easy a manner as you like. I have stuck to historical events exactly as they took place without taking any liberties with the basic facts of history. I have introduced sex as purely fiction or legitimately where I knew such events had taken place. As for the reader, honestly, I have never given a damn. As soon as a writer gets conscious of his audience, he is defeating his own purpose. I wrote it as it came.'

As to whether Bhagmati, the central character, was from the author's life or his own creation, Khushwant said: 'The incident about picking her up is real. I did, in fact, pick up a person lying on the road. It happened to be a hijra who had just been released from Delhi's Tihar jail whom I dropped at a bus stand. From there onwards my imagination got going. The hijra stands for a symbol of sterility. [The hijra] can never conceive and I thought it was a wonderful symbol for a city in which so much has happened, like a sexual intercourse that repeats itself. With Delhi too, with all that has happened to it in the way of violence, in the way of change of dynasties, it has still not produced anything as great as one would have expected of it. A city that is perhaps one of the oldest in the world is all you can think of it.'

'When literature is identified with life, a contemporary work reflects the political, economic and social issues of our times. How come you have not touched on such causes in your novel?' I asked him.

'I don't agree with this statement of yours,' he replied. 'Once you are conscious of the purpose of writing, then you are only becoming a propagandist. My only purpose in writing this novel was to get rid of my involvement with my city in the sense that I wanted to say something about it. I wanted to share with other people the emotions it arouses in me. And I have just done that in a series of episodes. I know that these have no social relevance to the problems of today, none whatsoever ...'

'But what about the last few chapters where you talk about Mahatma Gandhi, the assassination of Indira Gandhi and the riots that followed? I feel there certainly is a cause involved in it.'

'Yes. You are right. My one big emotional involvement is with Mahatma Gandhi and I wanted to portray that because the incident took place in Delhi.... These episodes are important and they mean a lot to me so they got included. Moreover, they also gave me a very neat ending.'

In October 1990, I spent a long weekend with Khushwant Singh and his wife Kaval (Bibiji to me) at their cottage Raj Villa in Kasauli. There, surrounded by books, rare maps and old paintings, he was working on his autobiography. He would write from early morning to noon. Go over it in the afternoon after a short siesta and then, at times, talk to me about it during our one-hour long walk starting at 4 or 5 p.m. depending on the weather.

The day I reached Kasauli he had just finished the fourth chapter, which took him to his marriage with Kaval Malik Singh in 1939. During the evening walk, he said: 'One thing I can tell you, my autobiography will be all truth – the way each and every event and incident took place in my life. I don't believe that one has to take recourse to imagination to fill in the gaps in the subject's psyche. That will become fiction and I am not writing fiction. I am writing about my life and I have to do it honestly. The only difference is that I am not really sure whether I will tell it all with names. If I do so

I [will] hurt a lot of people and I am not sure whether I have the right to do so. On the other hand, if I don't tell it all then I am not being an honest autobiographer. But this is only in the case of those with whom I was emotionally involved. As far as the rest of my life is concerned I have no intention of sparing anyone whatsoever – whether it is Indira Gandhi, Zail Singh, Sanjay [Gandhi], Maneka [Gandhi], [V. K.] Krishna Menon or anybody.'

The next morning Khushwant gave me the four chapters to read and also peep into the voluminous notes that were the main source material for his autobiography. It was some gossip, some titillation, some tearing apart of reputations.... I published it as an 'exclusive preview' in the *Sunday Review* of *The Times of India* of 2 December 1990. Six months later, on 23 June 1991, *Sunday Review* published another preview by me under the headline 'Sex, Scotch and Scholarship', by which time Khushwant had finished nine chapters. I asked him if he had thought of any title. 'Not yet...' he answered and asked: 'Any ideas?' I suggested 'A Child of Ageing Loins'. He had a good laugh. So did Bibiji. 'It's a good title ... catchy', he remarked. It became his working title though finally it was dropped in favour of *Truth, Love & a Little Malice.*

This was not the first time that a title, suggested by me, had been dropped by Khushwant. In 1996 he had joined hands with one Sharda Kaushik, a resident of Chandigarh, to do an anthology of poetry in four languages – English, Hindi, Urdu and Punjabi. On 7 October 1997, Khushwant and I had gone to Chandigarh for an event at Vivek High School, where he was presiding. That evening I was introduced to Sharda and her husband, a senior police officer posted in Patiala. Over drinks in his room at Hotel Shivalik in Sector 17, where we were staying, they discussed the book, which was in the final stages and were deciding on a suitable title. Khushwant asked my opinion. 'Making Love in Four Languages' was my suggestion. Sharda looked scandalized. Her husband was shocked. Khushwant approved it. Over dinner that night in the rooftop Chinese restaurant Yangste, with as charming and gracious hosts as there can be, Rani and Vijai Lal, owners of that beauty of a property 'The Judge's Court' in Pragpur, Himachal Pradesh, Khushwant said to me: 'That will be a saleable title ... very apt.'

I don't know what happened after that. A few months later when this 206-page book was published by Penguin Books India under its Viking imprint the title was: *Declaring Love in Four Languages: A Selection of the Finest Love Poems in English, Hindi, Urdu and Punjabi.*

'Immensely boring ... flat. Dull. And what a long subtitle? Who will buy it?' I asked Khushwant later. 'I agree but Sharda just wouldn't agree to your title ... I failed to convince her ... I think she was concerned about what her family and in-laws would think with the words "making love" in the title.... And her husband was of no help either', Khushwant explained.

'Silly lady', I thought to myself.

Of course, the book did not do well!

Coming back to Khushwant's autobiography, it was finally released after a seven-year-long legal battle with Maneka Gandhi on 10 February 2003. It was, as Sagarika Ghose had written earlier when the case was filed, in *Outlook* magazine of 27 December 1995: '... an example of a once close friendship further estranged because of the spilling, she would have us believe, of some defamatory beans.' Maneka who had objected to certain portions in the book, finally lost the case in a verdict given by a two-judge bench of the Delhi High Court (Justice Devinder Gupta and Justice S. K. Kaul) on 18 September 2001. In fact, she was asked to pay Rs 10,000 as litigation cost to Khushwant.

As expected *Truth, Love & a Little Malice* was a phenomenal success.

This was not the first time that Khushwant Singh had been dragged to court for one of his books.

On 1 June 1995 I had published his *Women and Men in My Life* under the UBSPD imprint. This 210-page book comprised profiles of the twelve women and fifteen men who came into Khushwant's life – whom he met, befriended and fell out with some of them, during various phases of his life. These included politicians, industrialists, lawyers, civil servants, actors, film-makers as well as relatively unknown people. Within a few weeks of the book's release, one Neelam Mahajan Singh, associated then with *The Times of India* (I can't recall in what capacity!), filed a case in the Delhi High Court and asked in her writ petition for 'banning the book, seizure of its remaining print order and for direction to the commissioner of police for registration of a case under Sections 292, 509 read with Section 34 of the Indian Penal Code.' The charge: '... some of the passages from the book have a tendency to deprave the character of the persons in whose hands the book is likely to fall' and the writer had 'discussed sex in a manner which is offensive to public decency and morality and likely to "pander to lascivious prurient, or sexually precocious minds"'.

Eminent jurist Soli Sorabjee fought the case on our behalf (Khushwant and UBSPD). As was expected to happen the demand for the book shot up overnight. On 1 March 1996, Justice Jaspal Singh dismissed the petition saying:

> ... (20) It was probably Koestler [Arthur Koestler, an Hungarian-British author] who said that Indians have a notoriously ambivalent attitude towards sex. On the one hand, the cult of lingam, the erotic temple carvings, the Kama Sutra; and on the other, prudery, hypocrisy, lip service to the ideal of chastity combined with spermal anxiety.
>
> (21) Khushwant Singh has no place for such prudery and hypocrisy. We may not sometimes agree with his choice of words. At places the language employed may have the tendency to shock or disgust but then revulsion is not corruption....
>
> (23) His are life stories of new styles of life, challenging traditional norms and values. What he has stated has to be tested by the current standards of ordinary decent people. I say so because the book being in English and with a high price tag is likely to

> be read only by well-educated persons in high-income brackets like the petitioner herself. Some of them may find some stray words or passages shocking or disgusting but not obscene. Even the petitioner only felt aghast and shocked. This does not prove obscenity. Let us not forget that freedom of expression requires adequate 'breathing space'. I do not think Khushwant Singh has crossed the permissible limits. The question of violation of right to privacy, dignity, fair treatment or reputation as enshrined under Article 21 of the Constitution thus also does not arise. In any case right of privacy under Article 21 is enforceable only qua the state.
>
> (24) The petition is dismissed but with no order as to costs.

However, I have also had a little shikwa (complaint) against Khushwant.

End-March 1980. I was up in Kasauli (in Himachal Pradesh) staying at Raj Villa as a guest of Khushwant Singh, where he would 'retire' at least thrice a year, if not more, for a holiday. Holiday perhaps is a wrong word to use, for his daily schedule there too would remain the same: Wake up well before sunrise, work till breakfast, read newspapers, work till lunch, short siesta, work again till 5 p.m., before taking an hour-long walk through which he would be stopped in Kasauli market by autograph hunters, holiday makers who wanted to be photographed with him, or just those who wanted to say hello. Back home it was time for his three drinks alone, or in the company of some of Kasauli's gentry, and to bed by 9 p.m.

During this trip, Khushwant was working on the translation of the renowned poet Muhammad Iqbal's *Shikwa* and *Jawab-i-Shikwa*, which according to him 'are two of Iqbal's most controversial and remarkable poems in Urdu. They extol the legacy of Islam, its civilizing role in history, and squarely confront the dilemmas of

Islam in modern times.' *Shikwa* is in the form of a complaint to Allah for having let his followers down, while *Jawab-i-Shikwa* is Allah's reply to the complaint.

During our regular evening walk I asked Khushwant if I (under the Vikas imprint, where I worked at that time) could publish *Shikwa* and *Jawab-i-Shikwa*. His immediate reply was: 'Why not?'

A few months passed. Khushwant had finished the book. When I brought up the subject of publishing it, he said: 'I am sorry ... I have given it to Ravi'. Ravi Dayal was his son-in-law and a reputed publisher who was the head of Oxford University Press (OUP) in India. I was upset but realized that the son-in-law took precedence over me. The ninety-six-page book *Muhammad Iqbal: Complaint and Answer – Iqbal's Dialogue with Allah* was published in paperback by OUP in June 1981, and sells to this day. It has a foreword by Rafiq Zakaria (a noted Islamic scholar).

Years later, on a trip to Dehradun, Khushwant told me the real reason for not giving the book to me: 'I don't like that man Narendra Kumar, who was your boss....' The matter was left there.

Khushwant Singh passed away on the afternoon of Thursday, 20 March 2014, at the age of ninety-nine. As was to be expected, his death made headlines. For days, newspapers, magazines and journals carried obituaries, apart from a slew of articles and write-ups on him. TV channels roped in many celebrities and others, who shared their memories of, and experiences with, Khushwant Singh. Most of these obits and articles were boring and lacking insights; they had less of Khushwant and more of the writer or speaker – all bragging about his or her closeness to Khushwant. The fact is that most of those who claimed closeness did not *really* know him. However, perhaps the best and the most memorable obituary was by Shobhaa Dé and the most poignant one by Fakir Syed Aijazuddin – both straight from the heart. Here is an extract from each:

From Shobhaa Dé [11]:

... Let me start by busting one or two popular myths. Come on, Singh, you were no Lothario. You didn't qualify as the Great Indian Lover. No way! You were not lecherous. You didn't grope. You were disappointingly well behaved! What the world did not know was that you probably suffered from low self-worth. That much-touted libido was all inside the turban. Your strike rate with all those lovely ladies in your durbar was verbal and non-intrusive. In that sense, you would never have had to 'recuse' or lacerate yourself. You, dear Khushwant, were an incurable romantic ... mushy, sentimental and gullible. Women used you ... your contacts ... your influence, much more than you ever 'used' them. All you really ached for was to be surrounded by beauty ... and lashings of female flattery ... God was kind! You received both generously ...

Let's talk about your branding. I wonder, were you a party to it! Or did it happen by default? Because, you know what, it may have sold zillions of books, but it did you enormous disservice. And you, dear Khushwant, were to the manor born. You were a rich man. You didn't need the money. And how many people know how generous you were with the royalties you received? Or how many favours you doled out each time you heard a sob story? How many people know about your mentoring young writers – some with merit, but most without? How many people were lucky enough to learn the nuts and bolts of magazine publishing under your dynamic stewardship? Not many.

And this is my big *shikayat* against you, Khushwant Singh. You played up and played into all the wrong things, when you could have highlighted your many achievements and qualities. Your legendary generosity – of spirit ... and ... spirits ... and more! And your blind trust in sycophants who flocked to your salon and took full advantage of your position. Khushwant Singh, let's face it, you were a sucker for praise, flattery, chamchagiri.

Many great men fall into this very trap, much to the chagrin of their family members. But what the hell – at least you lived your life Sardar size … no regrets, no explanations, no apologies.

Here's to you, Khushwant Singh – the Patiala Peg of publishing is no more! But we will continue to raise our glasses and thank you for liberating us from our idiotic, hypocritical, fake, humourless lives … for making us laugh at ourselves … for ridding us of quaint sexual hang-ups … for chucking old rules into the waste basket … for caring a damn! *Jeena isi ka naam hai*! I am sure you are enjoying your evening Chhota right now … with at least half a dozen celestial *apsaras* fawning over you. Heaven just got sexier! Thank you, Khushwant Singh …

From Fakir Syed Aijazuddin[12]:

To get a measure of Khushwant Singh's life one needs to remember that when he was born in 1915, the First World War had just begun. And if one goes back another 99 years, to 1816, Maharaja Ranjit Singh was still on the throne of Lahore. Khushwant Singh managed to telescope through his writings that two-hundred-year gap into one seamless narrative of Punjabiat.

Throughout his life he regarded his birth village of Hadali (now part of Pakistan's Punjab) with inordinate affection. He felt it qualified him to be a Pakistani. When we last met on 4 March, a fortnight before he died, he told me: 'You know that I am a Pakistani by birth and at heart.' I replied: 'You are a better Pakistani than most of us.' He laughed: 'I have told them I want to be buried in Hadali …'

I had gone to see him … to present him with a copy of my latest book *The Resourceful Fakirs: Three Muslim Brothers at the Sikh Court of Lahore*…. He recognized me within a second. I gave him my book. 'Inscribe it for me,' he said, adding after I had done so: 'Now write it in Urdu.' He demonstrated (as if I could ever forget) his mastery of Urdu and Persian by reciting a couplet of Iqbal's. 'You know that I am 99 years old.' I replied: 'May my years be added to yours.' He looked up at me with the softest expression, and said: 'No, but may you live as long as I have.'

I held his hand, the hand that had spent a lifetime writing books and inimitable articles, and kissed it. He brushed his cheek with mine. Both of us knew that it was a farewell. I left and stood on the gravel outside …

He has been cremated in New Delhi. His family has agreed that some of his ashes may be brought to Pakistan, for burial as he wished in his birth village Hadali. The son of Punjab will be returned to its soil.

It was Aijaz who carried a part of the last remains of Khushwant to his village Hadali in Pakistan. Extracts[13]:

Khushwant Singh's final journey was by train, to Pakistan. He did not require documents to cross the border. Ashes do not need visas…. To travel from New Delhi to Lahore now, one has to go to Amritsar, catch the Samjhauta or Friendship Express, change trains again at the Wagah/Attari border, and complete the journey in yet another train. The goodwill inherent in the train's title evaporates even over the short 42-kilometre distance between Amritsar and Lahore.

I took the less troublesome route and walked across the border at Wagah/Attari. No official on either side of the divisive white line seemed interested in the contents of the stainless steel urn I carried. Whatever attention Khushwant would receive would be at his birth village of Hadali, some 250 kilometres northwest of Lahore.

… [Hadali's] most prominent building would appear to be its Government Boys' School…. The main school hall is still, according to the bearded headmaster, as Khushwant left it as a young pupil in 1920…. Could there have been a better location for the marble memorial plaque I had brought with me? A niche was gouged out of the external wall of the school hall and the marble slab grouted in it. His grey ashes were merged and lost within the wet grey cement. The commemorative inscription read:

IN MEMORY OF
SARDAR KHUSHWANT SINGH
(1915 - 2014)
A SIKH, A SCHOLAR AND A SON OF HADALI (PUNJAB).

After the mason had applied the finishing touches, rounding the corners carefully with his fingers, I read the opening lines from Khushwant Singh's translation of the *Japji*: 'There is one God. He is the Supreme Truth. He the Creator is without fear and without hate.'

I ended with the *Shloka* or Epilogue, one line of which would have been requiem enough: 'The toils have ended of those that have worshipped Thee.'

While I was reciting these verses, I knew Khushwant would not have objected. He was only an arm-chair agnostic. Which truly believing agnostic would have laboured, as he did, to translate the *Sacred Writings of the Sikhs*? Which agnostic would have straddled the spiritual divide and translated with such understanding Allama Iqbal's epic remonstrance *Shikwa* as well as God's riposte *Jawab-i-Shikwa*? Which self-respecting agnostic would have, in the final year of his long life of ostensible disbelief, translated the *Japji* and the *Rehras* with such feeling and sensitivity?

Khushwant Singh did not need to make peace with his Maker with such gestures of conciliation, no more than he needed to be a literary *enfant terrible*. Khushwant Singh was above that. He had outgrown his time, overwhelmed his contemporaries with his expansive humanity.

If there was anything he never outgrew it was his affection for Hadali. It was of this cradle, this crucible of his life that he wrote:

> This is where my roots are. I have nourished them with tears of nostalgia.

And these are the closing lines you can read on his memorial plaque at Hadali, placed there on 22 April 2014.

Over the last couple of years I met Khushwant every now and then, with these visits being mostly dependent on his health and limited to just about fifteen- to thirty-odd minutes. He would invariably inquire regarding the status of this book and keep emphasizing that I should not conceal facts nor hesitate to take names. When I gave him a large chunk of the first draft, he took a long time to read it, while I waited patiently to get his feedback. Finally, he endorsed it. It was perhaps the last manuscript he read.

I had met Khushwant three days before he passed away. He was in his bedroom, sitting in his chair, his outstretched legs covered in his favourite green blanket with a beige-colour woollen cap on his head to keep him warm. '*Aa baith*' – come sit – he said. I had hardly sat down on the wicker stool next to him when he said, sounding serious: 'What is this I hear, you still have no lover in your life?' I was taken aback for he had never ever asked me such a question in all the years I had known him.

'Who's been telling you all this?' I asked.

'I have my sources … they tell me that they see you … meet you … regularly … everywhere, but you are always alone … I am concerned about you….' He then recited a Persian couplet, which loosely translated meant: A man who has no lover is no man at all!

Later that evening I narrated to his son Rahul what his father had told me. He replied: 'I promise I have not said anything to him …'

That was Khushwant. Even at ninety-nine, physically frail but mentally active, thinking about life and beauty, about poets and poetry, about love and lovers, and much else.... But more than all this, he was still, as always, concerned about everyone he knew.

On 20 March, late afternoon, as I helped carry the bier with his body on it, out of the door of his ground-floor apartment at New Delhi's Sujan Singh Park, to the waiting hearse, I realized that it was the last time I was going out of that door with him, through which he and I had walked in and out so many times. He would never walk *in* through it any more. A couplet by the renowned Urdu poet, and one of Khushwant's favourites, Mir Taqi Mir (1723–1810), which he had once recited to me, came to mind:

Ab to jaate hain maikade se Mir,
Phir milenge agar Khuda laaya
(I am now leaving the tavern Mir
We shall meet again, God willing.)

12

I. S. Johar

Sex Obsessed

I had never met him before. My only introduction to him was through the Hindi films where he occasionally played a comedian and did manage to raise a laugh or two. He was also a producer and director of some B- and C-grade Hindi films (except perhaps for that Ajit–Nalini Jaywant starrer *Nastik*, 1954). His manuscript came to me at Vikas Publishing House in June 1978 with the reference of Khushwant Singh.

The man was I. S. Johar (1920–84), the manuscript his autobiography.

Soon I was to learn more about him. A master in politics and economics, he had graduated in law also from Panjab University in Lahore, following which he moved to Bombay after Partition in 1947. He made his acting debut with Roop K. Shorey's *Ek Thi Ladki* in 1949. Thereafter, he went on to act in thirty-six Hindi and five Punjabi films. However, what he claimed, and rightly so, to be the resplendent 'feather in my cap' was the fact that he was the first Indian actor to be signed by Hollywood and that too by big banners and famous directors, opposite international stars of the time. He did cameos in films like Hugo Fregonese's *Harry Black* (1958), J. Lee Thompson's *North West Frontier* (1959), David Lean's magnum opus *Lawrence of Arabia* (1962) starring Peter O'Toole, Omar Sharif, Alec

Guinness, Anthony Quinn, Jack Hawkins amongst others, and Jack Guillermin's *Death on the Nile* (1978), based on Agatha Christie's classic of the same name, starring Peter Ustinov, Mia Farrow and Betty Davis.

Johar 'was an idiosyncratic, a lifelong liberal (if not libertine: he had five [official] marriages, an extraordinary number by Indian standards, both then and now) who poked fun at all forms of institutionalized self-satisfying smugness.... He also made and starred in films with his own surname in the title such as *Johar-Mehmood in Goa* (1964), *Johar in Kashmir* (1966), *Johar in Bombay* (1967). These movies are a testament both to his immense egotism, as well as popularity with the masses of that time – for whom a movie with the Johar name was a guarantee of easy laughs, as well as subtle ironic or frankly sarcastic jibes at Indian customs, mores, superstitions and institutions'.[1] His column 'Question Box' in *Filmfare* was widely read and suffused with acerbic wit and pithy replies!

I don't recall if there was any title given to this autobiography, but, even thirty-six years after reading it, I do remember the contents clearly. It was one sexual orgy after another. It was like a blue film on paper – enjoyable for the first few minutes or so, sick after that. However, one credit I must give to Johar: He had churned out 50,000 words or so on his sexual orgies and each one was more descriptive than the previous one, with graphic details and names of all the ladies involved with him – big or small, known or unknown. The manuscript came with one condition: 'You will not change or delete anything'.

Apparently, Johar had first shown the manuscript to Khushwant Singh for serialization in the *Illustrated Weekly of India*, which the latter was editing at that time. Khushwant refused to publish it. Johar labelled him a 'coward'. Khushwant charged him with having 'a sick mind'. Later, he wrote a profile of Johar, which was a part of his book *Women and Men in My Life*, which I mentioned in the previous chapter. I quote an extract from it to give an idea of what Johar's manuscript read like:

Johar sent me the manuscript of his autobiography for serialization.... It was difficult to say how much of it was factual, how much the creation of his sick fantasies. In any case there was more sex in it than was permissible for journals at that time. If Johar was to be believed, he started his sexapades at the age of twelve. He was spending his vacation with his uncle and aunt who had no children of their own. One night he had (or pretended to have) nightmares and started whimpering in his sleep. His aunt brought him to her bed. He snuggled into her bosom and soon had an erection. He tried to push into her. She slapped him and told him to behave himself. The next morning he was afraid he would be scolded and sent back home. However, his aunt was sweetness itself. After her husband had left for his office, she offered to bathe him. While she was soaping him, he again got sexually aroused. This time his aunt taught him what to do with it. It became his daily morning routine. Nevertheless, Johar confessed that in his years of adolescence what he enjoyed most was being buggered by older boys.

... he wrote of a starlet (now a star I won't name) whom he set up in a flat in Malabar Hill [Bombay]. Whenever he felt like it, he would drop in on her, have a drink or two, and then bed her. One evening he was in a particularly horny mood. When he got to the lady's flat, he was informed by her young Goan maidservant: '*Memsahib bahar gaya*' (madam has gone out).

'*Kab ayega*?' (When will she get back?)

'*Kya maloom? Bahut* late *hoga*' (I don't know, she will be late), replied the maid. So Johar simply pushed the girl on the bed and mounted her. The girl protested: '*Memsahib ayega to hum bolega*' (when madam returns I will tell her), and at the same time opened her legs to her mistress' paramour.

Even more bizarre was his story of how he bedded two sisters and their mother. One sister had been his mistress for some years before she left him to get married. She introduced her younger sister to Johar and asked him to help her get into films. He not only got her a few minor roles but also asked her to stay in his

> flat. One evening she came back from the studios looking very tired. Johar asked if she would like a hot cup of tea or something stronger to cheer her up. She replied: 'If you really want to know what I would like best, I'd like a nice fuck.' The girl left Johar to become a star. Her mother wrote to Johar to thank him for what he had done for her daughters and asked him if she could stay with him for a couple of days when visiting Bombay. One night she came to his bed, stark naked. 'I did not want to hurt the old lady's feelings', wrote Johar and 'obliged her the same way I had obliged her daughters.'[2]

In the first case mentioned above the lady concerned became a big star, got married and is happily settled today. The second case was of the two Punjabi Sikh sisters from Delhi. The elder acted in a couple of C-grade films, got married, divorced, and did return to Johar's bed for sometime when Johar 'got bored with her, with the routine of her monotonous love-making … and had to ask her to leave … for few realize that even in bed you have to be imaginative….' wrote Johar. The younger sister, prettier, graceful, and more talented, went on to become a star, got some prominent roles in big-banner films. Just when her career was taking off, she married a rich businessman, much sought after in the marriage market, divorced him, but never got to act in films again. She had no choice but to dabble with television for sometime.

There were many more examples. One more explicit than the other. Each more inventive and descriptive than the previous one. Some of his expressions have remained with me since. For example:

> As I entered S … it was like the charge of a light brigade into a valley of darkness …
>
> As I lay on top of K … with my eyes closed I realized that I may have entered a dark cave but there was golden light all over. Stars were suddenly shinning in my head …

> As I unhooked the tight black bra of … I noticed that her one breast was slightly smaller than the other …

Johar had not hesitated in mentioning names and giving out how each of them was in bed. I dare not mention any here. No publisher would have handled the book even with a pair of tongs. I met Johar during his trip to Delhi and expressed my inability to publish him. If he was disappointed he did not show it. He was an actor after all. His curt reply was: 'One needs balls of steel. Why don't you admit you have none!'

I wonder whatever happened to that manuscript. Perhaps, I may like to publish it today!

13

J. N. Dixit

Diplomat-Turned-Writer

I first met Jyotindra Nath Dixit (Mani to his friends) on the evening of 9 June 1978 along with his wife Vijayalaxmi Sundaram (Baby) through T. N. Kaul. Tikki Kaul, as he was known to one and all, one of India's foremost diplomats, had retired from service and decided to put his pen to paper for his first book, *Diplomacy in Peace and War: Recollections and Reflections* (Vikas, October 1978), which I edited. Referred to as 'sly and arrogant by birth' by the former US ambassador to India, Daniel Patrick Moynihan, Tikki Kaul was a 'great friend' of Ram Prasad, the then proprietor of that fabulous colonial-charm-inspired Ambassador Hotel next to Khan Market in New Delhi, where he always stayed in Suite 101, during his long or short visits to the city.

Mani and I soon became friends – a friendship that lasted till his sudden demise of a cardiac arrest in the early hours of 3 January 2005 – in fact, he was like a family elder in my life, whom I miss even today. The rotund, safari-suit-clad, pipe-smoking Mani was without doubt, one of India's finest tacticians and strategists and 'in many ways one of the last surviving diplomats from the Nehruvian era who truly understood India's role and place in the modern world. He wasn't for playing second fiddle to the United States nor was he for lapping up failed ideologies to prove a point. Neither was he for diplomacy steeped in petty communal arguments that have crowded several policy issues in recent times. The affable diplomat-turned-prolific writer was a warm-hearted old school Indian who read widely, spoke without jargon, and laughed loud with his friends even as he was trying to navigate the complex web of politics and power as the National Security Advisor'.[1]

Once I asked Mani as to what the 'J' in his name stood for. 'Jaldi', he replied with his usual laugh. Yes, Mani was always in a hurry to get his books written, and published, so that he could move on to the next project. No wonder, in ten years after retirement as India's foreign secretary he had eight books to his credit – four of which I published. Mani had a superb memory and a very disciplined work schedule. Early in the morning, he would be in his study, working in his DLF Phase-I house in Gurgaon (outside Delhi), checking the previous day's typed pages of his manuscript, which his secretary would have left on his desk the previous evening. At 9 a.m. his secretary would report and the dictation would start and carry on till 12.30 p.m. No telephone calls. No visitors. No meetings. No distractions whatsoever. His books provided not only relevant details with facts but were also acclaimed for their 'useful content and balanced analyses which stood out as a landmark in the sphere of foreign policy'.

Sometime in January 1995, during one of our regular casual evening dinners, Mani mentioned how he had published three books with a small-time, little-known publisher, only to help him out but had been taken for a bit of a ride. He was most unhappy with not only the production quality and the editorial inputs but also with the marketing and sales arrangements. That is when I asked Mani if he would like to do a book for me. The result was *My South Block Years: Memoirs of a Foreign Secretary*, which was published a year later under the UBSPD imprint. This 486-page book in hardback was a great success and went into three reprints followed by a paperback edition, which had another three reprints. It was reviewed extensively:

> [The reader is] ... introduced to the countries covered, given a brief background, developments during the author's tenure in the foreign service and what he did to further India's interests and finally, how he expects the situation to develop in the future. The book covers in relevant detail an important period of transition in India's foreign policy.... Dixit is pragmatic to the core – accepting reality, shedding much of the ideological baggage we have burdened ourselves with ...[2]

In early 1998, I quit UBS to start my own imprint Picus Books. The first authors to offer their books to me were Khushwant Singh and Mani. This was their contribution to my effort. Mani did *Across Borders: Fifty Years of India's Foreign Policy*, which was published on 1 September 1998. Distributed exclusively by my friend, Om Arora, through his Variety Book Depot, who too went out of his way to help me set up Picus Books, this 436-page volume in hardcover was one of the biggest successes I have had. The retail sales and bulk orders from the government agencies were large. Even diplomatic missions in India, I was told, bought multiple copies. Every newspaper and magazine reviewed the book, giving it a great exposure.

The book went into many reprints and the updated edition, three years later, too sold a few thousand copies. However, the most memorable moments connected with this book came months later – something I have never forgotten and today retain as the most precious treasure of my life.

At the best of times, Om Arora is a man of few words. However, he is the man to turn to for any news or gossip or help, all depending on what your need is – for he is totally clued into the goings-on in the book trade. He may or may not know everyone but everyone knows him. Most seek him out to inform him or take advice from him or just to say a quick hello. An exceptionally generous man, he is known for his lunch 'invites', which are extended at the drop of a hat. For years Om and I have been travelling together to book fairs across the world or just on holidays – now more holidays than book fairs. And, as per an unwritten rule, we try and meet every alternate Thursday for dinner, though left to him, he would like to meet every Thursday. As mentioned above, Om was handling the sales of Mani's book for me across the country and the exports, since there was demand for it from overseas also.

Even today I remember the evening of Thursday, 25 March 1999. Om and I met for our customary dinner at Larry's China, the Chinese restaurant at the Ambassador Hotel in New Delhi. After dinner, as we were leaving, he slipped into my pocket a small envelope saying: 'This is for the sales of the Dixit book.' It was my first payment for Picus! But I was in for a huge surprise!

Om had not charged his customary 50 per cent distributors' commission. Whatever he had received on selling the book to the wholesalers and retailers had been passed on to me. And there was more to come. I soon realized that he had paid me even for the stock he still had in his warehouse. I was totally overwhelmed and couldn't sleep the whole night. The next morning I went to meet him to point out that I could not possibly accept such a huge amount, but he would have none of it.

May 1999. Time had come to clear Mani's royalties for the financial year 1998-99. The book having sold well the royalty amount was naturally a sizeable one. I went over to Mani's house and handed him the cheque. Mani opened some beers and we celebrated, for apparently this was the highest royalty he had ever received 'in comparison to a couple of thousands that he had received for his previous books' from other publishers. However, the next evening Mani and his wife, who lived close by in Gurgaon, came over to see us. Mani returned the cheque saying: 'You gave me my royalty. I am giving you a gift for running Picus. Just give me Rs 100 as a guru dakshina. And the subject is closed. Now let's have a drink.'

I had still not got over Om's magnanimous gesture. And now Mani's ... I got emotional and made a fool of myself. If Om is my *habib*, my *hafeez*, my *humkadam*,[3] then Mani was my *rafiq*, my *mohsin*, my *rehnuma*.[4]

I never ever gave the guru dakshina of Rs 100 to Mani. It did occur to me at times but somehow it would slip my mind whenever we met. When Mani suddenly passed away on 3 January 2005, I was travelling. On return I went to meet Anu on 11 January. She was looking for Rs 100 in her wallet, which contained only 500-rupee note, to pay a taxi driver standing outside. I took out a 100-rupee note from my pocket and gave it to her!

14

N. Iqbal Singh

The Ladies' Man

I don't recall how and where I first met N. Iqbal Singh – Iqqy, as he was commonly known. Perhaps it was in the summer of 1978 at Vikas Publishing House in New Delhi, which was about to release his book *The Andaman Story* – an illustrated coffee-table volume which had on its blood-red jacket three large-sized women, with huge buttocks and thighs and perhaps the largest breasts and darkest nipples ever seen, covering them with nothing but just some beads and tiny jockstraps on their pubes. Or perhaps it was at the Defence Colony house of the ever-smiling and pleasant writer Uma Vasudev.

Iqqy was about thirty years my senior but we soon became friends and would meet and socialize regularly. It seemed he knew every second woman in Delhi and each one who met him went out of her way to hug him and plant a kiss in public and invite him over to her house for dinner. I was impressed, but also envied him immensely. 'What did they find in him?' I often asked myself. He was small, hardly 5 ft or so, very effeminate, sported long, grey hair at a time when it was not in fashion. He had a neatly trimmed beard, which was more Chinese with a French style added to it or French with a Chinese style added to it, for I could never make up my mind which one it was. When he would put on his thin, round rimmed glasses, John Lennon (Beatles) style, it certainly looked more Chinese. He wore good-quality aftershaves and perfumes and a different one every time one met him. Gentle and well mannered, he would dress nattily and, almost always, carry a woman on his arm. Rumour had it that ladies found him 'fabulous' and 'very satisfying' in bed.

Having travelled around the world including 'the South Pole and other godforsaken places' he was an excellent raconteur who could easily hold one's attention with his stories ranging from various drinking binges to the sex habits of the Ongi tribe in the Andaman Islands to how and what women of various nationalities preferred while making love. 'If you are small and short like me then the best place to make love is in the back seat of a car', he once explained to me. His adventures with women, particularly those in the Andamans, where he was posted as the station director of All India Radio in Port Blair for a number of years, were lucid, evocative and always descriptive. He narrated them with a straight face, like a professor lecturing on the Mughal invasion of Hindustan. Surprisingly, women, it seemed, were always his biggest audience.

According to Khushwant Singh, who had been a friend of his since college days: 'Iqqy was about the most popular student in Government College, Lahore, and was ever-willing to share other people's problems. He never seemed to have any of his own. A small man then he was far from being a ladies' man as any man I knew. Evidently, I did not sense any masculinity in his small frame. How wrong I was?'[1]

In Delhi one comes across many freeloaders. If one was to make a list, Iqqy would perhaps be somewhere on the top. He never said 'no' to an invite, even if it was to a couple of them over one evening, but never thought of returning his hosts' hospitality. This, despite the fact that he was a fabulous cook and loved cooking. Yet, he was certainly the most dined-and-wined man I knew. But one thing to his credit: he never ever gossiped nor spoke against anyone. Never even took part in any conversation that tore apart a reputation. He always had a good, warm word about every person he knew.

'How can you trust a person who has nothing to say against anyone?' I often asked myself.

I was quite surprised when Satish Gujral once asked me: 'You know Iqqy well … why don't you ask him to do a biography of Amrita Sher-Gil? He can do a great job … he is the only one who knew her the most and can give all the details…. He was the only permanent lover she had.'

'Amrita Sher-Gil? And Iqqy … her permanent lover … but how come he has never ever mentioned her during all our meetings?' I asked.

Each day is a learning experience!

Amrita, if one is to believe all the talk about her, was very oversexed, 'who was said to give appointments to her lovers at intervals of few hours. Sex mattered to her and she made no pretence about it.'[2] I decided to ask Khushwant who knew both Iqqy and Amrita and had even written on her and her love affairs. In fact, it was he who had once narrated to me about the time when the famous author and journalist Malcolm Muggeridge had spent a week with Amrita's parents – the aristocrat Sardar Umrao Singh Sher-Gil and the Hungarian Marie Antoniette Gottesmann – at their huge cottage, The Holme, in Summer Hill, on the outskirts of Simla town. Today, the cottage belongs to Rajan and Ritu Nanda of Escorts, which, besides a few cosmetic changes, retains its original character. Malcolm was in his twenties. In less than a week Amrita had reduced him 'into a limp.' 'I could not cope with her and was glad to get back to Calcutta', he confessed.[3]

Khushwant confirmed: 'Yes, we all knew that Amrita granted Iqqy certain favours she never granted to her other lovers … I don't know if it was love or anything like that, but it was a special relationship between the two'.

One day as we sat in the coffee lounge of the India International Centre in New Delhi, I casually asked Iqqy about his relationship with Amrita and if he would like to do her biography. Iqqy, being Iqqy, completely denied having had any lover's relationship with her. 'She was a good friend … a very dear friend … we cared for each other … in fact, I was the only friend she would confide in … don't believe anything beyond that,' he replied. I was looking for some spicy, juicy 'inside' details … the intimate story. Since I got none, I left it at that. My main interest was an intimate biography of Amrita. Iqqy refused.

However, much to my surprise Iqqy had a change of heart a few months later. Perhaps, he had given it a second thought. Vikas signed a contract with him on 26 March 1980. *Amrita Sher-Gil: An Intimate Biography*, a 208-page book, in hardback, was released in November 1984, by which time I had left Vikas to join Macmillan India. Though at that time there were only four major books on Amrita in the market, including one by Karl Khandalavala and another by Baldoon Dhingra, besides a special 116-page issue of the *Usha* magazine,[4] Iqqy's book, though the most 'authoritative and personal', which could have been a great contribution to the life and times of the gifted painter, just failed to create any impact. Iqqy had concealed more than he had revealed. Moreover, shabbily published with poorly reproduced photographs in black and white of the painter's colourful work, the book only made matters worse. It was a miserable volume, one that no one, least of all the author, could be proud of.

A pity indeed!

On 13 October 2012, at the first Khushwant Singh Literary Festival in Kasauli, there was a keynote address by Yashodhara Dalmia, author of that handsomely produced book *Amrita Sher-Gil: A Life.*[5] Yashodhara gave a wonderfully informative insight into Amrita's work with the help of slides of the painter's art to a packed-to-capacity hall. During the question-answer session someone from the audience asked Yashodhara if there were any pencil or charcoal drawings or any rough sketches of Amrita that she knew of, which could perhaps give more insight into the painter's mind. Yashodhara did not know of any.

Being the introducer of the session, I took permission from Yashodhara and answered the question by saying that I had seen drawings and rough sketches, quite a few of them, with Iqqy in his personal collection, which also contained some exquisite paintings gifted to him by Amrita herself. What happened to Iqqy's collection, few knew. I asked Iqqy's niece Bonnie Sodhi, who happened to be in the audience. She could not, or did not, want to answer the question. At that stage, art critic Alka Pande stood up to inform that Iqqy 'had sold them all one by one'. That was true. Every time Iqqy wanted to travel abroad, mostly to Europe, he would sell 'an Amrita', collecting just about enough that was sufficient for his needs.

In October 1988, at the age of seventy-four, Iqqy shifted to Chandigarh bag and baggage, where he lived alone in the sprawling house of his friend, Sunder Singh, in Sector 5, close to his elder brother's family and two nieces. Sunder Singh had passed away. His son Gullu lived in London while daughter Priya Rajvansh, a divorcee, on return from England, moved to Bombay to try her luck as a film actress. She met the producer-director Chetan Anand, fell in love and moved in with him to finally act only in his films – more out of necessity than choice. Her films under this banner include: India's first authentic war film *Haqeeqat* (1964) with Dharmendra; India's first film in verse *Heer Ranjha* (1970) and *Hindustan Ki Kasam* (1973), both with Raaj Kumar in the lead; *Hanste Zakhm* (1973), the only film where she displayed her limited acting abilities opposite Navin Nischal; the multi-starrer *Kudrat* (1981), with Raaj Kumar, Rajesh Khanna, Vinod Khanna, Hema Malini, and the highly forgettable *Hathon Ki Lakeeren* (1986).

Chetan's wife Uma moved to Delhi where she met the theatre legend E. Alkazi, fell in love with him, and the two established their own home.

Iqqy's baggage contained the works of Amrita Sher-Gil – four oils on canvas, one in pencil and charcoal, besides the line drawings and rough sketches. Once firmly settled in Chandigarh, the urge to travel took over. Once again, he sold an Amrita oil, which got him enough money to travel around in style and comfort, dividing 'his time between the nobility and the well-to-do he had befriended' over the years. After about four months he returned and sold another oil to live in the style he was used to. The first thing he did was to buy himself a two-door, mustard colour, Standard Herald car.

However, one work of Amrita's that Iqqy really loved, and which was very dear to him, was a black-and-white drawing done in pencil and charcoal. It was a self-portrait, nude, amply displaying her large rounded breasts with erect nipples on the dark areolae and the beautiful formation of the cleavage, a light shade of a thin muslin cloth covering her densely haired pube. It was one of the finest 'nudes' I have ever seen – pure, sublime, pious, captivating. Amrita looked gorgeous – 'a goddess of beauty'. Nothing like that had I seen ever before. Nor have seen since. It was rare and exquisite, enticing and adoring, exotic and sensuous. What wouldn't have I given to possess it! But Iqqy was categorical: 'No. I can't sell this. It's just too precious. I have an emotional attachment to it … I have to see it every day till I die'. I could see a slight mist in his eyes. Beautifully framed, it hung in his bedroom above the door so that he could see it the first thing in the morning when he got up and last thing before he retired every night. For him it had taken the form of a devi – a goddess – whom he had come to worship. In fact, it was this 'nude' by Amrita that motivated me to collect a series of nudes by different artists in the years to come.

But, emotional attachment not withstanding, nor the slight mist in his eyes that I had seen, Iqqy did sell the devi – his goddess of beauty!

In November 1995, Gullu Sunder Singh, the estranged brother of actress Priya Rajvansh, came to Chandigarh to explore the possibility of selling off his share of the property. He was able to buy the nude off Iqqy and took it back with him to England. A year or so later, Gullu Sunder Singh was detected with cancer. Treatment in England started to drain him off his finances. And what better way to raise money than to sell of a rare Amrita 'nude'? Whom did he sell it to? At what price? Where is it today? No one, it seems, knows. Gullu died soon after, on 17 November 1997. Six months later, on 31 May 1998, Iqqy, the one-time Amrita king who sold his empire piece by piece, too passed away as an Amrita pauper.

15

Patwant Singh

A Friend to None

If there is one author whom I could never understand it was Patwant Singh.

Writer, publisher, political commentator, conservationist and philanthropist, Patwant was born in luxury with the proverbial 'silver spoon in his mouth'. He lived lavishly, entertained stylishly, dressed dapperly. He drove around in a Mercedes Benz even in the good old 1960s and 1970s, when the Merc was a real status symbol and that too driven by a white-uniformed chauffeur. He travelled overseas first-class, which only a handful could afford. He knew all the so-called 'high and mighty' of the glitterati but liked to mix only with the literati, and that too only those who had some 'status'. In short, he had everything. And yet nothing. He died friendless!

I first met Patwant sometime in the mid-1980s, and then after a gap of nearly twenty years, in June 1999, through his 'close and dear' friends, the charming and courteous N. P. Singh (Nippie) and Mala Sekhri – my colleagues at the India Today Group. I soon realized that he had not only strong but very rigid likes and dislikes, almost childlike. He never ever had a good word about anyone, not even his closest friend, if there was one. There was no exception to this rule. His pet hate was Khushwant Singh, and Iqqy (N. Iqbal Singh) was 'not even worth a mention'. Once, during an interview with a journal I had said in reply to a question: 'Yes, [Nani] Palkhivala [the famous advocate] was certainly my godfather. But Khushwant Singh is my God, whom I worship every morning. Both played a silent but vital role in my life and for making me what I am today....'[1] Patwant remarked to a common friend: 'May God help him!' and did not talk to me for over a couple of months after that.

Patwant had an encyclopedic knowledge on the flora and fauna of Delhi. His interests were varied and so were the subjects he wrote on, ranging from history to religion to politics. According to Antony Wood of the *Guardian*, 'he had a very rare ability to communicate compellingly with the wider world on many issues without losing touch with his deeply held faith....'[2] Patwant was a good writer, who worked hard on his books. He was well informed and passionate about the subjects he wrote on. His books, at least most of them, certainly deserved a better exposure and fate than they got at the hands of insignificant publishers who had no sense of, nor were equipped for, any professional editorial work. But it all suited Patwant for he hated his writing to be touched by 'Indian' editors. For him it was only the British who could edit. And he paid them from his pocket.

He authored quite a few books, most of them good and readable. But few knew about them and yet fewer read them, for no one knew who the publishers were and where to buy them from. Every time he had a book ready he would invite me for dinner, always served with the choicest of wines or his favourite single malt – Glenlivet; or for breakfast, served on the first-floor deck outside his giant, round-shaped living room with a circular sitting arrangement, overlooking the lush green lawns of his luxurious home situated in the most exclusive residential area of Amrita Shergill Marg in Central Delhi. Two old loyal retainers, in starch-white uniforms and gloves, were always at hand to serve. If I said 'yes' to his book, I would be invited the next time too, and the next. If I said 'no' he would dismiss me as an 'upstart' or an 'elitist snob' and sulk till the next book was ready.

However, I must hasten to clarify that whenever I said 'no' to a project it was not because the book was not worth publication, but simply because it would not fit into my time schedules. Patwant was always in a hurry. He would take two years writing a book but would want it published within two months. The result was that he never ever bothered who the publisher was and which the imprint, as long as the book came out 'yesterday'. All a publisher had to do was 'lay it thick' and praise his manuscript. Strangely, like a pampered child, he was immensely hungry for praise. Sitting in his favourite chair-sofa of his book-lined study, overlooking his desk, overburdened with books, files, papers and a pen stand with neatly sharpened dozen or so pencils, with 'Biba' – his handsome and disciplined Labrador – faithfully sitting next to him, he would enjoy every word from the flatterer. No wonder, all sorts of unknown, unheard-of or faceless booksellers-turned-fly-by-night-publishers would walk away from his house with a signed contract in one hand and the manuscript in the other. A pity indeed!

Take, for example, his book *Gurdwaras: In India and around the World*. This wonderful, coffee-table book, which was a visual treat and at that time the only book of its kind in the market, was his labour of love on which he spent four years of his life. But he wanted it out in four months. Such was the fate of many of his books.

Patwant wrote over a dozen books in addition to two that he co-authored – *History of the Sikhs* (1998) with Joseph Davey Cunningham and *Empire of the Sikhs: The Life and Times of Maharaja Ranjit Singh* (2008) with Jyoti M. Rai, who not only co-authored the book with him but single-handedly did the entire research. But of all these only two remain memorable – *The History of the Sikhs* had a good run, while *Empire of the Sikhs* survived the daily onslaught of books on the shelves, and sells internationally to this day.

Patwant's books certainly deserved a better deal. Wish he had more patience. And less ego!

16

General V. P. Malik

A Soldier-Turned-Author

He has enormous patience. And no ego!

Yet I failed to understand him too.

On 23 August 2005, I had signed General V. P. Malik, the highly decorated former chief of army staff, for his book, *Kargil: From Surprise to Victory*, to be published by HarperCollins India. It was his first book. Despite being ramrod straight, he was very flexible and accommodating. The Kargil war of May-July 1999 had taken place during his tenure as the army chief and I had already published one title, *A Soldier's Diary: Kargil, The Inside Story* by Harinder Baweja in 2000 under the Books Today imprint, which was finally dissolved as a result of the India Today Group-HarperCollins joint venture coming into being on 1 December 2003.

General Malik's *Kargil* was an authoritative, detailed and authentic chronicle of the three-month war between Pakistan and India. The general's analyses, suggestions and conclusions were based on his vast and varied army experience. From a series of interactions I had with him, I could discern that he was not very happy with the politicians, especially with their attempts to imbue the army with communal colours.

General Malik did not mince words when it came to taking on his counterpart from Pakistan – General Pervez Musharraf, who, on 12 October 1999, took over power in Pakistan by ousting Prime Minister Nawaz Sharif. General Malik worked hard on his book as few authors do. He would spend hours going through the edited manuscript, answering editorial queries or giving clarifications and reading final proofs in my office in Hamilton House, Rajiv Chowk, New Delhi.

For the cover of *Kargil* I wanted to try out something new, something different, more unconventional. So I briefed the designer Smruthi Gargi Eswar to keep the front cover in blood red with just a two-inch-wide strip comprising images, in jet black, depicting soldiers fighting in the mountains and a Bofors gun placed in a valley. The title *Kargil* was to be taken over it again in red, but flat and 70 per cent diffused, about four inches wide, which we covered with UV (gloss varnish). The author's name – General V. P. Malik – was in black, small letters, to fit on top of just the two letters 'K' and 'A' of the word Kargil, while the subtitle was below the image.

I explained it to General Malik over the phone but he could not visualize it and was rather apprehensive. I doubt if he slept that night, for the very next morning, accompanied by his wife Ranjana (Dr Ranjana Malik, who had also contributed a chapter to the book), he came down to Delhi from Panchkula, near Chandigarh, where he has settled after retirement. That was the level of his involvement with his book. His face lit up when he saw the proof of the cover. 'I couldn't imagine it would be like this ... this is beautiful ... I love it', he remarked. When the advance copies of the book came out, General Malik was in for another surprise. While I had flowed the blood-red colour from the cover on to the spine, with the author's name and the title in the middle and the publisher's logo at the bottom, as is the norm, for the top of the spine I had the reversed rifle with a soldier's helmet on it, photographed from the Amar Jawan Jyoti memorial at the India Gate on Rajpath in New Delhi. The back cover was in jet black, with a photograph of Captain Rajshree Bisht against a setting sun, in uniform, saluting the tricolour-covered, wreath-laden coffin and bidding a soldier's farewell to her husband Major Vivek Gupta, MVC.[1] Below were printed in red:

When You Go Home, Tell Them of Us And Say,
For Their Tomorrow, We Gave Our Today.

The moment General Malik saw and read it, he stood up. He became a bit emotional. So did his wife. A soldier remains a soldier and that was the soldier in him feeling his tender moments within – quietly, with dignity and grace. The same emotions, which had, perhaps, made him dedicate his book thus:

For every single brave deed noticed and recognized
there are many that go unnoticed in the fog of war.
To
those unnoticed deeds and to the gallant individuals
who performed them

On 31 March 2006, General V. P. Malik's *Kargil: From Surprise to Victory* was out. And so was I from HarperCollins, India. He never forgave me for it.

After that, every time we met he would remind me that 'after producing a beautiful baby you abandoned it as a laawaris ...' and would always repeat 'you let me down ...' to me and make me feel pretty miserable and, at times, quite guilty. This despite the fact that I would always assure him: 'Sir, next time I will give you a better book and a superb post-publication service.'

Over the next few years I would ring him up, off and on, to remain in touch. Once, I suggested a subject for his next book but he did not seem enthused. Then in April 2012 he informed me of his wanting to do a book on 'security'. I was excited and told him so. In January 2013 he informed that he was just about three months away from finishing it. Over those three months I would call him in Panchkula regularly and he would inform me about the book's status.

The shock came on Friday, 12 April 2013!

I called General Malik only to be informed that, once again, he had signed the book, *India's Military Conflicts and Diplomacy: An Inside View of Decision Making*, with HarperCollins just two days earlier on Wednesday, 10 April 2013. I was shocked. And confused. How could he, when he was so unhappy with them regarding his earlier book? But there was no answer. However, General Malik did say during the conversation that 'after all HarperCollins is a much bigger name than Hay House'.

True indeed!

The general perhaps had not heard the old saying: 'Small is beautiful' too.

17

Rajinder Singh Bedi

Burning Passions

TWO OF THE MOST PROMINENT FIGURES OF THE INDIAN LITERARY world whom I was fortunate to meet, and in a way to be adopted by, though for a short time, were Rajinder Singh Bedi and Sahir Ludhianvi. One a novelist and short story writer; the other a poet and lyricist. Both were an important part of the Bombay film industry where they created names for themselves. Both were very creative and intensely sensitive.

Bedi, one of the leading twentieth-century progressive writers of Urdu fiction, is today considered the second most prominent Urdu fiction writer, after Saadat Hasan Manto.

Gian Sachdev, the estranged husband of film actress Achala Sachdev, known for her motherly roles, introduced me to Rajinder Singh Bedi. It seemed Gian, who had wasted, like numerous others, many years and a good deal of money trying to produce some film or the other, knew everyone in the film industry. Bedi had been in the industry for a long time, writing scripts, dialogues and stories. With the release of Bimal Roy's immortal *Devdas* in 1955 (starring Dilip Kumar, Vyjayanthimala and Suchitra Sen), Bedi, who had written its dialogues, shot into instant fame. According to Dilip Kumar: '... the dialogues of *Devdas* are replete with a haunting sensitivity, spontaneity and meaning. They came from the pen of Rajinder Singh Bedi, one of those rare writers whose syntax was so perfect that the simple lines he wrote inspired actors to build up deep emotions in their rendering. Being myself not given to superfluous speech, I appreciated the precision and brevity of the lines he wrote for *Devdas*. They were lines of profound meaning at times, but they were so simply and sensitively worded that generations of viewers have found pleasure in repeating them lovingly.'[1]

By 1970, Bedi was riding high on the success of his first directorial venture *Dastak* (The Knock) starring Sanjeev Kumar and Rehana Sultan, which had an unusual storyline set in a red-light area. This 'classic' went on to bag three national awards, including Best Actor for Sanjeev Kumar, Best Actress for Rehana and Best Music Director for Madan Mohan. Bedi now wanted to make a bigger film and signed up stars like Dharmendra, Waheeda Rehman and the then sensation, Jaya Bhaduri opposite Vijay Arora in his film titled *Phagun*. 'Wait and see how my heroine Shanta will beat even Nargis playing Radha in Mehboob Khan's *Mother India* (1957)', he boasted to one and all. Initially, Waheeda was reluctant to play Shanta Damle – Jaya's mother. After all she was only thirty-seven – an age at which actresses played lead roles those days. Bedi apparently was able to persuade her by citing Nargis playing Radha – mother to Sunil Dutt and Rajinder Kumar (both in her age group) in *Mother India* – at the age of only twenty-eight, a role that immortalized her. Finally, Waheeda signed on the dotted line. And perhaps never forgave herself for it. Nor did Dharmendra!

'Success' is a very fragile word in the world of films and you are only as good as your last hit. *Phagun*, released in 1973, was a disaster at the box office. Bedi, who had stretched himself financially to the core, was shocked beyond belief.

Then something happened that shocked his family too, beyond belief. Bedi fell in love. He was fifty-eight. The girl just nineteen. Bedi's wife, children and grandchildren couldn't believe it. Nor take it. The atmosphere at home became very ugly and to avoid it, he moved out. In the winter of 1973-74, Gian, Balwant Gargi and I had dinner with him in his shack in Juhu where Bedi, after many drinks and innumerable cigarettes, and Balwant after one drink and half-a-cigarette, started narrating their tales straight from the heart. For me it was somewhat embarrassing to see Bedi become rather emotional – a scene best described by Gargi:

> [Bedi:] This son[2] of mine who till yesterday ran my errands is rolling in money. He is illiterate. The mother and son have joined hands. They denounce me as a fool, with no talent for film making. Why? Because I've made a flop. These very people used to call me a genius, a super director. I can't believe my son can treat me like that. It's money. It has turned his brain upside down, corrupted them. My wife abuses me … calls me a bastard. A sex maniac. The other day the whole family gathered. My son and daughters. My wife shouted: 'If you meet that whore I'll throw acid on her face. I'll pick her eyes. I'll strip you in public. You are not a man. You are a monster …'
>
> Bedi got up. His cigarette had turned into an ash pencil. He picked up his black leather briefcase, clicked it open and brought out an envelope. He took out three photographs and showed them to me.
>
> The girl was plain looking. She had lacklustre eyes and a big bosom.
>
> He said: 'She is marvellous. You know … when she first met me I did not care for her. She rang me up many times. Once she came to see me here … in this shack. She said she liked me. Not because I was a great writer or a filmmaker. But as a man. I laughed and teased her. Then why don't you become a woman? She looked at me, her lips half-parted. She opened her blouse and revealed her large firm breasts…. I had never seen such breasts. They blinded me. It was not her face or intelligence but her breasts which maddened me. She held me and started kissing.
>
> 'For the first time I realized what I was missing in life. I was living like a barren person. This young woman revived me. My friends started a whispering campaign against me. They suddenly

> turned into medieval priests. What do they know of me? Most of them are busy piling up money and have lost [their] taste for life. Their minds are soggy.... They call my passion simple physical lust and condemn me. But it's the greatest spiritual reality.... This girl has revived me.... They won't understand that in order to live, to breathe, to create, I must taste life – the evil that lies chained in my body ... [I am] thrice her age. But believe me there is no difference of age in passion. When she is with me we become one ... the same height, mind and body.'[3]

Bedi was truly in love. Total love ... immersed in deep passion. He could see nothing beyond that girl. He told us: 'There is opium on her nipples ... when I suck them I get totally intoxicated ... it's a nasha I have never experienced before ... ("Opium on her nipples" was an expression Balwant had later used for one of his lovers in his autobiographical novel *The Naked Triangle.*) We cover our emotions and our inner reality by dressing them too much. We hide things and thereby make them ugly. I find no shame in speaking of my inner tortures, creative moments and the great passion of this young girl ... a great woman who can rise to the burning passion of love.'

'What if she were to leave you ... would you hate her?' I asked.

'I know she will leave me ... for someone else ... she will betray me ... but why would I hate her? By hating a woman or feeling betrayed by her, a man does not cease loving her. A woman is a multiple being with great seductive power, terrifying, made more hypnotic by the constant fear of her betraying the man ... it is all mental witchery, this subtle shadow of the fear of betrayal which sometimes becomes a source of attraction.'

Whether the opium on the nipples of this woman in Bedi's life was in reality an inspiration for him or not, I don't know, but he did want to make a film with her in the lead on the theme of untouchability. However, there was no financier to back his 'dream project'. Despite having worked in the film industry for nearly twenty-five years and that too with some of the biggest banners and names, financiers judged him by his last film – the flop *Phagun*. The success of his award-winning venture *Dastak* had been wiped off the slate of his career.

That is when Bedi decided to make *Ek Chadar Maili Si* (*I Take This Woman*) and was hopeful of financial backing from the Punjab government, which apparently had sponsored, substantially, Chetan Anand's film in verse: *Heer Ranjha* (1970). Bedi came to Chandigarh in October 1974 and stayed with me. Getting an appointment with Chief Minister Giani Zail Singh was just not working out. I spoke to the powerful bureaucrat Suraj Bagla, then principal secretary to the chief minister, whom I knew a little. He assured me that he would fix a meeting with Zail Singh, but to no avail. Bedi was getting impatient. I then decided to speak to my friend, the ever-helpful and resourceful Rashpal Malhotra, chairman of the Chandigarh-based Centre for Research on Rural and Industrial Development (CRRID), who had personal contacts with every known politician in Chandigarh. A few months earlier (in June 1974) he had not only helped arrange a meeting of writer-producer-director K. A. Abbas with Zail Singh but also helped get tax exemption for his film *Faasla* (1974) starring newcomers Shabana Azmi and Raman Khanna.

Once again, overnight, Rashpal fixed a breakfast meeting at his home in Sector 11 with the chief minister for the next morning. Zail Singh, immaculately dressed in white churidars and sherwani, with a red rose in the buttonhole, Nehru-style, met Bedi like an old, long-lost friend. Zail Singh told Bedi about the Punjab Film and News Corporation, which had been set up about a year earlier (26 June 1973) especially to promote, finance and establish a film industry in Mohali, then an upcoming suburb of Chandigarh. He also ordered an urgent meeting of Bedi with the corporation's managing director, one Krishnamurthy, whose full name I forget now.

However, nothing came out of the meeting. The government machinery moved at its own pace. Having burnt its fingers with Chetan Anand, the corporation was moving extra-cautiously with Bedi's file, which had a big 'burden' on it: the flop *Phagun*. Bedi lost patience and hope for *Ek Chadar Maili Si*! He did make two short films in 1978, *Aankhin Dekhi* and *Nawab Sahib*, but both tanked at the box office. One by one all producers and directors, for whom he wrote either award-winning or successful stories, screenplays and dialogues once, left him. So did his girl for another film-maker, whom she later married and is today happily settled with.

Bedi's professional life had come to an end. Soon he got lost in the big, wide, wicked and merciless world of Bollywood as a 'had been'. His saga reminds me of the lines by the poet Wasim Bareillvi:

Mili hawaaon mein udne ki woh saaza yaaron
Ki main zameen ke rishton se kat gaya yaaron
(For flying high I was meted out this punishment
My ties with the ground were severed.)

18

Zail Singh

The Loyal Courtier. And Friend

THANKS TO THE BREAKFAST MEETINGS AT RASHPAL MALHOTRA'S home, coupled with two stories that I was able to 'smuggle' on to the front page of *The Tribune*, Chandigarh, where I worked then as a junior sub-editor, and that too each with a large photograph of his, Chief Minister Giani Zail Singh was thrilled with me. P. D. Mohindra, then special correspondent of the paper for Punjab, a compulsive book purchaser who mutilated each one by underlining pages heavily, without reading perhaps even one page, fumed. He threatened to have me sacked and complained to the paper's editor R. Madhavan Nair.

Nothing happened.

Over the years Zail Singh developed a parental fondness for me. He even went out of his way to issue me a 500-square-yard residential plot in Mohali, in comparison to 200-square-yard ones that he gave to other journalists of *The Tribune*, out of his 'discretionary quota' just a couple of weeks before he lost power on 30 April 1977. Not only that, he even lent me Rs 24,750 that had to be immediately paid up – an amount I did not readily have. But we kept in touch off and on.

In April 1978, Chhotu Karadia, the managing editor of *India Today*, commissioned me to cover the CPI and CPM sessions at Punjab's dustbowl Bhatinda, and the hotbed of Punjab's politics

Jullundur (now spelt as Jalandhar), respectively. Jawaid Laiq of the *Indian Express*, M. H. Jadhav of *The Statesman* and I shared a taxi to travel together to the two towns. On 9 April, Giani Zail Singh came down to meet me at Jullundur's Skylark Hotel where we were all staying. Jawaid and Jadhav interviewed, separately, the former Punjab chief minister, who then was completely out of the news. While Jawaid's story was carried in the next day's *Indian Express* on the front page, much to Zail Singh's delight a day later, *The Statesman* too had one. In return, Zail Singh gave me some 'masala' about the communists, which was carried, without naming him of course, in the *India Today* edition of 16-30 April 1978 much to the delight of Chhotu. That was the beginning of my writing regularly for the magazine.

About two years later, the political situation in the country changed and so did the fortunes of Zail Singh who took over as the country's home minister on 14 January 1980 after Indira Gandhi came back to power at the Centre. He invited me for lunch on Sunday, 5 October 1980. He seemed to be a little disturbed about not 'getting the right press coverage'. I spoke to Khushwant Singh, who was then editing *New Delhi* magazine for the Ananda Bazar Patrika Group. Khushwant formed a team comprising his staffers Madhu Jain, Chaitanya Kalbagh and photographer N. K. Sareen, along with me. While Madhu and I covered Zail Singh in Delhi, Chaitanya and I flew with him over four days to various parts of Punjab. Khushwant carried the coverage as a cover-page story in the *New Delhi* of 12 November 1980. Later, Vimla Patil, then editor of *Femina*, and M. V. Kamath of *The Illustrated Weekly of India* featured two different stories of mine on Zail Singh prominently in their issues in December 1980 and January 1981 respectively. Zail Singh couldn't have been a happier man.

Zail Singh moved at a nawabi (royal) pace. He was a great orator who spiced his speeches with shairi (poetry), and thus managed to diffuse many difficult and complex situations, be it at a public rally in the Punjab Vidhan Sabha or in Parliament. Few know that Zail Singh wrote poetry and kirtans. But much that I tried to convince him, he refused to have them published. Homespun rhetoric and folksy logic would often win over facts, figures and arguments, thus disarming his opponents, at times mercilessly. In 1980, the north-east was perpetually on the brink of exploding, communal riots were rife and the situation in Kashmir, where the tough and far-from-shaky Sheikh Abdullah was the chief minister, was tense. But as Giani Zail Singh used to say, morning kirtan and poetry 'help me take the mind off such matters'.

Giani Zail Singh was also Prime Minister Indira Gandhi's 'most loyal soldier' – a phrase he often used to describe his relationship with her. He'd press on, regardless, under orders, into any battlefield, no matter how heavily mined. The rather big jump from the arena of Punjab politics to the Centre and on to Rashtrapati Bhavan as the seventh president of the country (25 July 1982–25 July 1987) had also been taken in with typical aplomb. Zail Singh, with his fierce black beard, spotless white turban, immaculately ironed clothes – which he changed three times a day – and eyes that glinted shrewdly behind steel-framed glasses, always appeared a picture of unflappability, whether it was in that rather imposing office in the North Block or in the posh and sprawling Rashtrapati Bhavan. And he was firm in his saddle.

However, wherever he was, there was always a whiff of the Punjab secretariat in the atmosphere in his particular corner of North Block. Rows of Sikhs waited outside his office. And inside, our interview proceeded from the scheduled half-hour to three hours, the generous hospitality extending through lunch, as several bureaucrats, all crisply turbaned, took turns to sit in.

Nobody could ever accuse Giani Zail Singh of not being bold. I recall his inaugural address at the International Anthropological Congress on the Panjab University campus in Chandigarh in November 1975. He came with a printed speech in English, which was distributed to the journalists and the participating anthropologists from around the world. But Zail Singh spoke in Punjabi with vehemence and brilliance: 'You say man is the son of a monkey. You may be, I am not! (*Laughter*). It's a lie cooked up by you people. If you say that man has evolved from the monkey, then tell me whose son is a parrot? How did the parrot come into existence? Why are its beak and green feathers still intact? Why hasn't it dissolved into a monkey or evolved into a man? And if monkeys change and their tails disappear and they assume the human form, then tell me why are monkeys still alive? Look at Ajanta and Ellora. Our ancient caves ... the statues of Gautam Buddha. His face is more beautiful than ours. Was he the son of a monkey? Utter nonsense.'[1]

Imagine what Zail Singh's address would have sounded in Punjabi!

> *Tussi kehende ho ki insaan bandar da puttar hai. Taain tussi hovo gey, main nahin hain ...*

His challenge left the anthropologists stunned.

Dr S. R. K. Chopra, then head of the anthropology department at the university, and his team, who had discovered traces of the early man in the Shivalik ranges of the western Himalayas in 1974 and were to present their findings at the first session of the congress, did not know what had hit them and how to make the presentation and clarify matters. Perhaps even Charles Darwin in their place would have been hard put that day to defend his theory.

Coming back to the *New Delhi* story, Madhu Jain and I tried to corner Zail Singh with a variety of questions ranging from the north-east to Bangladesh migrants to Kashmir, but to no avail. Before we could start, he looked at Madhu and disarmed her completely by saying: 'So you are also a Punjabi ... no wonder you are so pretty!' Extracts from the interview:

Q. Why has Sheikh Abdullah [the chief minister of Jammu and Kashmir] made such statements [against the Central Government]? Please clairify.
A. I will not tell you the reason. If I do so you will print it. And when you print it, it will be all over. You people from *New Delhi* magazine are very liberal. You keep no copyright. Any newspaper can then pick it up. Why should all newspapers pick it from you?

Q. What action are you planning to take against the Sheikh?
A. Why should I tell you? I believe in the theory that a man of action should take action and not just talk. I can't tell you anything at the moment.

Q. People say that you have failed to provide a government that works [as promised in the election manifesto]...
A. Have you ever seen a juggler's show where the juggler always keeps on repeating: 'I don't believe it. I don't believe it.' You must have gone to the circus also. This is the same element that says 'we don't believe it, the government is not working'.

Q. It is said that you are the best-dressed person in the Union cabinet.
A. (He beams and preens, a bit like a peacock). It is said or do you think so yourself? Yes, I love wearing spotlessly clean and well-stitched clothes. The dressing of the body should be perfect and should look very graceful. One must find a good tailor ... I've been always lucky.

Q. You wear khadi?
A. No, only my pajama and kurta are khadi. My sherwani is always of polyster-cotton as it gets a good fall, a comfortable crease and, most important doesn't crush easily.

Q. But khadi is so difficult to maintain ...
A. Oh, yes, it is. But I dare not suggest another dress symbol. My Congress friends will get angry with me. My policy is to live well, but within my means ...

Q. You are known to be a lover of fragrances and perfumes. Which is your favourite?
A. I like khusbhoo (fragrance) because I love beauty, I like pretty streets, people, houses. Beauty should be respected. But I have no knowledge of the various brands of ittars (fragrances). I wear whatever I get.

Q. How do you distinguish chamchas [sycophants] from friends?
A. I have completely failed in this. People have continued with me for more than twenty years, even more – even polished my shoes, but in the end I realized they were matlabis (opportunists). But I can be proud of the fact that I have not dropped a friend or a leader. Even if I have suffered because of them, I have overlooked their mistakes.

Q. How do you define a follower?
A. A follower should be able to tell his leader if he has made a mistake, but he should not talk about it to others or against the leader.... I believe one must follow one's mother and father, one's guru, one's leader – and never talk against them. A follower must do what the leader says even if it goes against his own wishes. A politician who says he does not lie is telling the biggest lie – you have to tell lies in politics ...

Giani Zail Singh had a great hunger for publicity. During the internal Emergency of 25 June 1975 to 21 March 1977, when he was chief minister of Punjab, 'his photographs started appearing daily in the press. Every billboard, magazine and calendar carried his grinning portrait. One of the universities conferred on him a doctorate to wipe out his well-known illiteracy. He ordered his press chief to drop the word Giani from his name and prefix it with Doctor. Though Giani means a learned person he wanted to be known as Doctor. He had reduced the entire Public Relations Department with its budget of millions to a department of self-publicity. He suffered from two diseases: diabetes and public speaking. Generally his throat was hoarse from spouting speeches from morning till late evening. And he kept sucking lozenges'.[2]

Everyone knows that Zail Singh had an enormous store of Urdu and Punjabi couplets in his repertoire, for every possible occasion. Few know that his biggest love was reading – history and poetry. Though he insisted 'I am no poet, but a patron of poetry', he used to write poetry. Whenever I would ask him to 'write a book' and fill it up with his poetry he would always reply: 'Where is the time?' After he left the Rashtrapati Bhavan on 25 July 1987 to settle down on Circular Road (now Pt Uma Shankar Dixit Marg) on Shanti Path in Chanakyapuri (the diplomatic section of New Delhi), he had the time but no inclination. I would repeatedy ask him to write, or at least, narrate his autobiography. 'How can I?' he once asked. 'It's best if I keep out of everything … I cover up more than you think!' Suddenly, with these words, he seemed to have become like La Ponica, the sturdy and faithful housekeeper of Bernarda in the Spanish playwright Federico Garcia Lorca's famous play *The House of Bernarda Alba*, who guarded many a secret within her. Then he recited a few couplets of Muhammad Iqbal:

Taskeen na ho jis se wo raaz badal dalo
Jo raaz na rakh paye hamraaz badal dalo
Dushman ke iradon ko hai zahir agar karna
Tum khel wohi khelo andaz badal dalo

(If you are uncomfortable with a particular secret, then change it
Change the confidant who cannot keep a secret
If you want to expose the intentions of your enemies
Play the same game, but change your style of playing.)

I once asked him about his favourite poets. 'Don't ask that. My poet friends will get angry', he replied. When the youthful singer-dreamer Shiv Batalvi – 'the Punjabi language poet, who was most known for his romantic poetry, noted for its heightened passion, pathos, separation and lover's agony'[3] – died on 23 July 1973 at the young age of thirty-six, Zail Singh felt the loss immensely. He also loved the romantic-realist poetry of Bhai Mohan Singh and Amrita Pritam.

He once desired to meet Shobhaa Dé to discuss with her something she had written in one of her columns that he did not agree with. Unfortunately, I could not arrange that meeting, though I wish I had!

19

Shobhaa Dé

Seductive! Soulful! Spicy! Sensuous!

SHE HAS MAGIC. SHE HAS MYSTIQUE!

She is the delight of every publisher. And the envy of every author.

She is, the one and only, Shobhaa Dé.

Period.

A question repeatedly asked is what has made Shobhaa the literary sensation that she is for a quarter of a century, over which period she has written more than eighteen books. My experience would say that she has two factors that have made her a perennial favourite among a cross section of readers – men and women alike.

First, the 'newness' or the magic formula of making her writing new. And which remains new with every read, year after year. Take her *Socialite Evenings*, published in 1989. It sells even today. As do all her other books. Second, frankness with no holds barred on any topic, issue or subject that was hitherto the exclusive preserve of 'the men'. With her, all subjects were open for discussion, nothing was confined to the closet. For the first time a woman had come out and told it all, from a woman's perspective, in a male-dominated society. And every time she wrote, the readers wanted more. And more.

Take the brew of mass-market best-sellers based on sex, suspense, wealth, celebrities and unbridled violence. It was all a male monopoly, which Shobhaa broke into for the first time with stories told with unusual candour that would match the best writers of the high-society scene. Where at times even male writers feared to tread, Shobhaa Dé dared to.

What's so new about the content, one might ask? Sex and high jinks are passé, but what made Shobhaa's writing different – and therefore new – was her directness. She didn't mince her words, and gave it, as it was, warts and all. Even when she wrote those descriptive sex scenes in her novels – all raw and rustic – there was freshness in them that readers liked and devoured, because, for her, there was no point in beating about the bush. Particularly, when the reality was known to all.

Soon, Shobhaa Dé the writer became seductive! Soulful! Spicy! Sensuous! Her writings engaged, provoked, enthralled and hypnotized readers with the range of subjects she took on. From the mirch-masala of Bollywood to Hollywood, from the petty doings of our netas (leaders) to the sordid crimes of passion, from the 'O' woes of women to the shenanigans of the menfolk, Shobhaa covered it all, as she dexterously got into the minds of politicians, corporate honchos, film stars and the common man to nattily expose their kinks. She talked about marital issues that most are scared to even admit and confronted with elan the troubles of one's growing years. Shobhaa convinced her readers that urban women don't have it easy and rural ones have it even tougher: all that talk about emancipation is merely theoretical. Unabashedly, she debunked the use of nauseatingly old-fashioned terms like 'keep' by an erudite judge, which, in turn, elicited a quick reaction from legal luminaries.

Shobhaa revealed the secret of Shah Rukh Khan's six-packs; the bare-all story of the starlet who made it to the cover of *Playboy*; the small-town incidents that rarely find a spot on the front page; and poignant stories about women politicos that have made it big and the 'chak de!' moments that elicit a 'whoop!'

In short, her writing is layered, which makes it hard-hitting and socially relevant. Few authors have that wide a range and that extensive a reach. And if there are any, they are merely copies, and who wants copies when the original is there?

When I joined UBSPD in January 1992 to start its publishing programme, the first names I thought of were Khushwant Singh and Shobhaa Dé. Khushwant, in his typical generous style said: 'Go ahead. Take whatever you want.' But Shobhaa's case was different. First, I had never even met her. Second, I was told, 'It's difficult to contact her and even if you do she will say an outright "*no*" like she says to every other publisher'. She was a Penguin author and David Davidar (the then Penguin India chief), who had published five of her novels and was ready with the sixth one, had drawn a 'David rekha (line)', which Shobhaa would not cross. Third, she first talks about money.

Armed with the thought that if Valmiki made Sita cross the Lakshman Rekha, why won't Shobhaa cross the 'David rekha', I met up with her on 18 September 1992 at the coffee shop of the President Hotel in Colaba in Bombay. It was a pleasant meeting at which I explained to her about UBS – a name she had not even heard of. I expressed my interest in exploring the possibility of publishing her – something, I knew, she was, and is even today, used to hearing from every publisher. She just listened. And smiled! At least, she had not said '*no*', which I had been cautioned about, I thought to myself.

I met up with her again on 3 December 1992, this time at her large apartment in Maker Towers, Cuffe Parade, Bombay, overlooking the sea. It was a meeting I will never forget – a day every publisher waits for. Every point about her that I had been warned against turned out to be untrue. I am now five Shobhaa-books old and I must admit that to this day she has never ever talked to me about money – advances and/or royalties. She has signed all the five contracts without even reading a single line. And every time I have sent her a royalty cheque she has, always, made me feel as though I have done her a great favour, instead of the other way around. It speaks volumes for Shobhaa the person. Hence, when on 13 October 2012, I introduced Shobhaa at the first Khushwant Singh Litfest in Kasauli by saying: 'First, a confession. I love Shobhaa. I love Shobhaa. I love Shobhaa. I love Shobhaa not only for being a woman who has lived life on her own terms, a writer who is read and respected widely, an author who writes candidly ... but Shobhaa for being a wonderful, wonderful human being.' I meant every word of what I said. And do so even more now. (There was a standing ovation, much to Shobhaa's thrill-cum-embarrassment.) May there be more Shobhaas on this planet!

How did I manage it? How and why did Shobhaa cross the David-drawn David rekha? To this day I have no answers to these questions. Hence, I'll just quote what Shobhaa wrote in her memoir, *Selective Memory: Stories from My Life*:

> If I was to single out two occasions when I felt great about being an author, I would pick my visit to the Calcutta Book Fair in 1994 ... when I published two books with UBSPD, a Delhi-based publishing house. I did so because I appreciated the publisher's approach. Ashok Chopra is a low-key individual whose publishing list is middle-brow and sensible. I get the feeling he doesn't really care what his contemporaries think of him – he knows his business and he's obviously good at it. Not for him the five large Scotches at a plush five-star bar and self-conscious pseudo-literary talk over roasted almonds. Chopra recognizes the unromantic fact that publishing is a business like any other – books must sell. And if they have to move from the shelves, the publisher in India has to know his marketing. The two books I did for his company (he has since left UBSPD) were different in that one was a collection of my columns over the years. And the other, a volume of short stories.
>
> *Shooting from the Hip* was a triumph of persistence over resistance and nothing else. It was Chopra's idea to put a few

representative columns together. But how? I hadn't followed a filing system. My clippings were scattered all over the place. I didn't have the time and energy to sift through twenty years of printed material. I wouldn't have known where to begin. I thought this fact alone would put him off. It didn't.

'Leave it to me', he said, 'just stuff what you can easily access into a suitcase and I'll have my man pick it up.'

This is exactly what I did. I didn't have the slightest idea of what that black-and-grey suitcase contained. I was certain that Chopra would find the task of sifting through it far too daunting, and give up. A month or so later he called to say he had managed to go through everything and give it some kind of order. He'd divided the material into segments: People, Politics, Travel and Social Issues. It was hanging together quite well. Before we knew it, we had a book. All it needed was a spicy title. *Spice* was too obvious. I came up with *Shooting from the Hip*. My superstition about the letter 'S' was also taken care of. Plus it had a zingy ring to it. We were in business. As always Gautam [Rajadhyaksha] 'donated' the cover transparency and the book was ready. As I went through the advance copy it came to me that I'd forgotten I'd even written some of those columns. Seeing them like this, neatly titled and effectively tabulated, I felt the efforts (Ashok's) had been well worth it. They provide a healthy chuckle when I read them now.

Small Betrayals was my idea. David didn't have much faith in the short story genre, mainly because, as he pointed out when I floated the idea of doing a volume, there is no market for it – not in India, not anywhere in the world. I wasn't convinced. Besides, I was keen to write it, regardless. I did. For Ashok, instead of David.

There was nothing controversial about either of the books, and Ashok didn't really have a strong peg to hang his marketing on. When he suggested that I launch *Small Betrayals* at what is the largest book fair in India (in terms of visitors), I was keen to do so for two reasons. One, I regard Calcutta as my second home; two,

Calcutta has a large and a very interested book-buying public. But nothing at all could have prepared me for what Chopra had lined up. He'd wanted it to be a complete surprise – and so it was. When we landed at Dum Dum [airport] we were greeted by large bouquets, which is a standard and accepted practice. But it was an enormous blue-and-silver satin banner right outside the arrival lounge that caught my attention. It said: 'Calcutta Welcomes Shobha[1] Dé – The Queen of Indian Fiction'. It was eye-catching and impressive, even if I did feel immodest, staring at it with undisguised glee. Such was his planning, when we got to the hotel the same banner-carrying men were present at the lobby, with more flowers and garlands. Chopra whispered: 'This is only the beginning'.

I was to get to the venue – the UBS stall – at a certain time that afternoon. I discovered that special permission was required for the car to be driven into the fair grounds. Chopra had got the requisite clearance and hired six security guards who were very enthusiastic about their job. When the car stopped at a particular point, I wondered why we weren't taking it right up to the stall entrance. I found out soon enough. As I emerged from the vehicle, a red carpet was rolled out, leading up to the stall. And right there, under a bright sun, were six dancers from Santiniketan, attired in all their traditional finery. Two of them held a beautifully decorated ceremonial umbrella over my head while the others sang a specially composed song of welcome. Rose petals were strewn in my path as musicians and dancers escorted me up the carpet and into the stall, which had been cleverly done up with large posters announcing my presence and eye-catching display of my two books. In a specially cordoned-off area, I was asked to sit on a throne-like chair with the guards standing around, ready to leap into instant action.

Cameras whirred as the crowds surged forward to have a look at what was going on. We sold and signed a record number of books in just an hour. And believe me, the sales had to do more with the manner in which Chopra had planned the signing session than just people's eagerness to buy my books. He pulled off a major coup that afternoon and demonstrated that with enough thought and planning it was possible to organize an event that generated excitement and interest in a business that for the average person is not all that riveting.

I was presented a memento in the shape of an open book. I thought that was a great touch – it is one memento I'm very sentimental about since it reminds me of the high I experienced for that one weekend when I felt all the effort that had gone into establishing my identity as a writer had been well rewarded after all. I felt appreciated and respected in the best way imaginable. All the barbs and taunts that had preceded this moment melted away as I took time off to revel in the heady sweetness of this well-orchestrated treat. Writing is an extraordinarily lonely experience. It is only at a time like this that one realizes how it is really perceived by those very people for whom you've been toiling away for years. It's a good feeling, I can tell you. Even now, when I recall the sight of those graceful dancers, my hair stands on end. Yes, I know they'd been hired by Chopra and were only doing their job – but I did feel deeply honoured and nothing can take away the pleasure of that emotion from me.[2]

Both the books, *Shooting from the Hips: Selected Writings* released on 14 April 1994 and *Small Betrayals* launched on 23 January 1995, were kept a secret throughout the editing and production stages and, when announced, did surprise many and shocked some. The first deadly missile came from David Davidar who was all ready to release Shobhaa's new novel *Sultry Days*. He was really furious and wrote a very angry, I would even say nasty, letter to me on 27 January 1995, with copies to Khushwant Singh, the Penguin editorial consultant, and Shobhaa, stating how it was unethical of me to publish *Small Betrayals* before Penguin came into the market with *Sultry Days*. An enraged David whose Shobhaa had crossed the David-set rekha was understandable, but the angry letter was not. While Shobhaa just laughed it off, Khushwant asked me to 'forget about it … he can be very childish'. I followed Khushwant's advice. But apparently David did not. The coldness continues!

As expected, both the books were huge sellers and went in for several reprints but it was the success of *Shooting from the Hip* that was surprising. After all, the book was recycled from her columns. Yet, it proved that, like Khushwant Singh, Shobhaa too had a large and loyal following. The reviews too helped. For example:

> … Out of her colossal collection, a suitable range of Shobha Dé's works has been carefully selected and arranged in this volume. It covers a versatility of Dé's writings, be it on politics, media, food, festivals, books, people, travels; or articles pertaining to her city of joy and pain (Bombay); and much more…. A mélange of themes, personalities, random thoughts all forcefully, even colourfully expressed – there is much that is amusing, outrageous, thought-provoking, even shocking.[3]

Here I must also mention that with the addition of three more stories, a revised and enlarged edition of *Small Betrayals* was relaunched on 11 October 2014 at the Khushwant Singh Literary Festival in Kasauli. This volume, in a new format and with a striking cover, now comprises seventeen fierce, honest, moving portraits of women wherein Shobhaa unfolds the betrayals and intimacies, the needs and regrets, the secrets that sustain relationships, and the ones that threaten to destroy it. One is confronted with vaguely familiar scents and images that draw us deeper into a world filled with eccentricities, darkness, love, and sorrows – a world that strangely mirrors our own.

With lyrical precision and suspenseful storytelling, Shobhaa gives us a volume rich with contemporary characters that wonderfully integrate different emotions, newly analysed, examined and experienced. Part dystopian, part dreamy, part romance, part drama, she managed to bring forward a remarkable account of the power of possibility and a woman's sense of self.

It is one book I am proud of, for it is a good read that forces a reader to question and accept his or her own society, attitude, purpose, and life.

It was, in many ways, a great learning experience to work with Shobhaa, and I looked forward to working with her again. It came, fifteen years later, on 3 May 2007, when she signed with Hay House India for two books – *Shobhaa at Sixty: Secrets of Getting It Right At Any Age* and *Shobhaa: Never a Dull Dé* – released on Friday, 30 October 2010 and Monday, 9 December 2013, respectively.

Shobhaa at Sixty was released in Chandigarh on the campus of Vivek High School, one of the largest educational institutions run in the city. And what a launch it was!

We at Hay House thought of dressing Shobhaa in typical Punjabi clothes – kameezes and Patiala salwars, complete with chunnis, parandis and Punjabi jooties – all in strong, colourful and vibrant colours and designs accompanied with matching glass bangles. Shobhaa, who had not worn the same in thirty-odd years, was game. In fact, very excited. I personally went around with my young colleagues, Aeshna Roy and Aditi Chaudhary, hunting for the materials in the shops of New Delhi and then sat with the tailor to explain what designs I had in mind. Five sets, each different from the other, for five different occasions, were stitched.

From Delhi, Shobhaa and I travelled by the Shatabdi Express to Chandigarh. Right on the platform, outside the Shatabdi coaches were banners welcoming Shobhaa and announcing that she was on the train. We had a few staff members of the sales team on the train selling the book. Suddenly, there was a crowd wanting Shobhaa's autographs on the copies, or on a plain piece of paper. Some wanted to just say 'hello' or have themselves photographed with her. Initially, Shobhaa was somewhat puzzled how and where so many people had acquired her book for her autograph, soon to learn that we had made special arrangements for the book to be available on the train. I think she was impressed, though she sounded amused.

In Chandigarh, Shobhaa was given a royal treatment from the minute she landed to the time she flew back two days later. The media had a field day. Every newspaper, English, Hindi, Punjabi and Urdu had her on the front page in her Punjabi attire while TV channels were seeking an 'exclusive'. Nearly two thousand Vivek High School students and teachers coupled with parents and guests received her to the beats of dhols and Punjabi giddas and bhangra. Shobhaa was dragged in and she joined them merrily. A thousand balloons in different colours printed with the cover of her book lined both sides of the route at the end of which a life-size poster with 150 gas-filled balloons was handed to her, to be let off amidst thunderous applause, cheers and whistles.

The finale was a talk by Shobhaa for the Chandigarhites at the Vivek High School auditorium, at which a record number of books were sold. Shobhaa went back happy. Before boarding her flight back to Mumbai at 1.25 p.m. on Sunday, 31 October 2010, she sent an SMS to me: 'Thanks Ashok for a dream launch. Bless you 4 every single thing you undertook to make me feel like a REAL QUEEN'.

For any publisher, it's a feel-good factor when an author appreciates (and very few do) the hard work put in. Shobhaa is one of the few who is generous with her words. In *Shobhaa: Never a Dull Dé* she wrote: 'Ashok Chopra … what can I say about this man with twinkling eyes and a scary sense of observation? His quiet strength and determination, his innate confidence and resolve to publish books he believes in … all these lovely qualities have provided much needed nurturing to countless authors.'

Today, I don't refer to Shobhaa Dé as the 'Queen' any more. Her rightful sobriquet: 'The Empress of the Hearts and Minds of the Reading Masses'.

20
Uma Vasudev

The Oriental Octopus

Sometime in April 1971, I got a letter from one Uma Vasudev, editor of *Surge* magazine, asking me to write an article on 'Theatre in Punjab' for her magazine. I had heard about Uma and read an occasional article by her in some newspaper or the other. I wrote back to her to ask how much would she pay. She never replied!

Months later, I met Uma in Delhi. That was the beginning of a warm, affectionate, loving and almost a family relationship. One of the finest persons in my life, with no ill will against anyone, Uma, I soon discovered, was an enigma. As Balwant Gargi said: 'Uma hynotizes people without involvement. Her eyes have a strange fascination. She is also called 303 – a deadly rifle. She holds her durbar in the Coffee House [in New Delhi] discussing politics, music, and scandals. She has a lust to see people and show herself to them ...'[1]

Uma is certainly all that and much more. She is like a beautiful oriental octopus who does a number of jobs at the same time. A multiple personality, she knows everyone who matters, 'she could be present at different places at the same time'. Uma has published over a dozen books including biographies, novels and on current affairs. At least three other projects she was 'serious' about never took off. *Two Faces of Indira Gandhi* (1977) was her most prominent work, and to a lesser extent, her novel *Shreya of Sonagarh* (1993). The rest had varied degrees of success or failure, depending on which way one looks at them.

Since the ever-smiling and cheerful Uma always has a dozen things to do simultaneously, the first casualty is her writing, or one would have seen many more books from her pen. She always takes a long, very long, time to finish a book, but once over, she wants to have it published 'yesterday'. A contradiction, but that is Uma! She gives birth to a book after a long labour but has no concern as to who would be the midwife to handle the delivery and who the nanny to help bring up the baby. Impatient to wait in the queue of the publisher's publishing schedule, in the last decade or more, she has been publishing with all sorts of unheard-of or small-time publishers. For example, she worked for years doing an authorized biography of the flute maestro Pandit Hari Prasad Chaurasia but couldn't wait for me to publish under the HarperCollins imprint because she was in a 'great hurry' to have it out without 'any editing'. It was her dream project and she had worked on it – with sensitivity, feeling and passion. I had gone through portions of it while it was being written and was keen to publish it. My colleague Nandita Aggarwal, one of the finest editors in the publishing industry, too recommended it but did not want to schedule it for press as she felt that the manuscript, particularly the second half, needed editorial work, for it seemed to have been written in a hurry.

Uma did not want to wait. Nor was she sure what sort of editorial work would be done on it. I failed to convince her that editorial inputs would only enhance the quality of the book. I suspect she was put off with my response. Hence, I was very surprised to learn that Uma's 'prestigious' 350-page *Hari Prasad Chaurasia: Romance of the Bamboo Reed – A Biography* was being published by some unknown publisher, somewhere in Gurgaon, whose name had not even been heard of. The company was hardly a publisher, but an exporter of multi-volume books of English literature, religion, philosophy, history and world literature.

The result was obvious. So also the reason for its fast disappearance.

I can't take any credit for Uma's first three books – *Indira Gandhi: Revolution in Restraint* (1974), *Two Faces of Indira Gandhi* (1977) and *The Song of Anasuya: A Novel* (1978). Though the three were published under the Vikas imprint, I was not associated with any of them as editor. However, her next novel, *Shreya of Sonagarh*, was my project for UBSPD in 1993. The novel was, as I wrote in its blurb, based on 'the story of a woman who emerges from the rigid traditionalities of a feudal order to become a politician. Set against the backdrop of state politics, it spans the traumatic period of India's emergence as a volatile, controversial, dilemma-ridden, multilevel society in the 1950s, a decade after Independence. It is also the story of a woman's growth. *Shreya of Sonagarh* brought alive all the pageantry of India's rituals, the crumbling of an old princely order and the dharma of a woman as conditioned in her thinking as any stereotype.'

The book was released on 25 September 1993 at an event designed by L. K. Malhotra, Uma's estranged husband, of which I have written in Chapter 36.

While on L. K. Malhotra, I must mention here that he was the man responsible for getting Begum Akhtar back into singing.

I am reminded of my first meeting with the ghazal queen sometime in the winter of 1972. It was LK who had introduced me to her at her sprawling house in Lucknow, the capital of Uttar Pradesh. By then Akhtari Bai Faizabadi, who was christened Bibbi by her parents at birth, had acted in eight films due to her 'sensitive voice and good looks', only to move away from the world of glamour for a career in Indian classical music and then into domesticity.

In 1945, she had fallen in love and married a known barrister and a connoisseur of music and poetry of the time in Lucknow, Ishitiaq Ahmed Abbasi, whose only condition was that his Begum would not sing any more. Overnight, Akhtari Bai, the classical singer, became Begum Akhtar, a housewife. The tanpura was wrapped up in its thick blue cotton cover and stored behind a door of one of the many rooms of her new home. Instead of keeping an account of her singing tones she started maintaining accounts of the Abbasi kitchen and the household with its retinue of servants. Instead of entertaining music lovers at musical evenings she now acted as a hostess to Abbasi's clients and guests to regular dinners at home. The housewife in her had taken over, as the artiste in her got relegated to the backwaters of the Gomati flowing through Lucknow.

Life moved on. With the passage of time, as normally happens, the romance of marriage started waning. Begum Akhtar realized that she might have given her heart to Ishitiaq Abbasi, but her soul belonged only to her music. And music alone! Without music her health started failing. So did the doctors prescriptions. At this point, a concerned LK whose sixth sense told him that perhaps music could save the Begum, told a worried Ishitiaq Abbasi that no amount of 'dava' or 'dua' [medicine or blessings of well-being] would help as music was the only remedy which needed to be tried out. LK had based his reading on the fact that a few weeks earlier he had been able to persuade the Begum to at least visit the studios of All India Radio sometime just to meet her old friends and teammates. Finally, she came and met all those who used to accompany her on various instruments when she sang. LK was able to persuade her to sing for them with a promise 'it will not be aired ... not even recorded'. The Begum consented. She sang as she wept. She wept as she sang. She sang as they too wept. They too wept as she sang.

A helpless Abbasi, much against his pride and so-called family honour, agreed but with a rider: 'You can sing, but only outside the city of Lucknow. In Lucknow you can record only in the studios of All India Radio. Nothing more'.

Begum Akhtar called LK, who was then station director of All India Radio at Lucknow, and asked him to prepare the studio for recording. It was truly an occasion to celebrate and everyone at the radio station was much excited. For LK 'it was a very special day ... a dream come true'. Begum Akhtar arrived. As she breezed into the studio, the air was filled with the fragrance of the ittar [perfume] she was wearing and a light aroma of the zarda [tobacco] that she ate with her paan [betel leaf]. The tanpura was tuned, and as her fingers glided over its strings, a spark from the big diamond in her finger ring travelled up and down the studio walls, reminding all present that a diamond is a diamond, whichever angle you see it from, whichever side you look at it from, after howsoever long you may pick it up, it only shines.

LK told me: 'Begum Akhtar began with a thumri [a classical form of singing] in [raga] Bhairavi followed by two dadras [another classical form of singing]. She did not have children and perhaps this personal sorrow mingled with the poignancy of Urdu ghazal to lift her music to celestial heights. The walls of the studio had not echoed with such a glorious voice for years. It was a great day. When the recording was played back, her eyes were full. So were mine. As also of so many others.'

That was the start of a long musical innings.

After that meeting I met Begum Akhtar a few times. The first was on 29 May 1974, when she came to participate in the Simla Summer Festival. I was her local unofficial chaperone and guide rolled into one. She came home to meet my parents and have some home-made Punjabi food. Listening to her was always great and talking to her greater still. According to her: 'Music helped me see life more deeply and get to the root of things.... I was eight years old when a [travelling] theatre came visiting the romantic town of Faizabad. One of its artistes, Chandan Bai, became a craze. I also went with my mother and what followed was a lifetime experience. For weeks the tune of the nat [a devotional song], addressed to the Prophet [Muhammad], echoed and re-echoed in my mind, my heart, my soul. I hummed it all the time, to the point it annoyed my mother.... But a career had been made for me.'

My last meeting with Begum Akhtar was in September 1974 at LK and Uma Vasudev's first-floor apartment, in New Delhi's Sujan Singh Park. By then LK had been transferred to the capital and posted in the Central government. There was a dinner get-together on at their house. As Uma was welcoming guests and her two young daughters Raka, then just about eight, and Kamia, about three, were serving snacks, in walked the one and only Begum Akhtar, much to everyone's pleasant surprise. Suddenly there was silence. Uma got up and gave her a warm hug. I greeted her with my customary feet touching as she blessed me lovingly and asked about my parents. Drinks flowed like waters of the Yamuna, drowning many of the journalist guests, one of whom was found in a ditch the next morning while another reached home only to find he had lost the house keys and spent the night outside his door with a stray dog for company and warmth, who woke him up in the morning by repeatedly licking his face. A third banged his car into a tree and just about miraculously escaped with a few minor injuries, with the car more or less written off. However, all that happened much later that night. The evening, as many others at Uma's, before and since, was an unforgettable one. It belonged only to Begum Akhtar who filled it with her music, singing one number after another. Yet, seeing her sitting there, one could make out that something was not quite right. There was something on her mind – a little worry, a little tension, a little concern, a little stress, or perhaps all rolled into one – sheer pain.

Soon it came out!

Uma and LK were at that stage going through marital problems. Begum Akhtar, more of a family elder to both, had immense affection for them. She loved them deeply, and cared for them dearly. She was highly disturbed about their marriage heading for a break-up. She had tried to persuade Uma, as she must have done with LK too, to settle the issue somehow. Finally, as Begum Akhtar was about to leave that evening, Uma and I came down to see her off. This was perhaps the moment the Begum, over twenty years her elder, was waiting for – to be alone with Uma for a few moments. She looked at Uma, put her hand on her cheek, then suddenly bent down, touched Uma's feet and begged: 'Uma, *main tumhare paon padti hoon yeh shaadi mat tootne do … maat todo … Beta, khuda ke wastee mat todo*' (Uma, I beg of you not to let this marriage break up … my child, for

God's sake don't let it break up). Uma, shell-shocked, broke down as she hugged the Begum in a warm embrace which it seemed, lasted a long, long time.

I saw Begum Akhtar to the car. As I touched her feet, she put her right hand on my head, lightly kissed my forehead and blessed: '*Khush raho … Khuda lambi umar dey*' (be happy … may God give you a long life), got into the car and drove off.

That was the last time I saw Begum Akhtar – sad and broken, with tears in her eyes. I was reminded of Shakeel Badayuni's heart-touching lyrics, which she had immortalized:

Aye mohabat tere anjaam pe rona aaya
Jaaney kyon aaj tere naam pe rona aaya …
(O Love, your outcome makes me weep.
Today, I don't know why your name makes me weep.)

Touching the feet of the elders and getting blessings in return is a normal tradition in many parts of the country and considered an important mark of respect, a sign of good upbringing. For me it has been part and parcel of my growing-up years. However, Begum Akhtar's blessings with her hand on my head, a light kiss on the forehead and the words '*Khush raho … Khuda lambi umar dey*' have remained embedded in my psyche to this day simply because the blessings were a totally different experience, an indescribable feeling, an enchanting sensation, which even today evokes layers of emotion in me. I had never felt anything like that before. Nor since. Until recently.

On Thursday, 24 April 2014, I had gone to Mumbai during the course of my work on the autobiography of the Hindi film industry's legend Dilip Kumar – *Dilip Kumar: The Substance and the Shadow*, which we published under the Hay House imprint. Meeting 'Sahab', as he is commonly known among his family and friends, is always a pleasure and there is much to listen to, and learn from him. That day as I was about to leave from their massive, sprawling bunglow, with over a hundred trees in their back lawns, on Pali Hill, Saira Banu, his doting wife, asked me to meet Sahab before leaving. He was taking his afternoon siesta. She woke him up despite my protests. 'I have come to take your leave,' I said in Punjabi – a language in which Sahab and I normally converse. 'Kyun'? (why?) he asked. Then, he took my left hand in his, put it on the left side of his chest, and asked: 'Can you hear what my heart is saying? It's saying I am always very happy to meet you … I love it when you come and will wait for your next visit…. Please do come soon.' It was straight from the heart. I got emotional.

'Yes, I will', I said. 'And I will bring the first copy of your book with me, which will be my chadawa [offering] to you'. Then, as I bent down to touch his feet, he put his right hand on my head, lightly kissed my forehead and said: '*Khush raho … Khuda lambi umar dave*', as Saira, controlling her tears said: 'Ameen' (so be it!).

It took me back forty years!

21

Dilip Kumar

The Longest Wait

The publishing of a book is like the making of a Hindi film, or a film in any language for that matter. It's a long and arduous journey – a journey whose final result no one can predict. Whether it will be a success or a failure only time will tell. By the time an author finishes writing his or her manuscript and the publisher brings it out in the shape of a book and puts it into the market, the average time gap can be anything between two and five years.

However, for any publisher to wait for twenty-four years to get a manuscript in hand is, to the best of my knowledge, unheard of – far too long by any standards. Something not only exceptional but rare too. That is precisely the time I waited for to publish the legendary actor Dilip Kumar's autobiography, *The Substance and the Shadow,* in June 2014.

Dilip Kumar (born Yousuf Khan) needs no introduction, as he stands out as a colossus in the field of film acting. Beginning as a diffident novice in *Jawar Bhata* (1944), he soon went on to attain the peak of stardom within a few years. He came up with spellbinding performances in one hit film after another in his almost six-decade-long career in which he developed a style of his own that left cinema-goers spellbound. It would not be out of place to mention here that he has been the most imitated actor in Hindi cinema.

I first met Dilip Sahab way back in the summer of 1990 when he was up in Manali in Himachal Pradesh shooting for the Mukta Arts film *Saudagar* (1991). This Subhash Ghai-directed film was publicized as 'A Clash of the Giants', as it had the eccentric Raaj Kumar opposite Dilip Sahab. Raaj Kumar, who had a gravelly voice, was known for his powerful dialogue delivery, which was unique in style and helped him steal scenes, which would amply substantiate his otherwise mediocre acting abilities. Films were specially written with him in mind and dialogues created exclusively for him, which he would improvise or improve, as the need be. The result was that the frontbenchers wolf-whistled in joy every time he appeared on the screen, while the backbenchers applauded in appreciation. With feet of clay and insecurity writ large, even the top stars of the time would normally think twice, even thrice, before signing on a project with him, for he was almost always sure to walk away with the film, and the honours, whatever his role be, whosoever be acting with him in it. On the other hand, so confident would he be that he was always ready to sign with anyone pitted against him. Hence, the casting of the 'two giants' was a coup for Subhash Ghai as Dilip Sahab and Raaj Kumar were working together in a film after a gap of over thirty years, having first come together in the S. S. Vasan-directed Gemini Pictures, *Paigham* (1959). Both *Paigham* and *Saudagar* went on to be huge successes at the box office.

I met up with Dilip Sahab one evening in Ambassador Hotel in Manali and spent a little time trying to explore the possibility of his writing his autobiography. A voracious reader with an elephant's memory, he is known for his great love for literature and poetry, be it in English, Urdu or Persian. A great orator, anything he has read he can easily recall, quote, or refer to, in his conversations, as I was to discover later. Sahab showed no inclination to write his autobiography. 'Why would anyone want to know anything about my life … what's so great about it that people would want to read about it?' he asked. I failed to convince him that there are plenty of readers who would give anything to read about his zealously guarded life, his times, his craft, his films, and above all, the making of a legend.

As we were talking, Raaj Kumar walked by in his inimitable style – cat-eye glasses, a scarf loosely thrown around his neck, his pipe in one hand and a walking stick with a heavily carved head of a lion in silver as its handle in the other, wearing a burgundy-coloured long coat made of velvet. He was most unconcerned about everyone around who, in turn, seemed to be in complete awe of him. His walk was regal. His looks fearful. As Subhash Ghai aptly described him: 'Raaj Kumar is a king. He lives like one. He behaves like one.' Looking at him, Dilip Sahab said: 'Well, there's the man you should talk to … his life is fascinating and perfect for a book.'

While on Raaj Kumar, I might as well mention here a little more of my personal experience with him, though very limited, and the numerous stories that one had heard about him, his moods, his temperament and eccentricities. How many of these were true and how many were just rumours floating around, few knew, including how he used to decline roles. The famous example often quoted is how he refused the role of the police inspector for the film *Zanjeer* (eventually released in 1973) just because he did not like the smell of the oil that the film's well-known producer-director Prakash Mehra used in his hair. As is now part of film lore, *Zanjeer* went on to become a blockbuster that gave Indian cinema the one and only Amitabh Bachchan.

Born as Kulbhushan Pandit (on 8 October 1926), Raaj Kumar was a sub-inspector in the Bombay Police when he was noticed and offered a role in the 1952 film, *Rangeeli*. Three films later, all of which tanked at the box office, and just when he was seriously thinking of quitting, came the role that was to change his life. It was an offer from none other than the great Mehboob Khan, who had to his credit many box office blockbusters including *Andaz* (1949) with Dilip Kumar, Raj Kapoor and Nargis, and *Aan* (1951) with Dilip Kumar, Nadira and Nimmi in the lead. Mehboob Khan was now venturing on the most ambitious project of his career, *Mother India*, which released in 1957 and went on to become legendary in the history of Hindi cinema.

Initially, Mehboob Khan wanted Dilip Kumar in a double role, as the heroine Nargis's husband and also her son, but he refused. Mehboob then signed Raaj Kumar, Nargis, Sunil Dutt and Rajendra Kumar. Raaj Kumar played husband to Nargis, and disappeared after losing his arms in an accident, never to make an appearance again. It was a small role but Raaj Kumar had made a distinct impression. He was now in demand. He had as many as five releases in 1957, three in 1958, six in 1959 in a career that saw seventy-one films in nearly four decades.

However, it was with F. C. Mehra's *Ujala* (1959) opposite Shammi Kapoor and Mala Sinha that Raaj Kumar adopted his own style of acting, heavily depending on the delivery of dialogues, which was further highlighted in Sridhar's *Dil Ek Mandir* (1963) opposite Meena Kumari and Rajendra Kumar. He was awarded the Filmfare Best Supporting Actor award for his role as a cancer patient, which he refused saying he was in the main lead and not a supporting actor. In between, he had a number of big hits, including Kishore Sahu's *Dil Apna aur Preet Parai* (1960) opposite Meena Kumari, with its evergreen music, which enhanced his career.

Then came the role of a lifetime – a role that is the dream of any actor, a role that every actor aspires for, but only someone born for it can play. It was that negative role as the eldest brother Raja in B. R. Chopra's multi-starrer *Waqt* (1965), directed by Yash Chopra, which had in its cast stalwarts like Balraj Sahni and Rehman and established stars like Sunil Dutt, Sadhana, Shashi Kapoor and Sharmila Tagore. But the film belonged to Raaj Kumar. And Raaj Kumar alone. He walked away with the honours. His dialogues from the film, rendered powerfully and authoritatively, like royal commands, became a rage. Overnight, the dialogues were being mimicked, his voice copied and his mannerisms followed closely by the masses. They had become his hallmark. Raaj Kumar the actor had turned into Raaj Kumar the 'King' as he projected himself as a confident, defiant, fearless, regal personality.

With success came the eccentricities, the mood swings, the quirky habits and the unpredictability – an impenetrable carapace that made him somewhat of an enigma. At the best of times no one could fathom his thoughts – his colleagues, his friends, his staff, even his family. By the time Ram Maheshwari's *Kaajal* (1965) with Meena Kumari, Dharmendra and Padmini, Vinod Kumar's *Mere Huzoor* (1968) with Jeetendra and Mala Sinha, F. C. Mehra's *Lal Patthar* (1971) with Hema Malini and Rakhee, and Kamal Amrohi's *Pakeezah* (1972) with Ashok Kumar and Meena Kumari were released, Raaj Kumar was signing only those memorable roles which had a 'royal feel' to them, as was evident from his later films, during the second phase of his career, where he was not a character actor, but the protagonist. Even in his day-to-day life he would address himself as 'Hum' and all others 'Tum' or simply 'Jaani'.

I first met Raaj Kumar in 1979 in Simla during the shooting of that multi-starrer *Kudrat* (1981) produced and directed by Chetan Anand, whom I had helped a year earlier with location hunting in and around Simla and Chail for the film. Raaj Kumar was most unpredictable and nobody dare approach him, come in his way or say anything in his presence – not even his co-stars in the film including the superstar Rajesh Khanna. In any case, he never ever mixed with any of the cast or crew of the film and rarely talked to them. The only exception was perhaps Hema Malini.

During the film's shooting, a senior bureaucrat of the Himachal Pradesh government who had also helped in giving various permissions for the shooting, perhaps wanting to show off to his colleagues, invited Chetan Anand and the cast for a dinner at his house. 'Raaj is most elusive and will not come but do send him an invite as a matter of courtesy,' advised Chetan Anand. The formality was duly carried out. That evening as Raaj Kumar and I were walking back from the YMCA (Young Men's Christian Association) on the

Ridge after a game of badminton, he said: 'Let's go to the dinner that chap has invited us for.' We did. I as a cheap guest of the chief guest!

The minute Raaj Kumar entered, the overjoyed bureaucrat and his wife, as also most of the guests, who were not in the least expecting him, rushed forward to receive him. Raaj Kumar looked around and said: '*Jaani, yahan koi tharre ki party chal rahi hai?*' (Is this a party where country liquor is being served?)

'No, Raaj Saab, I have Scotch – both Black Label and Chivas Regal, especially for this evening', said the host. Those were the days when Scotch was difficult to get and in any case few could afford to serve it.

'*To phir yeh phaltu ke log kyoon ikkatah hain*?' (So what have these useless people gathered here for?) he asked, looking at, and referring to, his co-stars Rajesh Khanna, Vinod Khanna, Priya Rajvansh, Aruna Irani and a couple of others, who were there with the guests.

The discomfited host, as also some of the guests who heard Raj Kumar's words, did not know what had hit them and how to react. Collecting his wits he asked: 'Raaj Saab, what will you have? Chivas?'

'No, I drink only Royal Salute and I carry it with me. Just get me a glass!' he answered.

Yes, Raaj Kumar was carrying Royal Salute in his hip flask and, surprisingly, a bottle of soda too in his coat pocket. However, before the glass could come, he left. Later, he told me: 'I don't like to drink in a crowd. The best way to enjoy a drink is by yourself. Alone.' Then why did he go at all, I thought to myself. How the host and the guests felt, one can well imagine.

Like many others, Chetan Anand, who had cast Raaj Kumar in two of his earlier films – *Heer Ranjha* (1970) and *Hindustan Ki Kasam* (1973) – had numerous anecdotes to narrate of the actor's moods and behaviour. Apparently, at a film party in Bombay, when the famous producer-director B. R. Chopra, who had cast Raaj Kumar in two of his earlier hugely successful films – the multi-starrer *Waqt* (1965) and *Hamraaz* (1967) – introduced Zeenat Aman, who had just acted in the lead in Chopra's another successful film *Insaf Ka Tarazu* (1980), Raaj Kumar would just not look at her and carried on with his conversation with someone else. Finally, when Chopra introduced Zeenat for the third time, Raaj Kumar looked at her, shook her hand and after a few moments said: 'You are a pretty girl, why don't you join films?'

However, Raaj Kumar's most classic barb was aimed at Shatrughan Sinha. Because of his powerful one-liners, Sinha had just walked away with all the applause from the front benchers, even against senior actors like Amitabh Bachchan and Shashi Kapoor, in the recently released *Kala Patthar* (1979), made by Yash Chopra. At a party, when Shatrughan walked in, everybody clapped and surrounded him – some hugging him, others shaking hands or just complimenting him for his 'great' performance. Shatrughan (commonly known as Shotgun) was certainly on top of the world. It was his day and he knew it. So did all the other guests. Seeing Raaj Kumar on one side, Shatrughan walked towards him, bent down to take his blessings, when Raaj Kumar said: '*Jaani, suna hai ki aaj kal tum jahan bhi jaate ho log bahut taalian bajate hain … lekin yeh maat bhoolo ki jab circus mein joker aata hain tab bhi bahut taalian bajti hain.*' (I hear wherever you go these days people welcome you with great applause … but don't forget there is also a huge applause when a joker enters a circus.)

I am sure, it completely ruined Shatrughan's evening and deflated his enormous, over-bloated ego, which he was, and still is, known for.

Raaj Kumar was a voracious reader. His love for novels, plays, biographies, history and travelogues was foremost. Due to his passion for classic literature I took him a couple of times to Maria Brothers on the Mall in Simla – that once famous bookshop known for stocking some of the most precious antique literature. He would spend a long time talking to the shop's owner, the well-informed and knowledgeable O. C. Sud, and gaining as much information he could get on books, particularly of the Raj days.

Dilip Kumar gives a special insight about Raaj Kumar in his autobiography:

When Subhash visited my home to talk to me about *Saudagar* and he briefed me about the interesting plot revolving round two thick friends that he was developing, I could see that he was slightly fidgety and he was waiting for the right moment to say something that was on his mind. Sure enough, he came out with it when he was about to leave. He told me rather nervously that he had the veteran Raaj Kumar in mind to play my friend who turns hostile in the dramatic twist that would surface in the critical juncture of the plot build-up. Apparently, he expected me to react adversely. I eased his mind by telling him it would be a pleasure working with Raaj and I had quite enjoyed his company whenever he was on the sets of *Paigham* (1959). Instead, I suggested he should ask Raaj if he welcomed the idea of working with me. Smiling naughtily, Subhash said he had already spoken to Raaj, who was looking forward to working with me.

... The media was on the alert during the entire shooting of *Saudagar* to smell any kind of conflict between me and Raaj, thanks to the many silly stories circulating about Raaj's temperament. Come to think about it, in some ways, Raaj was different from most of us actors of his age. During the shooting of *Saudagar*, he insisted on two heavy vehicles following him to the places marked by the art director and cameraman for the shooting. Raaj sat in a car alone, in solitary splendour, without an attendant while the vehicles trailing behind his car carried the entire wardrobe of costumes created for him for the entire film and his browbeaten attendant in charge of the suitcases and trunks filled with items such as clothes, footwear and wigs. It amazed me, and the others, and led to all kinds of hush-hush talk behind his back. Subhash stoically dismissed it as a quirk and had given standing instructions to his assistants to see that the vehicles were ready each day and the clothes and accessories were transported exactly the way Raaj wished.

One evening at Mahabaleshwar (a hill station in Maharashtra), the cameraman, his assistants and all the young spot boys were in a nervous flutter because Raaj was missing at the actual location and they found him seated on a chair on the perilous edge of a cliff. If he took one step forward from the chair, it would have plunged him into the dark mysterious chasm below. The boys came running to Subhash and the rest of us seated comfortably at the shooting spot to tell us what they had seen. Subhash asked them what they thought he was doing there and they said he was seated on his chair with a faraway expression in his eyes that were fixed on the misty horizon.

Subhash requested me to accompany him to the spot where Raaj was sitting. We went up to him quietly and engaged him in conversation, which distracted him from the hazy horizon he was staring at. Fortunately, he always responded to me in a friendly manner. So I managed to bring him back to the shooting location without much ado.

Raaj, I could see, was a thinking man. He preferred to be alone at times perhaps to immerse his mind in thoughts. He also read books and discussed the contents with me when he was in the mood to do so. He was known for his idiosyncrasies and eccentricities but I found him always very normal and gentlemanly. He was among the many friends who arrived early at my house on the day of my *nikah* (marriage) with Saira. When Saira and I invited him for our silver wedding anniversary, he came to attend the party with his wife but seeing the large gathering of film personalities, he left quietly without meeting us. He was perhaps not keen to mingle with the others. He left a gift for us, a beautiful silver platter with an inscribed message: 'To Lalay and Lalay ki Jaan, many happy returns!'[1]

I met Raaj Kumar on and off during my visits to Bombay. In November 1991, I had lunch with him at the Mehboob Studio in Bandra where he was shooting for Mehul Kumar's *Tirangaa* (1992), starring Nana Patekar and Mamta Kulkarni. I brought up the subject of his writing his autobiography. He was categorical: 'No ... Never! I guard my privacy very carefully ... I am an actor. My acting should speak to the masses. Not my life ... my life is not for public consumption.'

Coming back to Dilip Sahab's autobiography, where I failed, the woman behind the man succeeded. Yes, finally it was his shareek-e-hayat, his loving wife Saira Banu, who was able to persuade him to write.

By this time four books had come out on Sahab – Bunny Reuben's *Dilip Kumar: The Star Legend of Indian Cinema – A Definitive Biography* in December 2003; *The Thespian: Life and Films of Dilip Kumar* by Urmila Lamba (2003); Sanjit Narwekar's *Dilip Kumar: The Last Emperor* (2004); and *Nehru's Hero: Dilip Kumar in the Life of India* by Lord Meghnad Desai in 2004. Bunny's biography was published by me under the HarperCollins imprint. According to Udayatara Nayar (Tara to most of us), a well-known film journalist:

> It was a sultry afternoon in Mumbai's midsummer. The year was 2004. I was helping Saira Banu to rearrange the books on the bookshelf in her bedroom when Dilip Sahab picked up a book written by an author who claimed to have known him as no one else did. 'This is supposed to be my biography and it is full of distortions and misinformation,' he told Saira. 'Why don't you write the story of your life yourself?' Saira queried, gladly seizing the opportunity to pursue her continuous effort to pin him down to write his autobiography.... After a moment's silence, Dilip Sahab spoke, turning to both of us as we waited for his reply.
>
> 'All right I will narrate my story. It has to be compiled by someone who is enlightened and ready to put in the hard work that goes into anything that I do and it would be someone who knows us really well,' he said ...
>
> 'She is right here', Saira pointed out, looking at me.

Dilip Sahab too looked at me and laughed gently, seeing the disbelief on my face.

'When do we start?' he asked me …

Once Dilip Sahab said 'yes', Tara starting taking the narration – day after day, week after week, month after moth. In between, I met Saira and Tara, whom I had known a little, and written for, when she was editing *Screen* for the *Indian Express* group of newspapers, a few times just to check the status of the book but basically to keep emphasizing that I, only I, had to publish the autobiography, lest it go to some other publisher.

I am no film authority but just a film buff who has always maintained, rightly or wrongly, that Hindi cinema has produced many greats, some who became icons, a few geniuses, but only two legends – Dilip Kumar and Lata Mangeshkar. And legends are born once in a lifetime. I still hold this view. I had already published an 'authoritative biography' of Lata penned by Raju Bharatan (see Chapter 9), and I *had* to publish the autobiography of Sahab. For me it was no run-of-the-mill book, which a publisher brings out regularly. For me it had become a granth – my spiritual text. My religion. I could not afford to lose it.

I did not.

For getting the book I must give the credit to both Tara and Saira. While Tara, as she says, was quite clear in her mind that only I could handle Sahab's book, Saira I suspect took the decision in my favour, over other publishers, just seeing my passion, my perseverance, and my long involvement with it. Both perhaps also kept Sahab's wishes in mind, who, by now ninety-two, had not been keeping well. Regular visits to the doctors, hospitalizations, at times for long durations, the fluctuating pulse rate and heavy medication had started taking their toll on his health. Yet, he was looking forward to his book in its printed form. Finally, Dilip Sahab's autobiography came out of the press on Friday, 30 May 2014. As promised, the next morning I flew down to Mumbai with the first copy to present to Sahab as my chadawa – my offering. He was sitting in his room looking at an old black-and-white picture of his, as a young handsome Pathan boy, with his Amma (also published in the book on page 81) in his hands. Seeing me, his face lit up. When I presented him the book, he held my hand and pressed it to his chest as a tear or two of joy and happiness rolled down his cheeks, as also Saira's who was sitting on his left. He was happy as happy he could be. Behind him Tara, who had always felt blessed that she had been chosen by him to take down his narrations, was completely overwhelmed. Speechless, she too could hardly control her emotions.

The 456-page book was finally released on Monday, 9 June 2014, at a glittering event at the Grand Hyatt in Mumbai. Entire Bollywood, it seemed, had turned up to honour the first legend of Hindi cinema. Amitabh Bachchan, who holds the view that the history of Indian cinema shall be 'before Dilip Sahab' and 'after Dilip Sahab', did the honours along with Dharmendra and Aamir Khan. Karan Johar was the master of ceremonies while Priyanka Chopra and Madhuri Dixit lit the lamp. Every TV channel, every newspaper, every magazine and news agency covered the event.

For me, my longest wait ever for a book was over.

Since Sahab's autobiography – *The Substance and the Shadow* – was my granth, my spiritual text, my religion, I decided that it would be befitting for the publisher to donate all the profits from it to the Khushwant Singh Foundation for the education of the girl child. It was my offering for the work I had got from the mind of one legend to serve the cause that was so very dear to the heart of the other. Many a girl child of the future, I am sure, will bless Dilip Kumar and Khushwant Singh, with a prayer of thanks, for having made their lives. It was my little way of honouring the two legends whom I worship!

Ameen!

Part Two

Writers have always tended to write about the worlds they come from.

– Jhumpa Lahiri

22

Shimla

A Paradise Lost

For me Shimla is just a scrapbook of memories – some pleasant, some unpleasant. It evokes both joy and pain – at what it was and what it is.

It is no more the 'queen of hill stations' that I once knew. Everything here has changed beyond recognition, from its name (Simla to Shimla), the landscape (from lush green to dull grey), and the people to the monkeys. Up to the early 1970s, Simla was a far more exquisite and sensitive place. Today, it is forlorn and withdrawn. Were the British, the founders of this town, to revisit, they would be shocked beyond belief to see the mushrooming growth of concrete structures, the squalor of the so-called posh green areas, the neglected thoroughfares and choked drains. In fact, everything new in Shimla – the one-time summer capital of the country – is positively repulsive.

No longer do writers, artists and poets visit Shimla to write and paint. And if at all any of them does, he or she goes back painting or 'writing lines of pain, images of thorns, bleeding birds, black nights, lacerated flesh, smoking boxes....' They all wonder what Rudyard Kipling or Octavio Paz and so many others saw in Shimla, which inspired them to write all those poems or what made Edward Buck sit down to write the monumental *Simla: Past and Present*. In fact, what did the British see that they made Simla their 'summer capital'?

Only those who saw and lived in Simla from those early 1900s up to the late 1960s can give an answer.

In 1945, Henry Sharp wrote in his famous book *Goodbye India*: 'Anyone who visits Simla for the first time is bound to be struck by two things: it is silent, it is scenic. Its silence you can get nowhere else, and when I say it is scenic I mean it wears the appearance of a stage-setting, for example as in the first act of a light opera.'[1]

Today, Shimla is neither silent nor scenic. It is no more a town. It is like a city, still growing rapidly and expanding in all possible directions. It has already devoured the old, happy and colourful past, as also the unpolluted environment, the silent cool air. It is bursting. Everywhere one sees high-rise buildings with more concrete and glass structures covering areas where streams flowed. There is more traffic, more pollution, more dirt and filth, more politics and more society gossip.

Its air is thick with putrescence, kutcha lanes littered with human and animal excreta and stinking cesspools formed by the overflow of the drains of the Middle, Lower and Ram Bazaars. These areas house the town's bakeries, vegetable, fruit, egg, meat and fish markets coupled with halwai shops, tacky hotels and restaurants, medicine stores, and those ancient structures that are an apology for hospitals – unswept, uncleaned and unwashed. The sight of rubbish heaps dotting the area with nauseating frequency and knots of dogs and mules greedily hovering over them is sure to turn the hardest of stomachs. It is precisely in these subhuman conditions that nearly two-thirds of Shimla's ever-growing population live. Not exactly slums, but no better.

I recall that even in the mid-1960s the roads and streets, lanes and bylanes, of this one-time quaint town were washed and kept clean. There was this fire brigade chief, Mr Dhir, who, along with his small army of about twenty-odd firemen (they were not called firefighters then) and his beauty of an Alsatian (I think his name was Peter), would, early morning, every alternate Sunday, test their equipment and the hydrants by washing the Mall Road from Scandal Point to the Ladies Park. Satisfied that the Mall had been washed, his men were fit and the equipment working well to handle an emergency, he would stand at attention, say a few words of encouragement to his men, take a salute and disburse them. All this while Peter would be at his side and we youngsters would watch the whole exercise with rapt attention.

There was a time when, at the entry 'barrier' to Simla, the inoculator of the municipal health department did not let anyone enter the town without the customary smallpox shots. The sanitary inspectors regularly visited hotels, restaurants, halwai shops, vegetable and meat markets for checking. The local bakery was kept spotlessly clean. Garbage and refuse were emptied into twenty-four incinerators around the town. Fortnightly tests were conducted to ensure the potability of water and the results pasted on the public notice board of the municipal committee office on the Mall. Alas! None of that exists any more.

This 'town-city' is bereft of any cultural or sports activity. Ironically, when the British left, the first casualty was that beauty of a bookshop J. Roy & Sons, spread over nearly 5,000 square feet of space – one of the largest bookshops at the time – next to Grindlays House opposite the Scandal Point. It closed down on 18 October 1959, as there were hardly any lovers and buyers of books. However, an institution, born just after 1947, that has survived to this day is the India Coffee House run by the India Coffee Workers Cooperative Society from Kerala, which serves the cheapest and the best south Indian coffee and dry dosas. In fact, few know that it is from Shimla that this coffee establishment spread its wings across the small towns of the northern region of the country – to Dharamshala, Ludhiana, Jalandhar, Chandigarh, and Dehradun, right through to Delhi. It is still one of the most popular hang-outs of the intelligentsia in the respective towns. It is the adda for college and university dropouts, the disillusioned artists, culture vultures, and of course the news correspondents. Here one comes across many 'unknown' and often subsequently 'famous' or one-time 'famous' and now 'unknown' creative people. One may come across many an artist on his or her fifth cup of coffee and seventh meeting or the other way around. Each of the coffee houses is like a second-class railway compartment, where conversatations from the neighbouring tables overlap all the time. There are times when one almost answers questions addressed to someone else, as the non-stop chatter and the proximity created by the crush of people gives the place a sense of intimacy and camaraderie. It is a free-for-all vent-house, and plays a significant role in the social life of the town.

The playgrounds have disappeared. Thanks to the army, by some quirk of fate, the Annandale ground has survived. Left to the state government, there would have been a housing colony on the grounds today, as per a proposal of 1980-81. Annandale has a unique history. In 1847, a cricket ground was laid and the same year an improvised race course came into being. In 1869, an archery society was organized which held regular competitions amongst the fair sex. Then croquet made its appearance and 'became quite a fashionable game'. William Taylor in his *Thirty-Eight Years in India: From Jaganath to the Himalaya Mountains* wrote: 'It was delightful to see Sir [John] Lawrence with other high and mighty statesmen, at the close of a laborious day, entering with the zest of a boy, into the intricacies of the laborious game.'[2] In May 1888, Sir Mortimer Durand, British India's foreign member, started the first football tournament on this ground, which to this day is played as the 'Durand Cup'.

In 1902, the Annandale was christened as a sports club, which organized regular races and horse and dog shows apart from polo and cricket matches.

Simla was made the summer capital of the Raj in 1864. 'In its youth it had an eagle's eye. It could swoop down anywhere in the country to pick up chunks to feed her chicks. But today, with age, her vision is blurred,' comments an old resident in a fine, nostalgic analogy. One did not have to go looking for love. It came looking for you as it did in the case of one Samuel Evans Stokes. Born on 16 August 1882 into a Quaker family in Philadelphia, USA, he came to the Simla hills with a bagful of apple seeds. He fell in love with the mountains here and the simple hillbillies. While sowing the apple seeds, he ran into a charming local Rajput Christian girl, Agnes. Their love story is now a part of the local folklore. He became an Indian, participated actively in the freedom movement and married Agnes on 12 September 1912. He was greatly influenced by the Hindu faith and changed his name to Satyanand Stokes. Agnes became Priyadevi. He raised a family of four and encouraged the local farmers to cultivate apples.

Their third-born, Lal Chand, followed in his father's footsteps and joined the Indian National Congress. He died rather young at the age of forty-eight on 12 September 1973, and the seat he represented in the Himachal Pradesh Legislative Assembly went to his wife Vidya Stokes, who still occupies it. The love story of their second-born, Satyavati, is a tad juicier than that of her parents. She became Satyavati Dang after her marriage to an air force pilot Omkar Dang, who later became director of civil aviation. She, like her brother Lal Chand, too joined politics. The early death of Omkar Dang, of a heart attack in London, where he was attending Queen Elizabeth II's coronation on 2 June 1953 on behalf of International Civil Aviation Organization (ICAO), Canada, saw her come close to Chief Minister Dr Y. S. Parmar, a widower.

On 25 January 1971, Himachal Pradesh became the eighteenth state of the Union of India. Dr Parmar not only outsmarted but also outmanoeuvred his bitter opponent Thakur Karam Singh to once again become the chief minister. During his tenures in power (March 1952 to October 1956, when he had to step down as Himachal became a Union territory, and from July 1963 to January 1977), Satyavati became an extra-constitutional authority who, it was said, wielded more power than the chief minister and had more control over Dr Parmar than Sanjay Gandhi had over his mother Indira Gandhi. L. H. Naqvi, the *Hindustan Times* correspondent, did a number of stories – more in a paparazzi style than news –

on their love affair that amused Dr Parmar but annoyed Satyavati Dang. To end political rumour-mongering and public criticism, the sixty-eight-year-old Dr Parmar tied the knot with the fifty-one-year-old Satyavati on 16 October 1974 at the chief minister's official residence, Oakover – the one-time summer residence of Maharaja Rajinder Singh of Patiala.[3] Rumour had it that he married her at the insistence of Prime Minister Indira Gandhi who was fed up with the loose talk that was ruining the image of the party in the state and outside. Rumour also had it that Dr Parmar never forgave himself. Nor did his two daughters and four sons. All grown-up!

I joined as Himachal Pradesh state correspondent of the *Indian Express* newspaper in Simla on 1 June 1975. Internal Emergency was imposed by Prime Minister Indira Gandhi on 25 June. All political reporting stopped. This gave me an opportunity to travel extensively in the state.

Himachal Pradesh is known as 'The Land of Gods'. Every village has its own devi (goddess) and devta (male deity) and they all assemble in Kulu for the week-long Dussehra festival, which normally takes place in October every year. I visited every part of the state I could, courtesy the state PWD (Public Works Department), the army, the Deepak Project of the Border Roads Organization and of course, Thakur Ram Lal, who was to later succeed Dr Parmar. Himachal's temples, monasteries, forts and ancient monuments house (or at least used to) some of the most exquisite and priceless treasures of the world. Remaining in an undisturbed atmosphere for centuries, they were unique in having escaped the attention of the outside world. According to Dr N. Haertel, a former director of the Museum of Indian Art, Berlin: 'The entire belt is an archaeological paradise … digging must go on for a hundred years to unravel the history of her ancient art and culture.' However, with art theft having become a billion-dollar racket, many of the objects – bronzes, stones, paintings, masks, miniatures, woodcarvings and jewellery – started vanishing.

On 17 May 1976, the celebrated author, Lady Penelope Chetwode, who had earlier published: *Kulu: The End of the Habitable World*[4] and was obsessed with Himachal Pradesh, arrived in Simla. I travelled with her twice – once for eleven days (21 May to 31 May 1976) and later for twelve days (12 June to 23 June 1976). And what a privilege it was to see the art and culture of my state through her eyes and mind.

Lady Chetwode first came to India on 30 November 1930 as the eighteen-year-old daughter of the then British commander-in-chief in India, Field Marshal Sir Philip Chetwode, whose residence was at the Teen Murti House in New Delhi, later occupied by Prime Minister Jawaharlal Nehru after the partition of the country in 1947. In 1961, by which time she married John Betjeman who was later to become the Poet Laureate of England (1972-84), she returned to do an extensive mule trek through the western Himalayas.

Lady Chetwode, whose immense knowledge on the area was amazing, took me to see some of the hidden temples in remote villages. I soon realized the poor state of our art and culture. Nobody, it seemed, was interested in them. Materials that could have enriched museums and library shelves lay decaying in the company of spiders and birds and rodents. Villages whose beauty was once their stone edifices lay destroyed – sacked by vandals. In many a village, almost all the temples were disintegrating. For example, sheep and dogs wandered around in Hatkoti – the Valley of Stone Idols in the Jubbal area – while children played cricket amongst the relics. This mother centre of Himalayan culture, like many historical sites, was just a waste heap.

The locals of the area had forgotten their rich past and knew not the value of their art treasures. The attitude of the officials was lamentable and depressing. In Masrur – the land of rock-cut temples – and Udaipur, known for its exquisite woodwork, the carvings and the paintings had been whitewashed in a misguided zeal to make the walls look clean. Udaipur, in the Lahaul-Spiti Valley, is a fine example of the most unique woodcarvings – a study of which could be the ambition of any art scholar. But Udaipur was like a decaying corpse. Lady Chetwode believed that this miserably dirty place held the greatest treasure of wood art, for the carvings were so beautiful and alive as the day they were carved hundreds of years ago – no two alike, carved by expert craftsmen, each with a different sculptured motif.

I did a number of news stories and features for the *Indian Express* on most of these monuments and temples, detailing the history of each and highlighting the conditions of neglect. A year later, on 29 May 1977, when the *Express* editor-in-chief S. Mulgaonkar came to Simla for a holiday with his soft-spoken and charming wife Krishna and her relatives, the Kitchlus, Mulgaonkar wanted to go trout fishing. Krishna told me that trout fishing was a great passion with him for which he would go regularly to Kashmir, courtesy D. P. Dhar – the prominent Kashmiri politician-diplomat who had once been a confidant of Prime Minister Indira Gandhi. After his untimely death on 6 December 1975 at the young age of fifty-seven, Mulgaonkar had stopped going to Kashmir and had not indulged in his passion either.

I drove Mulgaonkar to Rohru, en route stopping at Khara Pathar to show him the centuries-old 'standing stone' and the wood palace of Jubbal, whose gracious owner, Raja Yogendra Singh Jubbal, hosted a private lunch. At Khara Pathar, I tried to show off my recently acquired little knowledge with the authority of an ignorant hoping to impress my boss. He said nothing. He was obviously more interested in trouts and looked forward to fishing than listening to the history of a 'standing stone' from an upstart. I was wrong!

Three days later, satisfied with his catch of three trouts, Mulgaonkar wanted to stop at Khara Pathar and know all about it, on our journey back to Simla.

Khara Pathar, a slender, black-and-white stone stands on the left side of the dirty Shimla–Jubbal state highway, 9,000 feet above sea level, overlooking one of the most beautiful valleys the state has. Worshipped by the locals, Khara Pathar, which is associated with a 'bloody past', also marks the spot where the upward mountainous journey ends and the descent to Rohru, via Hatkoti, starts. The path that it overlooks has been trodden by armies down the ages. From there Khara Pathar has mutely watched soldiers praying before it after sharpening their swords and khukris (curved daggers), spears and arrows, and marching to glory; it has also seen conquering hordes sweeping down to the rich valleys, as well as blood being shed of hundreds of soldiers.

The earliest mention of Khara Pathar is made by the Scottish travel writer and artist, James Baillie Fraser,[5] in 1820, which drew historians, travellers and writers from various parts of the world. So impressed was the British traveller Katherine Hart that she reportedly said: 'I wish I could take it back home for the Royal Museum. At least, they will take proper care of it.' According to Fraser: 'At this gorge there was a remarkable stone which the natives call "Oddee". It is about ten feet high and two feet broad. It appears to have been marked some time in a serrated manner and has deep cuts on it. It is today disfigured by the sharpening of hill axes for which indeed it is favourable, being made of soft species of sandstone quite differing from the rocks of the surrounding hills. This stone was placed here by the Sikhs to commemorate a successful invasion of these hills under Guru Nanak.'[6]

Fraser was wrong. Guru Nanak, the first Sikh Guru, was no warrior. Nor did the Sikhs penetrate the hills during his time. Perhaps, his reference is to the tenth Sikh Guru, Gobind Singh. He did go up to Paonta, on the banks of the River Yamuna. Whether he went to Khara Pathar or not is not documented, but he could have as Paonta is just about 20 miles away from there in the Pabbar Valley.

There is a second account, given by the locals, which is more commonly accepted and is documented in the records of the Jubbal Palace. According to it, during the years 1801 to 1806, the Gurkhas fought a 'bloody battle' here while advancing towards Jubbal and then Hatkoti. While they fought during the day, after sunset they sharpened their battleaxes and swords on Khara Pathar.

As for the cuts on this stone there are two views recorded. First, at times warriors used to test the sharpness of their weapons by hitting hard on this stone. Second, every morning, before the warriors went into battle they offered prayers to the Khara Pathar, at the end of which each hit it with his sword in respect. One point to be noted is that each and every member of the fighting army was referred to as 'warrior', not 'soldier'.

Today, the locals have caged their 'standing stone' behind thick, ugly iron bars. Khara Pathar, which once looked strong and majestic, free to breathe the air and get a 360-degree view of the mountains and valleys all around, has been humbled and dwarfed in its cell, by foolish and ignorant villagers. The 'standing stone', which has proudly witnessed history being made and written, today stands as a mute spectator, in a cage, with little natural light, breathing foul air left behind by 100-odd local worshippers daily.

Himalayan art is largely religious and expresses the faith of the people. Examples of it can be seen in northern India, Bhutan, Sikkim, Nepal and Myanmar. The frescoes contain a wealth of information about the local dress and customs of the tenth century. They also depict a variety of fairs, festivals, traditions, processions and birds and animals that bring a bygone era to life. Kings and queens have also been depicted. These historical and cultural remains speak eloquently of the ancient art and culture that flourished all along the western Himalayan belt.

Lady Chetwode and I travelled to the town of Kangra, in whose vicinity a village sleeps remembering its glorious past and sad present. It is Masrur – dead to the outside world. In the eighth century, its heyday, Masrur was a prosperous, busy and happy place. The rock-cut temples here are out of this world. Conditions in Dattanagar in the Sutlej Valley, which has fourteen temples with priceless and unique bronzes, were no better. Three bronzes vanished. One could see water seeping through the walls and the ceiling, which, in the case of the Dakhani Mahadev temple, had eroded the carvings around the doorway. Another doorway with a window of classical beauty, built in the seventh century, went missing.

Up in the hills of Mandi, there is a three-storey Parashar Rishi temple, standing beside a lake with a floating island. The temple has some of the most exquisite carvings seen in the hills. The iconography is very peculiar and should be studied by experts in the field. It also needs expert photographers who can capture the minutest details of the temple of this calibre. Lady Chetwode took me to an ancient temple, about 10 km from Kulu, which is not very easy to reach. Entry to the temple is 'only for virgins'. We did reach there only after making friends with the local Brahmin family but of course were not allowed into the temple. Photography was strictly prohibited, even from the outside. A better piece of art and design I had not seen. Neither the state of neglect.

Lady Chetwode observed: 'It is all fine for some foreigners to come, write and get a book published back home, but their knowledge is so shallow because they work from five-star hotels. People are losing their sense of travel and discovery. Why doesn't the state government feel the need to get some scholars to research and write seriously about its neglected culture and heritage? Why can't it look after these monuments and display them to the world? Why can't these be documented and turned into tourism sites? Everything is borrowed from old gazetteers. Why can't these scholars get up from their cushy chairs and travel to the interior to make extensive on-the-spot studies? Why can't the local youngsters in each area band together, collect and contribute funds, and maintain these temples? In England, as in Europe, we have many such societies which are dedicated to the preservation of our heritage.'

There were too many questions and few, if any, answers!

Lady Chetwode revisited Himachal Pradesh many times, particularly the Kulu region where 'she was deeply admired and respected by the locals, due to her love for the area and her vast knowledge of the local temples and their architecture'.[7] She loved the Kulu area and wanted to breathe her last there – a wish that was granted in 1986. She was cremated according to local rites, and 'her last remains scattered in the Beas river, which had been her request if ever she was to die in the Himalayas.'[8]

Lady Penelope Chetwode left behind in me a love for monuments – their design and architecture. Since then I have travelled a lot into the interiors – and still do. A lot has changed over the years. Tiny villages have grown and expanded. Modern-day electronic comforts have intruded into the homes of the locals everywhere. If something has not changed, it is the state of neglect of the monuments and temples of the area.

23

The Gaiety Theatre

Rise and Fall into Oblivion

Few writers, while visiting Shimla, past and present, have written anything much of significance on an important and a vital part of life during the Raj days – the Gaiety Theatre.

Simla theatre, known as 'the Mecca of amateur actors in the East' for over a century, now lies in dust – its moguls dead or deposed. This one-time best-equipped amateur theatre club in the world, which used to fetch some 9,500 to 11,000 rupees – an astronomical amount in those days – from the boxes alone on the first and second night of each play, opened in 1837 with *Time Will Tell*.

Ironically, time does tell a story. A sad one!

The Gaiety Theatre in Simla, designed by the renowned English architect, Henry Irwin, and constructed in the Gothic style – the only Gothic theatre in Asia, and amongst just six in the world, where bandmasters to field marshals, captains to commanders-in-chief, viceroys to poets worked. The theatre that brought to fame men like Lord Baden Powell, the chief scout, the celebrated poet and writer Rudyard Kipling, Field Marshal Douglas Haig, Commander-in-Chief Lord Robert Bulwer-Kitchener and Viceroy Lord Robert Lytton is perhaps the only amateur theatre in the world for which a viceroy wrote, produced and directed a play. It was here that the eminent painter Amrita Sher-Gil acted in her first and only play. However, the theatre from where actors and singers launched their acting/musical careers, which used to produce and stage the best London plays, and no other part of the country succeeded in proving the talent of its actors or the all-round excellence of its plays, which was without doubt, according to the centenary brochure 1837–1937,[1] the first home of amateur acting in India, is today relegated to the backwaters of art and culture.

The Simla Amateur Dramatic Club (ADC), which occupied a place of pride in the hearts of the Simlaites, is dead. The 'mummy' remains. Since the early 1960s, the condition of the Gaiety Theatre grew from bad to miserable. Properties, costumes, furniture, backdrops, sets, equipment and photographs – all vanished, gradually. No one knows where. No records are available. Layers of dust settled on the precious maroon curtains. The damp green rooms were used for stocking liquor by the authorities for use by the members in the bar upstairs. The backstage stank. Finally, the authorities decided to renovate the twin heritage structures of the municipal corporation on the Mall Road, which also housed the Simla ADC. Looking and feeling as grand as it was in the days of the Raj it was a great job done but the inseparable Simla ADC and the Gaiety Theatre got divorced from each other after a bond of almost 175 years.

The Gaiety Theatre, in its new avatar, inaugurated on 25 June 2009, is today used for staging amateur variety entertainment programmes by local schools or holding boring seminars and dreary annual meetings of different governmental departments and corporations, inaugurated by dull-witted political netas who conclude them with pompous speeches, which few care to listen to. On the other side, The Simla Amateur Dramatic Club, which opened about two-and-a-half years earlier on 23 December 2006, got kicked upstairs, with its entry now from the side of the area that is commonly known as the Ridge. Ironically, the only thing dramatic about it today is the bar – dark, impersonal, gleaming and sterile – a straight lift from a C-grade Bollywood film. Whoever designed it certainly had a very wicked sense of humour with no feel for aesthetics. It may sound harsh, but the fact is, the 'Green Room', as it is commonly known, is today just a glorified adda humming with the hoarseness of drink punctuated with inane and trite local gossip. Bereft of a stage and an auditorium, it is just left with an apology of a tacky dinning room in the basement and a dingy card room in an attic where fat, ugly, heavily made-up women sit mercilessly on weak chairs, playing 'rummy' with their 'paploos'.

1837: It was the year Queen Victoria ascended the throne as the monarch of the United Kingdom of Great Britain and Ireland on 20 June. (She became Empress of India in 1876.) It was the year that the first play was staged by the British in Simla. It was also the year Miss Emily Eden, sister of George Eden, the earl of Auckland, who was then Governor General of India (4 March 1836 to 26 February 1842), started writing her diary,[2] which was to become immensely valuable for researchers and historians in later years. About theatre in India Emily Eden wrote on 9 June 1838: 'We went to the play last night. There is a sort of little theatre in Simla, small and hot and somewhat dirty, but it does very well'. On 18 August she noted:

> We had to go to another play last night. Luckily, they acted two farces [and] we were home at ten. But anything worse we never saw. There were three women's parts in the last farce and the clerks had made their bonnets out of their straw hats tied on, they had their gowns with no plains in them and no petticoats nor bustles. One of them stood presenting his enormous back to the audience and the other observed with great pathos: upon my soul that is the most interesting little girl.[3]

Later on, matters seemed to have improved. An entry from her diary dated 20 October 1839 reads: 'We had an excellent play last night or rather two farces. It is supposed that R [the viceroy] was never seen to laugh … which he certainly did last night. It is astonishing how good a real laugh is.'[4]

Except for this diary, the record of plays produced before 1888 is vague and sketchy. Sir John Edward Buck in his book *Simla: Past and Present*[5] wrote: 'Plays were occasionally produced at the residences of different viceroys and commanders-in-chief when these dignitaries were indulgent to the aspirations of the amateur players, and when charity stretched out an appealing hand. Certain records show that though Sir John Lawrence, the viceroy of India (1864–69), did not encourage acting, yet under his patronage one William Taylor produced scenes from Sir Walter Scott's novels *The Talisman* and *Ivanhoe* in 1865 at Peteroff,[6] the then residence of the viceroy. Lady Lawrence, too, took much interest in the preliminary arrangements and rehearsals.'[7]

However, it was only in 1876 that the proper viceregal encouragement came. Lord Robert Lytton, viceroy of India (1876–80), took so much interest in amateur theatre that in 1878 he himself wrote and went on stage to produce a play: *Walpole*. Though 'this was an old-fashioned play dealing with Jacobite plots and was written in rhymed Alexandrine verse, still a viceroy as a producer and a stage manager, supervising a stage production from an especially resplendent sofa – all gilding and yellow satin and placed conveniently facing the stage – doesn't appear every day.'[8] Lady Lytton appeared in person in two pieces staged at the Viceregal Lodge – *Alexander's Horse* and *Maker of Dreams: A Fantasy in One Act*. From then onwards viceroys encouraged stage productions earnestly. In June 1889, Lord Landsdowne (Henry Petty-Fitzmaurice), the viceroy (1888–94), and later Lord Curzon (George Nathaniel Curzon, viceroy during 1899–1905) had a special stage built at the Viceregal Lodge and permission to stage plays here was also given by future viceroys – Lord Elgin (Victor Alexander Bruce, 1905–08), and Lord Reading (Rufus Daniel Saacs, 1921–26). It was under the direction of Lady Reading that a 'splendid performance' of the comedy drama *Quinneys*, written by Horace Annesley Vachell, was put up in 1922.

Theatre performances were also regularly staged at Snowdown, which today houses, in its expanded form, the Snowdown Hospital, at Oakover, at present the official residence of the state chief minister, and Kennedy House – the first house built in Simla in 1822 by Lieutenant Charles Kennedy – which was destroyed in a devastating fire in the 1980s. The area is today used as a parking lot for the state Vidhan Sabha vehicles.

The year 1887 marked the golden jubilee of Queen Victoria's reign, celebrations for which took place on 20 and 21 June. In Simla the celebrations coincided with the opening of the Gaiety Theatre on 30 May 1887 and, on 20 June, Colonel Neville Chamberlain, the man who invented the game of 'snooker' in Jubbulpore (now in Madhya Pradesh) in 1875, produced a burlesque titled *Lucia de Lammermoor*. The prologue to it was written by no other than the celebrated Rudyard Kipling and spoken by his sister, Miss Kipling. The Gaiety had 'become a centre of cultural activities and art,'[9] and not a week passed without a performance.

In 1888, the theatre took another turn and 'The Old Lady' (as it came to be known soon) was born on a breakfast talk in the shape of a joint company – The Simla Amateur Dramatic Club was to run the Gaiety Theatre. This gave it the professionalism it needed as also a big boost to its activities. The result was that in 1896 as many as twenty-one plays were staged, with many, like the Edwardian musical comedy *Floradora* written by Jimmy Davis under the pseudonym Owen Hall, running for eleven nights. The play was, in the years to come, one of the most successful Broadway musicals of the twentieth century.

Amongst the pictorial records of the club, the earliest photograph is one dated 1876 showing a group from the play *Cast* by one Robertson. The women are dressed in black stuffed gowns with bustles and the men wear six-bottom coats with shapeless trousers, and all look very earnest. Another point noticeable is the facial disguise that was taken very seriously. An interesting picture pertains to the year 1897 that shows a geisha pulling the pigtail of Lord Baden Powell, the chief scout.

A word about the extravagance of 'The Old Lady' would perhaps not be out of place. In those days money flowed in and out of its coffers with little check. In 1894 the season opened with a credit balance of Rs 3,660 but by the end turned into a debit balance of Rs 1,600. During this season no less than Rs 7,000 was spent on dresses alone, of which one play, *Burlesque*, absorbed Rs 1,500 and the band had cost Rs 2,100.

However, the funniest year in many ways was 1896. It saw the largest number of comedies staged at the Gaiety Theatre, receipts for which totalled Rs 50,000 and the balance in hand on 31 December amounted to ten annas (about sixty paise today). Though, in 1899, receipts totalled Rs 44,000, of which the boxes alone realized Rs 10,653, the season closed with a debit balance of Rs 1,100. The fact becomes comprehensive when we learn that *The Yeoman of the Guard* (or *The Merryman and His Maid*), a savoy opera, took Rs 50,000 and lost Rs 4,400. Felix Mendelssohn's *The Wedding March* (1842) could peal out to a tune of expenses covering the income.

Tales about 'The Old Lady' being taken out of the red by her fond lovers are numerous. In 1891, the ADC owed two years' rent and lacked the wherewithal to pay. Lord William Beresford, military secretary to Viceroy Lord Lansdowne, came to the rescue and personally shouldered responsibility for the debt. In 1898, Lieutenant General Sir Gerald de Courcy Morton, adjutant-general in India advanced Rs 2,000 to 'avoid having to pay interest on overdraft'.[10]

Strict discipline was enforced at the club in those days. An example: for holding the disciplinary tradition was the decision taken 'not to employ the 5th D.G. Band owing to the very unsatisfactory behaviour of the band master'.[11] Even the fair sex was not immune. Two ladies, who absented themselves from the chorus of *Solanthe* on the last night, were placed in the blacklist, never to be asked to perform again.

The year 1936 was marked by the production of the most successful play ever staged by the club – *Mary Rose* by Major W. H.

Crichton and a splendid cast that included the viceroy's (Lord Victor Hope's) daughter, Anne. The last play, before the British left India in 1947 was Noel Coward's *Harvey,* directed by Edward Everard.

One man who, according to records, stuck loyally to the Simla ADC was B. N. Brown. He was for forty-three years – till his death in 1932 at the age of eighty-five – business manager, guide, philosopher and friend to producers and directors. He was such an able man that Sir Edward Buck could not finish his book *Simla: Past and Present* without mentioning him: 'He is not on the committee but what he thinks today the committee are believed to think tomorrow. He is invariably invited to stage suppers and he always makes a speech. No one can believe that a show would go well without his ceremonial handshake and "Wish you luck, Sir" just before the curtain goes up on the first night. His motto is: "It will be all right on the first night" and he is not often wrong.'[12]

The year 1947 saw the decline of the theatre of dreams of this town as the Simla ADC went into hibernation and took quite some time to come up with a play. In 1954, Uma Anand (wife of producer-director Chetan Anand) took the initiative to produce an all-female-cast comedy *Charity Begins*, while in 1955, Anand Majumdar produced M. Stephen's *Nerves* and later, Harold Brooke's *All for Mary* in 1964 [13].

Along with the Simla ADC, four other theatre groups sprouted, all featuring the letters 'ADC' to stress their link with the popular and original Simla ADC. All the four groups came into being in the 1920s and collapsed by the mid-1940s. The first of these was 'Edward ADC', started by one Banerjee, more popularly known as Bacha Babu. Some of its important members were names like Rai Sahib Shiv Charan Das (Kaka Babu), Kunwar Mohinder Singh Bedi, and Yogesh Banerjee. The other three were 'Indian ADC', 'Premier ADC' and 'National ADC'. The last one was the most prominent of the four and survived the longest. In sharp contrast to the Simla ADC plays, the performances by these four ADCs had a certain disadvantage. Though Margaret Hughes, playing Desdemona in William Shakespeare's *Othello* was the first woman to make a public appearance on the stage in England as far back as 1660, and Edward Kyanston in 1706 was the last male actor to play a woman on the serious English stage, these ADCs had men acting female roles. Females on stage were 'a scandal' and considered 'vulgar'. Parents prevented their daughters from being on the stage on the pretext that the 'virginal purity of their ... daughters would be sullied forever'.

The other ADCs staged mostly religious or social plays, which enjoyed, at times, a fair amount of success. The most important play of the 1930s was *Shahida Naaz* by Agha Hashar Kashmiri, who was proclaimed on the billboards as India's Shakespeare. Groups led by prominent actors of the time like Prithviraj Kapoor, Zohra Sehgal, Balraj Sahni and Manmohan Krishna too performed at the Gaiety with 'moderate to good success'. But it was National ADC's six-hour-long play with two intervals, *Puran Bakht*, which became the most famous of all plays in 1932. The play was running successfully when its lead male singer fell sick with an acute attack of diarrhoea. The management went into a panic till one of the unit hands suggested that there was a young 'clerk' in the local Remington Typewriter Company who had a 'good' voice and knew all the songs by heart as he had been coming every night to watch the play. The youngster was brought in and was an instant hit. The audience was mesmerized by his voice and returned to just hear him sing day after day. The play was a huge success.

While performing on the stage of the Gaiety Theatre, this youngster was noticed by Harishchandra Bali, the classical music wizard, who took him to Calcutta and introduced him to R. C. Boral – the 'father of film music'. B. R. Sircar's studio New Theatres hired him immediately on a salary of Rs 200 a month – a big amount in those days. The rest is history! The youngster went to become a singing legend.

He was K. L. Saigal. The one and only Kundan Lal Saigal!

24

The Exit

A Blessing in Disguise

On 23 January 1977, the unthinkable happened. Prime Minister Indira Gandhi, to the surprise of one and all, announced general elections in the country. On 24 March 1977 the maverick and eccentric eighty-two-year-old Morarji Desai achieved his life's ambition and became the sixth prime minister of India. In the wake of the anti-Congress wave, in Simla the senior Jan Sangh (now Bharatiya Janata Party or BJP) leader, Shanta Kumar, was sworn in as the third (and first non-Congress) chief minister of Himachal Pradesh on 22 June 1977. In the first phase, he inducted into his cabinet nine members, including the lone woman legislator in a sixty-eight-member legislative assembly, the thirty-one-year-old Shyama Sharma as minister of state for law and panchayats. For him, that was the beginning of unending problems during a two-and-half-year reign. For me, it was the beginning of the end of my career as a newspaper correspondent.

Finally, it turned out to be a great blessing in disguise.

One of the most interesting places in the heart of Simla town is Scandal Point on the Mall Road. Its claim to fame, according to the locals, is that it was from here that the then Maharaja of Patiala eloped with the daughter of the viceroy. The maharaja was banished from entering Simla and set up for himself an alternative place of love and luxury in Chail, just 45 kilometres away. But this is more fiction that fact. There are no records existing of any such incident. Even Sir Edward Buck in his book *Simla: Past and Present*, the most authoritative record of its time, does not mention this episode. Perhaps, the name comes from it being at the intersection on the Mall Road, which is the broadest, where four roads meet, and even to this day people meet there to exchange society gossip and news. Whatever the story, or myth, Scandal Point has seen much over the decades.

Anything can happen at Scandal Point. Particularly when a wilful young woman minister plays all kinds of games to keep herself in power. And in the news!

Shyama Sharma led a quiet and insignificant life in the small, dusty surroundings of a little-known town called Nahan in Sirmour district in Himachal. She got catapulted into the political limelight during the Janata Party wave and soon came close to the one-time 'young Turk' and Congress rebel Chandra Shekhar – president of the newly formed Janata Party.

I first met Shyama Sharma at the Raj Bhavan in Simla a few minutes before she was sworn in as a minister of state in Shanta Kumar's cabinet on 22 June 1977. Those close to her informed me that she was a fiery orator whose speeches could sway audiences of thousands. She was fairly attractive, but reported to be calculating in the use of her charms. She could hypnotize people, was enigmatic and difficult to comprehend. Local poets composed verses in praise of her looks. Lots of young men lost their hearts to her; one even lost his secure government job and landed in jail. Another went looney. One could see her at Scandal Point every other evening where she would be the cynosure of all eyes. And she knew it. It was apparent that she liked to see people as much as she liked to be seen by them. She was mostly dressed in a leather jacket and woollen trousers or the other way around, leather trousers and a woollen jacket, with high-heeled boots. Press photographers hounded her and the vernacular newspapers published her photographs on the front pages. The simple, tradition-bound Himachalis could not believe their eyes that a young lady, who till yesterday was a poorly paid lawyer with a small practice in the district courts of Nahan, who made more noise in labour meetings than in the courtroom, the once simple daughter of orthodox Brahmin parents, could parade herself in such 'outlandish' clothes. All sorts of gossip, some believable, mostly not, followed. Little did one know that the lady seen at Scandal Point would soon be involved in scandals herself.

Shyama Sharma was highly ambitious and had higher goals in mind. But she had no patience, so very essential an ingredient in politics. She wanted to be in the headlines of the national newspapers. And soon she was!

Within a month or so of her becoming a minister, Shyama Sharma was assaulted by a young man at Scandal Point in full view of Simla's Sunday evening crowd. She summoned the press and alleged that the assault was preplanned 'to harass and defame her'[1] ... that ever since she joined the state cabinet she was being pressurized, and even threatened, to toe a particular political line to which she was ideologically opposed. She, however, refused to name those behind the incident, which she said, 'was politically motivated for assassinating my character'.[2]

The assaulter, a young man called Lakshmi Chand Kapoor, a junior engineer in the state electricity board, was suspended from service and put behind bars.

However, some inquisitive newsmen found it hard to digest the story and started their own investigation. It was soon revealed that Lakshmi Chand was an old friend and a close associate of Shyama Sharma. A few days prior to the incident he had been transferred to Simla, at her behest, and the 'Laila-Majnu' were frequently seen together in a local restaurant. As normally happens with a love story, there was a villain on the scene too. An aging lawyer of Nahan, one I. G. Gupta, who had been Shyama's guide and mentor, had suddenly assumed importance. He objected to her association (now that she was a minister) with a nondescript engineer. Shyama gave into the pressure and dropped Lakshmi Chand. The young engineer, who had good cause for hurt, on that Sunday evening slapped her in full public view. At the same time, it transpired that while the lady minister had called the press, she refused to file a complaint with the police. She was further embarrassed by the announcement of a judicial probe into the slapping incident. She shifted her camp to Delhi. Her plan worked.

The national press, hungry for sensational stories, swallowed every word of what she said without ascertaining the facts. Nobody asked why she had refused to file a complaint with the police. Why had she refused to see the chief minister? Why had she said that she could not identify her assaulter? Why had she shifted her base to Delhi to call a news conference? Shyama Sharma had achieved her goal. She succeeded in making the front-page headlines of newspapers across the country. Some women MPs too took up her cause and some leaders of the Central high command lent their shoulders for her to weep on.

On Chandra Shekhar's complaint to the prime minister, Shanta Kumar was summoned to Delhi where Morarji Desai gave him a dressing-down. Shanta Kumar, inexperienced in the art of handling women politicians and not knowing where their power lay, returned to Simla – humiliated and dejected. Shyama, on the other hand, returned with a fat scrapbook containing all that had been published about her in the national press. The judicial inquiry fizzled out.

Suddenly, Shyama Sharma had become powerful, more confident, and also more ambitious. She strutted the Himachal political scene like a 'queen in her queenland' with plenty of disgruntled legislators joining her as courtiers to raise a voice of rebellion with backing from Delhi. At a 'secret' meeting held on 4 January 1978, they proposed her name as the leader of the legislature party. The pro-Shyama fever was at its highest. A young legislator, who was a great Hindi film buff, cut his right-hand thumb and put his signature in blood pledging his support.

On 6 January 1978, two days before Shanta Kumar was to seek a vote of confidence, Shyama called the press, almost at the stroke of midnight, to announce that an attempt had been made to kidnap her. Her political adversaries, she claimed, wanted to put her out of circulation 'because of the surprise support extended to her as a contender for the leadership of the legislature party'. Once again Shyama Sharma had hit the headlines. The soft-spoken and courteous Shanta Kumar, a little more experienced now, acted swiftly this time. He got CID sleuths to look into the matter and a report was dispatched to the prime minister within four days. It was evident that Shyama's supporters in their enthusiasm to gain political sympathy and mileage had concocted the entire incident.

As the *Indian Express* correspondent in Simla, I filed three reports: on the first day, Shyama's version as given to me in an interview on 7 January 1978; second, the official version as given by the chief minister on 8 January; and third on 11 January, the CID report, a copy of which I was able to procure through my sources. The political advantage that Shyama Sharma sought had misfired. Political circles and the public read through the game. The entire episode boomeranged. Shyama Sharma was soon being labelled as 'The Lady of Scandals'. Once again she rushed to Delhi. Before she could call the press, Prime Minister Morarji Desai gave her a dressing-down on 13 January for trying to malign the state government and the Janata Party. He asked her to go back and 'do some constructive work instead of directing sensational dramas'.[3] I reported the same on 14 January 1978, which was again carried on the front page. She was not amused. Nor was Chandra Shekhar.

On 18 January 1978 evening, Kuldip Nayar, the then editor of Express News Service, and my immediate boss, called and blasted me for taking 'extra interest' in the Shyama story. My reply that I was only doing my job and that the *Express* coup had so annoyed Prem Bhatia (the editor-in-chief of the Chandigarh-based newspaper, *The Tribune*) that he had pulled up his correspondent, V. P. Prabhakar, just rubbed off him like water off a duck's back. I was ordered not to write anything more on the subject.

In any case, there was nothing left to report on it. The subject was closed. Or so I thought!

Apparently, in Delhi the matter had not been closed. On 30 January 1978, Ramnath Goenka (the proprietor of the *Indian Express* group of newspapers) drove up from Chandigarh to Simla with his confidant and *Jansatta* editor Prabash Joshi, and that too for a few hours. As planned, I met them in the lobby of Himland Hotel on Circular Road. Joshi whispered that Goenka was very angry with me and that I should just listen to him till he cools down. RNG came straight to the point and asked me as to why had I carried the CID report and how was I sure it was a genuine one and why was I taking so much interest in the Shyama Sharma story. I remained quiet. On one side were Joshi's words of caution. On the other side was the fact that a young, twenty-nine-year-old reporter was awestruck, face-to-face, for the first time, with his annadata, the lord and master, Ramnath Goenka. One said, 'Don't talk'. The other created fear. My reply, my story, my truth, got sandwiched between the two.

On the cold wintry evening of 9 February 1978, I got my orders for transfer to Jalandhar – 'the hotbed of Punjab politics' as Kuldip Nayar's marching orders put it. I spoke to the editor-in-chief, S. Mulgaonkar who said: 'I am sorry … Kuldip has let you down'. Nayar explained: 'Too many big people had got involved and I was just helpless'.

I resigned. In disgust.

25

Chance Encounters

Into the World of Publishing

LOOKING BACK AT MY WORKING LIFE, WHICH HAS BEEN OF words, words and words, I am often reminded of the poet T. S. Eliot's line: 'Our beginnings never know our ends'. Having started life as a small-time freelancer, slowly graduating into a correspondent of the *Indian Express*, I got pulled into book publishing, where I find myself busy even today – thirty-seven years later. However, I kept a foot in both camps right through till 23 March 1997, writing and reviewing, as at heart I was still a reporter, always curious to know 'what happened next' and where the story might finally lead.

The transit to book publishing happened almost unconsciously without much effort on my part. One can call it 'chance encounters' with publishing – Vikas, Macmillan, UBSPD, *India Today* Book Club, HarperCollins and Hay House – which seduced me to make the move to a world that on the surface looked like the other side of the coin because both were concerned with the written word. There were of course fundamental differences, as I soon discovered.

Journalism, I learnt soon enough, was by its very nature ephemeral. It cannot stand the test of time – and if it did, it was probably obsolete almost in no time after being published. In publishing terms, the shelf life of a news story was just about ten minutes. If one landed a story even an hour after the event, it was stale and fit only for the trash bin. Also, you just did not have the time to go into the nuances of a story – that had to be done later in weekly round-ups, if at all, because the reader first wants hard facts of what happened. As Tara Chand Gupta, an old hand at the game, once told me: 'In the journalism business "once you have shot, hanged, drawn and quartered the person you are writing about, you do not have to drown him".' Put simply, there was thrill and adventure in the chase, but when you looked back it was all over by the end of the day. Tomorrow was yet another day, and one started from scratch for another story that would end without an ending or analysis of why things happened as they did. Though I must admit variety did provide the spice to carry on day after day.

The world of books provided an alternative vision of events and people and that too without the intense pressure of deadlines; one could work at a more leisurely pace and produce 'literature' of more lasting value. Then there was the human factor or the kind of people one interacted with in the book world as distinct from those in journalism. Of course, both worlds have their rotten eggs, but on the whole, the book world has people who are certainly more stimulating. This is not being judgemental, or snobbish, but book publishing does demand better-informed editors than the rough-and-ready reporters who have little time for reflection on what they have done in a day's work.

Narendra Kumar, the managing director of Vikas Publishing House, was a great boss to work under and learn the ins and outs of book publishing from. From him I came to know what hard work is all about. S. G. Wasani, once chief of Macmillan India, whom I admire immensely, taught me the business of running a book-publishing house. But it was first Aroon Purie at the *India Today* Book Club and HarperCollins India who, behind his quiet exterior, has a razor-sharp brain; and now, the soft-spoken and man of few words, but astute and perspicacious, Reid Tracy, at Hay House, who have undoubtedly been the best bosses I have ever had. I never felt I was working under, or for, them. They always made me feel that

I was *working with* them. That was the essential difference. Hence, thirty-seven years in book publishing have been a very exciting phase of my life and I have enjoyed every moment of it. I fell in love with it and that affair, passionate in many ways, is still carrying on. It's been an unending romance. Sheer nasha! I only wish when the time comes, I can go reading a book, if not editing it.

Did I miss journalism? Yes, I did! Like all transitional states, it was marked by cross-currents. At one stage, journalism was my first love, and like all first loves, I both longed and dreaded to see her again. Hence, I did, as most do, the next best – an extramarital affair: Publishing at home. Journalism outside.

Sometime in December 1984, one Soumitra Chatterjee (Bobby) from *The Telegraph* of Calcutta, which was then edited by M. J. Akbar for the Ananda Bazar Patrika group, commissioned me to write a fortnightly column exclusively devoted to news and views about the book world: the focus was to be on books, writers, authors, poets, artists, publishers. It was an offer I couldn't refuse. The money was good enough to supplement my salary and I was going to get a byline. More importantly, it was here that I learned that the vast expansion of print and communication technology had led to diversification of media outlets, which had an inexhaustible appetite for raw material: gossip and discussion, debates and analysis, about books and writers. Along with my publishing job, I plunged into column-writing journalism, turning out a piece every fortnight. With the passage of time the column expanded its reach. In just a year it was being published as a syndicated column in nine newspapers across the country. For Dilip Padgaonkar, then editor of *The Times of India*, I wrote a fortnightly edit-page article for a year. Offers for regular book reviews, opinion pieces and features followed from *India Today* and *Indian Express* as also some Western newspapers and journals.

This writing went a long way in making me understand the business of books: who comes and who goes; what sells what does not; pricing, sales, marketing; where money was to be made and where the termites lurked. One can call it an ego trip, but I went along as the opportunities continued to come. I was now wanted both by the print media and the book publishers. The most satisfying aspect was when an opportunity came to review an outstanding or a very readable book and, more importantly, meet and interact with some of the greatest authors of our times. And I did meet many of them, or correspond with, both at home and abroad.

26

Isabel Allende

The Pain and the Agony

In reply to Vinita Dawra Nangia from *The Times of India* regarding my three favourite books of all time, I listed, on 25 October 2010: Leo Tolstoy's *Anna Karenina*, Gabriel García Márquez's *The General in His Labyrinth* and Isabel Allende's *Paula*.

Anna Karenina is perhaps the greatest work of imagination ever. It is the tragedy of a fashionable woman who abandons her husband, son and social position for a passionate liaison. As a piece of imaginative literature into the psychology of a woman – as a daughter, mother, sister, wife and mistress – it is unsurpassed. No wonder Nobel Prize winner American author William Faulkner, when asked to name three of the greatest works of imagination, famously said: '*Anna Karenina. Anna Karenina. Anna Karenina.*'

Though García Márquez's *One Hundred Years of Solitude* is considered his greatest work and *Love in the Time of Cholera* his most popular, for me it is *The General in His Labyrinth* that remains the most compelling. It is a lyrical description of an old man in the evening of his life, where he is left with only a pile of memories. It is the portrait of Simón Bolívar, the extraordinary general who pushed the Spanish out of South America and whose dreams of independence made him a hero in Latin America.

Allende's *Paula*[1] is the most tragic work I have ever read. It is more than a memoir. It is a tender, moving and vivid record of a mother's agony at the bedside of her daughter, Paula, which begins in the form of a long letter. The result is a mesmerizing story in which Isabel shares with us her most intimate feelings.

Paula is an experience not easy to describe. What is the substitute for lost love? What helps sorrows to be borne? Is it time?

The answer is memory. This is what one learns from *Paula*. As Allende says: 'It's so personal, so naked, so full of pain, of sorrow, and at the same time filled with such spirituality it shows that literature is more than just an idea. Literature is a mirror to life'.[2] So when Allende's twenty-eight-year-old daughter, Paula, fell ill with a hereditary metabolic disorder that quickly led her into a coma, she worked it out by writing three generations of family history, spanning four continents. It turned out to be a personal memoir, which further established her as a leading Latin American writer in a continent bristling with literary talent.

Paula is more than a memoir. It is a tender and moving account of a mother's heart-rending agony for a slowly dying child. Interspersed with episodes and anecdotes in a brilliant flood of autobiographical reminiscences, Allende tells her family history 'as the small part of her soul drifted into the abyss of her memories'.

Allende's father, a decadent aristocrat, disappeared when she was a child, and she was then brought up by a benevolent stepfather who taught her debating and social skills, and the pleasures of reading and writing. He was a diplomat, so she also got to travel the world. This gave her an opportunity to interview 'murderers, seers, prostitutes, necrophiliacs, jugglers, quasi-saints who performed nebulous miracles, demented psychiatrics and beggars with false stumps who rented babies to put a dent in charitable hearts'.[3] It was in this world that Allende saw the underbelly of real life, an experience which probably explains the knot of sex, violence and class hatred that underlies her novels.

Allende ranges over her own history and that of her family with tremendous honesty and verve. One reads these 'adventures' simply for the way the language flows – as if this alone would keep her daughter Paula's death at bay. Because Latin America has experienced so many forms of oppression and for so long, the Great Dictator is a central theme of almost all its great narratives. So in *Paula*, too, the Great Dictator puts in his mandatory appearance, and Allende, without the slightest trace of sentiment, describes the risks she and her family took to help fellow Chileans on General Augusto Pinochet's hit list.

Being a niece of President Salvador Allende of Chile, she also gives us an insight into what the man actually was – the man who, the world over, enjoyed the image of a leader determined to improve the lot of workers and overcome economic and social injustices, but, in his own country, was detested by half the population. Then there was the great Chilean poet with a distinct voice, Pablo Neruda, who chided her in the winter of 1972, when she was a young reporter: 'My dear child, you must be the worst journalist in the country. You are incapable of being objective, you place yourself at the centre of everything you do. I suspect you are not beyond fibbing, and when you don't have news, you invent it. Why don't you invent novels instead? In literature these defects are virtues.'[4]

However, it was not for another nine years, till 8 January 1981, that Allende wrote her first book. It was actually a letter, meant to be more of a goodbye to her grandfather, who was dying, leaving a hard-fought century behind him. The letter carried on and on. Allende wrote 'in a trance', with the sensation of unwinding a ball of yarn. At the end of the year, the pages had grown to 500, and Allende realized that it was no longer a letter, but a book. It was titled *The House of Spirits*. Thus was Allende 'initiated' into the incredible 'vice' of telling stories.

The book was published all over Europe and 'one of those rare miracles had happened that every author dreams of.' It was a 'scandalous success'.[5] Allende had arrived on the literary map of the world. When asked if she had ever dreamt of becoming a writer, she responded: 'No. I had energy to burn … but I was not sure what I was doing, because although my intention to write my grandfather a letter had quickly faded, I could not admit that I had launched into a novel. The idea seemed presumptuous. I had spent more than twenty years on the periphery of literature – journalism, theatre, television scripts, hundreds of letters – without daring to confess my true calling. I still remember the first question I was asked: "Can you explain the cyclical structure of your novel?" I hadn't any idea what he was talking about. In my vocabulary, only buildings had "structure", and the only "cyclical" I was familiar with referred to the moon or menstruation.'[6]

Mothers and daughters have a strange and paradoxical relationship. It is all-absorbing, all-transforming to begin with, but turns into a love-hate relationship of possessive jealousy in the adolescent years until it flowers into a loving companionship in adulthood and later years. And if the daughter falls critically ill in the formative years of young womanhood, 'love is tormented and interwoven with religious and various psychological currents of feeling which ends, sadly, in failure and pain'. Much of this anguish, as mentioned above, is because memory in its critical moments always goes back to the remotest origins of the lived experience, as with Paula. While Allende ranges over the labyrinths of her memory and Chilean history, Paula's deepening illness intrudes with unspoken pathos. Oddly enough, Allende's description of the slow, steady slant in Paula's journey towards death seems to fit Sigmund Freud's economic definition of wit. He says that 'we set aside a certain amount of energy to hear out a joke that threatens to go on and on' like life, and then suddenly the 'punch line cuts across it, freeing all that energy for a rush of pleasure.'[7]

The change in Allende, the vulnerability and strength of her spirit and courage, hopes and dreams, fear and pain, are all witnessed, making it an incredible journey of the soul that takes us to those rare moments in which the spirit is revealed. It is when she finds herself immobile that Allende's writing is at her best:

> The days are measured grain by grain in an hourglass of patient sand, so slow the calendar does not record them.... All the resources of magic are futile, messages in bottles thrown into the sea with the hope they will be found on some distant shore and someone will come to rescue us – until now, however, there has been no answer.... You Paula, have given me this silence in which to examine my path through the world, to return to the true and the fantastic pasts, to recover memories others have forgotten, to remember what never happened and what may still happen. Absent, mute, paralyzed, you are my guide. Time moves so slowly. Or perhaps it doesn't move at all and it is we who pass through it. I have day after day to reflect, with nothing to do, only wait, while you lie in this mysterious state, like an insect in a cocoon. I ask myself what kind of butterfly will emerge when you awake.[8]

We all invent stories in emergencies. Allende describes the tragic events as if to confine the catastrophe and to give her anxiety a shape. One story leads to another. As she recalls it, she once offered to buy Paula three new blouses. 'We go to our grave in a winding sheet', her daughter responded, 'why do we bother.'[9]

What *Paula* reveals is first-class reportage of 'a sickness and death'. And the 'understanding and sympathy of a novelist with everything that it takes: the ear, the eye, the mind, and the heart with an all-encompassing humanity'. It is often said that all a critically ill person needs is to be understood. If Paula could have read this memoir, 'she would have known that she had been understood'.[10]

27

Midnight and Them

The New Breed of Novelists

WITH *MIDNIGHT'S CHILDREN* (1981), SALMAN RUSHDIE established what has since remained the distinctive pattern for not only the Indian novel but also the subcontinental one: the family chronicle that is also the history of the nation and/or its fragments. Along with India, literary voices initially rose in Pakistan, Sri Lanka and later in Bangladesh too. And one has to look at the output of fiction to realize the dent it has made on the world literary scene.

Echoes of the partition of the Indian subcontinent have haunted almost all Indian novelists writing in English. Khushwant Singh's classic *Train to Pakistan* (1956) opened the floodgates of the most traumatic event of twentieth-century India (Bapsi Sidwa's *Ice Candy Man* on the same theme came three decades later), followed by the next generation of writers who have used family chronicles to describe the human costs of the partition and what it meant to the daily lives of common people. But a majority of these accounts have been provided from a male perspective, not from those who bore the brunt of Partition and dislocated homes – the women who have always suffered the most in such cataclysmic events. I would therefore say that our memories of Partition are fragmented – a phenomenon that can only be mended when the other half is given its proper place in history.

Perhaps the best came from Gita Mehta in 1989 – *Raj* [1]– and ten years later Shauna Singh Baldwin's *What the Body Remembers*[2] – two little gems that still shine.

Historical novels have always raised questions of factual accuracy and literary merit but rarely does one come across a work in which history and fiction have been so finely interwoven as in the case of *Raj* – a quintessential political novel on the struggle for independence, as seen through the eyes of a princess.

Gita Mehta reworked the Raj theme – an industry in itself. Instead of the moribund nostalgia that has been the landmark of Raj literature, she wrote what is essentially a political novel on India's struggle for independence. Seen through the main dramatis personae of the times – the princes, the British and national leaders – the book brought to life the machinations and intrigue of the big and the mighty as they manoeuvred towards freedom and the partition of India. But the years preceding independence are seen more as history from above, rather than a movement of the masses who remained substantially passive spectators in a feudal ethos, when elite groups decided the course of history.

The novel is spun around the central character of Jaya, the daughter of the (fictional) royal Balmer dynasty. Beginning from 1897, the book is divided into four main sections: first, the life and times of the royal Balmer household where Jaya is groomed as a princess; the second, her marriage into the Sirpur house in lower Assam, the travails of her marriage and her metamorphosis into a chic memsahib acceptable to the English; the third, as the Maharani of Sirpur with 'the cosmetics of power, not power itself'; and the finale, the coming of Independence and merger of the princely states with the Union of India.

The national movement and the description of princely India (hemmed into its own world of caste, religion, superstition and anachronisms) constantly mesh and it is the latter that in many ways is the most attractive feature of the novel. Gita Mehta picked up the lifestyle of the maharajas, their pride and prejudice, and the daily concerns inside the zenana (women's portion of the palaces) with rare and brilliant insight – as only an Indian could do – and she spun this into the novel to expose the decadence of the princes in a fast-changing world.

The woman's job was mainly to keep the man happy and the art of attraction – sola shringar (self-adorment) – became the most important part of grooming. In the Balmer kingdom, somewhere in the outback of Rajasthan, old feudal values were more strongly entrenched than in neighbouring Bikaner and Jodhpur and the Rajput woman's pride expressed itself most strongly in sati and/or her renunciation of the world during widowhood.

Jaya's grooming in Balmer, however, had an added dimension in that she learnt the arts of rajniti or politics (saam – serve the people; daan – provide for their welfare; dand – be even-handed in punishing injustice; and bhed – maintain secrecy to preserve the kingdom) and also to ride and shoot like any man. She is married off into the Sirpur house where Raja Pratap – an England-returned upstart – insisted that she be refashioned into a respectable lady capable of meeting the English gentry on their terms. So she is taught haute couture by a madame. Jaya's marriage is on the rocks from the start. Pratap is either drinking or womanizing and it is in the midst of the gathering domestic crisis that the national movement makes its first stirrings in the Sirpur house.

Hemmed in by a claustrophobic domestic environment, Jaya is initiated into the national movement by her tutor, Mrs Roy, who introduces her to national leaders in Calcutta (now Kolkata). British imperialism that was draining away the wealth of the country comes home poignantly in the Calcutta docks, where she sees goods sent to India from 'New Zealand-Australia-South Africa-Canada' that are of no use to the starving millions affected by the drought in Rajasthan, floods in Assam, and grinding poverty in the countryside.

The picture Gita Mehta paints of the main protagonists in the freedom struggle is not all good or all evil. They were princes who, despite the sordidness of their personal lifestyles, had championed the freedom struggle – like those from Patiala, Jodhpur and Balmer – while others, like her own husband, didn't want change. There were British sympathizers for the Indian cause – such as A. O. Hume and Annie Besant – and all the viceroys except Lord Louis Mountbatten were implacable enemies. The nationalists too were not all saints.

In a sense, the author's true hero is the 'iron man' Sardar Patel who organized the Instrument of Accession peacefully. Jaya, of course, with her royal upbringing believed that it was the Indian Union that merged with Sirpur and not Sirpur with the Indian Union! The guarantees of the privy purses, which were subsequently reneged on by Prime Minister Indira Gandhi in 1971, are highlighted. Jaya finally sees the writing on the wall and joins the mainstream of electoral politics.

As mentioned earlier in Chapter 11 in the case of Khushwant Singh's novel *Delhi*, historical novels of this kind can be assessed only in two ways: their literary merit and their authenticity. On purely literary merit, Gita Mehta can't be faulted. She captured the feudal, princely life with all its anachronisms in superb detail. Her descriptions of the lives of maharajas, their pride and passions, and that of the women, their ennui and frustrations, had not been portrayed with such vivid imagery in earlier Raj literature. For example, Paul Scott's *Raj Quartet* and M. M. Kaye's *Far Pavilions* or even Manohar Mulgaonkar's *Princes* portrayed the nostalgia felt at the passing of the old order. *Raj* was very different!

It's historical authenticity, however, did raise questions. Was the freedom movement essentially a game played by the elite with the masses not involved in any meaningful way? That was Gita Mehta's view of history, which was elitist and it didn't give sufficient weightage to the common people. The answer simply is that *Raj* is a novel, not a historical treatise. Her earlier book *Karma Cola* – 'a highly praised, acerbic account of the commercial exploitation of Indian traditions' – took her just three weeks to write. *Raj* took her eight years. Gita Mehta explained: '*Karma Cola* was full of jokes and aphorisms – it was fun to write. Since then I wanted to do something different, something that was more folk operative. There is a great storytelling tradition in India, that folk art, and the bards still exist. They were the genealogists of royal India for 2500 years. The accessibility of *Raj* is in this tradition. There isn't that separation in India between high art and low art. My aim was to cover (and convey) the tumult of events and the flavour of the country in all its contradictions – spiritual, earthy, sumptuous, ascetic, traditional, radical – to a wider readership. I wanted to challenge the idea that India is this impenetrable civilization that nobody is supposed to get the hang of.... Every time I visit India, I hear 600 stories in six weeks. *Raj* is just one story.... People have talked about Peter Brooks's production of *Mahabharata* as a great artistic event. In India the Mahabharata is not en event, it's an integral part of the culture. I just hoped *Raj* would join the general integration'[3]

All fiction has its autobiographical roots spreading through, as in *What the Body Remembers*, which dwells on the provincial world of pre-Partition Punjab, a limited, claustrophobic world. But it is also 'faction' – the artful mixing of fact and fiction. Baldwin employed the traditional structuring and intellectual hardware of plot, character, setting and theme.

The scene is the Punjab of the 1930s. Roop is a village girl of marriageable age. Her mother had died at childbirth and her father is in deep debt. She longs to break free from her trapped world, where she is hemmed in by tradition and lack of money. So when she learns she is to be married to a wealthy landlord, she is delighted.

But she is to be the second wife of a Sardarji, whose first wife, Satya, has borne him no children and is now well beyond child-bearing age. What follows is predictable: the struggle between the two women for control of the children to be born and the husband's attention. It is a ménage-à-trois, with all the tensions such arrangements entail. For young Roop, the arrangement turns out to be a nightmare. Satya, the more experienced of the two, knows how to bring the Sardarji around:

> Satya's lips move at Sardarji's diamond-studded earlobe. She offers him crumbly *pinni* sweets impressed with the marks of her fingers. 'Such a pity Roop is unwell', she whispers. 'How she would love this display!'[4]

This is Diwali night.

While *What the Body Remembers* was read as a story of familial relations, it will be remembered more as social history – the customs, traditions and mores of rural Punjab, many still unchanged. This is interspersed with the gathering storm of the nationalist movement that embraced all classes. But where were the women and why were they not at the barricades? The subtext provides the answers, which could be described as the stranglehold of tradition, legitimized by religion.

The novel is not just about the struggle for power between the two women. It is the Sardarji's story as well. And it is not merely his pathetic efforts to reconcile them that we need to sympathize with, but also with his changing perceptions of what the future may bring after independence. Would relations between landlords and Muslim peasants remain the same? And where would the Sikhs be? Shauna has described the scenes of the independence movement with great verve.

All 'good' novels are a hybrid form: part social inquiry or history, part fantasy, part confessional in search of an answer to 'who am I?': they cross frontiers of knowledge as well as topography. *Salt and Saffron*[5] by the young Pakistani-origin British writer Kamila Shamsie – one of the first outstanding young literary voices in English from her country – was precisely that: stories within stories that describe themselves not by birth, ethnicity or geographical location but by the confluence of all these factors with the facts of migration, transculturation and multiple identities.

The story is built around the homecoming of a young Pakistani girl, Aliya, a student in her early twenties who returns from her university in the United States to Karachi for the summer vacations. Distance has given her a perspective to look at her life that has been embedded in the Dard-e-Dil (literally, heartache) clan that spirals back to the Mughal times.

The clan is a garrulous lot. From it Aliya has picked up her storytelling abilities. She narrates her story and also that of the feudal class into which she was born and brought up and within which she finds her own voice, her own identity, or multiple identities, as she comes of age. The novel was not just a journey within but of externals too – of love and loss, the discovery (sometimes decades later) of the former, the continual presence of the latter, exemplified by the absence of a character called Mariam Apa (apa means elder sister) who appears mysteriously and disappears. Distance has then also provided Aliya the space to free herself of the ghosts of the past and look back unflinchingly and wryly and with a sense of humour at the stuff they are made of.

Shamsie's descriptions of the tyranny of the feudal class in Pakistan, and stratified Karachi, where to move up geographically was to move up socially, is social history at its best. 'Centuries of inbred snobbery'[6] meant there was no social mobility at all. Stifling social rules governed all aspects of their lives. The 'space' they inhabited as citizens of the world in London, or any city in the United States or the 'watering holes of Europe'[7], was unthinkable in Karachi, where invisible barriers divided men from women, one class from another.

For instance, there was no way Mariam Apa could indulge in small talk with Masood, the cook, though he had been there for decades; a writer falls in love with a youth from 'the wrong side of Karachi, where your life[style] says who you are'.[8] Much the same could be said about Delhi, Mumbai or Kolkata. Like all feudal structures, there are extended families on both sides with family mythologies that spin webs, and ensnare players, who can only free themselves when they begin spinning their own. Again, like all feudal families, there is great pride in their own cuisine, with its delicacies, all their own, which only they can provide. Masood's tantalizing delicacies, suffused with the right mix of salt and saffron, provide a thread that runs through the novel. In a sense, food becomes a metaphor for sexuality and desire, the urge to touch and taste the forbidden fruit.

In some ways, Kamila's novel reminds one of another Pakistani writer, Sara Suleri, whose *Meatless Days*[9] described Pakistani society of decades ago. However, what Kamila did for Karachi is what Salman Rushdie did for Bombay – bring it to life, warts and all. The similarities between Karachi and Bombay were there to see, maybe because in many senses they are both 'cities of the sea'. The ghosts of Rushdie are also present in subtle little ways but, having said that, Shamsie managed to retain her own literary identity.

Every good novel must have a philosophical subtext running through it and in *Salt and Saffron* it seemed to be about Great Divides: between India and Pakistan, exemplified by relatives on both sides across the border; the problematic nature of love; the divides in the Big City between class and colony; the generation gap between Dadi (paternal grandmother) and the girl – and the attempts to overcome them. The stories within the stories described Pakistani society, its people and its mores, better than anything that had, or has, come from that country for a long time, with the exception perhaps of Ali Sethi's *The Wish Maker.*[10]

28

Salman Rushdie

And His Credo

The Palestinian-American author Edward Said once poignantly observed: 'Exile ... is the unhealable rift forced between a human being and a native place, between the self and its true home: its essential sadness can never be healed'.[1] This applies more or less to all exiles – comprising those who are exiled by the state or those who go in for voluntary exile like Salman Rushdie who has been out of his homeland for fifty years or so.

Things happen when out in the cold and Rushdie has had a running love-hate relationship with India and Britain, which he has expressed in his trilogy – *Midnight's Children* (1981), *Shame* (1983) and *The Satanic Verses* (1988), which brought to an end the first phase of his writing – and numerous other little pieces that he has written here and there: *Step Across the Line*[2]; *Imaginary Homelands*[3]; and *The Jaguar Smile – A Nicaraguan Journey*[4].

What has been Salman Rushdie's credo, i.e., his ways of 'seeing' the world, so far?

Once in a private conversation Rushdie said that he had always been inspired by Qurratulain Hyder's (Ainee Apa) magnum opus *Aag Ka Darya*[5] (*River of Fire*[6]) that stretched from the fourth century BC to post-Partition India and was to become the most important novel of twentieth-century Urdu literature. Ainee had borrowed the title for her novel from Jigar Moradabadi's famous lines:

> *... Yeh ishq nahin aasan,*
> *bas, itna samaj lijiye*
> *Ik aag ka darya hai*
> *Aur doob ke jaana hai ...*
> (Love is not easy
> just think of it as if
> it is a river of fire
> and one has to drown in it and then emerge ...)

A continental history, before and after Independence, that would embrace India, Pakistan and Britain in its myriad relationships at all levels had been Rushdie's inspiration and this he brought out in his trilogy. Any such project would naturally embrace the interplay of religion and politics, the sham and reality of the interrelationships, the hypocrisy of the English ruling elites, which we, as ex-colonials, have deftly picked up, and all of which Rushdie tried to bring out in his novels.

Explained this way the themes sound simplistic, even banal, but human relationships exist at many different levels; good and evil are never easy to demarcate and define, and Rushdie, as an ex-colonial and a naturalized Britisher now, understands this all too well.

To bring out the criss-cross of relationships and attitudes, Rushdie borrowed the technique of the Latin American novel, in which memory goes back and forth, 'where past and future furiously chase each other in a journey of wonderful stories and astonishing flights of imagination.... The past that you know is in front of you and the future that is unknown recedes' as the narrative develops. There is no linear development of the novel. Everything is structurally loose and shifty and the attempt to find meanings, that literary critics often do, is at best hazardous because one meaning can be as valid as another. The non-linear technique, which the Latin Americans and the Europeans have specialized in because they identify literature with life, which is never linear, has been further complicated by using memory, dreams and fantasies that always intercede in the flow of the novel.

After the huge success of *Midnight's Children*, Rushdie acknowledged that he is heavily indebted to the Colombian novelist Gabriel García Márquez (who passed away on 17 April 2014) for his techniques, which he, like other newer writers, has picked up to explain the politics and religion of the subcontinent and British perfidy in strengthening obscurantism and fundamentalism in this part of the world. For even a simplistic understanding of Rushdie and his works, it is important to keep in mind that he isn't an easy novelist to read. None of his main characters is simple at all because they are all torn apart by their own contradictions. And the history of religion and politics of the subcontinent in this trilogy is not easy to decipher either because they are constantly interwoven.

Is *Midnight's Children* merely an account of the 'stroke of the midnight hour when India awoke to light and freedom', *Shame* a focus on Pakistan, and *The Satanic Verses* a picture of the subcontinent forty years after Independence, its relationship with the mother country, and of the mind of the ex-colonial? At a superficial level they are all this, but they are much, much more because there are so many strands – good and bad, some good contained in the bad, and vice versa – that it is difficult to say what is what!

Take *The Satanic Verses.* Like his earlier novels, this too has a lot to do with religion, especially with religious fundamentalism. But behind it all are the Big Questions of what is Good and Evil, the central theme of the inevitability of Death and whether life, as it is lived both here and in the West, with all the consumerism and 'yuppie' culture, is really worth it? These are, in my opinion, the questions that Rushdie is asking behind the spookiness of the novel, which is funny but has an undertone of sadness all through.

The narrative, shorn of the dreams and fantasies, wherein all the Big Questions are asked, is a simple one: Two characters, Gibreel Farishta who is a caricature of a famous Indian superstar, and Saladin Chamcha who is Rushdie himself, fall out of an exploding plane and land on a lonely coast of England, the promised land for ex-colonials of the subcontinent. Then start a series of adventures and chance encounters for both of them. Farishta, who is a little more than a country bumpkin, gets by in England, runs into old dames to protect and look after him, while Saladin, who considered himself more British than the British themselves, first runs into trouble with the British immigration authorities and then all kinds of strange things start happening to him. This is just another way of saying that he started asking questions about himself, his origins, where he was headed in life, and whether life as it was being lived was worth it, faced with the certitude of death. At this point Rushdie introduces dreams and fantasies like Jorge Luis Borges's *The Book of Imaginary Beings.*[7]

The dreams and fantasies take his characters down the corridors of time and memory, for Rushdie's characters have to do with religious fundamentalism and its role in contemporary politics. One may well ask: how did it all start, did the founders of religion (in this case, Islam) not go through doubts and vacillations? Was there not any opposition to their ideas, which is only natural when any new idea is born? How did the ideas get strengthened over time and what price had to be paid by the believers and the non-believers and whether society today reflects on the ideals of the true teachings of religion?

These are deeply philosophical questions that Rushdie raised in *The Satanic Verses*, though *Midnight's Children* and *Shame* had them too, but not in such a pointed manner – questions that touch upon the roots of a religious society, such as ours. As with all modern novelists, there are no answers provided – just a series of questions raised one after another.

Rushdie, when told of the objections of Muslim fundamentalists, clarified that his fictional character Mahound was rather like Greek writer Nikos Kazantzakis's Christ, who was wracked by questions and doubts when he was laying down laws for life and society. Superficially, it would appear to be blasphemous but underlying are the dreams and fantasies, the long conversations and soliloquies, in an attempt to understand the nature of religious fundamentalism that is beginning to have such a stronghold in large areas of the world. And this hold, Rushdie told us, is all the more difficult to understand when consumerism and the sweet life are what determine the private lives of most of us.

Is there then an inherent contradiction in all of us professing one thing and practising another, and can the same hypocrisy practised in the temporal sphere not be extended to the spiritual plane also? Rushdie has a fictional poet Baal – who was modelled after the poet Faiz Ahmed Faiz – who raises this doubt about the contradictory nature of good and evil, talking about good and doing just the opposite. Hence, I feel, that to reduce such a complex novel with its bewildering cast of characters to an attack on one religious group was to bring down the novel to the level of farce. *The Satanic Verses*, like Rushdie's earlier writings, basically dealt with religion and politics of the subcontinent, not the way it is preached but how it is practised – issues that affect our daily lives; issues that are more relevant today than ever before.

That censorship is a silent tribute that the state pays to the power of the written word has an element of perverse truth in it and this relates substantially to those regions, like the former Soviet Union, eastern Europe and Latin America, where literary traditions have been steeped into the marrow of their bones for decades or even centuries. Censorship elsewhere, especially in the 'Third World', including India, has little meaning simply because the tradition of reading – as distinct from the oral tradition – has simply not developed beyond the immediate needs of passing examinations and securing jobs.

The bare fact is that in the subcontinent there is no culture of reading for the sheer pleasure of it all, even among the elite who have both the time and the money on their hands. On this premise alone, that we are no nation of readers and that no revolution of any kind will ever come about because of the written word, the decision of the Indian government to invoke the Customs Act to prevent the entry of *The Satanic Verses* into the country in 1988 was yet another indication of how far removed our political-bureaucratic elite is from the realities on the ground.

In a dry, intellectual climate, where gossip, at times, is taken for high literary taste, the ban on the book in India made little sense because there are hardly any readers, where on an average the print run of a book is just about 2,000 copies, if not less! The average sales of titles is so abysmally low, the spread so narrow, and the impact so insignificant that perhaps it would have been advisable to have left the book unnoticed.

Coupled with this was the fact that, it is not an easy novel to read – for one thing it isn't linear and deals with too many fundamental questions on the nature of good and evil, the nature of the Self. For many, virtually the entire text went over their heads. The language too is not pucca English, but a mixture of spoken Indian English and British English, that only those who can appreciate the nuances of speech and word would understand and applaud. How many of such readers would wc have found here and how many of these would have taken to the streets to disturb communal peace and harmony?

True, riots are engineered on some pretext or the other and *The Satanic Verses* could have provided the excuse to start something. The fact also remains that, in January 2012, the proposed visit of Rushdie to the Jaipur Literature Festival as an invitee in itself generated so much of heat and dust that the state, the organizers and the hosts had to take a joint decision to call it off. The powers that be failed to balance the outrageous demands of fundamentalist groups on the one hand and the need of an open society on the other. And if they did succumb to the fundamentalists, should they not have extended the ban, for example, to the Nobel laureate Elias Canetti's *The Human Province* and to the French scholar Maxime Rodinson's works on Islam that are far more damning?

If Canetti and Rodinson got away earlier, it was simply because hardly anyone read them. The same was the case with Rushdie's book, which was not even read by those who were the first to propagate the idea of banning it. The upshot of all this baloney was that the book got so much of publicity the world over that it sold more than Rushdie or his publishers, the Penguin Group, could have ever imagined in their wildest dreams. Thanks to India, no book of Rushdie since then (and he has published eight more) has come to selling anywhere near the numbers of *The Satanic Verses.* I say 'thanks to India' because only India took the 'courage' to become leaders in ensuring Islamic purity and thought. The Iranian fatwa and the embargo by other Islamic countries, where fundamentalism is a part of state philosophy, came much later.

> Islam today sulks in the mosques and doesn't go beyond them to the outside world.... All of them are closed in circumstance, inclination, and ritual, and all of them distant from the true spirit of Islam ...

> Samia asked me about life in the land of Islam and about the role of women there and when I explained the situation she was extremely critical. She made comparisons with women at the time of the Prophet and the role they had played then. Then she said: 'Islam is wilting away at your hands and you are just standing and contemplating.... The difference between our Islam and yours is that ours has not closed the doors of independent judgment, and Islam without independent judgment means Islam without reason ...

> Excessive concern with religion seems to me to be the last resort of people who have been exhausted by life.... Religion is related to progress and civilization, not just emotions. Unfortunately, today's interpretations of religion are often backward and contradict the needs of civilization. It's clearly more important to

> treat one's fellow men well than to be always praying and fasting and touching one's head to a prayer mat. God did not intend religion to be an exercise club.

The first two quotes from the Nobel laureate Naguib Mahfouz's *The Journey of Ibn Fattouma*[8], are part of the Cairo trilogy, and the third expressed by him in an interview[9] to Charlotte El Snabrayy, came as a direct response to the threats to his life by Islamic fundamentalists in the Arab world, who were incensed by his repeated assertions that the boundaries of the Islamic constituency have been drawn too tightly for the postmodern world of science, reason and individuality. And when the threat was renewed with the publication of *The Journey of Ibn Fattouma* (his *Children of Gabelawi*[10] published in 1959 in Beirut was banned earlier in Egypt because in it Muhammad is clubbed along with other prophets), Mahfouz retorted: 'Every society has its tradition, laws and religious beliefs which it tries to preserve. From time to time individuals appear who demand changes. I believe that society has the right to defend itself just as the individual has the right to attack that with which he disagrees. If a writer comes to the conclusion that his society's laws are no longer valid or harmful, it is his or her duty to stand up.'[11]

Three decades earlier, an equally eminent Egyptian author, Taha Hussein, was forced to resign his teaching post at Cairo University. The crime for which he had earned the ire of the faithful was a work of literary criticism that cast doubt on the authenticity of some of the pre-Islamic poets. These poets are the source for the rules of grammar and syntax used in Quranic verses. It was feared that to cast doubt on them would be to call parts of the divine text itself into question. Many, if not most, of the books by scholars, which deal with the Quran and Islamic origins in a scientific manner, using the methods of textual analysis adopted from biblical scholarship, are banned in Muslim countries. Saudi Arabia – where the fundamentalist Wahhabite sect still holds sway in religious matters – even forbids such religious classics as the works of Al-Ghazali[12] and

Al-Ashari[13], because even these might lead the faithful to stray off the strict path of literalism. On the other side, we have Taslima Nasreen from Bangladesh, who, unfortunately, cannot speak out any more because she has no means to defend herself against fundamentalist hordes. And the reason is not that she is not a Nobel laureate like Mahfouz or an old invalid that no one would attack out of sheer pity but because she lived in 'an Islamic state' where religion and polity are one. It is the monotheism of Islam and the rigidities in its interpretation that drove Taslima underground and finally to seek asylum in India in 1994. After all, a state is a product of society, an expression and image of it. It is a structure that a society creates for itself as an instrument of its own self-realization.

Taslima's novel *Lajja*[14] tells the story of a Hindu family in Dacca (now Dhaka) following the events of December 1992 after the demolition of the Babri Masjid in Ayodhya. It is uncompromising in its denunciation of Hindu fundamentalists who hacked down the masjid, and is equally scathing in its attack on Bangladesh fundamentalists who attacked an innocent Hindu family, reminiscent of the violence during the partition in 1947. The novel – it is, in fact, more of a pamphlet – is really an attack on fundamentalists of all kinds: Hindu, Islamic et al. and all forms of religious bigotry that multiracial, multicultural societies are faced with when old ethnic 'boundaries' break up as in the former Soviet Union and Yugoslavia.

The theme still has its poignancy because the developments inescapably concern the entire subcontinent where communal boundaries – Hindu, Sikh, Christian, Muslim, and so many subgroups – criss-cross all over and there are no clear-cut constituencies any more. What happens in Bangladesh concerns us in India directly because we are, in fact, part of the same ethnic group.

The question of the literary merit of *Lajja* is really irrelevant – in fact, in its English translation the emotional surcharge of the Bengali is lost. The novel would not have been noticed if fundamentalists had not raked up the issue. What is important, however, are two key issues. First, the place of the minority in a contemporary nation state, which is becoming increasingly a global village thanks to the

IT revolution. Second, the monotheism of Islam and its intolerance of most forms of dissent in a modern state.

Minority rights, in many ways, is *the* central issue today. What do minorities do, especially women, who are the real minorities in all male-dominated societies? Turn to state and society for protection? And what happens when state and society are one because a religious reformation never took place in the Islamic world? Would we see more atrocities on the lines of Bosnia, or Gujarat nearer home, where Muslim minorities are at the receiving end?

In the melting pot of modern societies, where different communities merge into one another, many are 'outsiders' or minorities who need to be protected by the state when civil society breaks down as a result of the fanaticism of religious bigots. But in fundamentalist states, it is the state itself – like in Bangladesh – that leads the charge against dissent.

However, much more important is the question whether Islamic fundamentalism would not encourage the growth of alternative fundamentalisms to counter the perceived threat to their positions. Right or wrong, the growth of Hindu fundamentalist groups is partly because of the steady growth of Islamic fundamentalism, aided and abetted by the oil-rich Arab world that is prepared to go to any extent to fashion the world according to its own image.

Initially, the aggressiveness of minority groups in any society is a defence mechanism against the 'imperialism' of the majority but, sooner than later, both shed their pretensions and come face-to-face in street fights.

Among the liberals there is a totally wrong belief that since the minorities are finally the victims, they cannot also be the victimizers. In fact, to begin with, they are the victimizers because most live under a fear psychosis where even dissent is construed by them as an attack on their positions. So, they resort to aggression, which is met with counter-aggression and tyranny of the majority. In any confrontation, it is the minority that loses out.

What happened in Bangladesh, and happens elsewhere regularly, is an attack against the weaker minority in an Islamic theocratic state

– women. The state stands by because Islamic society demands a total submission to the Quran, as interpreted by the clergy. Whether Taslima actually said or wrote anything for or against the holy book is irrelevant because a rumour in circulation is worth a thousand truths. The connection is obvious: dissent in a theocratic state is not permitted, and so is the case with truth, which is in the minority.

It is said that some books are born great; others have greatness thrust upon them. Mahfouz's *The Journey of Ibn Fattouma* was born great in the hands of a great writer. Taslima Nasreen's *Lajja*, a third-rate novel, and Rushdie's *The Satanic Verses*, a clever one, had greatness thrust upon them by obscurantists who have often not seen the inside of a book. If they had, they would have let these pass and left them to their own fates.

29

State Terrorism

Literature and Its Intolerance

Censorship is not a unique Islamic contribution to literary creation and scholarship as many of us would like to believe. Literary and intellectual state terrorism is no longer confined to the borders of a nation but has been extended to embrace the whole world. All of us have seen it before and will do so in future – especially when 'internal peace and security' have been threatened. What has been the record of censorship on grounds of political and religious susceptibilities and what are the factors responsible for taking literary intolerance to such incomprehensible heights of insanity?

One would have thought that literary intolerance had reached its apogee with the Nazi leader Heinrich Himmler's boast that every time he heard the word 'culture' he would reach for his revolver. Heading the pack was the Soviet Union and the socialist countries where writers were gagged, or as a poet put it: 'The singer was killed and the song put away in museums.'

The record is too painful to recall. The list is long and wide. However, to name just a few, in Europe: Osip Mandelstam, Boris Pasternak, Joseph Brodsky, Franz Kafka and Milan Kundera; in South Africa: Alan Paton, Nadine Gordimer and Peter Abrahams; and in West Africa: Wole Soyinka and Chinua Achebe. And for Latin America one could include almost all the great writers like

Pablo Neruda, Isabel Allende and Gabriel García Márquez. In fact, the state repression of writers throughout Africa and Latin America was so terrifying that almost all the writers lived in exile and did their writing mostly from Britain and America.

However, even Britain and America – the so-called champions of free speech – have not been averse to clamping down on writers when they felt threatened. Their record of ban on books too is not all that clean as is often imagined and we tend to lose sight of intellectual terrorism by the state in the West. After all, D. H. Lawrence's *Lady Chatterley's Lover* (1928) remained banned till the early 1960s, and more recently, Peter Wright's *The Spycatcher* (1987) was not permitted to be published in Britain. America had John Steinbeck's *Of Mice and Men* (1937) banned in some of its states where they could impose their own censorship laws. It is only natural then that if the West has imposed censorship when the state felt threatened, the Islamic world did so too when its essentially theocratic state was challenged by writers.

Why has this come about?

A simplistic answer would be that the world has become a large melting pot where different nationalities mix outside their countries' borders. The scientific and technological revolution has made movement from one corner of the globe to another possible and immigration laws, however stringent, can quite easily be got around by posing as political dissidents.

The West, for its own reasons, welcomes political dissidents (after all Ayatollah Khomeini was also a dissident in France) as well as reactionary forces that hark back to medieval times because this keeps the 'Third World' in its place. Dissidents set up little ghettos of their own and, if you know the condition of the exile, they sustain themselves by clinging to the glories of the past and the call of religion and all its rituals. If exile in any way strengthens the roots of the past, the whole consumerist way of life in the West where everything is up for sale makes the weaponry of terrorism easily available – postal bombs, remote radio control devices, telescopic guns with silencers and much more. Guns and easy money only partially explain the rise of the youth to sacrifice themselves for a 'passage to Heaven'. What, I think, so far is more important is the insidious consumerist philosophy in the West, where as the poet says:

> Come to our well-run desert
> Where anguish arrives by cable
> And the deadly sins
> May be bought in tins
> With instructions on the label.[1]

With such precedents in mind, the barrage of hostility that writers face comes as no surprise. The main question is: Is any book worth giving life for? And is any book worth taking life for? A logical answer from any right-minded person would be: certainly not!

Censorship, then, is just a way of life for the modern state and both the East and the West have used it as a whip to bring writers in line when society has felt threatened. There is really nothing much to choose between the two. If there is any difference it is simply that in the West the clamp has been put down when internal security has been threatened – former spies spilling the beans, for example – whereas, in the East, it has always been when the predominant religion has been attacked or seriously questioned for its relevance to life in the modern world. In both cases, the writer has been told to 'fall in line or else'. However, never before in living memory had a writer ever been threatened by the state outside its national borders. But such is the world we are living in. Everything is up for sale. Love is bought ready-made and human relations reduced to a simple nexus, rather like: 'If you've got the money, I have got the stuff.' When rampant consumerism reaches the stage it has, critical faculty to think of one's conscience takes a backseat. All that is required to get things done is to arrange for the money for a turnkey job and it gets done. The same consumerist principle is also extended to the world of books and ideas.

When the dividing line between tragedy and farce becomes thin – as it often does in life – the best way to describe the shadow that falls between the dream and reality is satire: the exaggerated sense of the real, more often weird than the wildest fiction, which drives home the follies and foibles of the powers that be and the mess they create all around.

Here I am reminded of a weird case. Way back in the early 1980s, a Pakistani physician-historian, Dr Sadiq Hussain, decided to do a detailed study on the history of warriors. Nine years later, in 1989, he published his 'magnum opus' titled *Tehrik-e-Mujahideen*[2] in six volumes. Then all of a sudden, five years later, in April 1994, a Sikh professor of history of a college affiliated to Guru Nanak University in Amritsar learnt that the first of the six volumes distorted Sikh history and contained 'derogatory references to the Sikh gurus'. A frenzy got whipped up. The Punjab government, led by Chief Minister Beant Singh of the Congress, proscribed the book.

An unknown and obscure Amritsar-based organization, the 'Sikh Lower Court', announced an Ayatollah Khomeini-style reward of Rs 50 lakh to anyone who would kill Dr Sadiq Hussain. Two more unheard-of organizations, coupled with the 'Hindu Shiv Sena' of the Hindu nationalist organization, Shiv Sena, one of the many wings jumped into the fray, each announcing a 'suitable reward'. The then Youth Congress chief, Ramesh Singla, went a step further and offered Rs 1 crore for Dr Hussain's head. Where the money was to come from no one knew. But the main question was: had anyone seen a copy of the proscribed book? The Punjab government authorities were frantically trying to get hold of at least one copy of the book they had banned.

The most comic situation arose when the publisher of the book at Al-Meezan International in Lahore, whom I knew a little, informed me that since the book had failed to sell they had pulped the entire stock two years back. Moreover, the author, Dr Sadiq Hussain had died four years back on 19 June 1990. I wrote about the case in my column.

The Lahore publishers were thoroughly amused. The Punjab government was not, for it couldn't have looked more foolish than it did.

30

Writing Poetry

An Elitist Fashion without Takers

Writing poetry is in fashion, without any demand.

I have now lost count of the number of friends I have lost over the years simply because I did not publish their poems; poems that the wife (or the sister-in-law) wrote and the husband (or brother-in-law) said were 'excellent' – as if the poor fellow had any choice! Or the other way around. Once, years back, a childhood friend of mine invited me for drinks. His wife told me: 'You know my niece has heard so much about you … she is really looking forward to meeting you.' The niece, about fifteen years old, walked in and was asked to say 'hello' to uncle. 'You must read her poems. She is very good. Poetry comes naturally to her … go and get your poems dear, uncle will publish your book.' My drink suddenly tasted putrid!

'You see, we don't publish poetry', I clarified.

'But you did publish Keki Daruwalla … and Nissim, whatever his name is…?' (The reference was to Nissim Ezekiel.) What was I to say to that? That was the last I heard from them.

Yes, writing poetry in English is in fashion. Anyone and everyone is writing it and is fast on the way to becoming a poet. And everyone, who is anyone, does manage to get a platform to exhibit his or her poetic talents. The rest are children of the lesser gods. At every party, get-together, or function, one is sure to bump into a couple of individuals claiming pretensions to being poets who 'have publishers in hand' but are 'searching for one who is sensitive enough to recognize the depth of my poems'. Though we have a wealth of poetry in almost all our regional languages, comparable to the best in the world, there are unfortunately exceptional few who can claim to handle the English language well enough to write verse in it. Most of our 'poets' who write in English are considered commercially unviable. Hence, as a matter of policy, publishers do not touch poetry even with a pair of tongs. What lends a peculiar shabbiness to this scene that a whole slew of people still carry on writing poetry offering little or no hope.

One may well ask as to why so much of Indian poetry in English is derivative, banal and often, more as a rule than exception, downright trite? Is it because English, in the final analysis, is not our language and therefore we are incapable of expressing the intensity of feelings that poetry demands? Or is it because there is no culture of English poetry in India because 'poetry doesn't make anything happen'? Both factors are responsible for the pathetic state of the art, there could be others too, but to my mind, it is W. B. Yeats's famous comment – 'Out of our conflict with ourselves we get poetry' – that lies at the root of the intellectual wasteland in which we find ourselves.

Is there any Indian poet in English who could say like T. S. Eliot 'these fragments I have shored against my ruins'?[1] Or as Eliot's second wife, Valerie Fletcher, recorded: 'He felt he had paid too much a price to be a poet … that he had suffered too much'.[2] The fact is that our poets in English come from a background cushioned by all the trappings of material and emotional security that traditional kinship provides, where happiness and well-being become an obstacle to any kind of creativity. That could well be the reason why poetry in English by Indian 'poets' is limited by a sentimental view of life. All the idealism is beaten into a gooey pulp of sentimentalism and this ends up becoming a technical limitation. The result is that, there is no feeling, no passion in their poetry, nor in their thoughts.

In a word, the key catalyst to the creation of any worthwhile literature – suffering, alienation, loneliness (call it what you will) – is apparently absent from the private lives of our poets. I don't claim to have any intimate details about the private anguish of our English-speaking poets, but I do make this assertion on the basis of the general themes our poets have been choosing to write on and the manner in which most of the poetry anthologies have been published. The themes are pretty hackneyed or banal: domestic disharmony or the anguish of failed love. One can think of hardly any poem by any of our 'poets' that has gone beyond these two worn-out themes of home and 'exiled' love – a little has been done on 'games politicians play' – but, there is not a single one, for example, on the universal theme of loneliness and alienation that seeks to describe the human condition.

This shortcoming is conspicuous, especially if we consider how much the sheer poverty of everyday Indian life in cities and villages has to offer and how much of the universal has been expressed in our regional languages. Destitution and wretchedness and the compromises they demand have been written about most beautifully and touchingly, by our regional poets who have shown that poetry is 'language's highest degree of maturity ... a rhyme turns an idea into law'[3] that lives in our memories long after all the prose we have read is dead and forgotten.

Our poets writing in English have studiously kept away from these themes. My hunch is that it is because our English poets have no first-hand experience of these sufferings of the poor. I am not saying that nothing has been written, but the little that has been romanticizes poverty and somehow doesn't ring true.

If the themes our English poets have chosen to dwell on don't even touch the surface of things, the manner in which a majority of them hustled their way into publication is a strong pointer of how mediocre most of the stuff is. Agreed, poetry is the last thing our publishers want to touch because there are no takers, but these 'poets' have, in a very large number of cases, themselves financed publication of their anthologies just to get their few moments in the limelight. Many a publisher grew up on other people's funds, and reputations were made on an odd poem or a couple of them. Remember P. Lal and his Writers' Workshop in Calcutta?[4]

The bitter truth is that publishing poetry in English in India is mostly a veritable racket. It's vanity publishing at its peak. I recall how during my tenure with Macmillan India in the 1980s, we published a slim volume of poems by a professor of English only because he was very instrumental in recommending a number of English texts published by the company in various universities. Then there was this other professor of English from a university in Andhra Pradesh who too was influential in recommending texts to the three-year undergraduate courses of many universities. Macmillan, which never touched poetry, published his little volume with a print run of 500 copies so that he could submit it for a prestigious national award, which he did get, simply because he was the guide to the daughter of the government officer heading the award committee for her doctoral thesis. Or take the case of a printer, who had become a fly-by-night publisher too. He published for the first time, and the last too, a small edition of downright trite poetry of a senior Punjab government officer because with it came the 'reward' of a large print order of official publications. A case of 'poetical kickbacks' one can say. Such examples are legion!

However, this is not to say that there is no talent. There are exceptions like the Oxford poetry series as also the works of poets like A. K. Ramanujan, Dom Moraes, Pritish Nandy, Nissim Ezekiel, Keki N. Daruwalla and of course that genius, Vikram Seth. Here, I must not forget the *Poems of Gitanjali*, which were discovered by sheer accident and published by Oriel Press, USA, in 1982, after Gitanjali's death at the young age of seventeen.

The publication of *Poems of Gitanjali* is a story straight out of a Bollywood film.

At the age of fourteen, Gitanjali Ghei, who lived in Bombay, was diagnosed with terminal cancer. She died on 11 August 1977. After her death, several poems and notes, expressing her innermost thoughts and feelings, sorrow and grief, pain and agony, were discovered hidden in all kinds of improbable places – cupboards, draws, shelves, amongst books, in socks and pillow cases, under the mattresses, etc. The parents gave them to Pritish Nandy, who was then editing the poetry page of *The Illustrated Weekly of India.* He published six of them – touching and emotional, poignant and tender, at times heart-rending.

A few months later, a gentleman who was staying at the Taj Hotel in Bombay, stepped out in the evening to take a walk by the Gateway of India. Suddenly, he noticed that a piece of paper from the tin trunk of a roasted gram seller nearby flew and got stuck under his shoe. He picked it up. It was the poetry page of the *Weekly* issue which had carried Gitanjali's poems. The rest is history. The gentleman, if my memory serves me right, was Robert Giroux, a reputed publisher of the Farrar, Straus and Giroux publishing house in the US. He got in touch with Pritish, took the manuscript with him and published the thirty-seven poems, first in a hardback edition in 1978 and later in paperback.

However, though some copies were imported into India by India Book House Distributors, no Indian publisher bought the Indian rights. Later, much later, in 1992 the Gujarat Sahitya Prakash in Surat published thirty-one poems in a paperback edition which soon went out of print.

It is almost a cliché that poetry is born out of a conflict with ourselves; the greater the conflict, the more enduring the poetry. The problem with reviewing a poet's works, or his or her life for that matter, is that the poems are created with words that clothe ideas. If you break down the poem piecemeal, like lecturers in colleges and universities, you lose out on rhythm and music or just the feel of the poem.

Since poetry readings are crucial in projecting a poem, poets are unhappy with others, notably actors, reading out their works. Most readers treat poems as *text to be interpreted.* Few are tuned to the interplay between rhythm and meter in traditional verse, let alone be able to draw on, and draw out, the organic rhythmical resources of contemporary poetry.

By becoming better readers and presenters of their work, poets have now reclaimed the performer's role. Poets are different from each other. Vikram Seth or Keki Daruwalla read their poems to live audiences more powerfully, and with more feeling, than any performer would, retaining the sensibility and intellect, and registering music, tone and accent. The poet's own reading enhances the audience's appreciation of the poems.

Good poetry is a result of emotional turbulence, a miracle born of an exquisitely painful labour. It may make nothing happen and yet it moves us, maybe because the conflict within ourselves continues to grow. It is a reflection of intensity and is often disturbing. It is a pity that much of its essence is more often than not sacrificed in translation. In fact, one of the definitions of good poetry, as of good music, is that it cannot be translated. As the eminent author and translator Victor G. Kiernan remarked: 'All translation of poetry is a horn-window, allowing only a certain quantity of light to pass through it; a proposition in support of which innumerable quotations might be assembled.'[5]

And if an attempt is made, as indeed it should be, then every translator must consider what the English poet John Dryden stated: 'The liberty, not only to vary from the words and sense, but to forsake them both as he sees occasion; and taking only some general hints from the original, to run division on the groundwork, as he pleases.'[6] Though one may not agree entirely with this view, one fact is undebatable – that the translation should be from a 'poem to a poem', which stands on its own identity. There can be no dilution of identity because identity cannot be translated into anything other than itself. If all that happens is a line-for-line and word-for-word translation, we will get only the 'literals', with much of the original sweetness and sensitivity being lost en route. No wonder the unforgettable German poet Hans Magnus Enzensberger always, without exception, translates his own poems from the German into English. Like Bertolt Brecht, he combines an intense political imagination with lyrical gusto, in the anthology *Selected Poems*,[7]f ollowed by the formidable *The Sinking of the Titanic*.[8] Turning to the Indian subcontinent, let's take the following example where Faiz Ahmed Faiz's lines, translated by Waqas Ahmed Khwaja:

> *Mujh se pahli-si mohabbat, mĕri mahbūb, na māńg.*
> *Maine samajhā thā kē tū hai, to darakshān hai hayāt;*
> *Terā gham hai to gham-e-dahr kā jhagrā kyā hai?*
> *Teri sūrat se hai ālam men bahāāron ko ṣabāt,*
> *Terī ānkhon ke siwā duniyaā men rakhā kyā hai?*
> (Don't ask me dear for that first love again.
> I had believed with you life was illumined,
> Caring for you cares of the world had ceased,
> Your face affirmed the presence of spring,
> The world had nothing to match your eyes.[9])

Just for comparison, another translation of the same lines by Victor Kiernan:

> Love, do not ask me for that love again.
> Once, I thought life, because you lived, a prize
> The time's pain nothing, you alone were pain;
> Your beauty kept earth's springtimes from decay,
> My universe held only your bright eyes.[10]

True comparison for the literal translation that at times accompanies the verse is unavoidable. But the 'precise sense of shade of meaning in lines may be differently felt (as one saw in the example given above) by one reader or another … [because] a poetic phrase or image has, like each word by itself, not a single meaning but a band of related meanings for its inventor as well as for its listener.'[11]

Unfortunately, this is what happens to a substantial degree with most of our vernacular to English translations, because translators normally forget that each language has its own unique milieu, rhythm and cadence. Though a person equally proficient in, and with a feeling for both languages – which of course is an essential prerequisite – may succeed in transcribing the meaning of thoughts from one language to another, what well might be impossible to capture is the soul, the spirit behind them.

Besides Urdu to English, many valiant efforts have been made, in the recent past, to translate some of our rich poetry of other regional languages into English affording readers, totally unfamiliar with the language, a glimpse into its verse. Yet, the question still remains whether it is really possible to competently translate, for example, the famous Dogri or Punjabi works such as the folk tales of Shayer Pilloo's *Mirza Sahiban* or Sufi poet Hashim Shah's *Sassi-Punnu* or Sayyad Waris Shah's *Hir Ranjha* – immortal romances presented as long narratives in verse – with all their rustic earthiness, aggression, depth and drama. To date, we do not have a single good translation. Even the much publicized 1978 translation of *The Love of Hir and Ranjha* by Sant Singh Sekhon,[12] or *Sain Bulleh Shah: The Mystic Muse* by Kartar Singh Duggal,[13] disappeared unsung before their release, simply because the translation was, if it could be so termed, absolutely flat – without any emotion or feeling.

Modern Indian Love Poetry[14] featured the works of eighty-one Indian poets translated into English. Revolving around the theme of love, the hundred poems in this first volume (three were planned but the other two were never published) represented its many facets, exploring the intensity and incredible energy inherent in a man-woman relationship. Passionate, personal and often traumatic, the poems in various Indian languages, ranging from Hindi to Kannada to Urdu to Oriya and many more, possess an appeal that is universal and timeless. Unfortunately, this anthology too failed to become as timeless as expected, and the reasons were not far to seek. However, to be fair, the anthology had some good translations, for example, Pritish Nandy's translation of Kaifi Azmi's little gem, which was set by film director Chetan Anand to the music of Madan Mohan, in his 1964 film *Haqeeqat.*

When I went away I thought
She would try to stop me,

> Attempt to reconcile ...[15]

Or there's the example of D. R. Bendre's Kannada poem translated by K. Raghavendra Rao:

> As I gaze on your skin
> more delicate than the platinum leaf,
> I know the secret of the weaver's skill ...

But then came in the question of few wanting to read poetry and even fewer wanting to buy it.

The Penguin Book of Modern Urdu Poetry[16] comprises the works of seventeen modern Urdu poets from India and Pakistan – all of them radicals who speak the language of revolution, political action, the socialist aesthetic, in one poetic form: the nazm (free verse). The anthology opens with Faiz Ahmed Faiz and we once again have a taste of the translation of the lines (see above), which have become a part of our everyday life, this time by Mahmood Jamal:

> Do not ask me, my love ...
> ... there are other sorrows in the world than love,
> and other pleasures too.[17]

However, this should not be taken to mean that all translations are poor and should not be attempted. We in India have been singularly unlucky not to get our regional poetry in English reach a wider and larger readership; work on translations, nevertheless, must carry on, for poetry, even in translation, should be applauded if it transforms a poem into a poem and if it touches upon the universal themes of suffering, loneliness and alienation. After all, look at Khushwant Singh's superb translation of Muhammad Iqbal's *Shikwa* and *Jawab-e-Shikwa*[18] and the impact it has had on the readership which cannot read it in Urdu and yet has enjoyed the two poems, over the last few decades in English. The best of such poetry has, over the years, been coming from Latin America, Europe and, of course, from the Urdu world, probably because the world outside has nothing to do with reason and 'the bridge between a cause and an effect has collapsed and thought wanders off in sweet lazy liberty.'[19]

PART THREE

The wise man reads both books and life itself.

– Lin Yutang

31

The Shift

To a Higher Plane

A mid-life crisis has been loosely defined as 'an emotional crisis of self-confidence that occurs in middle age but is something that every working person goes through at some point or the other'. The crisis can take different forms – from interpersonal relationships to a crisis in the workplace, when things fall apart and the centre doesn't hold any more. I, too, went through a period of great doubt and hesitation, both personally and professionally, and more or less simultaneously, when the entire past suddenly felt repugnant and the urge to chuck it all up and move to some place else because of the unbearable pressures of a divided mind became stronger and firmer than ever before.

On the professional front, as the time came for me to leave HarperCollins India, which I was heading as its CEO, questions began to arise thick and fast, and the mind swung like a pendulum from one extreme to another: What have I been doing in the big corporate world that I found myself in? Where was I headed for? Shouldn't I have a change of scene, always assuming the security of a steady job that I was fortunate to have mostly had? Every job ultimately turns into a routine and most of us carry on because it is too much to shake ourselves out of the comfort we have got used to. But for how long? When relationships at the top level sour, for whatever reasons, boredom in some form or the other is an inevitable consequence: Would a switch from one corporate world to another (which, in any case, was not easy) make a substantial difference to my peace of mind? I found no answers anywhere, at least nothing that would satisfy my angst. Not even in literature – which normally does provide many an answer.

But literature, like music, was a palliative, not a solution to my existentialist problems. The answer finally, had to be found within.

I quit.

On 6 February 2006, I wrote to Aroon Purie, the chief of the *India Today* Group and the chairman of HarperCollins India:

> Dear Aroon,
>
> Further to our meeting of 16 January, I wish to inform that after serious thought I have decided to stick to my original plan to leave the group at the end of March 2006. It is with great regret that I have come to this decision. As you know I have immensely enjoyed working with you in particular and the group as a whole. The last eight years have been very rewarding and rich …

On 12 February, Aroon and I met over lunch at the 1911 restaurant of The Imperial Hotel on Janpath in New Delhi and talked about my letter. On 27 February 2006, he wrote:

> Dear Ashok,
>
> With reference to your letter of 6 February 2006, it is with regret that I accept your decision to leave the organization. I had hoped that we would continue to work together.
>
> I would like to express my appreciation for the dedication and honest way in which you worked for the best interest of the organization. I will not forget that it was your initiative that brought HarperCollins to us and also to bring it to its present state of success.

Please do remain in touch.
I wish you the very best in whatever you do next.

Best wishes.

I was without a job. But *free*!

For me, the climb up the greasy pole of publishing had been slow and steady. The question was what had kept me there for so long? Was it money and the sense of security that comes with it? Or the fact that I had engaged with the best that the corporate world of publishing had to offer? The truth is both.

The Indian book scene was opening up to American and European book publishers, who were looking for senior personnel to guide them through the thickets of the book trade's jungle. There were few around as most of the managers had risen from shop assistants or carried the shopkeeper's mentality; they did not have the larger view of the book world or, more importantly, the ability to 'connect' a forthcoming book to its potential in the market. That required an educational background, which these 'managers' did not have – harsh words, but the truth. The new entrants had few options but to poach the little talent available within the trade. In this poaching I too got solicited with offers that were a sort of 'embarrassment of riches' by almost all new North American and British book publishing houses that have opened offices in India. It may sound like an empty boast but I could have walked in through any of their doors, on my terms. Such a situation is certainly great for anyone's ego! I was no exception.

However, much to everyone's surprise, I chose a relatively little-known publishing imprint in India – Hay House – that specialized in 'mind-body-spirit', self-help and motivational publishing and is a world leader in these fields. These are quasi-spiritual books. I liked the philosophy of the company and one meeting with its president, Reid Tracy, at its offices in Carlsbad, California, and I knew it to be my calling. At that stage, it suited my craving for something more than the best life that money had to offer – a decision I have never regretted. Reid, whom I found to be incisive, quick-witted and dexterous, gave me a free hand and allowed me to publish more than what they did the world over. Hence, Hay House India today does publish every subject but fiction, including biographies, cinema and current affairs. The core business, however, is focused on mind-body-spirit books.

I am a religious sceptic and do not concern myself with the question of the existence (or non-existence) of God in everyday affairs. I don't look for Him and He doesn't for me. I have never found Him in any gurudwara, temple, church or mosque. But, I easily find Him every day in the music of a composer, in the voice of a singer, the painting of a painter, the writing of an author, the verse of a poet. He's there in a monument, in a sculpture, in a piece of fashion garment, in a manuscript that lands on my desk for publication. I see Him in the innocent smile of that child standing half-naked, with nose running, in some far-off village in the mountains. I find Him in my friends, who have taken me into their lives, their world, who are always there for me, who stand by me, who tolerate my various fluctuating moods and eccentricities. I would much rather look at the beautiful formation of a cleavage than the cross that hangs close to it.

You can discover God by reconciling your different selves – the good, the bad and the ugly. Let me quote the British author Graham Greene: 'If there is God who uses us and makes his saints out of such material as we are, the devil too may have his ambitions; he may dream of training even such a person as myself....'[1] I guard and protect myself from being influenced by the teachings and preachings of any baba or mataji, any guru, cleric or a moral brigade on how to be pious. For me, God is there within; certainly not in the distance, but here and *now*. I don't waste time and energy in prayers or in any sort of meditation. The only prayer to me is my work. My meditation is not to hurt anyone. And if by chance I do, I make it a point to apologize immediately. It helps me have a clear mind. It gives me a good night's sleep – God's biggest gift to me. And I enjoy the fruits of my work to the hilt.

Uncertainty and insecurity drive people to seek answers in religious practices. One turns to God, or so-called godmen and godwomen, to find solace from one's misfortunes, or seek favours by offering bribes for whatever one aspires for. Happiness, or that 'sense of inner peace', does not come from the realization of desires but by being content with what one has. I accept life, situations and people around me for what they are and not what they should be. I never think of yesterday. For me, everything is *now*. That's what makes my tomorrow.

This does not mean that one doesn't strive to improve life, to look into matters that are obviously wrong. It means that there are limits on how much an individual can do. It also means that we must limit our wants as there is no limit to greed. You cannot have God and Mammon on the same pedestal.

We all have our contradictions and multiple identities. There are many selves within each of us. Which self will assert itself at any given point depends on what influences us at that particular stage. We are constantly evolving. What we are today is not what we were yesterday. Life is like a stream that has to flow forward on its journey. The minute the water gets stagnant it gets polluted. Change is the only certainty and acceptance of it is what gives one peace of mind.

As a human being grows older, 'good health' becomes a central concern, which provides faith healers, homoeopaths, chiropractors (those who practise alternative medicine based on the manipulation of joints, especially the spinal column), yogis and plain, simple spiritualists a ready market for their books. Coupled with them are the so-called 'godmen' and the 'spiritual masters' as also the futurologists – palm readers, astrologers, handwriting experts and suchlike who claim to predict your future and/or give remedies to change the course of your life. This shouldn't come as a surprise because human beings have always had more faith and confidence in healers than in those who were better qualified and experienced.

Hippocratic literature has said much the same thing, emphasizing between the lines a patient's wish to please a doctor whom he or she admires: 'Some patients, though conscious that their condition is perilous, recover their health simply through their contentment with the goodness of the physician.'[2] This is the basis of the placebo effect – Latin for 'I will please' – which refers to a doctor's inclination to prescribe a cure when he knows that the drug (he or she has prescribed) has no active ingredients.

Then, why do ultra-sophisticated physicians of scientific medicine pooh-pooh such therapeutic attempts as so much hocus-pocus? And yet, why do spiritual books based on the relationship among the mind, body and spirit have a perennial demand, even at the expense of more scientific methods of research and inquiry?

A human being is essentially an irrational creature, guided more by his or her gut feelings, than by rational choice of pros and cons of what is good for him or her in a given situation. To stretch this argument a little further, when the future cannot be anticipated in all its variables, it is better to put your money in something that will make you feel better even if it gives just a temporary relief.

These are two standard reasons why spiritual books continue to come out in droves and both hold good. But they are not enough to explain the phenomenon for which we need a working definition of spiritualism and, perhaps, a couple of case studies of what these books contain as practical guides to 'the slings and arrows of life'. Publishers of spiritual books know that the common reader needs a simple formula to 'see it through', which means simple language without 'ifs' and 'buts'.

To the popular mind, it is the German philosopher and revolutionary socialist Karl Marx's definition, torn out of context, that religion was the opium of the people that sticks. But this was not all that he said. According to *Critique of Hegel's Philosophy of Right:*

> Religious distress is ... the expression of real distress.... Religion is the sigh of the oppressed creature, the heart of the heartless world, just as it is the spirit of a spiritless situation. It is the opium of the people.... The demand to give up the illusion about its condition is the demand to give up a condition that needs illusions.... Criticism has plucked the imaginary flowers on the chain not in order that man shall continue to bear that chain without fantasy or consolation, but so that he shall throw off the chain and cull the living flower.[3]

Ordinary people turn to religion or some supernatural forces in times of distress when nothing seems to work. Until antibiotics became generally available after World War II, the likelihood of a sick person getting better on his own or with the help of simple country-made herbs was less than 50 per cent: if it worked, well and good, if it didn't it was left to the mercy of God. On such occasions, literature that provided some semblance of hope went down well with the man in the street.

The question, however, is why does religion still hold good even in this day and age with all the medical advances during the last century and more? And not just with ordinary folk, but also with the intelligent, rational and the educated? The educated, who have had access to the best medical treatment, know when, for example, a malignant condition – cancer, Parkinson's, Alzheimer's and several others – occurs and the best that can be hoped for is to prolong the treatment with the least discomfort because there is no permanent solution to the problem. But this does not obviate the need for consolation that such literature holds out.

The intelligent and the educated also know that the healing or the prolongation of a painless life through drugs involves a complex mix of factors and the interaction of some seventy-five trillion cells in the human body. It may also involve removing the threat itself through surgery, strengthening the body's protective mechanism by blood transfusion or, say, by a combination of several other means. However, the way in which a body organizes its defence mechanisms remains obscure and here, too, success depends a lot on chance, on the hit-and-miss methods. One knows of numerous cases where patients have survived a terminal disease beyond all expert predictions and others who have succumbed fast, despite the best treatment.

When chances of recovery are uncertain, patients and those surrounding and caring for them, fall back on inspirational literature to comfort themselves. From experience in the publishing trade of the kind of people who buy the mind-body-spirit, health and self-motivational books, I can say that there are all kinds who do, and the buying of such books is not confined to the common reader alone. If the largest common denominator is worked out, I would say that it is the common people who always have some intractable problem on their hands, who are attracted to such books the most.

Are there any common features in these books? Are they the 'one-size-fits-all' variety or if 'you have read one, you have read them all'? Every book is addressed to specific segment/s of the market and so are those books that explore the relationships among 'the psyche, brain, peripheral and autonomic nervous systems, endocrine gland secretions, immune mechanisms and response to disease', according to Professor Sherwin Nukand, clinical professor of surgery, who teaches medical history at Yale University in Connecticut, USA. Although very different, at least as far as details are concerned, there are two common features. First, they are addressed to the common adult reader who has encountered out-of-the-teens or mid-life crises of some kind or the other – physical or emotional – that need, reassurance. Second, there is a strong element of yoga (and all its allies, like meditation) built into the text – both the philosophical and yogic aspects: breathing and asanas (postures). The kernel of these books, by and large, has to do with yogic practice and the lessons they teach. My conviction that yoga lies behind a majority of these texts was reinforced by the British scholar Tim Parks whose book *Teach Us to Sit Still*[4] drew upon yogic exercises, which he used to cure himself of an unexplained illness that persisted for years despite numerous visits to several doctors in different medical specializations. However, all said and done, written and read, seen and observed, the *main* and most crucial message, between the lines, is to have faith and confidence in your *own* self and the world around you and to get rid of anxiety, distrust and humiliation.

All mind-body-spirit books basically stress that calmness or awareness is the fundamental law of life, which forms the basis of true physical, mental and spiritual health. This is the one quality that leads to positive thinking. Since an ordinary human being lacks such thinking and is generally in an agitated or insecure mental state, mostly thinking of the past and worrying about his or her future, instead of enjoying his or her present, the first step is to acquire this state of consciousness. Spiritual texts stress that an ordinary person is deeply influenced by the interests and attractions created by life itself – health, wealth, pleasures, fame, security, vanity, pride and so on. It is the pursuit of those that give rise to negative emotions, such as violence, depression, anger, fear, envy, jealousy, frustration, suspicion, mistrust, anxiety and so on. Negative emotions take complete control of a human being and cause enormous damage to the human body, both physically and mentally. The task is to control the negative emotions, which can be done through critical self-awareness, a habit that needs to be cultivated.

In addition to the foregoing books are the other types – an extension of the mind-body-spirit category – the 'how to' books, on subjects ranging from dietary courses, specially for the obese, to cooking for vegans, from controlling your finances and planning for your retired life to handling a divorce or avoiding one. You name them and you can get them – ready-made formulas, beautifully packaged and marketed with the label 'only for you'. One may well ask where spiritualism fits into these books. Organized religion has no place. What takes its place is an emphasis on controlling your life, in every sphere, on simple and disciplined living that avoids injury to the body and the soul – both your own and others'. Publishers, and their authors, know that there are plenty of 'troubled souls' out there, and what better way to package all those ideas into books for them?

32

All Those Gods, Godmen and Godwomen

Babas and Swamis; Matas and Ammas

Given the vagaries of the book market where quality and relevance are often trumped by extraneous considerations, it would be foolish to make predictions on the commercial success or failure of new books. However, there is one category, more than even the spiritual and mind-body-spirit books (see the previous chapter), where I could stick my neck out because, in my publishing years, I have literally walked the streets to figure out what the market is looking for. It is for the good, bad or indifferent religious books that deal with any form of organized religion or the life, times and preachings of our godmen and godwomen. All of them invariably attain success. The barometer of success, in each case, may be different, but all do taste that sweet word. There is no other subject that elicits the same success rate consistently.

For example, the Bible always remains in print in numerous editions for all age groups – often given away gratis in hotel rooms and on special occasions, mainly in the West. Its stories are told and retold. Similarly, there are numerous editions of the Gita, the Ramayana and the Mahabharata, which are continuously in print. The Quran too has several editions, supplemented by dictionaries on Islam from various international publishers. (In fact, Islam and the Islamic world have been the most prolific of all subjects). In the past couple of decades or so, books on Buddhism have had good runs in different editions and this religion has seen the fastest number of new converts, followed by simple versions of the Upanishads and Indian systems of philosophy. I dare say the same story applies to other religions like Sikhism, Jainism and many others.

One could say that upmarket religious books have always had a perennial demand for decades but this does not account for the growth of popular religions that have been simplified by godmen and godwomen for the common reader, who has been bewildered by the happenings around him or her and by the pressures of everyday life. And it is not just comic strips of the Ramayana, the Mahabharata, the Bible or the Buddha's life and times as exemplified by the once enormously popular Amar Chitra Katha comics and others. I refer here to the great gush of simplified religious texts by godmen or godwomen (call them by whichever name you want) that have been replacing the 'originals' in the last decade or more.

Three questions arise. First, why have religious texts such a strong hold over readers, particularly in India? Second, what are these books by top godmen and godwomen and why have they taken over the originals to the point that most such persons have their own publishing units to popularize their teachings and are making money out of them? Third, and most important, will these versions replace the classical texts that have held the field so far because they are the 'made easies' for the lay person who doesn't have the time or the learning to go into the philosophy behind the scriptures?

Religion cannot be legislated away. Nor can the mere advances in social and economic emancipation make the supermarket redundant. In today's world, we live with doubts and compromises – even hard core believers do – and in this confused state, ordinary people find comfort in leaving it to God to solve their problems. Besides, as the British author G. K. Chesterton put it in his Father Brown stories, 'when people cease to believe in God, they do not believe in nothing – but rather they believe in anything.'[1] 'The common man may not be able to intellectualize his existential condition but he knows within himself that the world that he sees around him is thoughtless, normless, selfish hedonistic and individualistic', as Michael Harrington put it in his study of the question in his work, *The Politics at God's Funeral*.[2]

It would be redundant to state that the Gita, the Bible, the Quran, and other texts are essential reading for every believer and a copy would be found in every second home or so. But just how much of the message that is contained in these scriptures is understood by the believer or how much is followed in practice is debatable, though everyone would be able to recite a line or two or more from them. That in itself is sufficient to indicate how widely read they are and likely to remain so for generations to come.

Many non-believers ask whether there are any common features to be found in all religions that unites them in their belief in a common God. I am not a student of comparative religions, nor, as I mentioned in the previous chapter, one looking for Him anywhere. However, I do believe from what little I have read in some of the scriptures or seen in practice among believers of different faiths that there is 'something' that makes people stick to an unwritten code of what is right and what is wrong conduct. All religious texts insist on the primordial condition and absolute necessity to know oneself. To gain this knowledge, the beginner must learn to be alive to many-sided possibilities of the ego; he or she must eliminate all obstacles, personal as well as external. Silence and quietness are indispensable for concentration. It has nothing to do with mysticism that puts off many agnostics who describe it as jiggery-pokery.

The fact is, for the common people, it is not easy to read and comprehend the scriptures. Nor can they grasp the meaning between the lines or the underlying metaphors. They want to understand the philosophy provided in a capsule – something simpler, more direct, and easily digestible. Which explains the rise of godmen and godwomen and their literature.

Who are these godmen and godwomen who have proliferated all over? Should we take every self-appointed spiritual guru as God's representative on earth? Should we take each one of them seriously?

If meaning is derived from usage, that is, from the spoken language rather than the written dictionaries, the terms 'godmen' and 'godwomen' are often associated with those people who earn huge amounts and enjoy all the material comforts of life as a result of preaching an oversimplified version of religious texts. And often they have a personal lifestyle that compares in opulence and grandeur with the richest on earth, far removed from the image of a devout yogi who has renounced the way of all flesh. Far from it. Yet, their books (and audio CDs and DVDs) sell and their presence attracts hundreds of thousands of devotees with franchises extended to their close followers who spread the message to establish cults all over the world.

One wouldn't like to extend the definition of godmen and godwomen to genuine teachers who have simplified religious teachings for the common people and who lead an austere lifestyle away from the glitz and glamour. There are many such teachers who have been a source of great comfort to people in real pain or distress and yet they prefer to remain in the background.

Godmen and godwomen who have made it big believe in salesmanship. They sell not only their teachings in the form of books but a whole range of products that go along with it – audios, medicinal herbs, honey, potions that are supposed to cure pains and aches, scarves, badges, meditation cushions and what not. As they grow bigger and wealthier, they set up their own sprawling ashrams in salubrious surroundings, mostly in the mountains or on the banks of rivers, complete with auditoriums, yoga and meditation centres, and of course, their personal chambers.

Some of these godmen and godwomen who have 'arrived' in the consumer society don't hide their success. Let's take the case of two who really made it big, internationally – Maharishi Mahesh Yogi and Bhagwan Shree Rajneesh.

Mahesh Yogi preached 'yogic flying' (whatever that meant) and had a huge following in the late 1960s and early 1970s, ranging from celebrities like the rock-and-roll sensation Beatles. Whatever one may say about him, he was, after all, not a quack. He had studied mathematics and physics at Allahabad University in Uttar Pradesh and believed that 'one person practising transcendental meditation' could induce virtuous behaviour among ninety-nine non-meditators. He gathered hundreds of Vedic pundits to spread the message, which culminated in the Taste of Utopia conference in Fairfield, Iowa, USA, in 1984. Was he a 'crank' or a 'charlatan' or his followers a bunch of misfits who couldn't figure out the world around them? Nobody knows, but his movement fizzled out because he ran out of money. All the same, he did not use the money he got through donations, and he neither drank nor took drugs. At least that's to the best of one's knowledge. Such was not the case with Bhagwan Shree Rajneesh who accumulated scores of Rolls Royces, said to be donated by his devotees. His self-indulgence also included a helicopter that he used to fly in all over while in the US spreading 'the good word of hope and goodwill, not eternal damnation for the non-believer'. He did not promote a cult or mainstream religion because membership was open to all who were looking for peace of mind.

Sometimes, certain religious 'leaders' with a massive following have tarnished their own images, and a few have even been exposed for their acts of commission and omission, to finally land up behind bars. For instance, Asaram Bapu, who has been languishing in jail since September 2013 on rape charges and the self-styled godman, Sant Ram Rishi, who was awarded a seven-year jail term for rape and making threats to kill. The latest to join them is the sixty-three-year-old Sant Rampal Singh Jatin, who was arrested, after much drama, on 19 November 2014, from his ashram in Hissar district of Haryana. Wonder what the millions of their 'followers' and 'disciples' make of them now.

In contrast to such godmen are gurus like His Holiness the fourteenth Dalai Lama, who stand out as a symbol of compassion, love, peace and understanding the world over (see Chapter 33).

All kinds, as they say, make the world!

You name them and I have met them – published some, interacted with most. Over the years I have sold millions of copies of their books around the world in different languages. Most of these titles, published even ten or fifteen years back, sell to this day, generating a steady flow of profits for the publishers and royalties for the godmen and godwomen.

On a lighter vein, my biggest disappointment was a 'much looked forward to' meeting with Satya Sai Baba of Puttaparthi in Andhra Pradesh. I had heard numerous stories of the materialization of vibhuti (holy ash) and various items ranging from gold rings, necklaces to Rolex watches from the air 'along with reports of miraculous healings, resurrections, clairvoyance and omnipotence and omniscience'[3] for his devotees and the pilgrims who assembled at his ashram in thousands. My chance of meeting the 'godman' came on 22 June 1995, when the then chief election commissioner, T. N. Seshan (whose book I had published; see Chapter 36), who was known to him and had access to his inner chambers, took me with him to Baba's ashram. I prayed during the entire journey for the Rolex to be dropped into my hands by Baba, a watch that I immensely desired. Finally, face-to-face with Baba, with only Seshan and his wife present, the watch was forgotten. About half an hour later, on coming out of the meeting, I realized the Baba had not even blessed me with his famous vibhuti. Had he sensed I was on this pilgrimage to Puttaparthi only on 'mission greed'?

My earliest memories, which have meshed into my own being, are of visits to two monuments – Harmandir Sahib (Golden Temple) in Amritsar in Punjab and the Taj Mahal in Agra. Over the last three decades or so they have taken the form of an annual pilgrimage, although they have no religious connotation for me. I go there, simply, because they are there – more magnificent than ever. At times, they are covered with the winter dust, at times washed clean after a weak winter rain. But always majestic! As if to say:

> My name is Ozymandias,
> King of Kings:
> Look on my works,
> Ye mighty and despair.[4]

The Taj Mahal in Agra I visit every full moon in the month of February and the Golden Temple on Gurupurab – Guru Nanak's birthday, which falls in October or November.

Today the Taj is under a security threat and thus the night visits are allowed only on full-moon nights and a day before and a day after. Groups of 20-25 people are allowed, every forty-five minutes or so, after detailed verification and an intense security check. Each group is led into the Taj complex under heavy security cover of armed commandos. I see to it that I am in the last group of the night – the later the better for me. Once inside, after one crosses the gateway that frames the Taj – Darwaza-i-Rauza (the gate to the mausoleum), the main entrance to the tomb – and stands on the portico, till where one is allowed on these full-moon-night visits, the lights are switched off.

The sight is simply incredible!

Over the years I have seen the Taj Mahal in all its glory, in its varied moods and colours – on a cloudy day and under a hot sun; on a dark night and under a full moon; yellow at dusk and covered in a light emerald green early in the morning; I have seen it under thunder, lightning and heavy rain. Yet my greed to see it again and again has not been satisfied.

The hunger to visit the Golden Temple every year too is unlimited!

Built in the sixteenth century by the fifth Sikh guru, Arjan Dev, Harmandir Sahib is the holiest of the Sikh shrines. Guru Arjan also completed the Adi Granth – the holy book of the Sikhs comprising not only the compositions of the Sikh gurus but other saints too like Baba Farid, the twelfth-century Sufi preacher and saint of the Chisti order, Kabir, the mystic poet and saint whose writings influenced the Bhakti movement, as also passages from the Ramayana and the Gita.

Gurupurab at the Golden Temple is one day on which the entire complex is fully lit up. The reflection of a thousand-plus electric bulbs on the waters of the sarovar – the holy pond – around the temple, which then reflect on the domes and its gold-covered, heavily carved walls, is a sight to behold and treasure for a lifetime. There are hordes and hordes of people all around. Most of the times I have never reached the Dakshani Deori, the arch that stands at the beginning of the causeway to the sanctum sanctorum – 203 feet high and 20 feet wide. It is through this arch that the gold palki (palanquin), in all its finery, carrying the Adi Granth, enters every morning well before sunrise, to be installed by the priests in the main temple. This beautiful ceremony is watched by thousands of devotees from all over the world who brave the weather to stand there, bare feet, heads covered, in utter humility, with folded hands and a prayer on their lips.

These two getaways (that's what they are for me) don't fulfil any religious or spiritual need; nor do they provide advanced meditation lessons of any kind. It is not God or any embodiment of the supernatural that is beyond understanding. Basically, in both the places, I am alone with myself – never mind the milling crowds that gather there at any given time of the year – without the temptations of urban living that make life one damned struggle after another. Just the ambience makes it 'not the city of God or Marx, but a city called Peace of Mind'.[5] It is the beauty that accounts for their enduring quality. It is a humbling experience: for centuries the two have stood as a lasting testimony to the creativity of our ancestors that age 'cannot wither her, nor custom stale'.[6]

Perhaps, these visits mean 'coming to terms with myself', which is what philosophers meant when they said 'know thyself'. Whatever the calling, these visits for me are an annual debt that has to be repaid, without which I find myself in a void.

33

The Dalai Lama

The High Pontiff

BUDDHISM IS ONE OF THE FASTEST-GROWING RELIGIONS OF THE world. It is not Islam, despite all its claims, or Christianity, or Hinduism with its many offshoots but simple philosophy and ways of life that has attracted millions across the world.

Does this explain why the Dalai Lama holds his sway on the masses? Clearly it is not his 'battalions' or his wealth that has attracted people to him because it is the affluent West that has warmed up to him. The Dalai Lama is steeped in Tibetan art and culture, Sanskrit, medicine and Buddhist philosophy. The last is the most important and is further subdivided into five categories: Prajnaparamita, the perfection of wisdom; Madhyamika, the philosophy of the middle way; Vinaya, the canon of monastic discipline; Abidharma, metaphysics; and Pramana, logic and epistemology. Apart from these, there are minor subjects like poetry, music and drama.

Taken together, what we have is a well-rounded personality that is an integral part of the world and yet is untouched by its temptations. Everything about him is simple. There is not a trace of ostentation or affectation about him. This is the essence of his philosophy that has attracted people to him.

His Holiness the fourteenth Dalai Lama of Tibet was born on 6 July 1935 in Takster, in north-eastern Tibet. He started his monastic education at the age of six and, at the age of twenty-four, he was awarded the highest Geshe Lharampa degree, equivalent to a doctorate in Buddhist philosophy, at the Jokhang temple, Lhasa. A master of both sutra and tantra, of wisdom and practice, he is known to more than six million Tibetans, who look up to him as their spiritual and temporal leader, as Yeshi Norbu, the precious wish-fulfilling gem, an incarnation of Avalokiteshvara, the Buddha of Compassion. In his own description, however, he is just Tenzin Gyatso, a simple Buddhist Monk.

He was forced to seek political asylum in India on 31 March 1959, with more than a hundred thousand fellow Tibetans following him. Ever since, His Holiness has led the Tibetan refugees in a remarkable success story where even after more than fifty years in exile, the community has been able to retain its unique identity and remain welcome by their hosts.

His humanism has always triumphed over politics. Deeply committed to non-violence and the middle-path approach to the resolution of all disagreements, he formulated The Charter of Tibetans in Exile that has committed his people to genuine democracy including a provision for the Dalai Lama himself to be voted out of his temporal role. He has proposed numerous peace initiatives, including 'A Five Point Peace Plan' first presented to the European parliament that calls for Tibet to be a zone of peace. The Dalai Lama's appeal to the United Nations on the rights of Tibetans resulted in three resolutions adopted by the General Assembly in 1959, 1961, and 1965. He won the Nobel Peace Prize in December 1989, which was a global acknowledgement of his personal spiritual striving as also of his commitment to non-violence, his insistence on the interrelatedness of social and individual human rights, and him being amongst the first global leaders to urge the world to confront the threat of widespread environmental disaster.

He has been honoured with a hundred-odd awards, honorary doctorates, and prizes around the world in recognition of his message of peace, non-violence, inter-religious understanding, universal responsibility and compassion. He has also authored more than seventy-five books. In spite of all these accolades, he remains self-effacing and one of the most accessible public figures. As with all truly great and inspiring leaders, his life is his message and philosophy.

He is more than a Buddhist monk or the spiritual and temporal leader of the Tibetan people. His Holiness represents a progressive and logical continuum of a mind that has evolved through lifetimes and the institutions of the Dalai Lama, of whom he is the fourteenth incarnation. His message of compassion, altruism and peace has made him a powerful moral voice for our times. He works tirelessly for interfaith dialogue and understanding with the courage, humility and respect for other traditions to pray at the places of pilgrimage and worship of other faiths and perform their rituals. The Dalai Lama has embraced the role of science in both deepening our understanding of the human condition and improving it, but urging that this must never be at the cost of human values.

It was much easier to get an audience with His Holiness the fourteenth Dalai Lama, Tenzin Gyatso, those days. He was not the star sage that he is today. All that one had to do was write an official letter to his secretary seeking an appointment and, a week or so later, a telegram would come giving the date and time. That is precisely what I did in early November 1975, and was given an appointment for 19 November at 11.00 a.m. at his official residence in Mcleodganj, 11 km above Dharamshala, headquarters of the Kangra district of Himachal Pradesh in the western Himalayas. That was my first meeting with him.

His Holiness was warm and friendly. He answered all my questions and the story was carried on the front page of the *Indian Express* the next morning. Then onwards, I met him regularly for some news story or the other, and came back from one meeting with a Tibetan woollen jacket as a gift, which I have with me even today. Who was to know then that, thanks to the award-winning documentary film-maker and writer, my friend Rajiv Mehrotra, who is also the managing trustee of the Foundation for Universal Responsibility of His Holiness the Dalai Lama, one day I would be publishing the books of His Holiness! And of Rajiv Mehrotra himself.

The two crucial issues that have plagued the community since 1959 are: the continuity of the pontificate and the Tibetans' return to their homeland. The latter issue has hit the headlines once again, as all too often in the past, as recently as in October 2014 when Beijing issued a strong statement dismissing the possibility of the Dalai Lama returning to Tibet. This was following an indication from His Holiness that he had been in contact with Chinese officials regarding a historic pilgrimage.

It all started way back in July 1976. The repeated announcements by His Holiness that 'most probably he was the last Dalai Lama', coupled with his going into a four-month retreat, had caused distress and controversy in the Tibetan community. Quite a few of them took exception to his statement and went to the extent of questioning his right to close the line of incarnation. Since then His Holiness has repeatedly pointed out that the office of the Dalai Lama was instituted at a time when it proved to be 'beneficial to the nation'. At present, as the institution has changed dramatically, he doubts his own beneficence to his people.

The main question debated was whether the Dalai Lama should interfere with the continuity of the pontificate and whether he (then only forty-one years old) had the right to end the 500-year-old succession. *The Tibetan Review*, the official organ of the Tibetan community in exile, pointed out: 'The Dalai Lama's statement is rather premature and unwise' and added that it 'would not be proper' for His Holiness to end this dynasty 'either for his own good or for the Tibetan people'[1]. Professor Nirmal C. Sinha, founder director of the Sikkim Research Institute of Tibetology (SRIT) wrote: 'If any believers feel disturbed with the Dalai Lama's hints and suggestions, the believers are free to petition the Dalai Lama. When an incarnate lama expresses his desire to enter Nirvana, that is, when he does not like to be reborn, the believers petition him to change his mind.'[2]

However, in this particular case, at that time, the reaction was varied and strange. The believers even wanted to hold a plebiscite on the issue. During my meetings with the Dalai Lama, I had observed his strong leanings towards religious affairs as against political. In an interview, shortly before he went into retreat, he reiterated that he would lay down his political office, which he finally did on 26 April 2011, when the Tibetans elected the forty-three-year-old legal scholar and political activist Lobsang Sangay as the prime minister of the Tibetan government in exile.

I wrote an article for the editorial page of the *Indian Express* 'The Dalai Lama: To Be or Not To Be', wherein I mentioned that the Dalai Lama may be thinking of his own nirvana, after which the cycle of birth and rebirth ends.[3] The Tibetan faith in Mahayana Buddhism rests, among other things, on the first lesson imparted to Prince Siddhartha (who later became Lord Buddha) – 'for thyself and for the welfare of humanity'. It differs from Hinayana, in that a Hinayanaist monk is free to endeavour for his personal nirvana, while the Mahayanist is not. The Dalai Lama's announcement was therefore seen to go against the very faith of which he is the pontiff, and assumed added significance at a time when the fate of the whole community hung in the balance.

The institution of the Dalai Lama rests on the doctrine of transmigration of the soul. Such a phenomenon is beyond human control and does not cease except when the state of nirvana is reached. But then, the soul has to have attained 'Buddhahood' to be able to know (not decide) that nirvana is at hand. Various high lamas and scholars argue that even the Buddha, during his life, before he was born as Siddhartha, did not know whether or not there would be another physical existence – nor did he come to know of it till the precise moment was reached.

The high pontiff, according to the Tibetan belief, is the incarnation of the goddess of mercy, which, according to the Mahayana doctrine, represents the karuna (compassion) aspect of the Buddha himself. Can the incarnation decide that he or she will now cease to have further incarnations? Scholars believe it is for the deity and not for the Dalai Lama to take the decision.

A view has been put forth in certain quarters that the post of the institution came into being when Altan Khan, a descendant of Chengiz Khan, gave it recognition and vested the first Dalai Lama with temporal authority. That he was invested with such authority by Altan Khan is admitted by historians but recognition or no recognition, the institution, no matter what it may have been called, already existed. Equally erroneous is the attempt to describe the line of the Dalai Lamas as a dynasty and then to equate the announcement from the fourteenth high pontiff with the case of Queen Elizabeth II. A dynasty is a succession of rulers related by blood. The Dalai Lamas, as the concept goes, are not different persons in succession but a single individual appearing, disappearing and reappearing. In any case, the question that arises is: Does the British queen have the right to decide that the institution of monarchy should end with her?

There is, however, a school of thought that believes that the Dalai Lama has the right to end the institution. According to the Tibetan expert Eleanor Roos, the only fate awaiting the future Dalai Lamas is of 'figurehead' with reduced power or none at all. In such a case, the Dalai Lama should withdraw from public 'activity' that affects the cost of spiritual progress and be allowed to dedicate his life to a worthier cause.

This school also believes that the Dalai Lama's decision was not that unwise. It could be a 'timely and a kindly' warning to all Tibetans dictated by a wisdom that, in our ignorance, we may not be able to fathom. According to an old prophecy, there would never be more than thirteen Dalai Lamas. However, the saying that the 'Tibetan prophecies have a very special knack of coming true' has already been disproved in this case, for the present Dalai Lama is already the fourteenth in the line.

A question repeatedly asked is: Will the Dalai Lama and the Tibetans ever fulfil their dream of going back to Tibet – their homeland? And even if China were to soften its stand – as it did once way back in 1980 when the Dalai Lama sent three high-level delegations to Tibet in March, May and July of that year, at the Chinese invitation, to study the ground realities in Tibet – what will be the Dalai Lama's official position in the changed Tibet today? The March delegation, in fact, included His Holiness's elder brother Lobsang Samden. Even if the eighty-year-old high pontiff is content to be only the religious authority, which he will have to be, will the Chinese allow him to exercise it without restrictions? Also, how far will the new generations of Tibetans, who have grown up in their homeland without the guidance or even the physical presence of the Dalai Lama, but under the Chinese influence, respect his authority? Will the hierarchical pattern of the Tibetan religion be restored?

If the events of recent years are any barometer, the Dalai Lama's return, as also that of his people, to their homeland is a distant dream. Even if one was to go by the old saying that 'dreams are not ideal nothings, they are the parents of many possibilities', the fact is that the Chinese are unlikely to allow him much scope for reviving the traditional links of the lamas with the Tibetan people because the strength of that tradition now lying dormant can pose a challenge to the Han supremacy if checks are removed.

Lamaism and its institutions may also prove to be misfits in the changed socio-economic conditions. Perhaps, it was in recognition of these possibly irreversible changes that His Holiness had said that he was the last of the ancient line of Dalai Lamas.

Whatever the motive behind this announcement at that stage, the rumblings of protest did make the Dalai Lama more cautious. He has not repeated the point, perhaps realizing the impact of discordant voices of the radicals who had gone to the extent of describing the visits of the three groups of the Dalai Lama's representatives as 'sell-outs'. To eliminate any possible criticism from the younger generation, the second group comprised the then president of the Tibetan Youth Congress, Lesang Jinpa. Vis-à-vis the view of the radicals, His Holiness explained: 'Yes, there are people who may be called radicals. But since we are completely free, it is very helpful to have free discussion. Sometimes they criticize me.... Good.... that is the way to grow and make a sound decision.'[4]

Young Tibetans today argue, and perhaps rightly so, that return to their long-lost homeland is of course the finest dream of every one in exile. But what if the homeland has changed so much, which it certainly has, that the exiles no longer have a sense of belonging to it? What if they are looked upon as unwanted misfits by their own compatriots for whom they are, and will always be, practically strangers or aliens? With the tight Chinese control, or even otherwise, will the returning Tibetans be given a fair chance to merge into the mainstream of modern Tibet? The possibility of their being suspects in the eyes of the Chinese authorities in Tibet and even in those of the local Tibetans committed to follow the Chinese party line, and of their being discriminated against or treated worse, cannot be ruled out.

In going into exile way back in 1959, the Dalai Lama's main mission was to preserve the Tibetan identity, culture and spiritual tradition. If return to the homeland, still under tight Chinese control, results eventually in the loss of identity, it will be the end of the mission. It will be an all-or-nothing gamble. And the Dalai Lama and his followers may not get a second chance once they walk into the Chinese parlour. Even when he made his bid for freedom on 30 March 1959, he narrowly escaped capture.

By remaining in India, the Tibetans in exile at least hold on to what remains of Tibetan nationalism and the lama tradition. But the uncertainty of the future and the frustration of belonging neither here nor there has been increasingly telling on their future. A generation in exile has passed on, another is growing old and a new generation, more Indian (or whichever country they live in) than Tibetan, is growing up or has already grown up under the shadow of this question mark. Tibetan children educated in Indian schools and Indian institutions are totally different from what they would have been if they had been brought up in Tibet itself. The younger generation which lives, and enjoys, a modern jeans-and-MTV culture is technologically savvy, and has adopted a Western way of life. This has also involved an erosion of the Tibetan identity that the Dalai Lama has sought to preserve with monumental patience for over five decades.

Changes in the Dalai Lama's own thinking and outlook during this span testify to the effect of prolonged exile. However, as long as he is around, he certainly provides a great source of inspiration and is a rallying point to his people amidst the ups and downs of their lives in alien lands. What will happen and who will take his place, if and when he departs from the scene or abdicates his supreme leadership? That the twenty-eight-year-old seventeenth Karmapa, Ogyen Drodul Trinley Dorje, who fled from Tibet to India in January 2000, is already embroiled in embarrassing foreign currency cases, is second in line, and could be his successor, is more a myth than a reality. Hence, the vacuum is bound to have an unsettling effect on his people. Pressures will start building up on the leaderless community, which may get riven with group politics and faction fights. In such a situation, Tibetan exiles will have little bargaining power with Beijing. Much will also depend on the attitude of the Indian government, and the governments of the Western countries, and their relationship with China.

The destiny of a nation or race is ultimately decided by the strength of its character, its power of endurance and the will to overcome adversities. The Jews dreamt of an eventual return to Israel since the fall of Jerusalem and the great Exodus. They cherished this dream all through the ages, regardless of the blood and tears and humiliation of the intervening centuries, till the founding of the state of Israel in 1948. The saga of the Palestinian Arabs is the modern counterpart of the story of the Israelites. Despite overwhelming odds, they have kept alive the dream of a Palestinian state and fought their way to world recognition of their demands. But the fact remains that without their charismatic and courageous leader, Yasser Arafat, who died on 11 November 2004, today the cause is not recognized the way it was, say, just a decade back. Whether the peace-loving Tibetans, without the Dalai Lama, have the stamina and resolution to stick to their supreme objective – Tibetan freedom – is something that only the future will reveal.

34

Sourcing Manuscripts

The Art and Business of Publishing

Here are three fundamental facts of the book-publishing world today.

First, publishing is both an art and a business where the acceptance by the market is the final criterion of excellence as in all other businesses. The notion that, instead of catering to the public taste at its lowest side, publishers might seek to improve that taste has been tossed aside as too antiquated and absurd (not to mention 'patronizing') to be voiced in public. Success counts and success means what the market accepts.

Second, in order to achieve sales targets and profits, books have to be commissioned, which means: (a) authors have to be invited to write on specific subjects that publishers believe are wanted; (b) advances have to be paid to authors to deliver against deadlines; and (c) specifics of what the book should contain are clearly spelt out. These are worked out by the publishers on the basis of existing literature and the advice of experts in the field. Commissioning is done across board, from the textbooks in schools and colleges and beyond that includes reference books like dictionaries and atlases, advanced books in science, technology and medicine, accountancy, law and so on. Mass-market paperbacks that have now become a subdivision of the entertainment industry and spin off into television serials are also commissioned with guidelines on the mix of violence, sex and gossip. The non-commissioned books that authors submit to publishers on their own initiative are a very small percentage of a publisher's list, as the rejection rate can be as high as 99 per cent.

Third, advances in print technology and the communication revolution have made globalization a very real factor for publishers. Of late, e-books have been spreading their wings in the market, which is no longer confined merely to a limited geographical area. It extends to a much wider world that can be reached through co-publishing or joint imprints on a cost-sharing basis across clearly demarcated territories.

Insofar as the Indian market is concerned, there are four problems that inhibit the growth of the book industry.

First, distribution outlets and organized bookshops. Most of the bookshops are confined to the metros. Bookshops outside the metros, in small-town India, are undercapitalized and limited mostly to textbooks and newspapers and magazines; they also usually double up as general grocery stores for daily needs. This is reflected in poor cash flows and general liquidity.

Second, the all-India market is limited for English-language books; regional-language publishing is confined to the respective states. Although large in terms of numbers, it is mostly limited to newspapers/magazines or downmarket fiction. This is even true for Hindi, which still cannot boast of a series of textbooks in any subject in the social sciences and humanities beyond Class XII; in the sciences or the upper reaches of technology, it is a blank slate. If there has been any progress in the regional languages, it is confined to Bengali, Malayalam and Tamil, in which a few original works have been published.

Third, despite the huge expansion of educational institutions, good authors are difficult to commission for a number of reasons, but, most importantly, because we are still stuck in our oral traditions. As a general rule, Indians make good classroom teachers but fail the 'written test' that requires a different set of rules adhering strictly to the syllabi provided by the government agencies and the deadlines provided by the publisher. Often, the authors go awry as far as the details are concerned.

Fourth, apart from textbooks, general books for co-curricular reading have never been a priority with us; we stick to what is essential and leave the rest for the libraries to take care of. The result is that publishers stick to basic needs or to books that veer around the core subject areas. Hence, the textbook market is overcrowded and highly competitive where publishers offer discounts, credits, bonuses, substantial gifts and other facilities to entice the trade and the educational institutions, most of which have their own bookshops. The quality of the contents and their relevance do not really matter for the student as the book has been 'prescribed' by the educational institute.

Since the market is the prime determinant of what should or should not be published, it is necessary to define its parameters if one is to arrive at some kind of framework of what sells and why – and also why not. To get started, the market has to be broken down into its various segments: the school level, the undergraduate and tertiary levels, reference books and subject dictionaries; and trade publishing, which includes Indian writing in English covering all subject areas.

The School Market: The book market is like an inverted pyramid, the top layer occupied by the school market that tapers down as one goes to colleges, universities and the research institutions for higher education. The school sector is a mess – a sprawling, shifting mess – that defies rational analysis. This is quite understandable if one were to take into account the different languages in which instruction is provided across the length and breadth of the country – English is just a minuscule portion of the total market – and the unevenness of economic development is reflected in the educational structures. But a working model has to be constructed if one has to make a way through the labyrinth of different schools that coexist in our multilingual society.

If one were to keep aside the preschool sector (often described as playschools) that provides the first entry into the formal school structure, one can divide all schools between Classes I and XII into three types:

1. Schools affiliated to the state boards of education. This category constitutes the vast majority of schools where instruction is provided in the regional language, with English introduced as a subject only after Class V, or at the end of the primary school phase. We have the Delhi Board of School Education, the Punjab/Himachal Pradesh/Haryana/(and so on) boards of school education. Because the numbers involved are huge, these schools tend to be the poorer cousins of schools affiliated, say, to the Central Board of Secondary Education (CBSE).
2. Schools affiliated to CBSE are distributed throughout the country as also in some of the neighbouring countries like Nepal and the Gulf States. The medium of instruction is English with the state's primary regional language as a subject in lieu of Hindi. These schools, funded by the government in some form or the other, have much better facilities than the schools under the state boards.
3. Schools affiliated to the Indian Council of Secondary Education (ICSE) – a younger cousin of CBSE; comparatively, this is a small sector.

Apart from these three main categories, there are a limited number of schools that are affiliated to the International Baccalaureate (IB), headquartered in Geneva, Switzerland, and the 'A' level of the Cambridge Overseas Examination Board – a more recent development.

To cater to the vast numbers, which are rapidly growing, of the school-going population, the Central government has set up textbook boards to provide cheap textbooks. The National Council of Educational Research and Training (NCERT) and the similar state councils (SCERT) provide model textbooks, at all levels, for the subjects within the syllabi. The question that is often asked is whether school textbooks are nationalized or whether the private sector has any role to play in school publishing and how manuscripts are to be sourced in accordance with the syllabi laid down. There is no easy answer to this question because it is a mixed scene. As far as state board schools are concerned, there is a virtual monopoly of what and how subjects are to be taught. Hence, there is very little scope for private authorship, and private publishers, to gain an entry into this reserved sector.

There is, however, ample scope in the CBSE and ICSE for two reasons. Most of the large and well-known public schools are affiliated to either of them and most of the students are drawn from the more affluent sections of society. They can afford to buy higher-priced books marketed by private publishers. Here, one is talking of large numbers. For students in the plus-two stage – that is Classes XI and XII – which prepares them for university entrance, the NCERT books, which are especially tailored to their needs, are used as core texts. But for serious students, the norm of just one text is no longer followed. Hence, again the private publisher comes in.

One of the main reasons why standard textbooks provided by the NCERT and state textbook boards are no longer adequate is the increasing competition from tutorial coaching classes that prepare school-leaving students for entry into professional courses like engineering, medicine, technology and fashion designing. These courses are highly competitive, which demand a great deal more from students than the standard school curriculum.

This brings us to a whole new field of school (and college-level) textbooks. Also, reference books and guides have now become essential tools for a successful student. Language dictionaries that were the only reference books recommended once have now been supplemented by subject dictionaries and guides, which clarify concepts through high-quality photographs and illustrations. This is especially true for science, mathematics and medicine. Primary school textbooks that demand multicolour illustrations have also become the norm. Like it or not, 'guidebooks' of all kinds beginning with Q&As to sophisticated 'made-easy' varieties in almost all subjects, in most cases written and recommended by the teachers themselves, are widely in use. There are publishers whose lists comprise just guidebooks catering to students at every level, each assuring him or her of 'success' in examinations. In a world of increasing competition, where the pressure to do well so as to get admission into a reputed college or institution or university is enormous, that's what matters the most to the students.

While on schools, let's not forget that today there is a spectre haunting India's elite schools – the spectre of unbridled capitalism. Each major, and minor, industrial house or business empire has its own public school, or chains of schools, throughout the country. Every major 'property' developer has spun off a school or two. Many non-resident Indians too have built schools in 'sylvan surroundings'. In fact, whosoever has the funds to spare, or hide, has opened 'nurseries', which would end up as 'higher secondaries' in the years to come. What may have started off as 'philanthropy' in the 1960s, when industry moved into schools in an organized manner to replace or supplement missionaries as the major benefactors of the schooling system, is now big business with a burgeoning school population in the elite English-medium schools where donations, in cash or kind, both below and above the table, are often the basis of admissions. School fees are not a major hassle and regular contribution for school expansion is an accepted price for education. There is money, and big money, and with it comes power, and the smart operators know it.

Those in business know that there will be no let-up in the rapidly growing school population; parents will pay higher fees, donations and contributions; banks will always support them because the school is the best collateral to have these days, apart from tax benefits and social prestige (and power) for all time to come. Above all, the business class knows – like everyone else – that the government has lost its enthusiasm for promoting equality because, if you have equality, you sacrifice the concept of quality, and it is quality that is required in the job market.

However, can it be said that what is good for business is necessarily good for the schoolchild? Do better facilities – more lavish classrooms, airconditioned school buses and swimming pools and over-equipped labs with all the paraphernalia of audio-visual equipment – necessarily make for a more critical and curious mind? Is not much of school success a measure of parental advantage, where learning fills the air at home? Are not they the better teachers who teach the child that information is not as important as the adventure of private discovery and figuring it out yourself? In survey after survey, on school education in India and abroad, it is becoming increasingly clear that better facilities (which, with few exceptions, really boils down to spending more money indiscriminately) do not necessarily ensure better education.

All these are unseen factors, especially in the formative years till the end of the middle school, which matter more than anything else.

Why else is it being said that the public (i.e., elitist) school student does so poorly in national competitive examinations, beginning with the tests for entry to the professional courses, and ending with the civil services examinations in later life? Why is the place being taken over by the lower-middle-class government school student who does not enjoy even a fraction of the facilities available in the public schools? In fact, there seems to be a direct correlation between good facilities and poor students, and vice versa.

A majority of the 'public' schools are functioning like 'public' companies, which does not improve matters educationally simply because the methods of the boardrooms are not the methods of education. Business boardrooms discuss their commodities, marketing, profit-and-loss accounts, balance sheets, a cost-benefit analysis or management by objectives, which means, maximizing profits or returns on investments. These are not the methods of education boards, which (reportedly) discuss educational policies of how to generally improve the quality of instruction and how to perform better in examinations.

Of course, over the years with the economic crunch, more and more school boards are getting bogged down with disputes over wage and staff benefits (all at the expense of education) and, unfortunately, they have been totally oblivious to the earnings and expenditures of the schools. Hence, the need for more accountants and administrators on school administrative boards.

What may have been covert activity has now come out in the open with suggestions to go 'public' to raise funds for massive school expansion. What 'going public' will, no doubt, do is improve the existing facilities in public schools and provide room for more students and more amenities: better educational aids for teaching and, hopefully, better and more dedicated teachers who understand the limitations and potential of their pupils and gear their methods according to the latter's levels of comprehension and understanding of language and educational concepts.

However, apart from better facilities and better human resources, the urgent need is to provide for many more students in the coming decades. This expansion needs money that cannot be raised through raising school fees or 'donations' and 'contributions', or through some largesse by the Central government and state governments, which, in any case do not have it. In fact, the pressure on some elite English-medium schools is so great that many of them have resorted to a two-shift system like a factory. At this rate, perhaps, it is only a matter of time when there will even be 'night shifts' for senior classes. Contrary to what many believe, English-medium schools are considered a passport to immediate success, and this hankering after such schools is not confined to the privileged urban elite but extends all along the line to the newly rich rural classes as well.

In fact, today the real pressure for admissions to prestigious schools comes from the first-generation rural elite and not from the 'box-wallas', bureaucrats or old school students. The rural elite is prepared to pay the donations and also the regular/periodic contributions, apart from the school fees that keep rising every year.

Graduate and Tertiary Texts: 'Uneven development' is the term that economists have used to describe different levels of economic development in countries, though the same term can be used to describe the varying standards of educational development in colleges and universities throughout the country. It is virtually impossible to lay down a uniform educational standard that is found in all parts of the Indian subcontinent: what is obtained in Delhi is not what will be available in Chennai or Kolkata and elsewhere; in fact, even within a limited territory, there will be wide variations in standards.

That is not all. In a multilingual country where instruction is given in a combination of both the local language and English – hence 'Hinglish', that is a combination of both Hindi and English or 'Tinglish' (Tamil and English) or 'Benglish' (Bengali and English) and so on – it makes sourcing or commissioning of texts an almost impossible task. What do publishers provide authors when commissioning them? Is it just the syllabus laid down by the academic councils of universities and/or competing books that publishers hope to dislodge with their books? With wide variations in the linguistic standards between and within regions, what kind of linguistic guide do publishers provide? Publishers have figured out that books with simple linguistic structures work while others that have pitched their standards higher remain limited to the select elite schooled in English-medium institutions. The limits of our language have indeed become the limits of our thought and understanding.

However, these restraints confine the market only to a particular region, which often does not make a viable business proposition. Simply put, it is difficult to commission a book that would be acceptable to all parts of the country. Of course, there are exceptions but these are mainly limited to two categories. First, old texts that have been accepted by older generations of students and teachers and have been passed down as classics because they constitute the core texts on which examinations are based. Second, reprints of English and American textbooks, which are widely used in the universities. (This is especially true of science, technology and medicine, accountancy and other such professional courses, where Indian publishers are rather poorly represented.)

The real problem that confronts English publishers while sourcing manuscripts in educational areas – both in schools and universities – is how to navigate their way through all the restraints in order to achieve a viable print run, which, at the end of the day, will give a reasonable return in terms of profits for the author and the publisher? Unlike other countries in the West that have only to cope with a single language, we have a bewildering range, with uneven standards, which is reflected in uneven scholarship: publishers who commission authors simply can't be sure about the kind of final product they would bring about despite all the checks and balances they have come up with over the years to ensure they have made the right choice of author(s) for a subject.

One has often wondered why such is the state of affairs because there are so many brilliant teachers in our universities who, *potentially*, could deliver. In fact, not just our universities, even those in the West, particularly Britain and America, are full of Indian teachers in practically every discipline. Indian publishers are fully aware of the limits of the market and there is nothing they can do about it. They have to carry on and make the best of the existent situation because there is a potential to be exploited as educational facilities continue to expand, which is matched by advances in print and communication technologies that have cut production costs and made their wider distribution possible through direct sales.

A question that many would ask is whether there is a standard package, in terms of royalties and advances, that publishers would offer authors who are commissioned to write for them. The answer is both yes and no. An advance is normally given but the quantum varies, depending on the author's standing in the field and his or her reputation to deliver the manuscript (of acceptable quality) on time. The entire process is subject to negotiations before a formal contract is drawn up and signed. While a normal advance is given in three instalments – on signing, on handing in the manuscript, and on clearing the final proofs/on publication – more and more publishers are becoming aware of the fact that signing amounts should not be given as more and more authors either do not submit the manuscript on time or just delay it considerably. The normal royalty terms are 10 per cent for hardbacks and 6 to 7.5 per cent on paperbacks of the cost price, per copy sold.

The quantum of advance is worked out by the publisher on the number of copies he or she projects to sell of the first edition within about eighteen months of publication and whether the book would be reprinted and become a part of the backlist. There are many 'ifs' and 'buts' but an experienced publisher, who has worked closely with the sales and marketing teams, does arrive at a reasonable hunch on the potential of the project, despite all the vagaries of the market. Of course, there are titles that do not take off and some titles that become huge successes, but that's all a part of the book business, which in many ways is like making a Bollywood film – you never know till the last minute what will click and what will not. Hence, a working definition of success can loosely be defined as 'recovery of costs plus a reprint'. As mentioned above, publishing is both an art and a business and the art can only survive if the basic principle of business that provides a profit at the end of the day is ensured. The fact is that most of our authors, including the well-established ones, often fail to stick to their deadlines, or even more dangerously, to the brief provided by publishers like the extent of the manuscript, nature of illustrations, indexing and so on. Generally they tend to be lackadaisical in their whole approach. One could cite many examples of authors who were commissioned for a particular project, paid advances but either never submitted the manuscript or gave a manuscript totally different from the brief they were expected to follow. In either case, naturally the advance given is a bad investment that has to be written off, but worse is that the publisher loses the time for capturing the market with that particular project, something that Indian publishers can ill afford.

Yet, despite the fact that it is fraught with risks of undelivered and/or half-baked projects, commissioning authors is the only way to fill the huge gaps in our tertiary lists. Some publishers have argued forcefully that the gaps be filled by acquiring reprint rights from Western publishers. Many have done so over the years, but experience shows that though this may be a way out in some cases, it is not always possible, as there are problems that can't be brushed aside in the haste to make substitutes available. First, the number of titles that would justify acquiring reprint rights for a minimum reprint of 5,000 copies (or why would a Western publisher agree?) is few. Second, in a majority of Indian students, particularly in small-town India, where the actual market is, standards of English are not high and students find the language used, particularly in social science textbooks, too difficult and fall back on 'guidebooks' written mostly by their own teachers, culled from the Western texts, cheaply produced and lowly priced. Thus, a straight reprint is of limited use only to a select few.

Our greatest need for books is in science, technology and medicine (STM), but here reprint rights are difficult to come by; if they are obtained, these are for mostly outdated texts. STM books are with a minimum of 500 pages or so (considered big), in larger formats, and thus priced high with the result that the all-India demand gets limited, which, in turn, does not justify a viable print run.

Hence, with all the constraints, one way out is to negotiate special prices with Western publishers, 'for sale exclusively in the Indian subcontinent only'. That's what is being done more and more, not only for educational texts but also for reference books, journals and general trade titles.

Reference Books: As mentioned above, driven by market forces, publishers have made books a subdivision of the entertainment industry in anticipation of quick returns. The gamble doesn't always pay off and the shelf life, like all fast-moving consumer products, is limited to a few months from the date of publication. What publishers yearn for is a backlist of reference books for all age groups, like dictionaries of all kinds, atlases that are not merely geographical but also scientific that would supplement the main texts in various subjects, and supplementary readers. In fact, reference books constitute a whole new division in major publishing houses that has become a major profit centre, unlike trade publishers who bank more and more on evergreen 'classics', which, like reference books, are for all seasons as they satisfy the regular needs of all consumers – students, teachers or the common reader confounded by the explosion of knowledge.

Yet, reference books are never quite sufficient and difficult to bring out. They are generally 'authored' by a team, not a single author, with usually a chief or a general editor who coordinates the work of different specialists. Moreover, all reference books have fairly long gestation periods and require heavy investments, both in production and marketing. Both these factors apply a brake on our indigenous efforts. Indian publishers have contributed virtually nothing largely because they have not been able to commission authors, researchers, illustrators, indexers, cartographers, editors and proofreaders for the detailed and meticulous work required to be done.

Outside the formal educational structure of schools, colleges, universities and academic institutions at a higher level, where reference books are in constant demand, there is a vast unorganized sector where supplementary books that prepare students for the competitive world are required. It is impossible to categorize these books but the market for them can be divided into two distinct areas: preschool or playschool books and post-school-leaving books that supplement the requirements of competitive courses for various entrance tests.

Recent surveys of the school education scene have revealed that large numbers of middle-class families also supplement formal schooling of their wards with private tuitions that require intense drills in different subjects. Much the same approach is followed in coaching classes, where teachers prepare their own notes and sell them to students, who have no choice but to buy them. In fact, this has become quite a lucrative market.

The rapid computerization in all fields has also thrown up a range of computer reference books, at times beginning from preschool activities through different requirements of middle-school and school-leaving courses. Though computer studies is not yet a compulsory subject across the country, the more affluent schools, which can afford them, have included it in their courses, while the middle class is fast catching up. To fill this demand there are a vast number of books in the market ranging from locally written to those specially commissioned by publishers. This is a swiftly growing market and both authors and publishers know it.

Way back in 1997, the Ministry of Human Resource Development had asked for the establishment of a 'national consortium for higher education textbooks' under the University Grants Commission (UGC) to indigenously produce core textbooks with a 'truly Indian flavour', that would eventually shelve the need for foreign textbooks. The books, which were to be in English as the priority medium, were to 'be Indian not only in the sense that these are written by Indian authors but also they adopt the Indian perspective and use Indian examples and illustrations to make them intelligible and attractive to students'.

The scheme of a core textbook programme for undergraduate courses has been on the anvil since the mid-1960s. The UGC, the National Book Trust (NBT), the Indian Council of Historical Research (ICHR), the Indian Council of Social Science Research (ICSSR), the Indian Council of Agricultural Research (ICAR) and the publication bureaus of different universities have either commissioned or subsidized publications for almost fifty years now. Similarly, the larger Indian publishing houses, or their foreign partners, have consistently drawn up plans for textbooks in all the broad areas of undergraduate studies. The results, however, have been rather dismal. It has been an 'Academic wasteland [where] textbooks failed to make the grade'.[1] Little has changed since.

There are two reasons for the lack of progress in undergraduate publishing. First, a majority of the publishers and their authors in India have concentrated heavily on the school market that is ever-increasing and promises an assured rate of return on investments. As against this, undergraduate publishing takes a back seat. It is risky, time-consuming and calls for much larger investments. Rampant piracy under weak laws aggravates matters further. Perhaps, because Indian scholars know the harsh reality of the undergraduate market, they are reluctant to work on a core textbook, which may, or may not, sell and convert into financial gain for their time and energies spent.

That is, however, not the only deterrent. A greater handicap of publishers out to commission authors is that most serious scholars consider it beneath their dignity to write a textbook and get labelled as 'a textbook writer' for the rest of their careers. They would rather concentrate their efforts on research papers or a scholarly monograph, which few see and none read, but would certainly help them ascend the academic ladder as well as result in other spin-offs like visiting professorships, or invitation to seminars in foreign universities. This is a major factor that accounts for the large number of monographs that lie collecting dust in our universities, and simultaneous relative paucity of good, standard textbooks. One may call it academic snobbery or peer-group competition, but it is a fact that the Indian scholar, who can perhaps deliver the goods, will simply not work on a textbook or supplementary reader programme, whether sponsored by the Ministry of Human Resource Development or developed by a private publisher or a university publications bureau.

Unlike scholarly monographs that are aimed at a narrow, specialized market, textbook writing is a different ball game. In India where the standards of language have declined so sharply over the last fifty years, simplicity has become the first criterion of a 'good textbook'. The sad fact about Indian teachers is that they are very poor communicators in the written language. Years of classroom teaching may have given them some fluency in speech but this has been done at the cost of the written word. As any educational publisher will tell you, Indian textbook writing is too laboured and requires heavy editorial revisions and rewriting to make it suitable for students. But the author feels that since he has 'been teaching for decades' his writing 'is the best and should not be touched'. Such a stand-off leads to further delays in bringing out the book.

Three simple facts of the Indian academic book world are often lost in the rhetoric of the debate for shelving foreign books for 'truly Indian' ones. First, all major Indian publishers have close links with British and American publishers, in some form or the other, as their major distributors and agents and, without their support, their business would fall drastically. Second, barring a few exceptions, books in the English language sell much more than in the regional languages for the simple reason that English has an all-India market. Third, almost 80 per cent of Indian publishing caters to courses of higher studies at the undergraduate level and its equivalent. If one was to put these three basic facts together, there are obvious conclusions that follow. All the publishers who have achieved success in India have done so because of the high margins they have made on distribution of imported books, remainders included. More importantly, their links with Western publishers have provided them with the rights to reprint Western texts prescribed or recommended in colleges and other institutions. What is more, in a majority of cases, these reprints have provided 'models' on which Indian publishers and authors have based their own texts. All said and done, publishing and the writing of books are lonely activities. They cannot be done by committees or 'expert' bodies, which can, at best, draw up the blueprints of a publishing programme. The actual job of conceiving the details of the project, working them out in a presentable format and then writing the text can only be undertaken by two or three persons at the most. Bring in 'committees' and you can be sure that nothing will happen. We have over sixty barren years to prove it.

Academics and aristocratic people, it is often said, live in such an uncommon atmosphere that common sense rarely reaches them. But the growth of research institutions and news media has changed the battleground of ideas in unexpected ways. Today, professional intellectuals are outside the academic sphere; not inside it. And the old distrust of 'academic' intellectuals as free-floating cosmopolitans without any commitment and devoid of risk and depth, has once again asserted itself. That too in a big way. All academic institutions are under fire and the question is not why they have come under attack but how they have managed to remain immune to criticism for so long.

Almost everything with intellectual life comes from the formal institutions of higher learning. Government-run academic institutions luxuriate in the lap of semi-socialist institutions, with complete job security, high salary, elaborate perks and a system of poor review that protects them from outside scrutiny and the wrath that would descend on them if the public understood their functioning. Given the system of peer review, where teachers assess their own tribe by some loose quantitative yardsticks like the number of classes taken or the number of publications to their credit, there is no way to ensure impartiality in assessment of the *quality* of work done in universities and their affiliated colleges. Short of a thorough-going reformation, including the abolition of permanent appointment or its replacement by the tenure system along American lines – where permanency is given on the basis of an impartial peer review based on the quality and relevance of academic writings – there is little hope for any improvement in academic work.

Against the deep rot of formal academic institutions, a lot of vitality in the intellectual world today is to be found on the non-academic side. Independent research institutions, private colleges and universities that have mushroomed over the last decade or so across the length and breadth of the country, professional intellectuals in the media and even the bureaucrats who have to 'sell' their wares and are therefore more hard-working and honest are a much safer 'investment' in the communication of 'ideas' than the formal institutions of learning. Very simply, they are more disciplined by the marketplace and therefore better informed and more virtuous than the arid irrelevance and the intellectual dishonesty of their teaching cousins.

It is a sad but an amazing fact that in the entire field of social sciences and the humanities there would not be more than, say, 150 to 200 titles since Independence that have made any kind of intellectual impact – most of the enduring works of scholarship have come from outside the academic world – and are cited today as secondary sources of reference for any serious work in their respective disciplines. Equally, there are more than 200 titles written and published by Western scholars on Indian themes that are as relevant as ours, if not more, but have a much longer shelf life than the best of ours.

Under an increasingly global capitalist system, where the premium is on knowledge and a free movement of ideas, the only answer to academic stagnation lies in making research more relevant and the review of such literature by experts outside the cloistered corridors of academia. But how does one define 'relevance' under the diverse and highly differentiated and specialized academic world and from where does one find reviewers for respective subjects from outside the academic world preferably, or from within it, if necessary? These questions are not easy to answer in an environment where mediocrity is at a premium and where academic excellence is often measured by political skills than technical knowledge and the ability to communicate in a class where the standards of language – not necessarily English – are abysmally poor. For instance, what would be the relevance of Raymond Williams's *The Politics of Modernism,*[2] Clifford Geertz's *The Interpretation of Cultures*[3] and the *Eurasian Geography and Economics,*[4] and of biographies of well-known novelists like Charles Dickens, Graham Greene and John Steinbeck and how would one work out the criteria of their usefulness to academic courses where everything merges into everything else – politics into religion, economics, sociology, history and so on? The simple rule of thumb followed by small academic minds, which fail to see patterns and concepts from the welter of 'information overkill', is to relate books directly to what is required by courses of study, which were prescribed fifty to sixty years back. Sadly, this will not do any more because, to make sense of the highly fragmented world, we must resort to broad-based general theories. Concepts are necessary to give meanings to the tyranny of facts and theory has to take precedence over empirical studies that were the basic diet of the 1950s and 1960s. Literary, economic, political, sociological and linguistic theories are today the necessary tools for understanding the complexity of interrelationships between disciplines. For instance, charting the historic process is difficult but we will never understand it if we stick to naive romantic individualism because history is more than just the lives of kings, queens and heroes.

Similarly, is it possible to understand a novel without knowing the novelist or, specifically, is it possible to read, for example, John Steinbeck's *Grapes of Wrath* without knowing something of the life and times of the author? Would Michael Crichton's *Jurassic Park* or the works replete with sex, violence and glitz be relevant for the urban elite caught in the rush of daily life? Entertainment is an essential item of consumption in today's world even if it sounds infradig to dull academic minds. The fact is, relevance is an extremely difficult commodity to define and besides, one man's relevance may be another man's irrelevance.

How relevant or irrelevant a subject is, is often left to reviewers who are supposed to 'connect' the work with the potential reader. Sadly, we have not been able to build up a body of reviewers in different fields who should be able to not only assess the intrinsic merits of a work but also create a niche for it in the marketplace. The reasons for this paucity are many and complex but the dearth of reviewers has compelled book publishers and editors to look to foreign scholars to fill in the gaps in domestic scholarship. Ivory-tower academics who scowl when Western scholars review for us do not know the sheer paucity of intellectual talent readily available in India. Ask any educational publisher and he will clear the mist.

As universities and colleges go into a spin with the cutback in grants, and facing tough competition from the newly set up private institutions and universities, most of which claim to be affiliated to or recognized by some Western university or college, one of the most pathetic sights is to see hitherto laid-back professors coming to grips with demands of the market and the cost of the survival kit. How does one raise the resources – through tuitions, which cover less than 10 per cent of the running costs or through private donations that would never come unless there is a quid pro quo built into the deal? Or would universities have to lease out acres of prime land to real estate developers, build up a financial base and then manage within the available resources through management accountants rather than academic councils made up of tired old hands? Tough financial planning is necessary but the much tougher task is to face the crucial question of relevance. No longer can relevance be left to the eye of the beholder, it will have to be left to the marketplace of ideas.

E-Books: The crucial question today in the publishing world is whether e-books or digital books will replace traditional print editions in the near future. Definitions are needed first because we have to be clear what constitutes an e-book in an electronic age.

An electronic book (variously e-book, or digital book or even e-edition) is a book-length publication in digital form, consisting of a text, images, or both, readable on computers or other electronic devices. Although sometimes defined as 'an electronic version of a printed book' many electronic books are without any printed equivalent. Commercially produced and sold, e-books are usually intended to be read by dedicated e-book readers. However, almost any sophisticated electric device that features a controllable viewing screen, including computers, tablet computers, and smart phones, can also be used to read e-books. Actually, 'any device that can display a text on a screen may act as an e-book reader, but specialized e-book reader may optimize portability, readability (especially in sunlight), and battery life for this purpose. *A single e-book reader is capable of holding the digital equivalent of hundreds of printed texts with no added bulk or measurable mass* [emphasis added].'[5]

Although publishers today have specialized e-books catalogues, most of them issue simultaneous print and e-book editions at slightly differing prices. Customers are given a choice (especially useful when it comes to periodicals and magazines), which is important when you consider that many have a shelf life of just a few weeks given the flood of printed material that is churned out by publishers now.

Given this definition of e-books and its place in the publishers' list what will its impact be on the world of books? Technological developments have changed the perspectives of the existing world: the old world is not wiped out all together but its contours are altered so fundamentally that a new world, unrecognized by the old, is born to take over the shape of things to come.

If you go by the figures given out by Amazon and other wholesalers in the West, sales of e-books are almost catching up with printed editions and might even surpass them in the near future.

There are two main reasons why readers are switching their preferences; first, the ephemeral value of a great deal of printed material (why keep stuff that is not required beyond immediate needs or interests?); second, the lack of storage space, particularly in the West, for materials that have no resale value. A great deal of printed matter that is written off by Western publishers and pulped is recycled now because of technological advances.

From a publisher's point of view, e-books fulfil a perfect slot: the technological advances help to save a great deal of inventory space that is becoming more and more scarce because of the avalanche of print materials with short shelf lives. Floor space is a major item of expenditure now.

Books today are looked upon as commodities in a fast-moving consumer market that have to be moved along for others in the pipeline. It is for this reason that the remainder market (that is, books that are taken off the regular shelves and shoved into bargain counters before being sent for pulping) is a flourishing side business to the main lists now.

Of course, some of the conditions that I have described do not apply in their entirety to India because we still get a modest return for stuff we have written off. (Old newspapers, magazines and books are always in demand in the raddi market.) But for how long will such a state of affairs last with the rapid advances in technology?

Technological changes are so rapid that it will be difficult to predict what the future holds for e-publications. A clue can be glimpsed from the newspaper and magazine world in the West where circulation is rapidly declining because of digital editions and hand-held devices that give you what you want at the touch of a button. It is true that newspaper circulation is steadily increasing in India but once prices of electronic tablets and smart phones decline, it is likely that e-books/publications will fill in the gaps. If mobile phones today are replacing landlines, there is no logical reason why tablets will not do so for print editions in the future: they will cost less and occupy less space in an overcrowded world.

Trade Titles: In publishing parlance, trade titles cover a very wide range of subjects from fiction to non-fiction comprising biographies, current affairs, self-help, management, cookery, religion, travel and so on. It is aimed at the general reader of all age groups, who picks it up out of sheer interest, with or without any specific aim in mind; just for the sheer pleasure of reading. Comparatively, the readership here is small for there are very few readers in India who prefer to buy a book. These books are sold through different modes of publicity – reviews and extracts, the print, social and visual media, mail orders, book launches and book clubs, and most importantly, through word-of-mouth publicity. Hence, the rather loose-fitting label of 'trade books' unlike the rest of the above lists that were slotted into various definitive categories.

Fiction covers a vast field from serious stuff to classics to potboilers for the mass market and what has come to be called 'chick lit'. The top-end fiction sells because of its close links with the educational market; the downmarket variety is dependent entirely on the trade. A favourite category among trade books is the current political and economic scenario, both at home and abroad, and these, to an extent, are an extension of daily journalism, which cannot afford to give all sides of the picture. Most of these are with a historical background and a prognosis of the shape of things to come. Hence, their shelf life is rather limited – only a little more than the public interest in the subject.

Then there are coffee-table books, meant more for decoration than reading, and under whose weight many a table has collapsed. These are available on any and every subject you can think of: motor cars, watches and clocks, antiques, cookery, cigars, great moments in sports or history, great personalities of the twentieth century, guns used in the Second World War or the aircraft used in Vietnam, how to enjoy good sex, the Kama Sutra, or simply on anything affecting the daily lives of the people. With the entire emphasis on pictures and illustrations, these are lavishly produced in colour and marketed in fancy covers as gifts for all occasions.

Booksellers in the trade prefer trade books over the other categories listed above because of the favourable trade terms offered by publishers: high discounts, liberal credit terms with the facility to return unsold stocks after an initial stocking period, which could be anything between 120 and 180 days or, as is the normal trend, much beyond. In many ways, it is quite a disorganized sector where the bookseller pays virtually nothing except the space he leases out to a publisher's stock and, in the bargain, makes a killing. For him there is no risk element involved – that's the headache of the publisher and the author.

The bookseller has become an indispensable link in the publishing chain without whom it is impossible to service book buyers; they obtain their choice of book mainly through the bookshops, which supply the varied daily needs of their clientele, know what they want and procure it for them from different publishers. You can perhaps call them middlemen, but as with all trades, they perform a vital function. A recent trend is online shopping, where you order a book, for example through Flipkart or uRead, on line, which is delievcred at your doorstep, and you pay on delivery.

There are basically two ways of procuring manuscripts for trade titles. One, what flows into a publisher's office week after week, unsolicited and from unknown authors. As mentioned earlier, the rejection rate here would be around 99 per cent. Two, a multi-pronged method, which is the only way it works. This includes, being in touch with literary agents, which is happening in India also, and publishers overseas, so that one is on their radar when they are making submissions. This is a formula that may or may not work as today most agents have their favourites and submit, mostly, only to those publishers.

If it is a manuscript one is really desperate for, then, in some cases, the pre-emptive option is always available, but in that case the advance one offers has to be considerably higher than one's competitors.

The most important factor is for the publishers and the editors to keep themselves aware of the current political, cultural and social developments. This is one method that works well in India. For example, a publisher quite often comes across people who mention that they are working on their manuscripts. This is the time to move like lightning, establish contact with the person and get him or her before someone else does. Besides, a publisher or an editor who has an active and an alert mind will immediately spot book ideas even within articles in newspapers and magazines, visual and social media, and commission a potential author who would be most apt to write on the particular subject.

Finally, networking is very important. Over the years, one builds up a healthy network that comprises genuine warmth and not just air-kissing shallow relationships. You can be sure that, that group, however small, will always send your way, any potential author or a project they come across. This networking, I must admit, has helped me bag many a project over the years. Also, once a relationship has been built up with an author, he or she, I can say boastfully, has never gone to any other publisher. In fact, there are numerous well-known authors whom I can name, who moved with me from one publishing house to another including Kiran Bedi, Raju Bharatan, Uma Vasudev, Inder Malhotra, Fali S. Nariman, I. K. Gujral, Salman Khurshid, Shobhaa Dé, to name a few.

Earlier, while talking about various authors, I mentioned how manuscripts were sourced. Here I must mention that I have never felt so bad, and yet so happy, finally, on losing a book as I did, for example, with Tarun Tejpal's *The Story of My Assassins* and David Davidar's *Ithaca*.

In 2004, world rights for Tarun's first novel, *The Alchemy of Desire*, were sold by his agent Gillion Aitken to Andrew Kidd of Macmillan Publishers in the UK for, if I remember correctly, a six-digit figure in GBP, which was a good amount of advance at that time. I was able to buy the rights, for the Indian subcontinent, for HarperCollins India, which I was running at that time. However, the credit for that should not go to me. The fact is that Tarun was absolutely clear in his mind that the Indian rights would go to HarperCollins, as he wanted the book to be edited in India, and that too by my colleague Nandita Aggarwal whose editorial abilities he greatly admired and respected. Tarun could not have found a better editor for his novel! I signed the contract with Macmillan UK on 7 June 2004, for the India rights.

Working with Tarun was a sheer joy. He was personally involved with every aspect of pre-press work – editing, proofreading, selection of fonts, internal and cover designs, and marketing materials. For proofreading, besides the HarperCollins staff, he brought in two professionals, including the charming Vatsala Kaul, who later joined the Hachette Group along with Nandita, so that each page would be read by six pairs of eyes, including his and mine. It was this proof copy that was sent to Andrew in the UK to be published by Macmillan and other publishers the world over. The 518-page *Alchemy of Desire* was released on Tuesday, 15 March 2005, and was an instant commercial success in India. I recommended Marc Parent, who at that time was trying to launch works of Indian authors in France, to buy the French rights for his company Buchet-Chastel. He did. It was published under the title *Loin De Chandigarh.*

The lion had tasted the blood. The French edition of *Alchemy of Desire* became a phenomenal success the likes of which Buchet-Chastel had never had before. In a clever move, which took everyone by surprise, perhaps Gillon Aitken too, Marc Parent came to India in early 2006 and signed the world rights of Tarun's next book *The Story of My Assassins* on which he was working at an undisclosed price – 'an offer I couldn't refuse', Tarun later told me.

Marc was ready for the auction. I, who had by then left HarperCollins to start Hay House, bid for it. In fact, I was so keen on it that I asked my friend Om Arora to talk to Marc, a good friend of his for over two decades. So deep was their friendship that Om had christened Marc's daughter Maya and was her godfather. Om did talk to Marc. But for Marc what was important was the bottom line. And naturally so!

On Wednesday, 24 October 2007, I wrote to Marc giving my final offer. Late that night I got a mail from him:

> Dear Ashok,
>
> Many thanks for your offer and your enthusiasm.
>
> It was a pleasure to walk that path with you, along with 4 other publishers in the beginning, 2 others in the end – and to see your interest in this stunning new novel by Tarun.
>
> However, unfortunately, we have decided – after having thought it [over] extensively – not to accept your offer to publish *The Story of My Assassins* in India.
>
> It will finally be published, for your information, by HarperCollins India.
>
> I nevertheless hope to continue being in touch with you over more great books.
>
> Warm regards,
> Marc

I was very disappointed. Later Marc explained to Om: '... though Ashok's bid was the highest Tarun wanted it to be with HarperCollins not only because it's a bigger name but mainly because he wants the manuscript to be edited by Nandita Aggarwal.' The book was released in India in January 2009.

The rest is history! The book failed to generate much excitement or sales.

Seven months later, on a rainy evening, by which time the fate of the book had been decided, Om and I met for our customary fortnightly Thursday dinner, on 27 August 2009, at the Chinese restaurant The House of Ming at the Taj Mahal Hotel in New Delhi where he toasted my 'not having got the book', over French red wine.

Unlike Tarun Tejpal, I had not published David Davidar earlier. We knew each other but were not on the best of terms (see

Chapter 19). Yet, I was keen on publishing his hew book *Ithaca* that was being auctioned by his literary agent David Godwin.

In May 2010, David Davidar, who was the CEO of Penguin International based in Toronto, Canada, had made headlines in a 'sexual harassment case' brought against him by a colleague, Lisa Rundle, the rights and contracts director, who had filed a suit for damages to the tune of $ 523,000 on 9 June 2010. He was asked to quit and had to return to India.

Ithaca was supposed to be a thrilling account of the publishing world as seen by a publisher himself. David, much in the news with his book about publishing, would be a good sell, one thought. I bid and to make sure that I did not lose a book, I once again requested Om to talk to David. He did. My final bid, sent on Tuesday, 19 October 2010, ran into a seven-digit figure as advance against royalties.

On Friday, 29 October 2010, Charlotte Knight from Godwin Associates wrote to me:

> Dear Ashok,
>
> I'm sorry it's taken a while for me to get back to you. Unfortunately, we have decided to go with another publisher for David Davidar's book. HarperCollins came in with a very significant offer and so we decided to go with them. We are incredibly appreciative of your generous offer and the speed of your response. I'm really sorry that we haven't been able to work together on this title.

Once again, I was disappointed. So was Om. A day later, on Saturday, 30 October 2010, I got a mail from David Davidar:

> Dear Ashok,
>
> I wanted to write and thank you for your enthusiasm for *Ithaca*. I'm sorry you weren't able to publish it. I know you would have done a great job, it's only that the HarperCollins offer was too compelling for me to ignore. Best of luck with Hay House India

and I shall look forward to meeting up when we return at the end of the year.

Best wishes
David

Most gracious of David indeed!

The rest, once again, is history. David's book disappeared from the shelves before it could be noticed.

Once again, Om and I met for dinner on Thursday, 20 January 2011, this time at the rooftop Taipan restaurant at The Oberoi Hotel in Delhi. Once again, he ordered red wine and toasted: 'Here's to your not having got *Ithaca*. Cheers!'

Taking a walk with His Holiness, the fourteenth Dalai Lama, Tenzin Gyatso, on the lawns of his residence in McLeodganj, above Dharamshala, in Himachal Pradesh, on 19 November 1975 (left).

His Holiness, the Dalai Lama, sharing a piece of timeless wisdom on Friday, 21 March 2014, during a meeting in New Delhi.

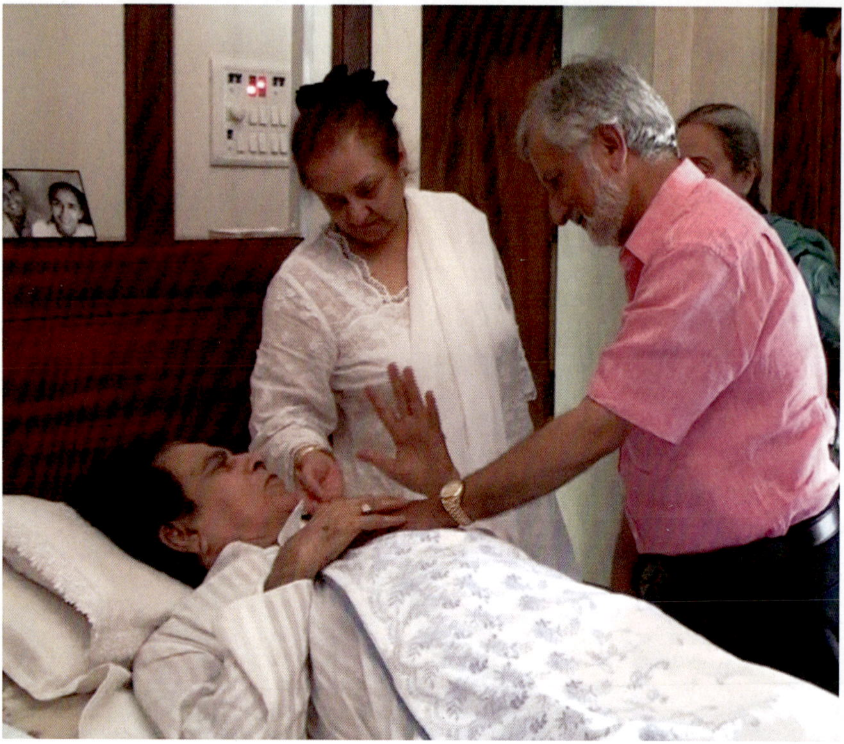

Dilip Kumar: 'Can you hear what my heart is saying…?'
Blessings from Dilip Kumar, a legend among Hindi film actors, that have stayed with me.

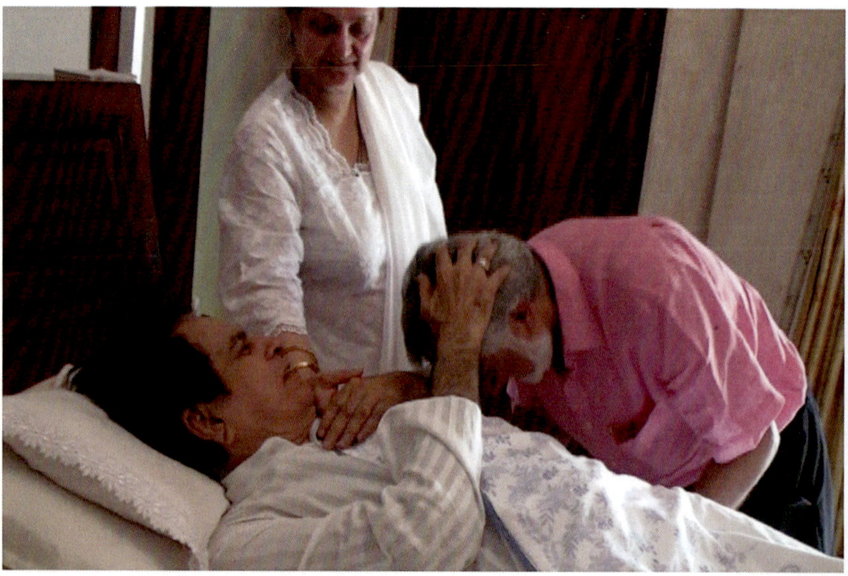

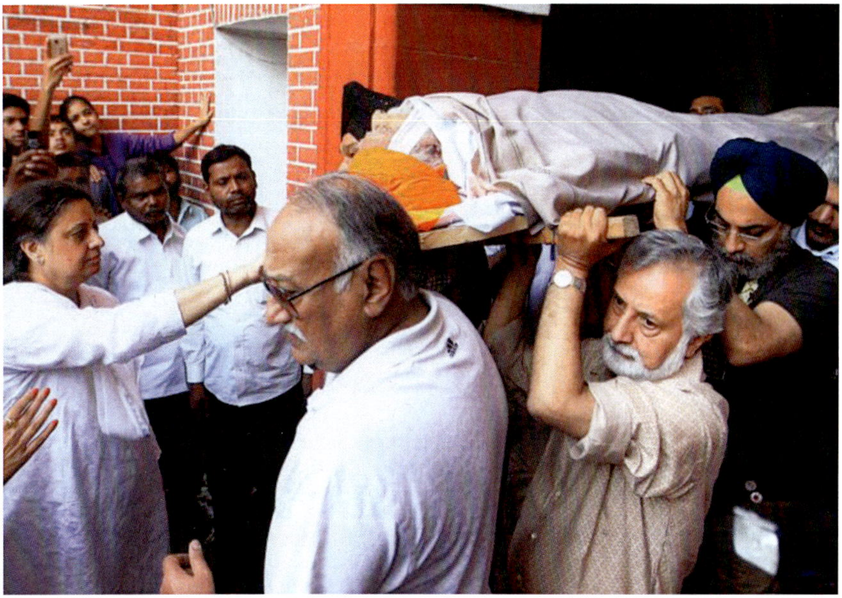

Helping carry the bier with Khushwant Singh's body on it out of his house on 20 March 2014 (above). The marble memorial plaque installed at the school in Hadali, Khushwant's native village in the Punjab province of Pakistan, where his last remains were buried by Fakir Syed Aijazuddin (below).

Two faces of Shimla – the quaint colonial charm of 1903 (above) and the crowded, modern city of 2014 (below).

The exterior of the Gaiety Theatre, Shimla, as it looked before renovation started in 2004.

Scenes from *Cast* (1876) (below, left) and *The Geisha* (1897) (below, right).

Welcoming the President of India, N. Sanjiva Reddy, on the stage of the Gaiety Theatre, where the Army Wives Welfare Association staged Alan Ayckbourn's play, *How the Other Half Loves*, on 21 June 1976.

The delight of every publisher and the envy of every author, Shobhaa Dé has been consistently the undisputed queen of popular fiction in India for nearly three decades.

A still from the movie *Shalimar*, showing Zeenat Aman (above). The book based on it was perhaps one of the biggest disasters of Indian publishing.

The evergreen Dev Anand whom I pursued for his memoirs for many years but did not get to publish eventually.

With Amitabh Bachchan and Anupam Kher at the launch of the latter's book, *The Best Thing About You Is YOU!*, in Mumbai, on 4 January 2012 (above). With Oprah Winfrey and Anupam Kher at the Jaipur Literature Festival on 27 January 2012 (below) and her comment in Kher's book: 'What a powerful title. I believe it' (inset).

Scenes from the World Book Fair (above), India's oldest book fair, held in Delhi, and the Kolkata Book Fair (below), considered to be the world's largest non-trade book fair. Daryaganj in Delhi and College Street in Kolkata are regarded as the hubs of textbook publishing in the two cities.

35

Delhi and Kolkata

A Tale of Two Markets

In a market-driven system, one just cannot ignore mass culture. Whether one likes it or not, it is only possible to stand in some relation to it – a little to the right or the left but it is the mass that sets off a chain reaction of demand that finally matters. At a time when the news of the death of the printed book is constantly being announced, and feared – because of rise of the electronic media as also of the e-book – the crucial question is: where does the mass culture and literature lie in India?

There is no specific instrument to measure the extent and depth of a prevailing culture but mass participation in book fairs, literary festivals, book launches and other book events is clearly as close an approximation as one can get of the crucial variables of the book trade. Unlike Mumbai and Chennai or Bengaluru, the two most important centres of the book trade in the Indian subcontinent are Kolkata and Delhi. Both cities are essentially an educational market with the school sector alone accounting for over half the business. The rest goes to higher education like colleges, universities and the professional courses in various disciplines. The 'book guides' have a place at the downend of the market – Nai Sarak in Delhi and College Street in Kolkata – followed by the trade lists. A great deal of the most sophisticated literature finds some response in both cities, among individual and institutional buyers.

Part of the reason for the greater response is the close linkages both Delhi and Kolkata have with educational inputs and the much greater emphasis placed by both cities on the need for quality education on par with the best in the West. Both are book-buying centres but here the similarities end because there is a vital difference between the 'buyers' in the two cities.

Delhi is primarily an educational market. With three universities – Delhi, Jawaharlal Nehru University (JNU) and Jamia Millia Islamia – and numerous other institutions deemed as universities as also a number of private universities, which have mushroomed under the umbrella of the industrial houses, apart from the presence of a large number of government libraries and research institutions, it is the key centre for library sales. Quite apart from the libraries in the capital that are usually better endowed than elsewhere, Delhi also acts as a clearing house for universities and institutions of the neighbouring states. Given the poor distribution of the book trade in India, Delhi has the largest concentration of library suppliers whose tentacles are spread throughout the country.

Most small towns do not have bookshops worth their name and those that do have are hopelessly undercapitalized to meet large institutional demands, say, from Roorkee University, or the Lal Bahadur Shastri National Academy of Administration, Mussoorie, the Indian Forest Research Institute, the Indian Military Academy, the Survey of India (all in and around Dehradun) and the number of schools and universities of Punjab, Haryana, Himachal Pradesh, Jammu and Kashmir, Chandigarh and Uttar Pradesh. Librarians have to come to Delhi to place their orders and make their purchases.

Kolkata and the neighbouring institutes and universities – the 'neighbourhood' goes all the way up to the north-east on one side and Bihar and Odisha on the other – present just the opposite picture: none of the institutions, which are largely funded by the respective state governments, have even half of the resources that Delhi and the adjoining states enjoy because they are centrally funded by the University Grants Commission (UGC). Institutional sales have hence never provided the badly needed prop to the book trade in east India. It has always come from the people or mass participation. Agreed, individual buying can never match up to huge institutional purchases and, in purely turnover figures, the east cannot boast of even a fraction of the sales in the north. Yet, turnover figures can never be taken as a sure guide to the health of the book trade. If the turnover comes primarily from institutional sales, it conceals two vital truths. First, almost all the business would depend on the availability of funds or, very simply: poor funds mean poor sales. Second, institutional sales in India mean poor liquidity because institutions have never been known to pay their bills within the stipulated credit period. Proper accounting that factors in overhead costs of operation and the loss incurred from delayed payment would show that profit margins are severely cut with an overdose of institutional sales.

This is where Kolkata scores over Delhi. In fact, over the rest of the country. For any culture to grow and flourish, it must have a mass base. And, obversely, if the base is eroded it will wither and die. Here, one must remember that a base is created not by money alone but also by language that determines the limits of our thoughts. In Mumbai, they only speak and read money. In Delhi there is money but no language, except officialese. In Kolkata there is little money, but a language with a strong base that communicates. There is a base made by a motley of individuals, even if they come and go speaking of Michelangelo or Rabindranath Tagore. In Delhi – a miserable city of subordinate existences and excessive snobbery – even the pretence is gone. Moreover, in Delhi everything is in the third person, future tense and with an irregular verb.

One could say that book buying and reading form part of a minority culture. In Kolkata this minority culture is still awake. Literary activity there is most overt, most theatrical and most attention-grabbing. Writers are recognized and accorded celebrity status. Publishers and booksellers have an obvious enthusiasm and elan for what each writer is doing.

While on institutional sales, I must mention here that in many ways March is the cruellest month for the Indian book trade. It is the month when sales to libraries are made before grants for the financial year are exhausted and fresh funds allocated on the basis of their utilization in the previous year. It is also the month in which everything is dredged out from the warehouses for the great library bazaar in the hope that the unwary buyer could be hyped into buying, apart from the new, also the old and the discarded

This literary situation has an upside and a downside. The upside is that it gives an opportunity to publishers and distributors to move out stocks to academics and librarians, which they missed during the course of the academic year. The downside is that in the desperation to exhaust the budget, a great deal of tripe gets sold that is of little relevance to teachers and students. Two questions arise. First, are the March sales, which constitute over 30 per cent of the annual turnover for major publishers, a sign of health for the book world? Second, who is primarily responsible for the injection of so much junk into the libraries – the publisher, the distributor, the librarian or the academic who is the real user?

To a great extent, the March 'drive' comes from the structure of the distribution trade, in which publishers and major distributors make the rules. Because of factors such as high prices, which are beyond the reach of the individual buyer, low discount to the retailer, tight credit policies and the low priority given to books outside the educational system, the retailer has little choice but to make the library the primary market. In this scenario, the individual customer, who pays across the counter or buys online, is just a bonus. Because the economics of book selling do not provide adequate returns on investments, the retailer has to go in for high-discount books that have remained unsold as well as to ensure adequate safeguards to return unsold stocks after months.

It is the inadequate returns on new publications that has driven the retail trade to go in for remainder books – that is, books sold at either a little over cost or, at times, even below cost by the publishers, just to get rid of the unsold stock from the inventory. Remainders have always been a normal trade practice but the pace of remaindering has increased enormously over the last decade or more. In the West, the remaindering period for a new book is small; that is, if the stock does not move within the first three to four weeks, the book is taken off the shelf and returned or put on the bargain counter.

The reasons for the accelerated pace of remaindering are many and complex but the three main factors are: high interest rates, increased costs of warehousing and the number of titles published every year, which shows that the literary world perpetuates itself like any other business enterprise that depends on product perceptions. The avalanche of books that come down the pipe means that every square inch of retail space has to be minutely monitored and books moved and removed to maximize profits. A non-selling title has simply to come off the shelf to make space for the new 'best-sellers'.

Given the low returns on new books and the very fast pace of remaindering by British, American and Australian publishers, the Indian distributors over the last few years have been remaindering in a big way. With heavy discounts on bulk purchases, they can make a decent margin after allowing for some handsome discount to libraries. It is a sad fact but remaindering by the so-called 'remainder kings' of the Indian book trade have made a difference to the health of the book trade.

There is a flip side to the whole business too. Most remainders are discards – books that have served their purpose and have been replaced by more updated versions, particularly in the educational and reference categories. The glut of world atlases in our market or those volumes in subjects such as science, technology and medicine, where updates are available every year, are shining examples of how irrelevant remainders can often be because the basic information is hopelessly outdated.

Because remainders have become a part and parcel of the general stock-in-trade, many believe that every book, new and old, is heavily discounted and, therefore, insist on hefty discounts. This is simply not true because new books and the backlist of steady sellers carry the normal trade discount, with freight and packing extra. So, the distributor cannot afford to give more than the standard terms and conditions laid down for the libraries. Since the distributor is desperate to sell, more often than not, he agrees to the librarian's terms but on one condition: the choice of books would be his. In other words, he would not supply new titles or 'throw' in just a few as a token. The notion that, instead of catering to public taste at the lower levels, publishers and retailers might seek to improve that taste has long been tossed aside as too antiquated and absurd (not to mention patronizing) to be voiced in public, as noted earlier. Success is what counts and success equals money.

Clearly, there are two consequences when the selection of books is reduced to the price-discount factor instead of quality and relevance, which should be the standard criteria. First, the library is cluttered with books that really are of little use to either the teacher or the student. They are there because the discount was attractive enough to buy. No critical judgement on how good or bad the book was or how useful would it be seems to have been applied. There is simply no other explanation for the mountains of unread books, which can easily be seen, almost in every institutional library, from the acquisition date and the number of withdrawals by the readers. Second, what the great library bazaar proves is that academics, who are the best judges of what should be acquired from both new and forthcoming titles, and who are normally a part of the acquisition committees, have in most cases abrogated their responsibilities. The job has been left to the librarians who want to prove their effectiveness by acquiring as many books as possible within the grants allocated to them.

36

Book Launches

Satisfying Egos or Increasing Sales?

A question that I have repeatedly been asked is: Do book launch functions help in the promotion and sales of the book? Frankly speaking, this is one question to which I have no precise answer. When I first got into publishing way back in 1978, a book release was de rigueur for a book to take off and get into the sales orbit. Of course, those days and right through the 1980s, book launches were few and far between. By the 1990s the trend had caught on and every author wanted a 'bash' and, in turn, the publisher had to agree – who, of course, did not mind as long as the author paid the expenses.

There are two types of book releases: The 'genuine releases' and the 'vanity launches'. The genuine ones are those where the publisher organizes an event for the release of a particular book whose author is a big name, where the function draws a big crowd not only comprising the family and friends but also genuine book lovers and fans of the author. Here, the numbers usually are large. The publisher may organize it jointly with organizations like the British Council or join hands with a five-star hotel, a prestigious restaurant or a liquor company to provide 'complimentary' booze for the evening.

'Vanity' releases are quite different. Though the invites go out in the name of the publisher, it is the author who pays for the entire event – the venue, the drinks, the dinner with complimentary copies of the book, duly autographed, thrown in as giveaways.

Over the years, I have seen the best and the worst of them, the lavish and the modest, the craziest and the funniest. And, of course, the most embarrassing ones too. I have attended a book release where the chief guest of the evening (naturally a VVIP politician) forgot to bring along his speech for the event and mumbled just a few lines much to his own and the host's embarrassment. Then there is this VIP, a regular guest at launches, who punctuates his immensely boring speeches at every book release that he is invited to, with some Sanskrit shlokas, which he has learnt by rote, despite the fact that nobody understands or is interested in them. But nothing was more absurd than a publisher failing to publish the book in time for the release date, and one of the most prominent political VVIPs in Delhi releasing a dummy of the book with just a jacket cover on it! He had been warned not to open the book as the pages were blank!

The question is whether a release event helps in the sales of the book or not. The fact is there are no hard and fast rules by which one can assess the returns. It is tempting to believe that those lavish parties end in 'great sales', but the fact that many books, despite a fancy launch over drinks and dinners, with VVIPs, glitterati, literati and at times even a film star or a cricketer or two thrown in, coupled with the relevant Page 3 coverage, have failed to click. On the other hand, there are books and books, which have had no release functions, but went on to become great hits and were on the 'best-seller lists' for weeks and months at a stretch. In both cases, one can cite numerous examples of such books by prominent or first-time authors. Let's take the case of Delhi. A lavish event may result in a few photographs and some lines on Page 3, but is so local – separate editions of newspapers are now being published for the satellite towns, like Gurgaon, Faridabad, Noida – that it, if at all, finally gets a coverage that few see or read. In fact, this Page 3 business is passé now as newspaper managements have become mercenary with the straight policy of 'pay and get yourself published'.

So why do many authors insist on release functions while an equal number of them insist on not having one? A simple answer is that the book world has been seduced by the consumerist/celebrity culture that has become the fashion of the day. Unlike the romantic notions that an author has about his or her book, the fact is that he brave new world of readers is not much different than the cut and thrust of business.

After nearly four decades in the profession, I can confidently claim that a 'good', readable book stands on its own. It is the content that will finally sell – nothing more nothing less. The biggest publicity for any book is through 'word of mouth', which was, and still remains, the most essential ingredient to the success recipe of any book. The middle class, the main consumer of books, wants value for money. If there is none, no amount of salesmanship or marketing gimmicks will make a person part with his or her money. Of course, impulsive buying is there but it is something more of an exception than a rule. The keys to a 'good' book are the age-old factors: the content, its relevance, and the support of a critical readership that passes on its views to equally critical readers. The terms – 'relevance', 'critical readership', 'word of mouth' – are hard to define, and even if one was to arrive at any definition, it would need to be changed regularly because what matters today need not matter tomorrow in a fast-changing book world where the shelf life of books is declining rapidly with the rise of mass media and other distractions that have become a part of our daily lives.

So, would book launches be so much honey and sweet words that brought no tangible returns? Not exactly! Those PR exercises could spin off in other directions at the appropriate time. Also, would release functions come as a damper to one's enthusiasm for the book world? Again, not exactly, but one realizes that the real book world is not as rosy as it is often made out to be. One has to take the rough with the smooth to run with the hare and hunt with the hound. Susan Sontag, America's leading critic, had famously said that 'literature was not an equal opportunity employer'. What she meant was that a good book stands on its own merits, and needs no props like the celebrity status of the author. I would add, even the price and the bluff and the bluster of publicity. I would strongly recommend to every author to leave it to the publisher for he knows when and where to spend, from his budget or yours, and which book to promote in which way to have a win-win situation at hand. After all, no publisher publishes to keep the book in the warehouse, where the inventory costs of storing are high and space expensive. He wants to get the book out there, and is more eager than the author for it to sell fast so that he recovers his returns as early as possible. Give him a *good* book and he will go out of his way to promote it, which he knows how, when and where. He knows what the value of each event would be for the book, and for its author, in return.

Most publishers and some authors too spend a lot of time 'cultivating' journalists, literary editors, columnists and the prominent reviewers who would help review and/or help place the reviews with 'friendly reviewers'. Having been a publisher and a books columnist, I do have a built-in advantage, and know how the system works, as also its strengths and weaknesses. I can simply say that, here again, nothing is straightforward and simple. There are reviews and there are reviews – some informed and critical, some favours done in anticipation of favours to be returned, and a great many just to fill in the slots of review pages, which, being the least read, are as good as not being there. No wonder, India's leader, *The Times of India*, removed its books page years ago, and many others have reduced its size.

One may as well ask what a good book is. How would one define it? It all depends from reader to reader. What may be good for me may not be good for you – particularly in the case of fiction, which is so very personal. However, for me, a good book is like good sex: It should drain you emotionally and physically – something you can go back to again and again. And still enjoy it !

At the best of times, we publishers are like midwives whose main job is to go from house to house to help deliever a baby. Once a baby has been delievered, the umbilical cord cut, the baby washed, dried and attired in new clothes, it is handed over to the proud parents. Then the midwife moves on to the next house to help deliever another baby. But, once in a while, even a midwife, after delievering a baby, holds it in her hands a few moments longer and says to herself: 'Wow! This baby is different.' That is precisely what I thought to myself when Anupam Kher first discussed his book project with me. Yes, it was different and what a success story it turned out to be!

Management guru Shiv Khera has a trademark statement: 'Successful people do not do different things. They do things differently.'[1] The highly talented Anupam Kher, one of the most versatile actors in Bollywood, who has successfully spread his wings into Hollywood too, is a man of ideas. And he certainly does things differently.

Anupam did not want a normal launch for his book *The Best Thing About You Is YOU!* over drinks and dinner with film stars and Mumbai's glitterati in attendance. He had a different idea. On 4 January 2012 his book was released in Mumbai by the eminent film actor Amitabh Bachchan with television anchors Arnab Goswami from Times Now, Nidhi Razdan from NDTV, Ashutosh from India TV, media personality and film-maker Pritish Nandy and Anupam's actor wife Kirron Kher as the guests of honour. Only the media – print, audio and visual – was invited. I for one had never seen such a large assembly of media assembled to cover an event. Each of the guests of honour for the evening spoke on Anupam and read out a chapter from the book.

Anupam achieved what he wanted to. So did we as publishers. That night and the next day the media covered Anupam's book so extensively that it was unbelievable – something every author dreams of but rarely gets. At the Jaipur Literature Festival that year, Oprah Winfrey, who had been presented a copy of the book, wrote: 'I love this title. I believe it.'

October 2002. Tensions between India and Pakistan, always on the edge, were escalating. As the Kashmir issue brought the two South Asian rivals close to a nuclear war, I published J. N. Dixit's (Mani to one and all) *India-Pakistan in War & Peace* under Books Today – an imprint of the *India Today* Group, which I had joined a year earlier to start its books division. This 504-page hardbound edition was later published in the UK and North America as an international edition by Taylor and Francis under its Routledge imprint. This, 'balanced and very readable account of the most tempestuous and potentially dangerous flashpoint in international politics',[2] was acclaimed by Western critics. Like Mani's previous books, it was once again reviewed by the media extensively. At home too reviewers were more or less unanimous in their praise. While *India Today* noted it as 'an account rich in detail',[3] the *Hindu* said it was 'an important, indeed remarkable contribution that takes a comprehensive look in a long perspective.... An insider's account and therefore an authoritative one.'[4] The *Hindustan Times* termed it 'one of the most significant books of India's relations with the outside world to be published since the Cold War....'[5]

The book was exported to Pakistan too. But it never reached the other side. The Pakistani authorities stopped its journey at the border itself. Ironically, it was the UK edition published by Taylor and Francis that did get an entry into Pakistan (and Bangladesh) a few months later.

Mani, whom I had published earlier also (see Chapter 13), was always against any book release function or a launch. Since *India-Pakistan in War & Peace* was the second major title from the Books Today imprint of the India Today Group, the first being Harinder (Shammi) Baweja's *A Soldier's Diary: Kargil – The Inside Story*, I requested Mani to agree to a book release function so that the book and the imprint got good coverage. Mani agreed, though most reluctantly, and got the then Union minister for finance and company affairs, Jaswant Singh, who had just two months earlier, on 1 July 2002, relinquished the charge of the Ministry of External Affairs after a stint there from December 1998, to attend.

It was one book release function, which, thanks to Jaswant Singh, turned out to be rather embarrassing and somewhat hilarious.

The Teen Murti House auditorium in New Delhi was filled to capacity. Those being the heyday of tension between India and Pakistan, the media, looking for a good story too, came in great strength. At the appointed time Aroon Purie, the chief of the *India Today* Group, Mani Dixit and I stood on the portico to receive our chief guest. He came on the dot. After pleasantries were exchanged, Jaswant Singh dropped a bombshell: 'I have decided not to speak on India-Pakistan relations or our foreign policy. Instead, I will talk on reviewing books.' We were shocked. Mani, very diplomatically said: 'Sir, it's a full house … the press is there … everyone is waiting to hear you on India–Pakistan and our foreign policy…' Jaswant Singh, for whatever reason, had made up his mind. He rambled on and on, with canned phrases, dull-witted and lifeless, on a subject, it was so obvious, he was not qualified to handle. Yet, he spoke with the authority of an ignorant. Time, it seemed, moved slowly. Each minute seemed like an hour. A bored audience grew restless. But Jaswant Singh, like a true politician, was in love with his own voice. His own words. By the time he finished the auditorium was half empty. Those present heaved a sigh of relief.

Jaswant Singh, it seemed, was happy with his performance. Mani was really upset. It was undoubtedly the most boring and lacklustre book release function of my career.

The other embarrassing book release was that of Narendra Singh Sarila's *The Shadow of the Great Game: The Untold Story of India's Partition*.[6]

Narendra Singh was the raja of the princely state of Sarila in central India. A former ADC to the last British viceroy of India, Lord Louis Mountbatten, he later joined the Indian Foreign Service in 1948 and served as the country's ambassador to Spain, Brazil, Libya, Switzerland and France. After retirement in 1985, he spent his time shunting between Sarila, Delhi and Switzerland, commenting on international affairs for numerous international journals or writing books, one of which – *Once a Prince of Sarila: Of Palaces and Tiger*

Hunts, Of Nehrus and Mountbattens – went on to be published internationally to good reviews in 2008.[7]

The Shadow of the Great Game was an authoritative work. Sarila's extensive research and meticulous chronology of events that led to the partition of the Indian subcontinent made for fascinating reading. He drove home the point that the shrewd British establishment wanted a buffer state between India and the oil wells of the Middle East. Consequently, the crafty British mandarins assiduously built up Muhammad Ali Jinnah and his Muslim League as a powerful opponent to the Indian National Congress (guided mainly by Mahatma Gandhi). Jinnah, on the basis of his two-nation theory, ultimately succeeded in creating a new nation, Pakistan, with disastrous consequences for the region, whose impact is still being felt after more than six decades.

On 10 September 2005, Sarila and HarperCollins organized a release function at the Taj Mahal Hotel in New Delhi with the cream of Delhi's who's who and the 'royalty' from many erstwhile Indian states present. The panelists for the evening were former diplomat-turned-politician K. Natwar Singh; the then leader of the opposition in the Rajya Sabha, none other than Jaswant Singh; the well-respected defence analyst, K. Subrahmanyam; the former Sadr-i-Riyasat of Jammu and Kashmir, Dr Karan Singh; and Aroon Purie.

After the book had been formally launched, each of the speakers put forth his views on the subject and complimented the author for writing a book that presented a totally new perspective on the partition of India in 1947. Some praised HarperCollins for the production quality of the book. With one exception!

Much to our and Sarila's embarrassment, Dr Karan Singh declared: 'Aroon, I must point out that there are errors in the book, which your editors should have checked....' He then referred to some obscure people of Kashmir whose names had been misspelt or designations given wrongly. One was his own Sanskrit teacher and another his one-time ADC in 1947. The names of the obscure people had been given by the author and no editor could have possibly spotted the error. As the chief guest of the evening, Dr Karan Singh could have discreetly told the author about the same, instead of embarrassing Aroon Purie openly. The damage had been done.

Why Dr Karan Singh did so is a mystery that never got solved.

If I were to pick out some of the best release functions I ever had, I would start with the one organized for the release of Uma Vasudev's novel *Shreya of Sonagarh* (published under the UBSPD imprint; see Chapter 20) on Saturday, 25 September 1993, at the brimming C. D. Deshmukh Auditorium at the India International Centre on Max Mueller Marg in New Delhi. The event was not a routine one that the Delhiwallahs witness every other day overflowing with boring speeches, followed by drinks. The leading Kathak exponent Uma Sharma interpreted scenes from the novel and danced to them to the accompaniment of the tabla beats of Jwala Prasad. As a prelude to each dance scene, L. K. Malhotra, Uma's estranged husband, read out the respective extract from the book to the accompaniment of soft, light music and appropriate lighting. His voice was captivating. Haunting. It was a very enchanting and memorable evening, which the audience did not want to end.

A month later, on Saturday, 30 October 1993, we organized a release in Bombay also. Author Mulk Raj Anand launched *Shreya of Sonagarh* while film actor Saeed Jaffrey and theatre personality Alyque Padamsee read extracts from it on the decks of a large double-decker customized boat which had been specially commissioned, and decorated, for a journey starting from the Gateway of India to wherever it would take us. There were over a hundred special invitees – writers, poets, artists, fashion designers, actors, composers, musicians and dancers. It was a 'tandoori night' with plenty of food, drinks and music. The mood, the ambience and the setting – never before experienced for the release of a book – could not have been better. As the singing started, it brought to mind the boat scene from Kishore Sahu's 1960 superhit *Dil Apna Aur Preet Parai* where Meena

Kumari sings that famous evergreen number, '*Ajeeb dastan hai yeh, kahan shuroo kahan khatam*', to actor Raaj Kumar and the others gathered to celebrate his wedding to Nadira. It seemed the evening, that was to soon merge into the full-moon night, would never end.

It did, but only in the early hours of the morning.

The other book release that stands out in my mind is that of Tarun Tejpal's first book *Alchemy of Desire* published under the HarperCollins imprint. It was released on Tuesday, 15 March 2005, in collaboration with the British Council in its auditorium on Kasturba Gandhi Marg in New Delhi. So large was the gathering that the British Council had to hurriedly open the lecture halls upstairs so that everyone could be accommodated and watch the proceedings on the specially set up video conference screens. The who's who of the city seemed to be there. Aroon Purie, the HarperCollins India chairman, released the book and the first copy was presented to Sir V. S. Naipaul who, in a rare gesture, had endorsed the book saying: 'At last – a new and brilliantly original novel from India'.

However, if I were to pick the grandest and the most graceful book release I have ever had, I would say it was for Admiral S. M. Nanda's *The Man Who Bombed Karachi: A Memoir*, published during my tenure with HarperCollins India. The manuscript had come to me through Khushwant Singh (who had suggested the title too), with the words: 'Take it. It will sell'.

It did!

The book was an instant success and came on the best-seller lists within just a couple of weeks of its release. The reviewers raved about it. The memoir is a 'seafarer's detached story about his life and time and serves as an important source of information about events of which there is no authoritative record....'[8] The author's millionaire hotelier son Suresh Nanda wanted the release function to take place in his flagship hotel The Claridges in New Delhi and gave me a free hand to organize it – all expenses paid for.

The release was organized on 4 December 2003 evening, to coincide with the day Admiral Nanda had organized the bombing of the Karachi port, thirty-two years earlier, under Operation Trident.

A thousand-plus attendees, both civilian and defence forces (mostly from the navy), the who's who of Delhi, a naval band in attendance with the naval police controlling the mile-long queue of cars. On both sides of the sprawling front lawns of the hotel were displayed large photographs of the 1971 Karachi attack. The entire evening was carried out with military precision. On the dot, at 6.55 p.m. arrived the author – Admiral S. M. Nanda, retired chief of naval staff – escorted by two retired naval officers, one his staff officer, the other his ADC. Aroon Purie and I received him, to the accompaniment of the naval band. On the dot at 7 p.m., as the band once again struck up its music, arrived Admiral Madhavendra Singh, the chief of naval staff, the chief guest of the evening. Aroon introduced him to Victoria Barnsley, the CEO, and John Bailey, the COO, of HarperCollins UK, who happened to be in Delhi for the company's board meeting, and led him to the dais, where he saluted his senior, Admiral Nanda. Aroon welcomed the guests, as two giant screens projected the proceedings followed by a fourteen-minute film of the Karachi expedition, put together with the help of the naval authorities.

The function ended on a great high, and for a change Aroon, a man difficult to please, was happy. A month later, another launch of the same book was arranged, this time on the decks of the INS *Vikrant*,[9] in Mumbai. It was a release of a lifetime. The setting was unique – the upper deck of the aircraft carrier. The naval arrangements were superb and left nothing to be desired.

Now I must write about the release of Mani Shankar Aiyar's *Pakistan Papers*.

How does one describe Mani? Highly knowledgeable, intelligent, brilliant, witty, humorous (to the point of being hilarious at times), acerbic, and above all, forthright and thus controversial, one of the few politicians who has a superb command over the English language and is one of the finest orators inside and outside

Parliament. During book release functions Mani is at his oratorical best with huge dollops of humour, at times very biting or immensely wicked, as the occasion demands. He can be candid, especially when it comes to blasting his political rivals. No wonder someone (I think it was lawyer-politician Arun Jaitley) correctly said: 'Mani is at his best when in the opposition.' And today he is there. I published two of Mani's books in addition to the four volumes of *Rajiv Gandhi's India* for the Rajiv Gandhi Foundation, of which Mani was the general editor. The most controversial of these was *Pakistan Papers* (UBSPD), a 248-page volume initially published in hardcover. It focused on how India and Pakistan needed to engage themselves in an 'uninterrupted and uninterruptible dialogue', which has, over the years, become a catchphrase.

Mani, a career-diplomat-turned-politician, spent a few years in Pakistan as India's first-ever consul general in Karachi (1978–82) and penned a long 'top secret' document for the Ministry of External Affairs, which this book *Pakistan Papers* comprised. In it, he examined the pros and cons of four alternative options in the context of the evolving realities of Pakistan over the last half a century: First, the destruction of Pakistan; second, its Balkanization; third, the acceptance of the inevitability of Pakistan as an intractably hostile neighbour; and fourth, the friendship option. The argument built a powerful plea for exploring the fourth option through dialogues. It was an 'outsider's view from the inside', with its perceptions indicating vistas for a relationship between the two countries in the twenty-first century, which might prove less barren than the latter half of the twentieth century.

Pakistan Papers was released at the main auditorium of New Delhi's India International Centre on Thursday, 8 December 1994. The speakers for the morning were Congress leader Salman Khurshid, the BJP stalwart Sikander Bakht – both excellent speakers who could keep any audience spellbound. But Mani's coup was to get the then Pakistan high commissioner in India, Riaz Husain Khokkar, to be the chief guest of the morning. The diplomatic corps of Delhi and the media came in full strength and, quite naturally, the auditorium proved to be a little too small for the large gathering, a majority of whom had to go back disappointed.

Riaz Khokkar came with his full contingent, each one of whom was seen taking notes of the scintillating debate on Indo-Pakistan relations, as each of the panelists pitched in with well-reasoned arguments. Ultimately, the morning belonged to Riaz Khokkar and his oratory. He had certainly read Mani's *Pakistan Papers*, from cover to cover, and had come fully prepared. Riaz Khokkar admitted at the outset that he had come 'without taking permission from Islamabad' to preside over the function and 'whether it would go well with Islamabad or not' he did not know. He had 'risked his job'. Had he? (He kept on climbing the greasy pole to finally become Pakistan's foreign secretary.)

Perhaps it was all theatrics! But the media, and the audience, lapped it all up, giving extensive coverage to the function with most of the papers displaying on their front page Mani and Riaz Khokkar in a bear hug and both with big smiles. At least, on the surface it was great bonhomie. The end result was that *Pakistan Papers* got so much publicity that it was a big commercial success – any publisher's dream wish, any author's desire.

Mani can be a great friend – ever helpful and always there for you – whose friendship one can treasure. Or a staunch opponent who is best avoided, if you know what is good for you. I recall an incident narrated to me by the then principal of St Stephen's College, New Delhi, Anil Wilson. At the college's annual dinner of old students, the guests as usual signed the visitor's book with a comment or two. K. Natwar Singh, also a former diplomat-turned-politician, known for having a chip on his shoulder whom Khushwant Singh once described as 'an overambitious mediocrity' in one of his columns, wrote: 'Whatever I have learnt and whatever I am today is because of this college.' When Mani's turn came, he read what Natwar Singh had written, put an asterik mark there, drew an arrow and wrote: 'Why blame the poor college!'

Mani and I have kept in touch off and on – more off than on. But whenever he hears of a good book for publishing, he informs me immediately and goes out of his way to get it for me – right from 1994, when he got me Salman Khurshid's *Beyond Terrorism: New Hope for Kashmir*, then an instant bestseller through to another best-seller in 2013, *What's Wrong with Pakistan*?, by the well-known Pakistani journalist Babar Ayaz. My biggest regret is that he never wrote another book. I have thrown numerous hints and even spoken to him directly, but Mani has not taken them seriously. I wish he would, for I would, like any other publisher, love to publish him again.

A mention of Salman Khurshid reminds me that few publishers can claim to have published the works of both the husband and the wife. I have: Salman (*Beyond Terrorism: New Hope for Kashmir*, 1994, and more recently *At Home in India: The Muslim Saga*, 2015), and his wife Louise Fernandes (*Travails of Chachi: Conversations with a DLY Taxi Driver*, 2014). It has been a great experience, and joy, working with both.

Trained as a lawyer, Salman, who hails from an eminent family (his maternal grandfather was Dr Zakir Husain, a renowned and respected scholar and freedom fighter and a former president of India), is a senior Congress party politician, who over the years has held several important ministerial portfolios in the Central government. Highly knowledgeable, articulate and a seasoned political commentator, and one of the finest speakers in the country, both in and outside Parliament, he does not shy away from dealing with crucial and extremely sensitive topics such as fundamentalism, communalism, terrorism and minority alienation. His command over the language, his grasp of the subject and his felicity of expression have enabled him to put forth his ideas, views, opinions and perspectives in a lucid and unambiguous manner.

Way back in early 1994, I had interacted with him many times during the course of the publication of his first book *Beyond*

Terrorism. He was then minister of state in the Ministry of External Affairs. I found him to be warm, easy-going and open to all editorial suggestions in the text.

At Home in India came out of an informal conversation at his home twenty years later, on the afternoon of Saturday, 18 January 2014, when we were exchanging views on minority rights in a democracy. The book had to be basically a candid and forthright account highlighting how Muslims *do* feel at home in India despite numerous provocations and allegations questioning their patriotism and commitment to the idea of India. Salman agreed to take up the project, despite the fact that he was busy, very busy. The 2014 general elections were round the corner. Besides, he also had a full-time job as the minister for external affairs. Frankly speaking, given this scenario, my colleagues in the office had no hope of the manuscript being completed. However, having worked with him earlier, I had no doubts about it and knew he would do it. And he did it – eight days in advance of his deadline. How did he find the time to work on his manuscript? When did he write? How did he meet the deadline, and that too ahead of time, is still a mystery for me. Indeed, a great lesson on the dedication and passion of an author to his commitment.

Presently, I am working on two more books with him and am very excited about them, both very contemporary and powerful subjects – provocative and revealing, informative and educative – which, gripping as they are, will be, I am sure, extensively discussed and widely studied, and reviewed.

Before I end this chapter on book launches I am reminded of another launch connected with Mani.

Most of us would recall that in the 1990s (1990–96) the then chief election commissioner, T. N. Seshan, had become the most talked-about, written-about and the most feared man by the political class though loved by the common man. He was also known for his sharp and crisp one-liners to his superiors and ministers or while handling the media.

Monday morning, 17 April 1995, was a wet one with intermittent showers through the day. We at UBSPD were to release Seshan's much awaited *A Heartful of Burden*, a 158-page volume in hardcover, comprising his views on various subjects including the Indian democratic electoral process and politics. The panelists were the irrepressible Khushwant Singh as the chief guest, supercop Dr Kiran Bedi, opposition leader Jaswant Singh and Mani Shankar Aiyar. The subject was 'What's Wrong with India?' It was once again one of those book releases where the auditorium of the India International Centre was overflowing. While the other panelists had arrived, as also T. N. Seshan, there was no sign of Mani who was to fly in from Madras that morning. Presuming that the flight had got delayed, we started the function.

Khushwant released the book, and in his remarks, was exceptionally complimentary to Seshan who, he pointed out, was the 'right person to be the next president of India', amidst huge applause, something he had written about in his column also. Kiran Bedi was in the middle of her speech when Mani entered wearing the traditional Tamilian dress – a white khadi shirt and a veshti (dhoti).

Mani, who was introduced by Khushwant as 'the finest speaker India has got' started dramatically: 'I am late by fifteen minutes but I make no apologies about it. I took off from Madras on time to be here on time. But once near Delhi, we kept hovering around for nearly half an hour, waiting for our turn to land, because of something known, and I quote, as "VVIP movement". And this VVIP movement is the singular gift to this nation, at the huge inconvenience to the common traveller and immense expense to the nation, of a person known as Mr T. N. Seshan. That, ladies and gentleman, is what is wrong with India. It is people like Mr T. N. Seshan, in seats of authority, that is wrong with India.'

For a few seconds there was dead silence and then, suddenly, the audience erupted into laughter, and applauded. That was the signal

Mani was perhaps waiting for. He went on to castigate Seshan for his domineering behaviour and other perceived shortcomings. He attacked Seshan for being a bully, like a schoolboy, giving one example after another. Mani, who had worked with Seshan in the former prime minister Rajiv Gandhi's office, went all out for Seshan for his role as the cabinet secretary and pointed out that while Seshan's role was to 'protect' the prime minister, his role as Rajiv Gandhi's election publicist, was to 'project' the prime minister. 'While Mr Seshan was busy shielding the prime minister from the media, my job required me to expose him to the media.' The issue formed the crux of the Mani-Seshan clash.

Mani was in full form and there was no stopping him. Seshan, sat through it all, very, very patiently, smiling a couple of times in between at Mani's barbs. Who knew what was going on in his mind?

Once Mani finished his peroration, Seshan got up slowly, walked to the podium and started by thanking the audience, Khushwant Singh, Jaswant Singh, Kiran Bedi and me in that order, and 'particularly Mani for having taken the trouble to come all the way from Madras for my book. I am very touched. I am honoured. And very grateful to Mr Mani Shankar Aiyar. And will always be.' There was no sarcasm in his tone. Nor any rancour, at least on the surface. It seemed he meant every word of what he said.

Seshan talked about this and that, about his book and how it was put together. Just when everyone thought that he was about to conclude, he took off by rebutting each of Mani's accusations, point by point, with tremendous patience and equanimity. And what a performance it was! He had been challenged and was not going to lose the battle under any circumstances. It was a verbal duel between the two south Indian Brahmins. He tore into each of the points Mani had made earlier. Seshan had an elephant's memory and could quote verbatim long passages, be it from the scriptures or prose or poetry. That morning he quoted the right one, at the right time, at the right point. He had all his facts right, as also his arguments. His one-liners were a real treat: 'The Indian Civil Service is neither Indian, nor civil nor service.' 'What is this IAS (Indian Administrative Service) except saying "I Am Sorry". I am saying in public that the civil service in India has got reduced to the condition of polished call girls.'

Another one: '... Mani, you bet your last penny that if it becomes necessary I shall grunt, I shall growl, I shall bark and ultimately I shall bite. And don't ask me why an *Alseshan* bites because it is customary for an *Alseshan* to bite'.

The audience loved every word, every sentence, every moment of it. The applause, at times, was deafening. But Seshan in his superfluous outburst perhaps got carried away and made a mistake that was to expose him later as a man of double meanings, of double standards. A man who changed his values as it suited him best.

Referring to Khushwant's remark that 'Seshan was the most suitable candidate for being the next president of India', which Mani had also touched upon very sarcastically, he said: 'Thank you, Sir... I also thank you all for your generous trust in me. Thank you very much. But no, Sir, no. No. I am not here to be the next president of India ... the next president of my country. I don't have any such ambitions. I am very happy to be the chief election commissioner.... I have my task set out before me and I just want to finish that. Then I will retire as a satisfied man to my modest home in Madras. But before I retire, I have to clean up this rotten system. Do you know how elections are run in this country? Liquor for the father, cloth for the mother and food for the baby.... In a booth in Bihar where the polling starts at seven o' clock in the morning, by 7.15, 105 per cent of the votes are cast.... And, there are rolls which are extremely defective. There are names which appear five times, there are names which don't appear at all, there are dead names which are still alive and there are live names which are dead ... I have to clean this for you all ... for my country. And I will do it whether you like it or not Mani ... whether anyone likes it or not.' (Huge applause.)

Then turning to Mani, he carried on: 'You really think, Mani ... you seriously think I want to be the next president and sit in the Rashtrapati Bhavan? Forget it ... forget it. Let me tell you, Mani, in the presence of the very respected Mr Khushwant Singh, in the presence of the honourable Mr Jaswant Singh, member of our great

Parliament, the illustrious Kiran Bedi … no Dr Kiran Bedi … in the presence of my young friend Mr Ashok Chopra … in the presence of this eminent gathering and the media, that not to talk of becoming the president of India, I don't even want to be the president of the Rotary Club or the president of this Max Mueller Marg club, if they have one. I just want to do my job and retire to my little home….'

That evening, at a dinner at my house, Seshan and Mani were cordial with each other. And yet cold. A year and a half later on retirement on 11 December 1996, Seshan, who in his own words, had 'the outstanding achievement of being universally hated by all the political parties', made a U-turn and did just the opposite of what he had been proclaiming all along. He desperately started mustering the support of all possible political parties – big or small, known or unknown – to be the eleventh president of the Republic of India. In July 1997 he even contested against K. R. Narayanan and, needless to say, lost, getting only 50,631 votes in comparison to Narayanan's 956,290. Overnight, the man who had once been the 'darling of the masses', whom the common people had come to perceive as an honest upright man with morals, whom they believed was a messiah come to clean up the rotten system, was dropped like a hot potato, and forgotten, only to become a footnote in the history of the election system of India.

Mani, of course, had the last laugh. And the last word. A month or so before the presidential poll took place, Mani gave it off to Seshan at another book launch function, whose details I don't recall, at the same venue, which draws more or less the same crowd for every function:

> … Don't you think Seshan's pathetic attempt to become our Rashtrapatiji proves everything that I have said about the old fraud? First, he describes his IAS colleagues as 'prostitutes', forgetting that since he made [it as] cabinet secretary, that makes him the madam of the cat house! Now, after getting the admiration of his fans by saying he will retire to his 'modest house' in Madras immediately on attaining superannuation from the chief election

commissionership, he is doing his damnedest to get into the most immodest palace in India. No wonder Gandhiji wanted to convert Rashtrapati Bhavan into a hospital. I doubt if that Seshan would have wished to become a male nurse.

37

AUTHORS

Their Quirks, Their Highs and Their Lows

WHAT COMPELS AN INDIVIDUAL TO TAKE UP WRITING? IS IT loneliness, suffering or as the Canadian-born American writer Saul Bellow felt 'ninety per cent spleen'?[1] And do writers have a central concern in their writings or are there dramatic departures in their basic passions? Can one write without a philosophical base, some kind of a meditative philosophy or a 'moral puzzle'? Above all, how do writers work – what are their schedules, idiosyncrasies and writing habits?

These were some of the questions that the *Paris Review* interviews in its 'Writers at Work' series (April 1990 onwards) asked some of the leading contemporary writers and provided fascinating insights into their compulsions, their 'highs and lows' and the very human qualities that keep them going at a time when the printed word has been assaulted by the visual culture and all serious literature is at a disadvantage in the marketplace. It was a fascinating study that provided an answer to their basic 'drives', their modus operandi and finally what keeps the writers going when the world around them is 'going to rack and ruin'. Is there a camaraderie in diversity – a common ground of profound seriousness about the writing predicament?

Yes, there is. First, the beginnings themselves. Almost all writers started off as journalists with some downtown newspaper, graduating into the mainstream, and when they realized that 'journalism is not literature in a hurry', they took to serious writing. It provided the first spark. However, many writers continued their journalistic pieces even after they were recognized as front-rank writers – that was combined with a 'cathartic experience', which drove them to describe the 'human condition' in whatever fragments they chose as their milieu. Some kind of catharsis is almost always there, which could be 'internal or external exile', suffering or the total helplessness to help someone you love, which provides 'some turn in the character' as a 'way of dealing with violence within oneself'.

If all writers try to impose structure on their individual experiences as an exercise in self-analysis, there is also a tremendous diversity simply because our reactions to them differ so greatly. Each writer 'sees' the fragmentation of reality in his or her particular way. Literature, it is said, is meant to show the fragmentation of truth – and it is their ways of seeing the kaleidoscope of life that makes their thoughts, their views and their ideas so interesting to follow.

For Joseph Brodsky, for example, brought up in the harsh realities of post-revolutionary Russia, the fundamental theme of his poetry was the nature of time: 'What time does to a man.' And since time is so transient and fleeting, the only thing that lasts for him is 'language.... If there's any deity to me, it's language.... In the works of better poets you get the sensation that they are not talking to people any more, or to some seraphical creature. What they are doing is simply talking back to language of which the poet is a clear mirror ...'[2]

For the art-historian-turned-novelist, Anita Brookner, brought up in a strict Jewish household, the whole writing game is about 'love ... what else is there? All the rest is mere literature!'[3] But love, to her, is almost always 'innocence betrayed – the duality of innocence versus experience.'[4] The chaos of emotions, 'the inexorable progress towards further loneliness'[5] drives one, according to her, 'towards existential position....' For her, based on her own experience and her own conditions, 'I am one of the loneliest women in London',[6] and life has to be lived 'in absence'. 'It is only under conditions of complete isolation that some of the big questions that literature should raise come up.'[7]

Going through the lives of poets and authors like George Orwell, Walt Whitman, Ernest Hemingway and William Faulkner, to name a few, we find how mentally turmoiled they were: suffering from depression and suicidal tendencies, alcoholism and 'seriously dysfunctional personality deviations.' According to Doreen Carvajal, 'Since Aristotle observed that "since no excellent soul is exempt from mixture of madness" speculation about the link between art and insanity has been a lingering topic, probed and studied by academics whose laboratory rats are literary biographies'.[8]

If creative writing can be described as a novel way of viewing the usual and mundane in everyday life, then eccentricity – something offbeat – becomes an essential trait of any writer, big or small. Eccentricity is an essential norm therefore of all writers and artists but the degree to which it approaches deviation – usually sexual – and sheer madness is something that comes to light when belated biographies of the dead and the famous come out, written either by those closest to them or by researchers who have delved into what they can call 'the springs of their genius'.

For instance, Leo Tolstoy was a sexual pervert who was involved in numerous affairs. Charles Dickens had a number of simultaneous affairs, and Ezra Pound, after his honeymoon, ended up in a loony bin. American philosopher-novelist, Ayn Rand, who most of us read as a 'must' during a certain phase of our lives, landed up in a lunatic asylum. Virginia Woolf, the English writer and one of the 'foremost modernists of twentieth century', was 'throughout her life plagued by periodic mood swings and associated illness'.[9] Her depression in March 1941 was so severe that on the twenty-eighth of that month she wrote a letter to her husband, Leonard Woolf, put on her house coat, filled its pockets with stones, walked into River Ouse in east Sussex and drowned herself . Then there was the American poet and novelist Sylvia Plath who suffered from depression for much of her adult life. Early one morning (11 February 1963) she placed her head in the oven, with the gas turned on. She was just thirty.

One can keep on writing about such examples endlessly. In fact, as more skeletons tumble out of cupboards, it appears that every writer has been slightly daft and has had his or her peculiar angularities – some innocent and childlike, others vicious and murderous. Says author Anne Hollander: 'Writers come under intense pressure to create, a process that others may not understand. You wake up every morning and say what am I doing? What is the point? I am going to have a drink. I am going to force myself to stare at the wall and write. You sit and you stare and you move a comma from here to there. This kind of thing is very, very taxing.'[10]

Our Indian authors are no better. However, one perforce has to avoid naming any of them, simply because I have no time for legal cases or money to engage lawyers, or the time and patience to collect witnesses to be present for those endless hearings in overcrowded courtrooms. Hence, instead of delving into the peccadillos of our writers, I will limit myself to mentioning the idiosyncrasies of some of the better-known ones, which have provided them with an outlet for their creative energies and given us some of the finest pieces of literature.

Perhaps the greatest short-story writer in Urdu, Saadat Hasan Manto, would always dress up in sparkling-white kurta-pajama, sit stooped in a chair with his legs drawn up under his body, its weight falling on them. Urdu novelist Ismat Chugtai once recounted: 'I saw a man stooped, like an insect in a big chair against a large table.'[11] Manto loved fountain pens. In Bombay, where he had plenty of money while working in the film industry, he would go around looking for the exorbitantly priced Parker and Sheaffer pens – the most prized brands at that time. It 'was their novelty, rather than utility that attracted him, for he seldom used them. To write radio plays and film scenarios, he used his Urdu typewriter, which was a slower process but gave him time to think, while for short stories he always preferred a soft pencil, which helped his hand keep pace with his thoughts'.[12] Ismat had a green 'ladies Parker' fountain pen gifted to her by Manto, which I finally inherited, and is one of my prized possessions, despite the fact that it doesn't work any more.

According to Manto's nephew Hamid Jalal: 'Though an agnostic, Manto would start every story, essay or play by inscribing the number 786 on top of the page, which means "In the Name of Allah". And if he ever forgot to do so, he would discard the paper and start afresh on a new sheet. Commenting on this, Manto once remarked: 'I who often deny the existence of God in one stroke, become a believer on paper'.[13] Shoes, sandals and gold embroidered jooties [footwear] were the love of his life, and he loved giving them away. Once, at a friend's house, the host praised his newly acquired jooties. That evening, on his way out, he quietly left them behind for his friend and walked back home barefoot. 'In fact, next to alcohol, footwear remained his abiding interest in life'.[14]

At his grave in Miyan Sahab cemetery in Lahore is the following epitaph which he chose himself:

> Here lies Saadat Hasan Manto. In his breast are buried all the secrets and nuances of the art of short-story writing. Even *now* weighed down by earth, he is wondering if he is the great story writer or God![15]

Ismat Chugtai too had her own peculiarities. She kept an old pack of playing cards near her with its greasy smell tickling her. She would always sit on a mattress on the floor of her study-cum-visitors' room where a bolster was used as back support and a munim's (accountant's) desk as her writing table. She would keep on playing cards with her left hand and writing with her right one. Punjabi prose writer Gurbaksh Singh inhaled fresh jasmine buds, which lay on his writing table. While poet-lyricist Sahir Ludhianvi wrote in a state of high excitement or frustration, Mulk Raj Anand (an author known for his realistic works) had a special chair – like a baby's high chair – on which he climbed to write.

Khushwant Singh was a star writer – the only one who was recognized on the streets of most cities and towns in India and stopped for photographs or autographs or both. He may have been a simple man going by his attire, but he had some of the most expensive writing habits. While for writing his columns he used any pen that came his way, he started every new book of his with the most expensive pen in the market – a luxury he could afford and enjoyed. I often asked him what he did with the pens once the project was over. He never took the hint! (Finally, I think, just to shut me up he gifted me a Cartier gold oval ballpoint pen.) He wrote only on yellow, ruled pads, always imported from a particular shop in Paris. He had a very small, in fact tiny, handwriting resembling ants crawling on paper. He never used a writing table – instead would sit in his living room, on an easy sofa-chair, next to the fireplace. He would put his feet on the spine of a cane stool and place his writing pad on his knees to write every day for hours together. When he worked at *The Illustrated Weekly of India* and later at the *National Herald, New Delhi,* and *Hindustan Times* offices, he would half pull out a drawer of his office table, put his feet on it and write with the pad on his knees. A man of strict habits and a slave of self-imposed timings, he had a very tight writing schedule and was exceptionally rigid with his deadlines. Few know that while writing he would always have paan (betel leaf) and chew tobacco.

Poet Amrita Pritam would lie in her bed for hours before she would spring up with the energy of a tigress and start writing either a sad poem or a happy love story.

Playwright Balwant Gargi could never work without a study table, though he would never write or type himself. He would always dictate directly to his secretary who would sit opposite him at the typewriter, with endless cups of boiling tea, though hardly consumed, being quietly placed and removed, at regular intervals by his cook. A telephone instrument, with its receiver off, was also a must next to him. In fact, it was the ticking sound of the electric typewriter, which he had imported from America, which set his thinking powers in motion making the words flow out. On the table had to be a dozen-odd imported ballpoint pens, in various colours, and reams of expensive typing paper. Mostly the page took just about six to eight typed lines. 'Rest of the space is for editing and corrections', he would say.

Shobhaa Dé is professional to the core who never interferes in the working of her editors. Like many authors I know, she too writes longhand and is very generous with her handwriting – long and big letters, with just about five lines or so fitting a page. Her handwriting reminds me of a cockroach, which, after a dip in a bottle of ink, is let loose on a sheet of paper.

Full of contradictions, writers are, mostly, ruthless and sensitive, emotional and uncaring, charming and unpleasant, who are in love with their own images. They have crazy habits and different ways to kick-start their imaginations and some of them have built up mnemonic devices to set them off on each day's writing task.

French writer Guy de Maupassant, considered as one of the fathers of the modern short story, loved to sit on a Turkish rug while writing his stories; German poet Friedrich Schiller kept overripe apples by his side while composing poems. Russian writer Maxim Gorky, constantly struck matchsticks while writing and held the burning sticks in his hand as he went on throwing these, at intervals, into an ash tray. Famous American composer-poet William Goyen, who always spoke of writing as 'singing', wrote only under bed sheets with a flashlight.

Probably the most bizarre case is that of the American author Ernest Hemingway, which was later supplemented by his biographer Carlos Baker.[16] Bitten by manic depression, which finally drove him to suicide, Hemingway would always 'work in his bedroom divided into two alcoves' by a part of a chest-high cluttered bookcase. It was on top of one of these that Hemingway had 'his work desk, a square foot of cramped area hemmed in by books on one side and on the other by a newspaper-covered heap of papers, manuscripts, pamphlets, bull-fighting journals and stocks of letters bound together by rubber bands.'

Hemingway always wrote while standing, 'in a pair of his oversized loafers on the worn skin of a kudu – the typewriter and the reading board chest-high opposite him.' He always worked 'in absolute concentration, moving only to shift from one foot to another, perspiring heavily when the work went well, excited as a boy, fretful, miserable when the artistic touch momentarily vanished.'[17]

American author and film-maker, Norman Mailer, had a 'writer's costume', that is, faded dungarees and an open-necked sport shirt. He worked in rooms with long views – sea, ships, anything with a vista to it. He disliked looking on to gardens. A disciplined writer, he wrote only four days a week – Monday, Tuesday, Thursday and Friday – and for a very definitive five hours.

Author of the famous classic *Dr Zhivago*, Russian novelist and poet Boris Pasternak, was, according to many, totally in love with his own image. He was a living legend – a hero to some and to others one who had sold himself to the enemies of Russia. He was available only on Sundays when he held an open house. Even his lectures and interviews had to be scheduled only on that day.

A regional American poet who achieved international stature and won the Pulitzer Prize for a record four times, Robert Frost, always wrote while seated in a blue overstuffed chair, which he had specially designed to write in. It had no arms, which left him the room he needed. He never had a table or a writing room. He wrote on anything and everything, including pieces of paper, bedsheets, handkerchiefs, walls, glass in the bathroom and even the sole of his shoe.

American playwright Tennessee Williams, who claimed to be a 'born writer', followed a daily routine he adhered to most of his adult life, that is, get up at dawn, go straight to the typewriter to work for four hours and then go for a swim.

Rebecca West's biggest eccentricity was to be at her 'bitchiest best'. She never had a good word for another writer. To her, the great Russian master Leo Tolstoy was highly overrated and his monumental *War and Peace* was 'no great novel'. She never ever 'admired the eminent English author E. M. Forster and never understood how could anyone read the French novelist Marcel Proust'. While she didn't like T. S. Eliot a bit because he was a 'poseur', the British novelist and master short-story writer Somerset Maugham 'couldn't write for toffee. He wrote conventional short stories, much inferior to the work of other people'.

The famous co-author of historical books like *Freedom at Midnight* and *Is Paris Burning?*, Dominique Lapierre (see Chapter 10), writes longhand even today, with a pen dipped in a bottle of ink. For his book *Beyond Love*, he once told me, he consumed thirty-four bottles of ink to write over 2,100 pages as the first draft. And it is always on the same quality of paper, which he has used for over five decades and the same ink – 'Parker Quink Permanent Black'. In his study, all along the walls are numerous small shelves, which, instead of books, display the hundreds of empty ink bottles used in the writing of his thirteen books over forty-five years – from *Is Paris Burning?* in1965 to *India mon amour* in 2010. And he has catalogued each one of them. He explained to me: 'I keep a necklace. I keep it in my study. In my office I have a number of necklaces, one for each book. I write longhand and then my wife Dominique [they share a common first name] puts it all on the computer. I never touch those machines. I don't even know how they work and I don't want to know. Computers, mobiles, faxes are all huge distractions for my writing. They keep you linked perpetually to the outside world, when all I want is to be really flying, swimming in my own atmosphere. When I am not progressing well with my writing, I saddle one of my horses and go riding in the hills ... that is my yoga ... my nirvana. Here, I resolve all my problems. I am able to find a better beginning for my chapter.'

Lapierre's biggest eccentricity is that he burns agarbatti (incense) day and night though only in his study and bedroom, which 'smell more of incense than a Hindu temple does'. For him, this 'is very important as smell captures a place. I am reminded of an atmosphere by smell, even more than my vision.... I am told that more agarbattis are made in India than ... we have cheese in France. Just as a great wine lover selects his own wine, I have my own brand of agarbatti, which is not easy to find so I always get them in large quantities'.

Chilean author Isabel Allende always, without exception, starts every new book of hers, only on the eighth day of January, 'partly out of superstition but also for reasons of discipline. I always write the first line of my books on that day. When the date approaches, I try to be alone and silent for many hours; I need a lot of time to rid my mind of the noise outside and to cleanse my mind of life's confusion. I light candles to summon the muses and guardian spirits, and place flowers on my desk to intimidate tedium and the complete works of Pablo Neruda beneath the computer with the hope they will inspire osmosis.... In a secret ceremony I prepare my mind and soul to receive the first sentence in a trance, so the door may open slightly and allow me to peer through and perceive the hazy outlines of the story waiting for me ... I do not determine the subject, the subject chooses me; my work consists simply of providing enough time, solitude, and discipline for the book to write itself.'[18]

Part Four

There comes a time when you have to choose between turning the page and closing the book.

– Josh Jameson

38
Past and Present

English Book Publishing in India

I favor the god, Janus, who faces
backward and forward at once. Without a
vivid link to the past, the present is chaos
and the future unreadable.[1]

After nearly seven decades since Independence, Indian publishing stands at the edge of a vast transformation. What was once a cottage industry, decentralized and improvisational, run by a small group of like-minded people, devoted to the need of writers and to the diverse interests of readers, has burgeoned into a giant communications industry that embraces myriad forms – books, newpapers, magazines, music – that have an inexhaustible appetite for ideas.

However, the situation has an upside and a downside. The upside is that the literary world is now open to anybody who can string two sentences together, whether they make sense or not. The downside is, as mentioned earlier, success has become the only criterion of excellence and success means money. Writers have become valuable assets like brand names, worth far more than the income they actually generate – though they could, in certain circumstances, generate a good deal.

Hence arise the following questions: In the current literary situation, has there been a contamination of literary values by considerations of fame and money? Is Indian publishing at the crossroads and, if we can see the future, does it work? Or will technology determine what goes in and how it is packaged rather than the content and its relevance to our needs? Or as the playwright asked: 'Will technology so arrange the book world that we no longer experience it?'

However, before I proceed further I must clarify that this is not a comprehensive report on the developments in Indian publishing since Independence, nor any thesis, nor an authoritative research paper. Nor does it cover the whole Indian publishing industry scenario. Necessary and urgent as such a survey would be, it is beyond my competence, even though Indian publishing is at the threshold of a 'great leap forward'. I can discuss only Indian publishing in English and how I have experienced and seen it. All in all, it is a personal assessment. Nothing more, nothing less.

Besides, reliable statistics of regional-language publishing are not available and without figures to support my views, it would be presumptuous to project one point of view against others. In a multilingual country like ours, due representation must be given to regional language publishing to provide a balanced picture of the state of literary activity; not to do so would smack of literary chauvinism in favour of one group against another. Hence, this section is a little more than reminiscences of an individual who had the good fortune of working with some of the leading publishing houses in senior capacities. While doing so, I have also usurped the observations of some of my senior colleagues in the publishing and print world, as also of journalists and columnists, who have had a wider range of experience than I could have possibly gathered in a lifetime.

Thomas Macaulay and his establishment of the English system of education with his 'Minute on Education'[2] of 1835 have had a profound impact on the internal market for books in the English language – a market that continues to grow quite rapidly.

There are two main reasons why books in English are in growing demand despite the end of colonial domination nearly seventy years ago. First, as mentioned earlier, India is primarily an educational market with a great emphasis on textbooks in all subjects and at all levels from schools to colleges to universities and beyond. Second, again, regional-language publishing has not quite kept pace with the explosion of knowledge, particularly in science, technology, medicine and other professional spheres. Without going into the reasons, which I have discussed earlier, regional-language publishers, taken together as a body, have very little to offer both in terms of quality and quantity, compared with their counterparts in English. Certainly unfortunate but a stark fact, which can be seen in the mad rush for admissions to English-medium schools and the mushrooming growth of English teaching shops not only in the metros but also in every corner of small-town India.

With a growing body of intellectuals, fluent in English, which is recognized as the language of international communication, books in English are preferred over those in the regional languages. 'The language of instruction, examinations and competitive examinations, as well as theses and dissertations',[3] is to a large extent, English. It is because of the continuing domination of English in the job market that over 40 per cent of all books published are in English, despite many attempts 'by government and non-governmental agencies to encourage the use of regional languages for official and academic purposes. It is this historical background that has made India the third-largest producer of books in English (in terms of the number of titles published annually) after the USA and Britain.'[4] And with advances in print technology and software development, India has become a major exporter of finished books apart from being a hub for typesetting, printing and binding.

There has been a considerable growth over the last three decades: the number of publishers of all-India standing has increased immensely with every publisher, big or small, having a presence in all the major cities. Delhi, for instance, with its growing middle class and the prosperous diplomatic community can boast of a couple of good bookshops, though the number is disappointing given the fairly large English-speaking population. The per capita consumption is still deplorably low.

The weakness of the situation doesn't arise from the fact that English has a very narrow base: there are other major reasons, like the fact that the English-speaking elite is more drawn to imported books rather than the indigenous variety.

In this scenario, what of the Indian languages and their share in the total volume of Indian publishing? Take Hindi, the 'official' language of the Indian Union. Prima facie, it enjoys a number of advantages as a publishing language: half of India's population, or over 500 million people, use Hindi or its variants; it is the language of the great majority of Indian films and numerous television serials, which are watched by millions all over the country. Hindi has been systematically promoted for educational and administrative purposes; the Central Hindi Directorate and six State Granth Akademis – in Himachal Pradesh, Haryana, Uttar Pradesh, Bihar, Rajasthan and Madhya Pradesh – publish and promote Hindi at all levels. If you go by numbers alone, the Hindi-speaking population has grown enormously.

Yet, where are the bookshops for Hindi books? Even in the Hindi heartland (the six states mentioned above coupled with Uttarakhand), there are virtually no bookshops that stock titles in Hindi; they are generally mixed with titles in English or with all those newspapers and magazines sold on the pavements or, worse still, in the kirana (general merchandise) stores. This stark fact is something that we have to face up to: production of books is meaningless unless matched by distribution networks of wholesalers and booksellers. Without their active support, no publishing programme can take off. What you normally see in Hindi are poor imitations of Western downmarket stuff: sex, violence, popular paperbacks or quickies, or, at the most, those cheaply translated and poorly produced editions of mind-body-spirit and self-improvement translations of Western best-sellers.

The state of Hindi publishing has often been commented upon but none of the fault lines have been identified. A telling story of what has gone wrong could be learned from the experience of Macmillan India that had embarked on a Hindi publishing programme in the late 1970s and early 1980s. There were original works as well as translations of standard English-language textbooks. The programme flopped and was finally scrapped.

Why?

In the post-mortem that invariably follows a disaster, there were just unconvincing answers: First, scholars capable 'of presenting scholarly material in Hindi often still preferred to write and publish in English, whether in India and abroad'.[5] There was no rational explanation for this failure to attract Hindi scholars to write in Hindi for a wider audience. Second, wrong kind of books were published, the prices were too high for the Hindi market and, above all, there was a marketing and promotional failure. Since then, both Penguin Books India and HarperCollins *Publishers* India launched Hindi-publishing programme, comprising translations of titles published by them in English but with limited success, if at all. These lists also include original Hindi titles. In my extended discussions with Hindi editors, I could find no convincing answers that would account for the failure of nearly fifteen years of Hindi publishing. So I have come up with answers of my own.

First, any publishing programme in India (which, as I have said, is essentially an educational market) will depend on the state of education in schools and colleges. If these are moribund, as they are in the Hindi belt, books will have a low premium. Where can publishers sell their books in the absence of bookshops on college campuses? This was a problem faced by Macmillan field representatives who could find very few outlets for their publications. Sadly, this is an academic apathy that is not encountered elsewhere in the country.

Yet there is a paradox: Hindi newspapers and popular magazines continue to outsell their English counterparts in ever-increasing numbers. And this is not merely because they are priced lower and trade incentives to newspaper vendors are more than for their English cousins: they are on par with the rest. So does the explanation lie in the quality of education in Hindi as against that in English?

Which leads to a bigger question: Why do books in Bengali and Malayalam, the two regional languages that top the list, sell more than those in English when the number of bookshops and trade outlets are as limited? Is there a historical explanation for this disparity? Both language groups have to be examined separately because generalizations will not explain the exceptions that crop up in the two markets.

Unlike the print media, Indian book publishing statistics are notoriously unreliable because of the fragmented nature of the industry in this multilingual country. English-language book publishing is somewhat better served because it has a longer recorded history since Independence, even though ours is an English-speaking country only to a very limited extent. Of a population of over 1.25 billion now, only about 30 per cent are literate, and of these only about 10 per cent are functionally literate in English, which makes a population of just a few million. This is a sizeable market and it is a population that is constantly growing because, as mentioned earlier, the higher echelons of education and subjects such as science, technology and medicine are taught in English, the regional languages having failed to provide adequate literature that would equip students for the job market.

The question one has to ask is: how far has English-language book publishing progressed since Independence and whether it has created sufficient literature over the years to provide students with core materials in different disciplines to cater to varied demands of the market? To answer this question, a brief background of the major Indian publishers in English and their evolution over the years would be necessary.

I have divided this chapter into two sections: the first from 1950 to mid-1980s and the second from mid-1980s to the present, during which computerization and the communications revolution changed the face of the publishing industry the world over. These dates are somewhat arbitrary but I have taken 1985 as the watershed because, by the mid-1980s, most Indian book publishers switched over from the traditional letterpress printing to computerized setting and offset printing that brought their production standards on par with English-language publishers the world over.

The dozen or so English-language publishers had direct or indirect links with book importers and distributors, and, in fact, were called 'agency houses'. In this group, the most prominent were the wholly British-owned Indian branches of Oxford University Press, which has been around for more than a century, Macmillan Company of India, the Longman Group in Orient Longman and Blackie of Glasgow, which was recently bought over by the powerful Delhi publishing house, S. Chand.

The American companies were comparative newcomers; in fact, US publishers were not directly represented in India till after the end of World War II. With the fast advances in science, technology and medicine (STM), the demand for American books grew rapidly and Indian distributors turned to them for their requirements of the Indian market. The initiative was taken by Asia Publishing House that pioneered tertiary-level books mainly by acquiring reprint rights for titles that had run their course in the American market but were still in demand in the Indian subcontinent.

The indigenization of Indian publishing really began with low-cost Japanese reprints of STM books, which were later reprinted under licence in India. To keep prices low, 'the production costs were subsidized by the USIS[6] (United States Information Services) with PL 480 funds that were generated from US Wheat Loan rupee interest funds'.[7] The subsidy models were later adopted by the National Book Trust (NBT) and other agencies to produce university-level textbooks. It was an experiment that worked for a while but eventually withered away because of bureaucratic red tape that private publishers found too cumbersome to deal with.

With the adoption of American textbooks, it was just a question of time before American companies came in with Indian partners. In this group were Prentice-Hall of India, Wiley Eastern, Affiliated East-West Press that was associated with Van Nostrand. The biggest catch was McGraw-Hill, which joined hands in India with the country's most reputed and credible name – the Tatas – and set up, what till recently was known as Tata McGraw-Hill – exclusively, for reprints of standard American texts adopted or recommended by Indian universities. It must be kept in mind that most of these companies concentrated more on distribution than on reprinting for two reasons: first, licences to reprint were not as easily given as is often made out; second, reprints of limited editions did not bring down unit cost of production on which pricing would be based. But the principle of foreign collaboration had been established, which led to spin-offs in other directions, like encouraging Indian authors to write their own stuff, despite the fact that most of the writing was adapted from Western texts.

The growing presence of English-language publishers led to wholly Indian companies being set up. One could call it 'the demonstration effect' but the real reason was that Indian publishers-cum-distributors (they were distributors of imported books first and publishers later) realized that the margins in imported books were small compared to our own books. This awareness that publishing too was a business and not a charitable activity undertaken by gentlemen of leisure may be said to be a silent revolution that led to modern management techniques being adopted by publishers.

Quite naturally, it led to wholly Indian companies that developed and concentrated on their own lists. The pioneer was Asia Publishing House (APH), that at the peak of its activity, was said to be publishing around 250 titles a year according to its then chief editor, Samuel Israel, the doyen of Indian pubishers. Most of these titles were scholarly monographs submitted for doctoral thesis, that had a subsidy attached to it for publication, which came in handy. There were also general titles that had a distinct educational bias. What was remarkable was that APH established a foothold in British and American markets that took care of a small proportion of the print run. With tight management and editorial control, this was enough to establish the APH imprint in the West too. Sadly, its fading away from the Indian market became an object lesson of trying to do too much too soon when the market wasn't ready for it.

Following closely was S. Chand & Co., which was soon to become the leading publisher of textbooks. A single-proprietor firm, Shyam Lal Gupta acquired exclusive reprint rights for a number of university-level texts primarily on accountancy and commerce and virtually dominated the market in the field. With this as a base, he moved into print machinery and real estate, buying up small firms that specialized in the primary- and middle-school market – in fact, any title that fitted the school curriculum. Gupta knew that schools were largely state subjects in our federal set-up, and he established his hold on state boards of education. Much of his success was because of his ruthless business acumen that left the well-established foreign publishing firms in the shade. He succeeded where Oxford-Macmillan-Longman failed simply because he represented the Indian face of publishing, which went down well with state boards still imbued with the 'nationalist spirit' that considered any linkages to the past as anathema to the growth of indigenous publishing.

In the early 1970s, Vikas Publishing House, set up by UBS Publishers' Distributors owner C. M. Chawla, with Narendra Kumar, poached from Asia Publishing House, as its editorial head, made a big splash. He published books on topical interest and once Vikas signed the reprint rights of Larry Collins and Dominique Lapierre's

Freedom at Midnight (discussed in Chapter 10) there was no looking back. Soon followed books on, or connected with, the internal Emergency from June 1975 to March 1977 and the Vikas imprint, supported by the well-oiled distribution machinery of UBS, got well entrenched. Narendra Kumar was a dynamo, publishing anything that lay in the borderland of journalism and gossip with 'an output of 250 to 300 titles a year'. However, Narendra Kumar, supported ably by Chawla's wife Sharda (the publisher of Vikas), like the French before the revolution, had 'forgotten nothing nor learnt anything' from the rise and fall of Asia Publishing House. The story of the rise and fall of Vikas, too, is a lesson of doing too much without professionalism to back the publishing programme.

Several medium-sized publishers sprang up: Jaico (founded by Jaman Shah in 1946 as a book distribution business for US publishers), India Book House (IBH), Oxford-IBH, Allied Publishers, Sterling Publishers, Popular Prakashan in Bombay, Pramod Kapoor's Roli Books, Academic Press and Scientific Book Agency, Calcutta, to name a few. But like their predecessors, they were primarily distributors of imported titles and publishers later. Quite apart from these newly emerging publishers, several professionals who were working in the bigger houses broke off and set up small establishments of their own.

Alongside, mass-market paperbacks also made a tentative appearance on subjects of popular interest – sex, celebrities, violence – that could spin off into sitcoms. To begin with, there were the paperbacks of established hardback publishers: Sangam (Orient Longman), Mayfair (Arnold Heinemann), Pearl (India Book House), Bell (Vikas) and Sterling. Most of these were simply paperbacks of established hardback titles that had done reasonably well in their first editions. In the absence of reliable sales figures, how well these were received by the public at large is difficult to say, but since most of them are still around, it means they have survived the vagaries of the market.

Perhaps the only imprint which not only survived the ups and downs of the market graphs, but also established itself well was

Rupa, which was founded by D. Mehra in Calcutta in 1936. Over the last nearly eight decades, it has been the most consistent of the Indian publishers and distributors and that too with an impeccable reputation. That in the Indian scenario is saying a great deal. Today, with its headquarters in Delhi it has a well-established sales network of its own, with branches across the country and, under the leadership of R. K. Mehra, still remains an imprint to reckon with.

In this scenario, the real change, for the better, came when Penguin Books India was set up in October 1987 by the young, ambitious and visionary David Davidar. Indian publishing never looked the same again. It's image in the world market too underwent a total change!

Mention must also be made of the emergence of government-financed organizations that have played an important role in publishing in the country: the National Book Trust (NBT), the Children's Book Trust (CBT), and the National Council of Educational Research and Training (NCERT) besides the educational bodies in the states – State Council of Educational Research and Training (SCERTs) – and the Sahitya Akademi. These institutions were established to promote education and book awareness in the broadest sense of the term, with heavy subsidies to place books within the reach of the common reader.

Of these, NCERT has had the greatest impact because it has specialized in school textbooks from the primary to the school-leaving stage up to classes XI and XII. The state education boards prepare books specifically for the requirements of their respective states' students. Almost all schools prescribe NCERT/SCERT books as the first option for two reasons: first, they are prepared by a team of experts drawn from schools all over the country and, hence, educationally sound; second, and more important, they are priced well within the reach of the common student. While there is no compulsion that non-government-aided schools use these books, the general consensus is that they need to be consulted if only to do well in examinations.

The mid-1980s and beyond marked a paradigm shift in English-language book publishing in India. There were four underlying factors that brought about this qualitative shift between the past and the present.

First, the computerization of the entire publication process – production, editorial and distribution – along with the communications revolution via satellite and the Internet led to globalization of English-language book publishing. Britain, and later the United States, were hooked on to real time to publishing centres in India. Co-publishing, special sheet deals and, in some cases, sharing of costs became immediately possible.

Second, a silent managerial revolution was taking place that led to a greater professionalism in the industry. Publishing that had hitherto been a gentleman's vocation became a hard-nosed business activity where management accountants became the real decision makers of what goes in and what stays out, how much to print and how much to maintain in the inventory. With this development, the notion that publishers should seek to improve public taste was tossed out of the window. Success was all that mattered and, at the end of the day, success meant the bottom line.

Third, the tremendous expansion of education with a growing awareness that without a functional knowledge of spoken and written English there was no future in the job market meant that university and professional courses in science, medicine, engineering, accountancy and law had to introduce English texts to cater to the growing and diverse demands of students. If Indian publishers couldn't deliver, as they hadn't for over the last twenty-odd years, books had to be imported or at least reprinted under licence. Restrictions on imports of plant and print machinery were considerably eased and that helped Indian publishers to improve the quality of book production.

Fourth, English-language publishing houses, especially those publishing school and university textbooks that were spread all over the country in state capitals and main educational centres, were now consolidated in the main metropolitan cities of New Delhi, Calcutta, Bombay, Madras and Bangalore, all of which also emerged as centres for high-quality printing.

The growing educational market led to two developments that had a direct impact on English-language book publishing. First came the establishment of printing facilities that could handle the very large print runs required. Second, the creation of school boards of education that served not merely as examining bodies with 'model textbooks' but also that could print, distribute and deliver books to school students on time across the length and breadth of the country.

For a market as large and diverse as India, it was not possible for a single organization to undertake the huge task of production and distribution on an all-India basis. Decentralization became necessary, though the results have not been entirely satisfactory because of the huge print runs and tight delivery schedules especially at the primary-school-level. But a beginning had been made and a message sent out to the political organizations (aided by some of our own publishers with vested interests) – that had demanded the abolition of English – that this language had come to stay. This was particularly significant in the hard core Hindi belt because there were a large number of English-medium schools and research-institutions where English was the only means of communication. The Hindi opposition to English was by and large snuffed out by the late 1990s.

However, there was a downside that was a natural corollary to the vast unplanned expansion of school education: the mushrooming growth of English-language teaching shops that were spearheaded by school bookshops producing 'guides' or 'kunjis' (as they are referred to in north India and used purely from an examination point of view) that guaranteed success within 'four weeks or money back'. Not surprisingly, they worked because they fulfilled the local demand, which in terms of numbers was quite considerable.

A silent revolution was taking place alongside. Many hard core professionals working with multinationals like Oxford University Press, Orient Longman and Macmillan India broke away and set up 'shop' of their own. This list was quite impressive not because of the number of titles published but because it meant two things: first professionalization and second the Indianization of their publishing programmes. These new entrants included Urvashi Butalia and Ritu Menon – Kali for Women – though they later separated to start their respective imprints; Ravi Dayal under his imprint confining himself to Indian writing in English; Rukun Advani – Permanent Black – in social sciences for the serious common reader; Naveen Kishore – Seagull Books – in theatre and the acquisitions for reprint rights of European classics in translation; Vinod Vashisht of Viva Books; and Pramod Kapoor – Roli Books – for lavishly produced coffee-table volumes, which he sold internationally. There were others too, but the significant point is that these publishers stuck to specific areas in literature and the social sciences.

Having said this, it must be pointed out that though there is a growing market for English-language books, it isn't anywhere near what is hyped in the popular media and the market. The fact is, when I joined the Indian publishing industry in 1977-78, the general print run of a trade title was around 2,000 copies. Today, on an average, it remains the same. The main difference being that there are many more publishing houses today and hence more titles published. The floor space for books in the retail sector too is more and better organized as also the online sales connectivity. On the other hand there are authors like Chetan Bhagat, Ravinder Singh, and Amish Tripathi who sell over 100,000 copies. A contradiction – but that's the Indian publishing scenario!

The progressive development of English-language book publishing has raised some awkward questions among critics that have to be faced by professionals who have waxed eloquent about the dynamics of the industry in the last two decades. Has this development come at the expense of Indian-language publishing that has lagged behind in every field, be it fiction or non-fiction? Some of these questions were raised by Samuel Israel, in an article, 'The Colonial Heritage of Indian Publishing'.[8] They have become increasingly relevant as we move towards universal education. Also, it is important that one examines the directions in which expansion has taken place through the medium of English language – religion, philosophy, fiction (what has been described as Indian writing in English) at the expense of modern scholarship in the humanities, the social sciences, the biological and physical sciences, technology and medicine, and the vital sectors in undergraduate and postgraduate subjects.

How many of the worthwhile books – those that become the bread-and-butter basis for publishers and students for years on end – have originated in India? Very few. Why is this so? Is it because we were unable to communicate in written English even as we became fluent in spoken English? Or as the eminent educationist, Dr S. Gopal, queried: 'Did we not educate our masters?'

Before we go on to answer these questions, it is necessary to set out the limits of the Indian *book publishing* industry, as distinct from publishing as a whole that includes the print and other media, which is much larger, with greater resources, and much higher returns, especially as it has branched out to embrace all branches of the communications industry – TV, film, mobile phones and its numerous applications. Also, it must be realized that book publishing in India is heavily dependent for its 'products' on the educational sector. Publishers do not write books; they solicit them from those who can write, which are later fashioned into a finished product.

If the intellectual climate is stagnant, publishers have only two courses of action open to them: to get the books from abroad by directly importing under special discounts or licensing them for reprints; or make do with what is available in the local market, edit it and then produce it in an attractive manner. 'Educating our masters' may be the ideal for any publishing house, but it is beyond the capacity of the resources that Indian publishers have, either individually or collectively. Besides, the book can at best supplement what the teachers provide by way of knowledge; it can never replace them.

Has English-language publishing eaten into the vitals of publishing in the vernacular languages, especially Hindi? The answer is emphatically *no*.

Writing is a solitary act; it is not possible to compel any writer to put his or her ideas on paper, even with the promise of handsome returns. It must come from within and the author must have something to say, based on his or her learning and experience. Of course, textbook writers can cut and paste, but this propensity shows up and the publisher soon learns from whom to solicit his works. No publisher wants to lose money on his investments and he takes all the care to see that his author-to-be has covered his ground well. This is done through reviews by peers, checking and cross-checking with existing literature and generally consulting a cross section of opinion.

As far as books in Hindi are concerned (the same would be true of other languages as well), funding was never a problem: adequate funds were and are available through the Hindi Sahitya Akademi and other bodies that either provided subsidies or guaranteed sales of a minimum number of copies. But Hindi publishers concentrated on a range of books, mainly fiction, and biography (that tended to be hagiographies) that simply didn't take off. Some publishers did produce general fiction for the common reader, but, by and large, the market didn't respond the way one had hoped for. Perhaps, one of the main reasons for lack of market support was that Hindi publishers kept away from educational publishing in the post-school sector. Most Hindi publishing was concentrated on primary and secondary schools (nursery rhymes, puzzles, drawing and painting books) and general fiction for the mass market. It didn't venture into university books, which raised more questions: Were the titles that were published either as originals or translations the wrong ones for the educational market in the Hindi belt? Were the prices and terms offered to the booksellers unattractive, as compared to those in English? Were the marketing efforts inadequate? Was the Hindi book distribution trade disorganized to handle sophisticated titles in that language?

I am often asked about the future of English-language book publishing in India. Is the printed word becoming increasingly marginalized in the electronic era? Is the whole familiar tradition of the book being swept away by technologies that will render it antiquated? Have we finally arrived at a breaking point at which the entire system of beliefs, values and cultural aspirations are about to be supplanted by something new, and in the full sweep of its implications, unknown? Is it true that India, never known to be a nation of book lovers, is reading even less? Is the demanding world of reading being shoved aside in favour of the easy world of the audio and visual that can do the imagining for us? After all, reading essentially demands that imagination is put to work; interactions or connections that need to be made to substitute the visual or aural images for the imagined ones require some effort. Reading is a lonely affair that requires, in the final analysis, an engagement between the reader and the text that many would rather not commit when the going gets tough. Given this psychological make-up of the reader, what has gone wrong with the middle and top end of the book market that have hitherto been the backbone of all publishing outside the lucrative educational market?

The rot really begins at school. Our entire schooling system is hidebound by the rigidities of the syllabus, outside of which little is read, if at all, or taught even in the pre-primary and primary classes. Teachers are not required to go outside the syllabus and are not encouraged to do much of their own innovations in classroom teaching.

Undergraduate studies are merely an extension of the schooling system. Observation, thinking and feeling about the world are stifled forever. Learning by rote, the predominance of a single textbook and the overwhelming 'presence' of the examiner who is the sole arbiter of right and wrong kill whatever curiosity that may have been felt after years in the wasteland. Why should the undergraduate read anything extra when the critical text is more important, more profitable than the poem, and the examination syllabus matters more than the adventure of private discovery? No wonder, we are such an information-filled society rather than one with knowledge.

India may not be a land of book lovers but we have a great tradition of storytelling – both oral and written. Even the most illiterate grandmother would come up with the most imaginative stories. However, with the sharp deterioration in the standards of language today, this rich oral tradition is bereft of all meaning because we no longer have a language to express it in. It is invariably a mixture of the regional language and a smattering of English. What the grandmother speaks is little understood by the grandchildren. Sadly, the limits of a language are the limits of thought and when language is so restricted, reading and thinking are the first casualties.

It is not just the educational system and the lack of meaningful debates about what is important and what is not, what should be in and what should be out, that are responsible for our poor reading habits. In a literary situation – thanks to the advances in print and communications, which have led to a vast expansion and diversification of media outlets with their inexhaustible appetite for material – there are two other factors that perhaps reflect the underlying reasons for the state of functional illiteracy. First, because of the continued state of insecurity, there is a conspiracy of courtesy among the elite where each side tells the other what the other wants to hear. There is no cut-and-thrust debate and without this, there are few takers. What all this is tantamount to is that we have not been able to build a 'community of readers' – a critical mass – that would stimulate others to take to the book for the sheer pleasure of reading.

The second reason is more substantive. Argentine scholar Alberto Manguel, while quoting a wide range of sources, says: 'We read in order to be quiet'. Solitude is what is required, he says, 'which does not mean loneliness but the desire to be left alone with your thoughts and feelings.'[9] The answer is not a simple one and would involve, in the least, a cursory examination of our family and kinship patterns. Family and kinship are what sustain us. The joint family structure may have broken down in the urban centres but family and friends are very much a part of our everyday lives. We are, for better or worse, never left alone. Solitude is an alien concept to us. More often than not, to be quiet and withdrawn is taken as an antisocial behaviour. For an average Indian, the move away from traditional patterns of social behaviour has been more in the direction of building bridges with those who would help in leading him or her towards the 'good life'.

Reading, it is said, is cumulative and proceeds by geometrical progression: each new reading builds on whatever the reader has read before. But this assumes coming to terms with your own self and being alone. Have you ever noticed that we, the average Indians, are scared to be left alone? Therein lies the crux of the problem. It is not a question of money or availability; but the moral strength to be alone 'with the beating of one's heart'.

39

The Last Word

What Is Book Publishing as a Career?

This is one question I am asked repeatedly. To be blunt, it is a wonderful profession if you are interested in books, and not too eager to earn quick money and perks (at least, to start with) or make a name in the form of a byline. Publishing can't afford the former and it doesn't give the latter. But the intellectual and other compensations, like meeting some of the finest contemporary minds, more than make up for the relative paucity of goodies. Also, in a fast-moving universe, where time has shrunk and the world has narrowed considerably, publishing is a very monotonous job and one needs to have an unimaginable amount of patience to deal with authors and their works. Can you imagine working on a manuscript or two, for weeks together, at times even months? Can you read one manuscript after another, in its raw form, which is very different from the book that you finally read? Imagine being totally disappointed by the manuscript of an author whom you otherwise loved or worshipped because of his/her previous books? The true answer to these questions lies within you.

Most authors are an eccentric, erratic, temperamental, egotist lot, who have no value for your time, patience and deadlines. Most of them are fragile and very sensitive by nature or are victims of their over-bloated egos. They take themselves most seriously. Each is different from the other, in every possible imaginable way. You have to handle them carefully. Diplomatically. Patiently. With care. With love. You may need to pamper them. Coax them. Yet once you come to know them, you will love them for these very qualities or eccentricities (whichever way you take them), simply because most of them are wonderful minds – thinkers, creators, ever germinating new ideas and giving their writing a beautiful shape and form. You will come to love and respect them, as I do. And who knows someone, some day, may instigate you enough, for you to take to writing too, to become an author, as publishers like David Davidar, Ratika Kapur, Kishwar Desai and Urvashi Butalia did – each one of them a good, readable writer and a wonderful, loving, human being.

I must admit that, in the last nearly four decades in publishing, I have come across hundreds of authors and writers whom I have published or interacted with – some of them debutants, some known and established, some great minds, some exceptionally creative, some real geniuses – but each of them very special, in his or her own way. The journey with each may have been varied, as it was bound to be, but was indeed memorable and enriching and I treasure it. If there is another life, as they say there is, and if I were to get one wish for it, I would without hesitation opt for publishing as a career, so as to be able to meet and know more authors and writers; so as to be able to publish those whom I could not in this life; so as to be able to go, once again, with the present ones, on even a longer journey with, and through, their written words.

Except for one – that ungrateful one! That shameless one! That faceless one! Whom I shall keep nameless for now!

Notes and References

There is a great deal of difference between an eager man who wants to read a book and the tired man who wants a book to read.

– Gilbert K. Chesterton

1. CHANDIGARH – A City that Never Was

1. Balwant Gargi, *Purple Moonlight* (New Delhi: UBS Publishers' Distributors, 1993).

2. SATISH GUJRAL – Painter of Images. And Words

1. Balwant Gargi, *Purple Moonlight* (New Delhi: UBS Publishers' Distributors, 1993).
2. Ibid.
3. Ibid.
4. Raj Thapar, *All These Years: A Memoir* (New Delhi: Penguin, 1991).
5. Satish Gujral, *The World of Satish Gujral: In His Own Words* (New Delhi: UBS Publishers' Distributors, 1993).

3. BALWANT GARGI – The Ornamental Cactus

1. With permission from Neelam Mansingh Chowdhry from her unpublished memoirs.
2. Ibid.
3. Khushwant Singh, 'With Malice Towards One and All', *Hindustan Times*.
4. http://www.indiaclub.com/Purple-Moonlight-Balwant-Gargi/dp/B00N82RI0W. Last accessed on 5 January 2014.
5. Neelam Mansingh Chowdhry, unpublished memoirs.
6. Elia Kazan, *A Life* (New York: Andre Deutsch Limited, 1988).
7. http://www.culturalindia.net/indian-art/painters/jatin-das.html. Last accessed on 5 January 2014.

4. M. F. HUSAIN – The Generous Gifter

1. William Grimes, 'Maqbool Fida Husain, India's Most Famous Painter, Dies at 95', *The New York Times*, 9 June 2011.

5. F. N. SOUZA – The Ungrateful One

1. Yashodhara Dalmia, 'God, Sex and Souza', *The Times of India*, 5 May 2010.
2. 'Expressionism was a modernist movement, initially in poetry and painting, originating in Germany at the beginning of the twentieth century. Its typical trait is to present the world solely from a subjective perspective, distorting it radically for emotional effect in order to evoke moods or ideas. Expressionist artists sought to express meaning or emotional experience rather than physical reality'. – Wikipedia (http://en.wikipedia.org/wiki/Expressionism). Last accessed on 5 January 2014.

3. Art Brut, or outsider art, was 'a label created by French artist Jean Dubuffet to describe art created outside the boundaries of official culture'. – Wikipedia (http://en.wikipedia.org/wiki/Outsider_art). Last accessed on 5 January 2014.
4. Yashodhara Dalmia, 'God, Sex and Souza'.
5. Morarji Desai was known for drinking his own urine.

6. DOM MORAES – The Devil within Authors

1. In the days before courier, fax and email, Registered A.D. (Acknowledgement Due) was the surest and only officially and legally recognized method of postal delivery.

8. SHALIMAR – The Mega Fiasco

1. OBIE awards are given annually to theatre artists and groups in New York City and cover the Off-Broadway and Off-Off Broadway productions.

9. RAJU BHARATAN – The Film Music Encyclopedia

1. Chandan Mitra, 'A Scrambled Record', *India Today*, 9 October 2010.

10. DOMINIQUE LAPIERRE AND LARRY COLLINS – Joide de Vivre

1. Sir Burke St John Trend was a British civil servant and later rector of Lincoln College, Oxford, who in 1974 was made a life peer as Baron Trend of Greenwich in Greater London.
2. British economist H. V. Hodson held numerous posts both in the government and outside. A one-time reforms commissioner of the Government of India, in the 1940s, he was also editor of *The Sunday Times* from 1950 to 1961. Author of many books, Hudson's 564-page *The Great Divide: Britain, India, Pakistan* was published in 1969 by Hutchinson.
3. Nicholas Mansergh, E. W. R. Lumby and Penderel Moon (eds), *The Transfer of Power, 1942-47*, 12 volumes, published by Her Majesty's Stationery Office in the UK, between 1970 and 1988.
4. Richard Hough, *Mountbatten: Hero of Our Time* (London: Weidenfeld & Nicolson, 1980).
5. Rajni Shaleen Chopra, 'One Hundred Years of Solitude', *The Indian Express*, Chandigarh, 19 June 2011.

11. KHUSHWANT SINGH – The Man for All Seasons

1. Geoffrey Strickland, 'Stendhal: The Education of a Novelist', *Truth and Lies in Literature: Essays and Reviews*, ed. Stephen Vizinczey (Chicago: University of Chicago Press, 1986).
2. Khushwant Singh with Ashok Chopra, *Agnostic Khushwant: There Is No God* (New Delhi: Hay House Publishers India, 2012).
3. Khushwant Singh, *Train to Pakistan* (New York: Grove Press, 1956).
4. Khushwant Singh, *Delhi: A Novel* (New Delhi: Penguin, 1990).
5. Ibid.
6. Ibid.
7. Ibid.
8. Ibid.
9. Ibid.
10. Ibid.
11. Shobhaa Dé, 'The Patiala Peg of Publishing Is No More', *India Today*, 27 March 2014.
12. Fakir Syed Aijazuddin, '99 Not Out', *Dawn*, 27 March 2014.
13. Fakir Syed Aijazuddin, 'Train to Pakistan – 2014', *Dawn*, 24 April 2014.

12. I. S. JOHAR – Sex Obsessed

1. http://en.wikipedia.org/wiki/I._S._Johar
2. Khushwant Singh, *Women and Men in My Life* (New Delhi: UBSPD, 1995).

13. J. N. DIXIT– Diplomat-turned-Writer

1. Josy Joseph, 'JN Dixit: Always India First', *The Times of India*, 3 January 2005.
2. Vandana Khare, 'India and the World,' *Outlook*, 30 October 1996.

3. My friend, my protector, my fellow traveller.
4. My companion, my patron, my guide.

14. N. IQBAL SINGH – The Ladies' Man

1. Khushwant Singh, *Women and Men in My Life* (New Delhi: UBSPD, 1995).
2. Ibid.
3. Ibid.
4. *Usha*, Vol. 3, No. 2, August 1942, Lahore.
5. Yasodhara Dalmia, *Amrita Sher-Gil: A Life* (New Delhi: Penguin, 2006).

15. PATWANT SINGH – A Friend to None

1. Surinder Ghai, *One to One: Glimpses of Indian Publishing Industry* (New Delhi: Sterling, 2013).
2. Antony Wood, 'Patwant Singh', *The Guardian*, 19 August 2009.

16. GENERAL V. P. MALIK – A Soldier-turned-Author

1. MVC, or the Maha Vir Chakra, is the second highest military decoration in India and is awarded for acts of conspicuous gallantry in the presence of the enemy, whether on land, sea or in the air. The medal may be awarded posthumously.

17. RAJINDER SINGH BEDI – Burning Passions

1. *Dilip Kumar: The Substance and the Shadow – An Autobiography*, (New Delhi: Hay House Publishers, 2014).
2. Narinder Bedi (who also spelt his name as Narender) was a film maker too who was riding a wave of success then. He had tasted triumph with his Randhir Kapoor-Jaya Bhaduri starrer *Jawani Diwani* (1972), followed by a crime thriller, *Benaam* (1974), with Amitabh Bachchan, Moushumi Chaterjee and Prem Chopra in the main roles.
3. Balwant Gargi, *The Naked Triangle: An Autobiographical Novel* (New Delhi: Vikas Publishing House, 1979).

18. ZAIL SINGH – The Loyal Courtier. And Friend

1. Balwant Gargi, *The Naked Triangle: An Autobiographical Novel* (New Delhi: Vikas Publishing House, 1979).
2. Ibid.
3. http://en.wikipedia.org/wiki/Shiv_Kumar_Batalvi. Last accessed on 5 January 2014.

19. SHOBHA DE – Seductive! Soulful! Spicy! Sensuous!

1. Shobha added an extra 'a' to her first name years later.
2. Shobha Dé, *Selective Memory: Stories from My Life* (New Delhi: Penguin, 1998).
3. *Hindustan Times*, New Delhi, 18 July 1994.

20. UMA VASUDEV – The Oriental Octopus

1. Balwant Gargi, *The Naked Triangle: An Autobiographical Novel* (New Delhi: Vikas Publishing House, 1979).

21. DILIP KUMAR – The Longest Wait

1. Dilip Kumar, *The Substance and the Shadow: An Autobiography* (New Delhi: Hay House Publishers, 2014).

22. SHIMLA – A Paradise Lost

1. Henry Sharp, *Goodbye India* (Oxford: Oxford University Press, 1945).
2. http://archive.org/stream/cu31924021024835/cu31924021024835_djvu.txt. Last accessed on 5 January 2014.
3. Rajinder Singh (1872-1900), the Maharaja of Patiala, had three houses in Simla, located near each other – Oakover, Cedar Lodge (now Punjab government's guest house in Shimla) and Rookwood (a private property). Given the title *Farzand-e-Khas-Daulat-e-Englishia* – the most favourite son of the English empire – by the British, he entertained the high and the mighty of the empire in Oakover. See Minakshi Chaudhry, *Love Stories of Shimla Hills* (New Delhi: Rupa & Co., 2010).
4. Penelope Chetwode, *Kulu: The End of the Habitable World* (London: John Murray Publishers, 1963).
5. James Baillie Fraser, *Journal of a Tour through Part of the Snowy Range of the Himala Mountains, and to the Sources of the River Jumna and Ganges* (London: Rodwell and Martin, 1820).
6. Ibid.
7. http://nityin.wordpress.com/2007/12/08/the-story-of-penelope-chetwode/. Last accessed on 5 January 2014.
8. Ibid.

23. THE GAIETY THEATRE – Rise and Fall into Oblivion

1. Major General G. H. Addison, *Simla Amateur Dramatic Club: 1837–1937* (Simla: Civil and Military Press, 1937).
2. Emily Eden, *Up the Country: Letters Written to Her Sister from the Upper Provinces of India*, two volumes, (UK: Cambridge University Press, 1867).
3. Ibid.
4. Ibid.
5. Sir John Edward Buck, *Simla: Past and Present* (Calcutta: Thacker Spinx, 1904).

6. Today Peteroff is run as a premium hotel by the Himachal Pradesh Tourism Development Corporation.
7. Sir John Edward Buck, *Simla*.
8. Major General G. H. Addison, *Simla Amateur Dramatic Club*.
9. Ibid.
10. Ibid.
11. Ibid.
12. Sir John Edward Buck, *Simla*.
13. Major General G. H. Addison, Simla Amateur Dramatic Club.

24. THE EXIT – A Blessing in Disguise

1. L. H. Naqvi, *Hindustan Times*, New Delhi, 6 January 1978.
2. V. P. Prabhakar, *The Tribune*, Chandigarh, 6 January 1978.
3. *The Indian Express*, 14 January 1978.

26. ISABEL ALLENDE – The Pain and the Agony

1. Isabel Allende, *Paula* (London: HarperCollins Publishers, 1999).
2. Anatole Broyard, *Intoxicated by My Illness: And Other Writings on Life and Death* (New York: Ballantine Books, 1992).
3. Steve King, 'The Allende Magic', *Review*: *Barnes and Noble*, New York, 2 August 2012.
4. Ibid.
5. Ibid.
6. Isabel Allende in an interview with the *New York Times*. (Date untraceable.)
7. Anatole Broyard, *Intoxicated by My Illness*.
8. Isabel Allende, *Paula*.
9. Ibid.
10. Suzanne Ruta, 'The Long Goodbye', *New York Times*, 21 May 1995.

27. MIDNIGHT AND THEM – The New Breed of Novelists

1. Gita Mehta, *Raj* (London: Jonathan Cape, 1989).
2. Shauna Singh Baldwin, *What the Body Remembers* (London: HarperCollins Publishers, 1999).
3. Gita Mehta, interview with *The Bookseller*, London, 15 May 1989.
4. Shauna Singh Baldwin, *What the Body Remembers*.
5. Kamila Shamsie, *Salt and Saffron* (London: Bloomsbury, 2000).
6. Ibid.
7. Ibid.
8. Ibid.

9. Sara Suleri, *Meatless Days* (Chicago: University of Chicago Press, 1991).
10. Ali Sethi, *The Wish Maker* (London: Riverhead, 2009).

28. SALMAN RUSHDIE – And His Credo

1. Edward Said, *Reflections on Exile: And Other Literary and Cultural Essays* (London: Granta, 2001).
2. Salman Rushdie, *Step Across the Line: Collected Non-Fiction 1992-2002* (London: Modern Library Paperbacks, 2003).
3. Salman Rushdie, *Imaginary Homelands – Essays and Criticism 1981- 1991* (London: Granta in association with Penguin, 1992).
4. Salman Rushdie, *The Jaguar Smile: A Nicaraguan Journey*, (London: Penguin, 1987).
5. Qurratulain Hyder, *Aag Ka Darya* (Lahore: Sang-e-Meel Publications, 1959).
6. Qurratulain Hyder, *River of Fire* (New Delhi: Kali for Women, 1998).
7. Jorge Luis Borges, *The Book of Imaginary Beings* (London: Penguin, 1957).
8. Naguib Mahfouz, *The Journey of Ibn Fattouma* (London: Anchor Books, 1983).
9. Naguib Mahfouz, 'The Art of Fiction No. 129', *The Paris Review*, No. 123, Summer, 1992.
10. Naguib Mahfouz, *Children of Gabelawi* (London: Three Continents Press, 1959).
11. Naguib Mahfouz, *The Paris Review*, No. 123.
12. Abū Sāmid Muhammad ibn Muhammad al-Ghazālī (c. 1058–1111), known as Al-Ghazali or Algazel to the Western medieval world, was a Muslim theologian, jurist, philosopher and mystic of Persian descent. He has sometimes been referred to by historians as the single most influential Muslim after the Islamic Prophet Muhammad (Source: Wikipedia).
13. Abū al-Hasan Alī ibn Ismā'īl al-Ash'arī (874–936) was a Shafi'i scholar and theologian who founded the school of tenets of faith that bears his name (Ash'ari). Muslims consider him to be the founder of the Sunni Ash'ari tradition of Aqeedah (Source: Wikipedia).
14. Taslima Nasreen, *Lajja* (New Delhi: Penguin, 1997).

29. STATE TERRORISM – Literature and Its Intolerance

1. W. H. Auden, 'The Flight into Egypt', *For the Time Being: A Christmas Oratorio* (London: Vintage, 1941).
2. Dr Sadiq Hussain, *Tehrik-e-Mujahideen* (Lahore: Al-Meezan, 1989).

30. WRITING POETRY – An Elitist Fashion without Takers

1. T. S. Eliot, *The Wasteland* (New York: Horace Liveright Publisher, 1922).
2. Valerie Fletcher, interview with *The New York Times*, 13 January 1985.
3. Joseph Brodsky, *Less Than One: Selected Essays* (London: Penguin, 2011).
4. Writers' Workshop, a Calcutta-based literary publisher, was founded by the poet-professor Purushottama Lal in 1958. Over the next few decades it published many new authors of post-Independence urban literature, by charging them a fee or making them buy copies, some of whom later became important, including A. K. Ramanujan, Agha Shahid Ali, Adil Jussawalla, Arvind Krishna Mehrotra, Keki N. Daruwalla, Kamala Das, Nissim Ezekiel, Pritish Nandy, Ruskin Bond, Shiv Kumar, Saleem Peeradina, Vikram Seth, and William Hull among others. Throughout its history, this alternative publishing venture published authors, without a distribution system to back it.
5. Victor G. Kiernan, *Poems of Faiz* (Lahore: Vanguard Books, 1971).
6. John Dryden, *The Poems of John Dryden: 1649-1681* (New York: Pearson, 1995).
7. Hans Magnus Enzensberger, *Selected Poems* (London: Paladin Books, 1999).
8. Hans Magnus Enzensberger, *The Sinking of the Titanic* (London: Paladin Books, 1994).
9. Waqas Ahmed Khwaja (ed.), *Mornings in the Wilderness* (Lahore: Sang-e-Meel Publications, 1988).
10. Victor Kiernan (trans.), *Poems by Faiz* (London: George Allen & Unwin, 1971).
11. Ibid.
12. Sant Singh Sekhon (trans.), *The Love of Hir and Ranjha* (Ludhiana: College of Agriculture, Punjab Agricultural University, 1978).
13. Kartar Singh Duggal (trans.), *Sain Bulleh Shah: The Mystic Muse* (New Delhi: Abhinav Publications, 1996).
14. Pritish Nandy (ed.), *Modern Indian Love Poetry* (New Delhi: Vikas Publishing House, 1980).
15. Ibid.
16. Mahmood Jamal (ed.), *The Penguin Book of Modern Urdu Poetry* (London: Penguin, 1986).
17. Ibid.
18. Khushwant Singh (trans.), *Muhammad Iqbal: Shikwa & Jawab-e-Shikwa: Complaint and Answer – Iqbal's Dialogue with Allah* (New Delhi: Oxford University Press, 1997).
19. Milan Kundera, *The Art of the Novel* (London: Faber and Faber, 1986).

31. THE SHIFT – To a Higher Plane

1. Graham Greene, *The End of the Affair* (London: Penguin, 1951).
2. *Writings of Hippocrates and Galen epitomized from the original Latin translations by John Redman Coxe* (Philadelphia: Lindsay and Blakistan, 1846).
3. Karl Marx, *Critique of Hegel's Philosophy of Right*, Annette Jocin and Joseph O' Malley (trans.) Cambridge University Press, USA; 1997.
4. Tim Parks, *Teach Us to Sit Still: A Sceptic's Search for Health and Healing* (London: Vintage Books, 2011).

32. ALL THOSE GODS, GODMEN AND GODWOMEN – Babas and Swamis; Matas and Ammas

1. Father Brown is a fictional character created by G. K. Chesterton, who starred in fifty-one detective stories, most of which were later compiled in a series of five books.
2. Michael Harrington, *The Politics at God's Funeral: The Spiritual Crisis of Western Civilization* (New York: Henry Holt & Co., 1989).
3. http://en.wikipedia.org/wiki/Sathya_Sai_Baba. Last accessed on 5 January 2014.
4. Percy Bysshe Shelley, 'Ozymandias'.
5. Graham Greene, *The Human Factor* (London: Penguin, 1978).
6. William Shakespeare, *Anthony and Cleopatra*, Act II, Scene II.

33. THE DALAI LAMA – The High Pontiff

1. *The Tibetan Review*, Mcleodganj, Dharamshala, Himachal Pradesh, 1 June 1976.
2. Nirmal C. Sinha, 'Why Not Petition His Holiness?', *Bulletin of Tibetology* (Gangtok: Namgyal Institute of Tibetology, July 1976).
3. *The Indian Express*, 19 July 1976.
4. Interview with *The New York Times*, 17 April 1980.

34. SOURCING MANUSCRIPTS – The Art of Publishing

1. Ashok Chopra, 'Academic Wasteland: Textbooks Fail to Make the Grade', *The Times of India*, 1 February 1997.
2. Raymond Williams, *The Politics of Modernism: Against the New Conformists* (London: Verso, 2007).
3. Clifford Geertz, *The Interpretation of Cultures* (New York: Basic Books, 1977).

4. Originally published as *Post-Soviet Geography* by the Kenan Institute for Advanced Russian Studies from 1992 to 1995, this journal went through a series of name changes. It is now published as *Eurasian Geography and Economics.*
5. http://en.wikipedia.org/wiki/E-reader. Last accessed on 5 January 2014.

36. BOOK LAUNCHES – Satisfying Egos or Increasing Sales?

1. Shiv Khera, *You Can Win: A Step by Step Tool for Top Achievers* (New Delhi: Macmillan, 1998).
2. J. N. Dixit, *India-Pakistan in War & Peace* (London: Taylor and Francis, 2003).
3. *India Today*, 3 June 2002.
4. *The Hindu*, 21 July 2002.
5. *Hindustan Times*, 11 July 2002.
6. Narendra Singh Sarila, *The Shadow of the Great Game: The Untold Story of India's Partition* (New Delhi: HarperCollins India, 2005).
7. Narendra Singh Sarila, *Once a Prince of Sarila: Of Palaces and Tiger Hunts, of Nehrus and Mountbattens* (London: I. B. Tauris, 2008).
8. Ashok K. Mehta, 'Sea Is the Limit', *India Today*, 29 December 2003.
9. INS *Vikrant*: a majestic, Asia's first, aircraft carrier that played a key rolc in enforcing the naval blockadc on East Pakistan during the 1971 operations. It was decommissioned in 1997. And, finally, which was torn apart piece by piece and turned into scrap on Friday, 21 November 2014.

37. AUTHORS – Their Quirks, Their Highs and Their Lows

1. Saul Bellow, *More Die of Heartbreak* (Surrey: Delta Publishing Company, 1997).
2. Joseph Brodsky, 'The Art of Poetry No. 28,' *The Paris Review*, No. 83, Spring 1982.
3. Anita Brookner, 'The Art of Fiction No. 98', *The Paris Review,* No. 104, Fall 1987.
4. Ibid.
5. Ibid.
6. Ibid.
7. Ibid.
8. Doreen Carvajal, 'Prose or Poetry, Writers Are Mad (Scientists Say)', *The New York Times*, 21 May 1996.
9. Ibid.
10. Ibid.

11. Hamid Jalal, 'The Agony of an Ecstasy', *Mornings in the Wilderness*, (Lahore: Sang-e-Meel Publications, 1988).
12. Ibid.
13. Ibid.
14. Ibid.
15. Ibid.
16. Carlos Baker, *Ernest Hemingway: A Life Story* (New York: Scribner, 1969).
17. Ernest Hemingway, 'The Art of Fiction No. 21', *The Paris Review*, No. 18, Spring, 1958.
18. Isabel Allende, *Paula*.

38. PAST AND PRESENT – English Book Publishing in India

1. John Epstein, 'The Battles of Pebbles', *The New York Review of Books*, April 2000.
2. Thomas Babington Macaulay, 'Minute in Education', *Through Indian Eyes: The Living Tradition*, Donald J. Johnson et al. (eds.) (New York: Cite Books, 1992).
3. Samuel Israel, 'The Colonial Heritage of Indian Publishing', *Literary Trends*, 26 (Spring, 1978).
4. Ibid
5. Ibid.
6. Unites States Information Services provided information on the American way of life – something that would enhance American influence. Its greatest contribution was in opening of American libraries in the main metros across the country that benefited a large number of students. It was the American response to the British Council libraries.
7. PL 480 – Public Law (1954) – is a legislation that was passed by Dwight D. Eisenhower, the thirty-fourth president of the United States of America in 1954, by which he laid the basis for the permanent expansion of American food imports to food-deficient, cash-strapped poor countries, which paid for these American food imports in their own currencies instead of US dollars. As a result of this, America built up huge rupee reserves, which were then parcelled out to various agencies in India. Substantial funds also went into reprinting American textbooks, which were somewhat outdated in the American market, but were used to great advantage, and commercial success, by many Indian publishers. PL 480 later morphed into other food programmes – Food for Peace Act (1966), Food, Agriculture, Conservation and Trade Act (1990), Emergency and Food Development Programmes. In India the PL 480 programme came under a great criticism from left-wing groups.

India's dependence on PL 480 dwindled as it became self-sufficient after the Green Revolution of the late 1960s.

8. Samuel Israel, 'The Colonial Heritage of Indian Publishing', *Literary Trends*, 26, Spring 1978.
9. Alberto Manguel, *A History of Reading* (London: Penguin Books, 1997).

Index

Keep reading books, but remember that a book is only a book, and you should learn to think for yourself.

– Maxim Gorky

Index

In gratitude

- To the ubiquitous Om Prakash, my man Friday, who, though younger to me, zealously guards my privacy and protects me against all intrusions like a caring and a loving family elder so that I can work undisturbed. And the ever-smiling Krishan Lal and his shy, but charming wife, Bina, who not only provide me with all the comforts of a home but look after me like mother hens, whenever I am up at my cottage in Rakkar (Dharamshala), in the western Himalayas.
- To the one and only, Om Arora, for taking many a straight, at times rocky, journey with me, and yet being there. *Always*!
- To Fakir Syed Aijazuddin, Raju Bharatan, Mala Dayal on behalf of Khushwant Singh, Shobhaa Dé, Neelam Mansingh, Rajiv Mehrotra, Lakkan Naqvi, and Ravi Vyas, for letting me use extracts from their published, and in some cases unpublished, works. I have also quoted from Balwant Gargi's *The Naked Triangle* and *Purple Moonlight*, the two works that I published. He is no more, but I have taken the liberty of presuming he would have never objected to my using them. Raja Bhasin, Lakshmi Reuben-Gopali, Prakash Loumi, Sudha Puaar, Sanjana Roychoudhury, Asha Sharma, Deepak Sood and Rakeshwar Lall Sood for collecting and readily providing various little details as and when I needed them.
- To Uma Vasudev, a special thanks, for letting me narrate, for the first time ever, a private moment from her life to which I was privy.

- To Abu Abraham, Bagga, Sudhir Dar, Gopi Gajwani, R. K. Laxman, Mario Miranda, Ajit Ninan, Rajinder Puri and Sudhir Tailang, for providing me, over the years, those exquisite caricatures of authors, some of which I have used here but all of which I treasure immensely.
- To all those newspapers and magazines in India and overseas where parts of this book have appeared, over a period of time, in different forms – articles, features, interviews or as my syndicated columns. The list being formidable, and lest I omit a name or two, I take the easy way out to acknowledge all of them jointly.
- To HarperCollins *Publishers* India, Hay House Publishers India, Penguin Books India, Ravi Dayal Publisher, UBS Publishers' Distributors and Vikas Publishing House India from whose publications I have used extracts.
- To the publishing family comprising the ever-helpful Udayan Mitra who was my first sounding board and who gave many a useful suggestion, K. J. Ravinder for his useful contributions, Rakesh Kumar for painstakingly designing the text, Raghav Khattar for the immense hard work that he put in lovingly, as also Ravi Grover, Hariharan, Rajalakshmi, Ruchita Ahuja and Bharat Singh for all their support. The exceptional team at HarperCollins *Publishers* India comprising, amongst others, its chief P. M. Sukumar, publisher Krishan Chopra, managing editor Somak Ghoshal, art director Bonita Shimray, Sameer Mahale, Iti Khurana, S.K. Ray Chaudhuri and my old colleague Girija Padmanabhan for not only believing in this project but also earnestly providing little nuggets of advice which went a long way in fine-tuning, chiselling and polishing the rougher edges, and most importantly, cutting it into their regular publishing and production schedules to bring it out at an unbelievable pace – professionally and expertly. Seeing their competence and dedication to the profession makes me feel that I wasted my years in publishing. God bless them and may their tribe increase!

Photo Credits

End paper photographs courtesy:
Dilip Kumar and Lata Mangeshkar (Gautam Rajadhyaksha); Satish Gujral (Gopi Gajwani); Uma Vasudev (Aruna Vasudev); Shobhaa Dé (Vikram Bawa); Fali S. Nariman (Ananth Padmanabhan); Anupam Kher (Atul Kasbekar); Nani A. Palkhivala (Dhiraj Chawda); Khushwant Singh (T. Narayan); Gita Mehta (*Times of India*); Shauna Singh Baldwin (*India Today*); Raaj Kumar (Mukta Arts); Kiran Bedi (Star Plus); F. N. Souza (Mala Photogallery); J. N. Dixit and Dom Moraes (*The Tribune*); Dominique Lapierre and Larry Collins (Library Thing); Manohar Malgonkar (Khabar); Tarun Tejpal (Yes Punjab); Salman Khurshid (Foreign and Commonwealth Office/Flickr). **Authors**: Patwant Singh, Balwant Gargi, Jyoti M. Rai, Raju Bharatan, Rajiv Mehrotra, General V. P. Malik, Jatin Das. **Wikipedia Creative Commons Licence**: Christopher: Dalai Lama; *New York World-Telegram* and the *Sun*: Elia Kazan; Kyle Cassidy: Salman Rushdie; Ahinsa Jain: Mani Shankar Aiyar; Bollywood Hungama: Dev Anand and Sunil Gavaskar; Ekabhishek: Rajinder Singh Bedi; Jaisingh Rathore: Giani Zail Singh; Mutari: Isabel Allende.

End-paper caricatures courtesy:
R. K. Laxman, Ajit Ninan

Photographs in inserts courtesy:
Rock Garden, Chandigarh: James Southorn, Flickr, Creative Commons licence; www.yespunjab.com.
Khushwant Singh: *The Indian Express*; Fakir Syed Aijazuddin.
Shimla: www.himachalwatcher.com
Shobhaa Dé: Vikram Bawa.
Dev Anand: Bollywood Hungama.
World Book Fair, Delhi: Kprateek88, Wikipedia, Creative Commons licence.
Kolkata Book Fair: Biswarup Ganguly, Wikipedia, Creative Commons licence.